WELLINGTON'S OPERATIONS
IN THE PENINSULA

Wellington's Operations in the Peninsula

1808–1814

By
Captain Lewis Butler
Late King's Royal Rifle Corps

WITH SKETCH MAPS

IN TWO VOLUMES

VOLUME TWO

The Naval & Military Press Ltd

published in association with

FIREPOWER
The Royal Artillery Museum
Woolwich

Published by
The Naval & Military Press Ltd
Unit 10 Ridgewood Industrial Park,
Uckfield, East Sussex,
TN22 5QE England
Tel: +44 (0) 1825 749494
Fax: +44 (0) 1825 765701
www.naval-military-press.com

in association with

FIREPOWER
The Royal Artillery Museum, Woolwich
www.firepower.org.uk

In reprinting in facsimile from the original, any imperfections are inevitably reproduced and the quality may fall short of modern type and cartographic standards.

Printed and bound by Antony Rowe Ltd, Eastbourne

Contents

PART IV

THE FRONTIER FORTRESSES (*continued*)

CHAPTER XXII
                                                  PAGE
Affairs in the northern and eastern provinces—Joseph resigns the throne—Resumes it 419

CHAPTER XXIII
Wellington invests Badajoz—Approach of Soult and Marmont—The siege raised—Wellington retires across the Guadiana—Takes up a position on the Caya—Soult retires . . 424

CHAPTER XXIV
Marmont retires into the valley of the Tagus—Napoleon's plans—Difficulties on either side—Wellington takes the bulk of his Army to the Coa—Advance of Marmont and Dorsenne—El Bodon—Aldea Ponte—The enemy retires—Blockade of Ciudad Rodrigo 439

CONTENTS

CHAPTER XXV

Napoleon's instructions to Marmont—Suchet captures Valencia—Operations in Andalusia—Hill surprises Girard at Aroyo des Molinos—Defence of Tarifa 457

CHAPTER XXVI

Wellington's plans—Siege and capture of Ciudad Rodrigo and Badajoz 471

PART V

THE SALAMANCA CAMPAIGN

CHAPTER XXVII

Repression of excesses in Badajoz—Approach and retirement of Soult—Lord W. Bentinck from Sicily proposes a diversion on the east coast of Spain — Marmont approaches the Agueda—Retreat of Victor Alten—Able conduct of Colonels Trant, Wilson and Le Cor—Marmont retires—His plans contrasted with those of the Emperor—Wellington's plans for an advance into Spain—Hill's surprise of Almaraz . 506

CHAPTER XXVIII

The war on the north coast—Formation of the French Army of the Ebro—Catalonia, Valencia and Andalusia — Lord W. Bentinck—Before starting for Russia Napoleon makes overtures of peace to the British Government—United States declare war against England—Lord Wellington devises means to feed the whole population of Portugal—His difficulties increased by the English Government—Comparative strength of the opposing forces . . 521

CHAPTER XXIX

Wellington's arrangements for taking the offensive—He concentrates on the Agueda—Counter movements of Marmont—Wellington crosses the Agueda and enters Salamanca—Siege and capture of the forts—Marmont retires across the Duero 532

CONTENTS

CHAPTER XXX

Marmont recrosses the Duero and Guarena, and turns Wellington's right—Wellington retires on Salamanca—General state of the Allied Army—Battle of Salamanca . 544

CHAPTER XXXI

Joseph abandons Madrid—Wellington enters it—Landing of an Anglo-Sicilian force at Alicante — Soult abandons the blockade of Cadiz and joins the King—Courses open to Wellington 574

CHAPTER XXXII

Clausel resumes the offensive—Wellington marches against him—Reaches Burgos—Siege of Burgos—Wellington's difficulties—Advance of the Armies of Portugal and the North—Retreat from Burgos 588

CHAPTER XXXIII

Soult and the King advance on Madrid—Hill abandons the line of the Tagus 605

CHAPTER XXXIV

Wellington retires behind the Tormes and is joined by Hill—Junction of the French Armies—Departure of the Army of the North—Soult turns Wellington's flank—Wellington retreats—Capture of Sir E. Paget—Wellington reaches Ciudad Rodrigo and puts his troops into winter quarters—His censure—Comments 610

CHAPTER XXXV

Position of the French Armies—The Anglo-Sicilian contingents at Alicante — Wellington's reinforcements—He goes to Cadiz—Reorganises the Spanish Army—Returns viâ Lisbon—Affairs of Portugal 629

CONTENTS

PART VI

THE VITORIA CAMPAIGN AND INVASION OF FRANCE

CHAPTER XXXVI

Position of the French forces at the beginning of 1813—Insurrection in the northern provinces—Sir J. Murray takes command of the Anglo-Sicilian force at Alicante—His action at Castalla—Plans suggested to him by Wellington—His failure at Tarragona—Lord W. Bentinck arrives and takes command 639

CHAPTER XXXVII

News of the French disasters in Russia—Forces on either side in Spain—Views of the Emperor—The French harassed by Partida warfare during the winter—Wellington's plans—State of his Army—Positions of the French forces . . 649

CHAPTER XXXVIII

Wellington's administrative difficulties — He assumes the offensive—The enemy retires—The wings of the Allied Army unite at Toro—Destruction of the Castle of Burgos—Wellington crosses the Ebro and marches down the left bank—Joseph retires into the "basin of Vitoria" . . 665

CHAPTER XXXIX

Position taken up by Joseph—Movements of the Allied Army—Wellington's orders for the 21st—Battle of Vitoria—Retreat of the French 680

CHAPTER XL

Wellington follows up the enemy—Movements of Foy and of Clausel—The French retire into France—Misconduct of Wellington's troops—Case of Captain Ramsay—Appointment of Marshal Soult as Lieutenant of the Emperor—

CONTENTS

ix

PAGE

Retirement of Joseph—State of the French Army of Spain—Dispositions on either side—The theatre of operations—Soult's plan of attack—His movements—Difficulties of the Allies on the defensive—Soult attacks—Defence of the Passes and retreat of the right wing of the Allies . . 694

CHAPTER XLI

Wellington joins his troops at Sorauren—Battle of Sorauren—Combat at Buenza—Second battle of Sorauren—Pursuit of the enemy, who narrowly escapes into French territory—Cessation of the pursuit 713

CHAPTER XLII

Lord W. Bentinck returns to Alicante—Suchet follows, but on hearing of the battle of Vitoria retires across the Ebro—Bentinck advances and invests Tarragona—Detaches Del Parque to join Wellington—Is defeated at Ordal—Relinquishes his command—Is succeeded by General William Clinton—Clinton's measures—Occupies the country about Villa Franca 725

CHAPTER XLIII

Siege of San Sebastian—Its capture—Attempt of Soult to relieve the fortress—Battle of San Marcial—Advance of Hill—Soult withdraws behind the Bidassoa . . . 730

CHAPTER XLIV

Passage of the Bidassoa—The Allies established within French territory—Sir T. Graham quits the Army and is succeeded by Sir John Hope 740

CHAPTER XLV

Wellington takes measures to restore discipline—He organises his troops in three Army Corps—Strength of the Allies—Position and strength of the enemy—Soult's plan of combined action is declined by Suchet — Pampeluna surrenders—Battle of the Nivelle—Retreat of the French to the Nive—Wellington forces the passage—The five days' fighting called the Battle of the Nive . . . 745

CHAPTER XLVI

Wellington's administration of the country occupied—Causes of friction with the Allies—Is urged from home to advance more rapidly—His reply—His financial distress—Casualties of the British Army in 1813—State of the Allied Army in January, 1814—Position and objects of the opposing forces —Wellington advances against Soult—Passage of the Adour by Sir J. Hope—Investment of Bayonne—Battle of Orthez —Retreat of Soult—Foils his pursuers . . . 766

CHAPTER XLVII

Beresford enters Bordeaux—Operations of Lord Dalhousie in the neighbourhood—Soult resumes the offensive against Wellington—Retires towards Toulouse—Wellington follows —Skirmish at Vic en Bigorre—Death of Col. Sturgeon, R.E. —Skirmish at Tarbes—Advance on Toulouse—Wellington fails to cross the Garonne above the town—Crosses it below —Battle of Toulouse—Soult evacuates the town—Abdication of Napoleon—Cessation of hostilities . . . 799

CHAPTER XLVIII

Operations in Catalonia—Treaty of Valençay—Release of King Ferdinand — Wellington directs Clinton to break up his Army and reinforce him with the British regiments—Conclusion of hostilities—Sortie from Bayonne—Capture of Sir J. Hope—End of the war—Wellington's farewell order to his troops—Sails for England—Conclusion . . 822

List of Sketch Maps

	PAGE
SKETCH OF CIUDAD RODRIGO . . . *Facing*	478
COUNTRY ROUND CIUDAD RODRIGO AND BADAJOZ. ,,	492
SKETCH OF BADAJOZ . . . . ,,	500
SKETCH OF THE SALAMANCA POSITION, JULY 22, 1812 .	569
THE SALAMANCA CAMPAIGN, 1812	638
SKETCH OF THE POSITION AT VITORIA, JUNE 21, 1813 .	689
SKETCH OF THE VITORIA CAMPAIGN, 1813. . .	692
SKETCH OF SAN SEBASTIAN	733
SKETCH OF GROUND COVERED IN THE BATTLES OF THE NIVE	761
SKETCH OF THE COUNTRY EMBRACING THE BATTLES OF THE PYRENEES, SAN MARCIAL AND THE NIVELLE . *Facing*	782
SKETCH OF THE GROUND AT ORTHEZ . . .	795
SKETCH OF TOULOUSE	821
CAMPAIGN IN THE SOUTH OF FRANCE . . *Facing*	822
SKETCH OF THE EAST COAST OF SPAIN . ,,	826

CHAPTER XXII

Affairs in the northern and eastern provinces—Joseph resigns his throne—Resumes it.

DURING the summer and autumn of 1810 minor operations had been carried on by the Galicians under Mahi; but little was achieved, and on the arrival of the French 9th Corps in October their feeble efforts died away.

In the Asturias, 8,000 men under Porlier gave a good deal of trouble to General Bonet. Naval and military expeditions under Admiral Sir H. Popham and General Walker were organised to assist the Spaniards on the north coast. Walker was anxious to occupy Santona as having a good winter harbour and being eminently defensible—built as it was "on a mountain promontory joined to the mainland by a narrow, sandy neck." "It would have cut Bonet's communications with France by the sea, given the British squadron a secure post from whence to vex the French coasts, and furnished a point of connection with the partidas of the Rioja, Biscay, and Navarre." Lord Liverpool, the Secretary of State, was ready to occupy it with 4,000 men, but desisted on Wellington's representations to the effect that a small force would be useless, and a large one would do little good "owing to the want of those equipments and supplies in which an army landed from its ships must be deficient.

420 WELLINGTON'S OPERATIONS

It is vain to hope for any assistance . . . from the Spaniards: the first thing they will require uniformly will be money; then arms, ammunition, clothing of all descriptions, provisions, forage, horses, means of transport, and everything which the expedition would have a right to require from them; and after all, this extraordinary and perverse people will scarcely allow the commander of the expedition to have a voice in the plan of operations to be followed when the whole shall be ready to undertake any, if indeed they ever should be ready." In point of fact the question settled itself, for Santona was shortly afterwards seized by the French and remained in their hands until the end of the war.

In the eastern provinces, Marshal Macdonald had replaced Augereau in command of the 7th Army Corps. The Partidas harassed his communications; the Spanish regular army in Catalonia was 30,000 strong, and the British vessels off the coast not only blockaded Barcelona, Rosas and the mouths of the Ebro, but landed parties of men to destroy the French convoys as they moved along the coast roads. Consequently Macdonald was principally taken up in provisioning Barcelona; but Suchet, who commanded the 3rd Corps, having tranquilised Aragon as successfully as Soult had tranquilised Andalusia, laid siege to Tortosa in December, 1810, and captured it in the first days of January, 1811, thus accounting for 8,000 Spanish soldiers, reducing the principal bulwarks of Catalonia and Valencia, and cutting off the communication between the two provinces. In May he proceeded to attack Tarragona, which, after a gallant defence, was taken by storm at the end of June with terrible slaughter. The capture of Tarragona gained for Suchet his bâton of Marshal. Montserrat fell a month later.

Six thousand regular soldiers, and 8,000 irregular, were taken or killed at Tarragona, and the Catalonian army was now reduced to 16,000 men. The fall of the city was a blot on the British honour. Three days before the end, a British squadron conveying 1,200 men under Colonel Skerrett appeared in the harbour. But Skerrett, despairing of the situation, declined to land his troops. By his pusillanimous conduct the ill-feeling entertained by the Spaniards for the English was—not without reason—greatly increased.

In August the fortress of Figueras, which had been cleverly surprised by the Spaniards in April, was recovered by Marshal Macdonald.

In Murcia and Andalusia nothing very noteworthy took place.

Meanwhile, political events of importance had occurred. In the autumn of 1810 the Spanish national Cortez assembled at Cadiz. The principles of its members were chiefly democratic, and inclined it in reality rather to the French than to the English alliance. As is the habit of parliamentary institutions, there was much talk, but little action except wrangling with the provincial Juntas and a disgraceful quarrel with the South American colonies, which was carried to such an extent that, incredible as it may appear, a proposal was actually made to employ British money and supplies to coerce the colonists by force of arms!

On the French side, Joseph had grown heartily tired of his turbulent kingdom. He was miserably poor; for the expense incurred by France on account of the war had been enormous, and Napoleon was not in a position to supply him with further subsidies. He was anxious to rule his subjects in a spirit of conciliation, and men such as Soult and Suchet showed admirable powers of administration; but others of the General Officers—who, nominally under his orders, paid very little heed to his authority—had in many cases thwarted his designs by tyranny and exactions. So greatly did Joseph dislike his position that in April, 1811, he resigned the throne and went off to France. His sudden absence tended to dislocate the military operations then in progress; Bessières abandoned the Asturias and concentrated the 70,000 men of the Northern Army in Leon and Castile, on the line of communications with France. Soult failed to get the support which he had expected from the Army of the Centre which was directly under Joseph's command, and the whole machinery of war was paralysed.

What took place in the interviews between Joseph and Napoleon is not quite clear. On the surface it appeared that Joseph wished to have nothing more to do with Spain, but that his brother persuaded him to return. Possibly Joseph merely used the threat of resignation for the purpose of extorting money or personal advantage, for at a later period Napoleon speaks of having desired Joseph to resign, and being unable to induce him to do so. At all events the upshot was that Napoleon concealed the Act of Abdication and gave out that his brother had merely come to confer on measures of state. In July, Joseph returned to Spain, having gained a good deal by his journey, for the Emperor gave him an additional six millions of francs for the maintenance of his Court: empowered him to remove officers whom he distrusted, and took measures to prevent the oppression of the Spaniards by ordering "the French military authorities to send the king daily reports of all requisitions and contributions exacted." The Emperor retained, however, in his own hands the general command of the French armies in Spain. It must also have been evident to him by this time that, in order to gain the best results, his personal presence in Spain was indispensable; but the shadow of the Russian war was now looming in the distance, and the enforcement of the Continental System in Northern Europe compelled Napoleon to remain in France. Hence, French politics were a favourable factor in Wellington's calculations, just as those of England were the reverse. In fact, it was the prospect of a war between France and Russia which to a great extent prevented Lord Wellington resigning his command; for "people in England were changing their opinions almost with the wind" (letter to Mr. Villiers, May 25th, 1811), he was ill-supported by his own Government, insulted by that of Portugal and by the exiled Prince Regent; and to such an extent were the most elementary details thrown upon his shoulders, that he and Mr. Stuart were obliged to continue to trade in the purchase of wheat from Egypt, Barbary, South America, etc., etc., for the subsistence, not only of the troops under his command, but even of the civil population of Portugal.

CHAPTER XXIII

Wellington invests Badajoz—Approach of Soult and Marmont—The siege raised—Wellington retires across the Guadiana—Takes up a position on the Caya—Soult retires.

THE Peninsular War may be divided into seven great periods. The first ended with the Convention of Cintra; the second, with Soult's expulsion from Portugal. The third was occupied in Wellington's advance to Talavera, and ended in his retirement within Portuguese territory. The fourth, the only one in which, for the most part, the British acted on the defensive, ended with Masséna's retreat into Spain. The fifth was a period of transition during which Wellington's principal object was the recovery of the Spanish frontier fortresses. The sixth showed the resumption of the offensive, followed by retreat; the seventh, the final advance and invasion of France.

Of these periods, four had now been completed. Wellington's mind dwelt on resuming the offensive. But as a preliminary, it was essential to re-capture the fortresses of Ciudad Rodrigo and Badajoz on the Spanish frontier, and by so doing gain a choice of routes for an advance into Spain. For the siege of Ciudad Rodrigo Wellington had at present no siege train; and, after carefully weighing the alternatives, he decided to resume the siege of Badajoz; for although in view of his scanty

IN THE PENINSULA 425

means of attack he could hardly doubt that Soult or Marmont would come to the relief of the place, yet the object was worth an attempt, and if by good fortune he were to succeed and could afterwards secure Rodrigo, it was his intention to advance during the autumn into Andalusia with the object of capturing Seville and raising the blockade of Cadiz.

At dusk on the 25th of May, the 7th Division, aided by three Portuguese battalions, invested Badajoz with 5,000 men on the right bank of the Guadiana. On the 27th, Picton with the 3rd Division reinforced Hamilton on the left bank; the force on that side amounting now to 10,000 men. The covering army under Hill consisted of the 2nd and 4th Divisions and the Spaniards. It extended from Merida to Albuera. The Cavalry was pushed forward in observation of Soult at Llerena.

Communication with the Army in Beira was maintained thus—

Stages.	Distances.
Sabugal ...	
Pedrogao	27 miles
St. Miguel d'Arche	8 ,,
Escalhas da Cima	10 ,,
Castello Branco	10 ,,
Sarnadas	10 ,,
Villa Velha, across the Tagus	10 ,,
Niza	11 ,,
Portalégre	24 ,,
Assumar	12 ,,
Santa Llaya	14 ,,
Elvas	10 ,,
Total distance from Sabugal to Elvas	146 miles.

From the nature of circumstances the siege operations could be little less than a farce. Some of the guns dated from the time of the Spanish Armada. The shot did not fit the bore. The gunners were few in number; there was no trained corps of sappers and miners; the Infantry was untaught in the art of making gabions and fascines. It was found necessary to adopt Beresford's lines of attack upon the Castle and San Christoval, but they were to "be pushed simultaneously and with more powerful means."

"San Christoval might thus be taken, and batteries from thence sweep the interior of the Castle, which was meanwhile to be breached; something also was to be hoped from the inhabitants, and something from the effect of Soult's retreat from Albuera" (Napier). Major Dickson rapidly prepared a battering train of 30 24-pounders, 4 16-pounders, and 12 8- and 10-inch howitzers used as mortars by placing them on trucks. Six iron Portuguese ship guns also arrived. "Some British artillery came from Lisbon to be mixed with the Portuguese, making a total of six hundred gunners. The regular engineer officers present were 29 in number; 11 volunteers from the line were joined as assistant engineers; and a draft of 300 intelligent Infantry, including 25 artificers of the Staff Corps, strengthened the force immediately under their command."

General Phillipon, the Governor, had not failed to make the best use of the interval allowed him, to repair breaches, level trenches, &c. The hopes reposed by Wellington in the inhabitants proved vain. In fact they helped to strengthen the fortifications. On the 6th of June two breaches had, however, been made in San Christoval, but an assault that night, and another on the 9th, failed. An intercepted letter from Soult to Marmont gave information of the approaching junction of the armies under the two Marshals, and Lord Wellington found himself compelled to turn the siege—which had cost him 500 men—into a blockade.

IN THE PENINSULA

The following return gives the amount of ammunition expended in the siege from the 3rd to the 10th of June—

24-pounder round shot	14,369
,, grape ,,	641
16-pounder round ,,	1,141
10-inch shells	702
8-inch ,,	2,079
Arrobas of powder; 32 lbs. each	4,344

"It was not strange," observes Napier, "that the siege failed. It was strange and culpable that the British Government after such long wars should have sent an engineer corps into the field so ill organised and equipped that all the officers' bravery and zeal could not render it efficient. The very tools used . . . were unfit for work; the captured French cutting instruments were eagerly sought for in preference; and when the soldiers' lives and the honour of England were at stake, English cutlery would not bear comparison with the French."

"Hence," observes the same writer in another passage, "the crimes of politicians were atoned for by the blood of the soldiers."

Modern authors attempt to discount Napier's scathing criticisms on the Government by the imputation of political prejudice. He was no doubt a Radical; but a Radical of his day had even less in common with the Whig than with the Tory. The fact, however, is that Napier was not a party man but a patriot, and he lashes both political parties with equal impartiality. It must be remembered also that the doctrine of the infallibility of a Conservative Government is of somewhat recent origin.

On the 14th of June, the 9th Corps, under Count d'Erlon, joined Soult, who thereupon advanced from Llerena with a view to meeting Marmont, for he knew

WELLINGTON'S OPERATIONS

that Marshal was marching southward with the Army of Portugal which, in pursuance of the Emperor's orders, had now been re-organised in six Divisions as follow, the titles of 2nd, 6th, and 8th Army Corps being given up.

1st Division	6th Light Infantry,		39th; 69th; 76th of the Line.
2nd ,,	25th ,,	,,	27th; 50th; 59th.
3rd ,,	31st ,,	,,	26th; 66th; 82nd. Legion of the South.
4th ,,		,, ,,	15th 47th; 70th; 86th.
5th ,,	17th ,,	,,	22nd; 65th. Hanoverian, Prussian, and Irish Legions.
6th ,,	2nd, 4th, 15th, 32nd L. I.; 36th; 130th.		

Marmont had started for the Tagus on the 6th, in two columns. Two Divisions under Reynier—his 2nd in command—proceed through the Pass of Banos; the other four, under Marmont in person, took the route of Perales. Thereupon Sir Brent Spencer, with the 1st, 5th, 6th, and Light Divisions, blew up the fortifications of Almeida and marched southwards by parallel roads, leaving Julian Sanchez to keep up a nominal blockade of Ciudad Rodrigo.

On the 18th Marmont effected his junction with Soult, and the two Marshals entered Badajoz next day. It was high time, for Phillipon had but one day's provision remaining. Although aware of that fact, Wellington, in view of the overwhelming numbers of the enemy now concentrated in his front, had raised the blockade three days previously, and had carried his army over the Guadiana. He was followed on the 23rd by the Marshals: the Army under Marmont comprising 36,000 men and 54 guns, that under Soult 28,000 men with 36 guns.

The "State" of the 24th of June gives the following figures for Wellington's Army:—

IN THE PENINSULA

Lieut.-General the Earl of Wellington, K.B.
Major Lord FitzRoy Somerset, Military Secretary.
Major-General the Hon. C. Stewart, Adjutant-General.
Colonel George Murray, Quartermaster-General.

Cavalry Division.

Lieut.-General Sir Stapleton Cotton, K.B.

		Effective Rank and File.
1st Brigade, Major-Gen. Sir W. Erskine, Bart.	3rd Dragoon Guards	332
	4th Dragoons	229
		561
2nd Brigade, Major-General Slade	Royal Dragoons	424
	13th Light Dragoons	287
		711
3rd Brigade, Brigdr.-General Anson	14th Light Dragoons	340
	16th ,, ,,	333
		673
4th Brigade, Major-Gen. Victor Alten	1st Light Dragoons, K.G.L.	429
	2nd Light Dragoons, K.G.L.	203
	11th Light Dragoons	550
		1,182

Portuguese Cavalry Division.

	Effective Rank and File.	Guns.
Provoa's Brigade	486	
Barbacena's Brigade	418	
Madden's Brigade	362	
	1,266	

Artillery.

British	2167 }	72
Portuguese	820 }	

1st *Infantry Division.*
Lieut.-General Sir B. Spencer.

		Effective Rank and File.	
Brigade of Guards Major-Gen. H. Campbell	1st Batt. Coldstream 1st Batt. 3rd Guards 1 Company 5th Batt. 60th Rifles	761 766 33	1,560
2nd Brigade Major-Gen. Hon. E. Stopford	2nd Batt. 24th 2nd ,, 42nd 1st ,, 79th 1 Company 60th	277 350 566 25	1,218
3rd Brigade Major-General Baron Low	1st Line Batt. K.G.L. 2nd ,, ,, ,, 5th ,, ,, ,, 7th ,, ,, ,,	440 390 344 339	1,813
			4,591

2nd *Division.*
Lieut.-General Hill.

1st Brigade Major-General Howard	1st Batt. 50th 1st ,, 71st 1st ,, 92nd	452 414 602	1,468
2nd Brigade Major-General Lumley	Provisional Battalion (Buffs, 79; 29th, 135; 31st, 202; 57th, 242; 66th, 155) 2nd Batt. 28th 2nd ,, 34th 2nd ,, 39th 3 Coys. 5th Batt. 60th 1 Coy. 3rd Batt. 95th	813 313 383 308 107 56	1,980
Portuguese Brigade Colonel Ashworth	6th and 18th Regts.		1,877
			5,325

IN THE PENINSULA

3rd Division.
Major-General Picton.

		Effective Rank and File.	
1st Brigade Colonel Mackinnon	1st Batt. 45th 1st ,, 74th 1st ,, 88th 3 Companies 60th	391 464 585 163	1,603
2nd Brigade Major-Gen. Hon. C. Colville	2nd Batt. 5th 2nd ,, 83rd 2nd ,, 88th 2nd ,, 94th	392 345 258 409	1,404
Portuguese Brigade Lieut.-Col. Sutton	9th and 21st Regts.		1,081
			4,088

4th Division.
Major-General Hon. G. L. Cole.

1st Brigade Major-General Kemmis	3rd Batt. 27th 1st ,, 40th 1st ,, 97th 1 Company 60th	576 585 289 28	1,478
2nd Brigade Brigdr.-Gen. Hon. E. Pakenham	1st Batt. 7th Fusiliers 2nd ,, 7th ,, 1st ,, 23rd ,, 1st ,, 48th 1 Coy. Brunswick L.I.	346 179 358 316 61	1,260
Portuguese Brigade Brigdr.-Gen. Harvey	11th and 23rd Regts.		2,667
			5,405

5th Division.
Major-General Dunlop.

1st Brigade Major-General Hay	3rd Batt. 1st Royals 1st ,, 9th 2nd ,, 38th 1 Coy. Brunswick L.I.	550 570 332 56	1,508

		Effective Rank and File.	
2nd Brigade Major-General Dunlop	1st Batt. 4th	543	
	2nd ,, 30th	399	
	2nd ,, 44th	350	
	1 Coy. Brunswick L.I.	56	1,348
Portuguese Brigade Brigdr.-General Spry	3rd and 15th Regts.		1,694
			4,545

6th Division.
Major-General Alexander Campbell.

1st Brigade Major-General Hulse	1st Batt. 11th	738	
	2nd ,, 53rd	404	
	1st ,, 61st	608	
	1 Company 60th	40	1,790
2nd Brigade Major-Gen. Burne	2nd	487	
	1st Batt. 36th	415	902
Portuguese Brigade Baron Eben	8th and 12th Regts.		1,878
			4,570

7th Division.
Major-General Sontag.

1st Brigade Major-Gen. Baron C. Alten	1st Light Batt. K.G.L.	537	
	2nd ,, ,, ,,	520	
	9 Coys. Brunswick L.I.	473	1,530
2nd Brigade Major-General Sontag	51st	360	
	5 Companies 85th	200	
	Chasseurs Britanniques	588	1,148
Portuguese Brigade Colonel Palmerini	7th and 19th		1,704
			4,882

IN THE PENINSULA 433

Light Division.

Major-General R. Crauford.

		Effective Rank and File.	
1st Brigade Colonel Beckwith	1st Batt. 43rd	651	
	1st ,, 95th (4 Coys.)	327	
	2nd ,, 95th (1 Coy.)	78	
			1,056
2nd Brigade Brigdr.-General Drummond	1st Batt. 52nd	723	
	2nd ,, 52nd	435	
	1st ,, 95th (4 Coys.)	332	
			1,490
Portuguese Brigade	2nd and 3rd Caçadores		783
			3,329

Portuguese Division.

Major-General Hamilton.

1st Brigade Major-General Fonseca	2nd; and 14th		2,322
2nd Brigade Brigdr.-General Campbell	4th and 10th Regts.		2,182
	13th Regt.	934	
	5th Caçadores	404	
			1,338
			5,842
Portuguese Brigade Brigdr.-General Pack	1st and 16th Regts.		1,886

Grand Total 51,343 men and 72 guns.

By adding one-eighth to these figures on account of officers, sergeants, &c., we get a total of all ranks of 57,760. The 2nd Battalion 58th (313 rank and file) was at Lisbon.

Reinforcements had been sent from England, but only the 11th Light Dragoons had arrived. The 12th Light Dragoons (460 sabres), 4th Dragoon Guards, and Infantry Drafts (3,800) were on their way; as were the 26th, 32nd, 68th, and 77th Regiments (2,950). The 1st Battalion

31st, 39th, and Watteville's Regiment (2,700) were to be brought from the Mediterranean; the 1st Battalion 28th (600) from Gibraltar; detachments of the 2nd Hussars K.G.L. (200), and 3rd Battalion 95th (300) from Cadiz. Watteville's Regiment was countermanded, but without reckoning it, about 17,000 officers and men had been ordered to the Peninsula.

The following Spanish troops, exclusive of those in Catalonia, were in the field.

Blake's Army	12,000
In Galicia	12,000
In Valencia	8,000
In Murcia	10,000
Total	42,000

The French Marshals, on crossing the Guadiana, found Wellington occupying a position astride the Caya river, between Campo Mayor and Elvas. His left, consisting of the Light, 5th and 6th Divisions, was strongly posted on the Gebora, and the line ran from the small fort of Ouguela through Campo Mayor — which formed the centre, being held by the 3rd and 7th Divisions under Picton — and was prolonged thence in the direction of Elvas by the 2nd, 4th, and Hamilton's Portuguese Division under Hill. The whole line extended over twelve miles of country. The plains in front were open, and the approach of the enemy at a distance could be plainly seen from the ancient watch towers built for the purpose.

In order to defeat any turning movement that might be made either on the right by Estremoz or on the left by Marvao, the 1st Division was posted at Portalégre, thirty miles in rear of Campo Mayor. This reduced by 5,000 men and 12 guns the numbers available for battle. The 5th Division also did not arrive till the 24th. Even then with 60 guns and 52,000 men—of whom the troops under Pack and Hamilton, the only ones supplied by the Portuguese Government, were starving—against 70,000 men and 90 guns * of the enemy, Wellington's position was one of "bluff"; but it was essential to maintain it as long as possible, for the Portuguese fortresses, owing to the neglect of the Government, were in no condition for defence. On the other hand the concentration of the French armies also gave the Spaniards another golden opportunity to strike a blow elsewhere. As usual, however, nothing of importance was effected in the country; and the large cities remained tranquil, in the enjoyment of good administration by the French.

Soult and Marmont, freed from anxiety as to their communications, were on the other hand in a position to strike a great strategic blow, which, if successful, might carry them to the gates of Lisbon and even ensure the evacuation of the Peninsula by the British Army. But, during the last few weeks, both armies had had experience of the fighting qualities of British troops, and were perhaps not over anxious to repeat the experiment unless under circumstances of exceptional advantage, and though such circumstances did in point of fact exist at this period, the Marshals did not realise the state of the case.

While his opponents hesitated, Wellington made the best use of the respite by sending his sick and baggage to the rear, and doing his utmost to place the Portuguese fortresses in a state of defence. An opportunity arose for making a diversion in his own favour. He had been

* Wellington understood this to be the strength of the combined armies. If Napier's 64,000 includes only sabres and bayonets the number would exceed 70,000, and in any case the garrison of Badajoz was available.

436 WELLINGTON'S OPERATIONS

unwilling to bring Blake's Spanish Corps of 13,000 men permanently into Portugal: partly because he feared quarrels between the Spaniards and Portuguese; partly that in the event of a general action he preferred to be without the former. Observing, therefore, that Soult's concentration had denuded Andalusia of troops, Wellington had asked Blake to cross the Guadiana on the 22nd at Mertola, on the borders of the Algarves, with a view to an attack on Seville which was now very weakly guarded. The result of this operation would be to destroy the magazines on which Victor depended for the blockade of Cadiz, and to threaten the flank and rear of Soult and Marmont. The co-operation of the Murcians and of a force from the lines of San Roque was arranged.

The plan was feebly executed, but its effect was immediate. Soult at once detached a Division of the 9th Corps to cut Blake off from Ayamonte, and with part of the rest of his army marched to the relief of Seville, which he effected on the 6th of July. The troops belonging to the 4th Corps were recalled from Badajoz to take the place of the garrisons in the larger towns which had been sent to repel insurgents.

Blake effected his escape; embarked his Corps, and, landing again at Almeria, reinforced the Murcians. Soult marched against the combined forces, and on the 10th of August routed them at Baza.

Speaking of Soult's campaign, Napier (bk. xiv. ch. 6) observes, "His vigour and ability had now been signally displayed for six months. Taking the field with a small force in the depth of winter he reduced Olivenza, Badajoz, Albuquerque, Valencia d'Alcantara, and Campo Mayor, defeated a large army on the Gebora, and captured 20,000 men. When unexpectedly assailed by Beresford from the north, by the Murcians on the east, by Ballesteros on the west, by Graham and Lapeña in the south, he found means to repel three of those attacks, to continue the blockade of Cadiz and to keep Seville tranquil while he marched against the fourth. At Albuera he lost one of the fiercest battles on record at a moment when the king by abandoning his throne had doubled every embarrassment; nevertheless, holding fast to Estremadura, he maintained the struggle, and again taking the offensive compelled the Allies to repass the Guadiana. If he did not then push his fortune it must be considered that his command was divided and his troops still impressed with the recollection of Albuera, while the genius of his adversary was working new troubles for him in Andalusia. With what resolution and activity he repressed those troubles has just been shown; and he is likewise to be commended for the prudent vigour of his administration which, despite the opposition of Joseph's Spanish counsellors, had impressed the Andalusians with such a notion of his power and resources that no revolt of any real consequence took place, and none of his civil guards or Escopeteros failed him in the hour of need. Let the wide extent of country he had to maintain be considered; the frontier fringed, as it were, with hostile armies, the interior shuddering under war requisitions, the people secretly hating the French, a constant insurrection in the Ronda, a national government and a powerful army in the Isla de Leon. Innumerable English and Spanish agents, prodigal of money and of arms, continually instigating the people to revolt, the coast covered with hostile vessels, Gibraltar sheltering beaten armies on one side, Portugal on another, Cadiz on a third, Murcia on a fourth; the communication with France difficult, two battles lost, the reinforcements few, and all the material means to be created in the country. Few men could have stood firm in such a whirlwind; yet Soult did not merely keep his ground but contemplated gigantic offensive enterprises, and was always to be dreaded. What though his skill in actual combat was not so remarkable as in some of his contemporaries; who can deny him firmness, activity, vigour, foresight, grand conceptions, and admirable arrangement?"

CHAPTER XXIV

Marmont retires into the valley of the Tagus—Napoleon's plans—
Difficulties on either side—Wellington takes the bulk of the army
to the Coa—Advance of Marmont and Dorsenne—El Bodon—
Aldea Ponte—The enemy retires—Blockade of Ciudad Rodrigo.

WITH the departure of Soult, Marmont realised that he was too weak to attack Wellington single-handed. In the early days of July he retired into the valley of the Tagus, and the crisis passed away.

But the general position of the French in Spain was improving. Joseph returned to Madrid. Reinforcements to the extent of 40,000 men were arriving in the north. The Young Guard re-occupied Leon and prepared to invade Galicia.

Marmont, based on Madrid, was ordered to assume a central position on the Tagus, whence he would be enabled to operate on Wellington's left flank, should that Commander march to the relief of Cadiz, or on his right flank should he advance on Salamanca. A junction of Soult and Marmont would concentrate 65,000; a junction between Marmont and Dorsenne—who had succeeded Bessières in command of the Army of the North—would concentrate 70,000. If—as a third alternative—Wellington should march straight on Madrid by the valley of the Tagus, Marmont, reinforced by Dorsenne as well as Soult, would oppose the Allies in far superior numbers.

The means of intercourse between the French armies had hitherto been very deficient; in fact they got hardly any information of each other's plans and movements except from Napoleon. In order to establish communication between himself and Soult, Marmont fortified the bridge of Almaraz on both banks of the Tagus; constructed a large fort on the Mirabete ridge to protect the road to Truxillo where Foy's Division was posted; and repaired the Castle of Medellin on the Guadiana. The line of communication with Soult was taken up thence by Girard's Division of the 5th Corps at Zafra.

Badajoz was garrisoned with detachments from each of the Armies of Portugal, the South and the Centre, in order to give each an equal interest in its maintenance, for the Emperor was well aware to what extent in the past his combinations had been marred by the mutual jealousies of his Marshals.

Between Dorsenne and Marmont communication was kept up by the passes of Banos and Bejar, and by the road along the Pino river.

It was Napoleon's intention that in September the offensive should be resumed and a simultaneous invasion of Portugal made by Dorsenne and Marmont north, and by Soult, south of the Tagus.

Against such a combination Wellington had the advantage of acting on interior lines with a force considerably larger than could be opposed to him by any of the French Commanders singly, and the power of utilising for purposes of transport all navigable rivers within his sphere of operations.

As regards what may be termed accessory circumstances, matters on either side were about evenly balanced; for although in places the action of the Guerilla bands harassed the French convoys, cut off their messengers and necessitated the detachment of large escorts for their protection, Wellington was suffering terribly from the neglect of his own Government to supply him with specie, and from that of the Portuguese to organise an efficient commissariat for their troops. Three-fourths of the Portuguese were fed by Wellington, the expense being deducted from the annual subsidy furnished by England. But the principal means of land transport was by pack mules, driven by Spanish muleteers. These muleteers, "by whose aid alone," as Wellington remarked, "we can exist," were six months in arrear of pay, and, what was worse, from their national contempt of the Portuguese refused to carry food for them, or to associate with them in any way; regarding them indeed as people of an inferior caste. Thus Wellington, writing on the 12th of June, 1811, to Colonel Gordon, Commissary in Chief, remarks that in addition to embarrassments of all kinds, he "had to contend with an ancient enmity between the two nations, which is more like cat and dog than anything else, of which no sense of common danger or common interest can get the better, even in individuals." And he adds that the Spanish Muleteers would prefer to quit the British Army and attend the French to being obliged to carry provisions for the Portuguese. The British Commander was able to get the Portuguese Brigades attached to British Divisions fed, by leading the Muleteers to believe that the supplies which they conveyed were for the British alone; but as regarded the rest of the Portuguese troops he was obliged to leave them to the arrangements made by their own Government, which were practically nil; and the consequence was that the Allied Army contained a large proportion of starving soldiers.

But though the Spaniards were too grand to associate with their neighbours the latter got on capitally with the

British troops. They ate the same food and adopted the same habits as our men, including in some cases the same disposition to intoxication!

The intelligence department was well organised both on the French and on the English side. To complete the comparison between the rival armies, it must be remembered that whereas Wellington was thoroughly and intelligently supported at home by no one except his brother, Lord Wellesley, at this time Foreign Secretary, the French Commanders were backed up by the whole available resources of France centralised under the greatest genius of that or probably any other age.

The position taken up by Marmont, and the prevalence of the Guadiana fever during the summer months (which had already affected his army), made it impossible to resume the siege of Badajoz. Wellington's plans in regard to Andalusia had to be perforce abandoned for the present; and the reflection that, but for Beresford's tardiness Badajoz should have been in his hands three months ago, must have added bitterness to the disappointment of the British Commander.

Wellington then turned his thoughts again to the capture of Ciudad Rodrigo, the northern gate into Spain, the possession of which was as essential a preliminary to an advance against Salamanca as was that of Badajoz for an invasion of the southern provinces.

By this time a siege train of sixty-eight heavy guns and mortars had arrived from England. Wellington re-embarked it at Lisbon to give the impression that it was intended for Cadiz; but, at sea, transferred the pieces to vessels of shallow draft which were brought to Oporto. Thence the guns were carried in boats up to Lamego, and from there over forty miles of mountains to Villa de Ponte near Celorico. The toil was stupendous : 5,000 bullocks were required to draw the train and 1,000 Militiamen were for several weeks employed in repairing the road. Yet as the route lay along a main channel of supply the operation attracted no attention on the part of the French.

On Marmont's retirement into the valley of the Tagus Wellington conformed to the movement by quartering the bulk of his army about Marvao and Castello de Vide; leaving Hill with a Division of Cavalry, two of Infantry and four batteries, in the country between Portalégre and Villa Viciosa, protected by the fortresses of Elvas, Campo Mayor, &c., and covered by the 5th Spanish Army under Castanos at Montijo on the Guadiana.

During this period the expected reinforcements arrived. Wellington's force actually in the field was raised to about 64,000 of all ranks. There was, however, a good deal of sickness among his troops, and the old difficulty recurred of officers—particularly general officers—wanting leave of absence to go home. Illness was the only claim that Wellington would admit; but Generals Nightingall, W. Stewart, De Grey, Lumley, and Howarth went home on medical certificate. Spencer, on being superseded by Graham as second in command, also departed. Leith had been long absent. Dunlop, Hay, Cole, and Alexander Campbell asked for leave on private affairs. "Till we get the minds of the officers of the army settled to their duty," said Wellington, "we shall not get on as we ought."

On the 18th of July, Picton was despatched northward with the 3rd and 6th Divisions and Slade's Cavalry Brigade. On the 1st of August he was followed by Lord Wellington with the 1st, 4th, 5th, 7th, and Light Divisions.

The Cavalry was now organised in two Divisions as follows :—

1st *Cavalry Division.*
Lieutenant-General Sir S. Cotton, K.B.

Royal Dragoons } Major-General Slade.
12th Light Dragoons

14th Light Dragoons } Major-General Anson.
16th   ,,   ,,

11th Light Dragoons } Major-General Victor Alten.
1st Hussars K.G.L.

Portuguese Brigade   Brigadier-General Madden.

2nd *Division.*
Major-General Sir W. Erskine.

3rd Dragoon Guards } Colonel Sir Granby Calcraft.
4th Dragoons

13th Light Dragoons } Major-General Long.
2nd Hussars K.G.L.

9th Light Dragoons, about to join.
Otway's and Barbacena's Portuguese Brigades.

Erskine's Division, excepting Calcraft's Brigade, remained with Hill at Portalégre. The rest of the Cavalry went northward with Wellington.

Early in August Lord Wellington received, as a compliment from the War Office, the local rank of General in Spain and Portugal. On the 9th of the same month General Graham arrived from Cadiz and took over command of the 1st Division from Sir Brent Spencer.

On the 12th of August, Headquarters were established at Fuente Guinaldo. The march had been unopposed; nor was its object comprehended by the enemy, who believed it due rather to a desire to disturb Dorsenne's operations in Galicia and to relieve Murcia by drawing Marmont from Soult, in which case the latter would be in no position to leave Andalusia. In point of fact, Wellington's march did recall Dorsenne, who had arrived within measurable distance of Corunna in pursuit of the Spanish General Abadia. "This saving of Galicia," observes Napier, "was a great thing. That kingdom was the base of all the operations against the French line of communication; from thence went forth British squadrons to nourish the guerillas of Biscay, of the Montana, Navarre, the Rioja, and the Asturias; it was the chief resource for the supply of cattle to the Allied Army, it was the outwork of Portugal; and if honestly and vigorously governed, would have been more important than Catalonia. But, like the rest of Spain, it was always weak from disorders, and there was nothing to prevent Dorsenne from conquering it. Had he only occupied St. Jago, Lugo, Villa Franca, and Orense, they would have given him entire command of the interior, and the Spaniards holding only the ports could not have dislodged him. . . . It was worthy of observation that Wellington (in his plans) did not comprise the Galician army as an auxiliary; he had no expectation that it would act at all, and was certain that it would not act effectually; yet this was in August, 1811, and Galicia had not seen an enemy since June, 1809!"

Wellington arrived on the Coa only to find the blockade relieved and Ciudad Rodrigo, but three days previously, provisioned for two months. He thereupon quartered his army near the sources of the Coa and Agueda, "close to the line of communication between Dorsenne and Marmont. . . . Thence if the enemy advanced in superior numbers there was a retreat through the strong country to a position of battle near Sabugal whence the communication with Hill was direct." By an advance on Almeida, Marmont would expose his left flank. The magazines at Celorico were protected; but there was a real danger that if Dorsenne knew of the position of the siege train he might capture it with impunity.

The British Commander was intent on besieging Ciudad Rodrigo; but finding that Dorsenne had an available force of 20,000 men, and knowing Marmont's strength and position, he felt himself unequal to the task. He therefore contented himself with blockading the fortress once more. Almeida was re-fortified and made into a depôt for stores. The Light Division was posted at Martiago; the 5th, with one of Hill's batteries, at Perales on the Sierra de Gata in observation of Marmont; with the 1st in support at Penamacor. The 2nd Division occupied the line of the Ponçul with a view to protecting the magazines on the Castello Branco road. Wellington had now the advantage of a broad base of operations from Lisbon to Coimbra, and a double line of supply by way of the Mondego and Castello Branco. His line of retreat ran through Sabugal and Castello Branco along the valleys of the Zezere and Tagus, communication with Hill being maintained by a detachment of that officer's Corps posted at Castello Branco.

But although occupying an advanced position and having under his command an army consisting nominally of over 90,000 officers and men and 90 guns, yet 25,000 of his men were in hospital; 12,000 or 14,000 were with Hill; 6,000 more were on detachment, and his available force would be about 45,000, much inferior to the combined armies of Dorsenne and Marmont, who had been largely reinforced. There was also still a chance that the Emperor would take the field in person. In such a case there could be no hesitation on the part of the Army of the South to combine with that of Portugal; and, to meet the contingency, the lines of Torres Vedras were strengthened on both sides, but particularly on the south of the Tagus. "On the southern bank," says Napier, "the double entrenchments of Almada had been continued on a gigantic scale. A defensive canal there was planned on a depth to float ships of 300 tons, and serve as a passage from the Tagus to Setuval by joining the navigation of the Sadao and Marateca rivers, thus conducing to objects of general utility as well as the military defence; and it will be found that Wellington did at all times sustain, not only the political and financial and military affairs, but also the agricultural, commercial, and charitable interests of Portugal. . . ." The Engineers had cleverly constructed four jetties capable of withstanding the worst storms, which secured the embarkation of the army at any season.

Other defensive measures were taken. The Militia was called out again. The regular army, now thoroughly seasoned, refilled its ranks and mustered 24,000 bayonets. But the Portuguese Regency once more displayed its combination of treachery and incompetence. The broken bridges were not repaired along the valley of the Mondego, which, as a line of retreat, was consequently useless. Nor was this all. By publishing confidential information which was promptly copied into English newspapers and thence speedily reached the French Government, the Regency silenced Wellington's sources of confidential intelligence. To add to the mortification of the British Commander, although neither money nor patriotism could induce his allies to procure aid, the French Generals " had only to issue their orders to the Spaniards through the prefects of provinces, and all kinds of aid possible to be obtained were surely provided on the day and at the place indicated " (Napier).

By the middle of September Ciudad Rodrigo began again to feel the pinch of famine. Reinforcements had raised Marmont's strength to 50,000 men. A combined movement for the relief of the fortress was arranged between him and Dorsenne, who concentrated at Salamanca a Cavalry Division under Wathier, two Infantry Divisions commanded by Thiébault and Souham, and two Divisions and a Cavalry Brigade of the Imperial Guard; the whole amounting to 26,000 men and 50 guns. In the south, Foy, relieved by a Division of the 5th Corps at Truxillo, took post at Plasencia. On the 21st, the bulk of the Armies of Portugal and the North, to the number of 60,000 men and 100 guns, formed a junction at Tamames.

Wellington concentrated his troops, but was not strong enough to stop the re-victualment of Rodrigo. He took up a position astride the Azava and Agueda, facing northeast. The Light Division, with some squadrons of Anson's Cavalry Brigade and a battery R.H.A., forming the right wing, was posted beyond the Agueda at Martiago on the Valdillo river, a confluence of the Agueda, 12 miles above the fortress. The 3rd Division, covered by Alten's Cavalry Brigade, was in the centre at El Bodon, on the high ground overlooking the left bank of the Agueda, with a detachment thrown forward to Pastores and the fortress beyond. Anson's Cavalry Brigade—whose outposts were at Marialva, Carpio, and the roads leading from Ciudad Rodrigo to Campillo—with the 6th Division, formed the left wing at Espeja; and still further to the left, Julian Sanchez watched the Lower Agueda.

On the evening of the 22nd further orders were issued, to take effect next morning. The 1st Division was to concentrate at Nava de Aver. The Portuguese Cavalry Brigades of MacMahon, Otway, and Madden to occupy the woods between Fuentes d'Onoro and Pozo Velho. Pack's Brigade to march to Campillo. The 4th Division to Fuente Guinaldo. The Cavalry Brigades of Calcraft and Slade, each with a battery Royal Horse Artillery, to

IN THE PENINSULA

connect the left and centre of the army by the occupation of Etuero and Puebla de Azava. The 7th Division to move on Alamedilla; the reserve ammunition to Aldea de Ponte. The 1st, 6th, and 7th Divisions, Anson's Brigade, and all troops to the left of a line drawn from Espeja to Nava de Aver were placed under command of Graham, who, in case of being attacked by superior numbers, was directed to concentrate his British and Portuguese troops at Nava de Aver and retire thence, if necessary, on Villa Maior and Aldea de Ribeira. The Spaniards on the Lower Agueda were to retire on Castello Bom and defend the passage of the river. The 5th Division remained at San Payo to hold in check Foy at Plasencia. Hill sent a Brigade to replace the 1st Division at Penamacor, and pushed Hamilton forward to Albuquerque in support of the Spanish Cavalry, which was being threatened by the 5th Corps.

Wellington's position, extending over ten miles, was too large for his force. He therefore threw up redoubts at Fuente Guinaldo, the apex of the triangle along the base of which the army was extended, and the point of convergence for his Divisions in case of retreat.

On the 23rd the enemy advanced from Tamames upon Ciudad Rodrigo. Wellington, although reinforced by the 4th Division, was not in a position to prevent the revictualment of the fortress next day.

At daybreak on the 25th, Marmont crossed the Agueda. Eight of his squadrons, fording the Azava, drove in Anson's picquets, but were checked by the fire of Hulse's Brigade of the 6th Division, and, being charged by the supports, were driven back over the river with some loss. Among the French Cavalry was a regiment of Lancers. The weapon was new to our men; but it was observed to become an encumbrance to its owner when once closed upon, and in the retreat it caught in the accoutrements of other men and pulled them from their horses. The lance of that date was, however, much longer and more cumbersome than the modern one.

Meanwhile, on the French left, Montbrun, with 14 battalions, 30 squadrons, and 12 guns, had crossed the Agueda close to Ciudad Rodrigo and marched on Guinaldo. His line of advance penetrated the British line between Graham and Picton, turning the left of the latter. Picton's Division had to cover a good deal of ground. The 74th and the three headquarter companies of the 60th were on outpost duty at Pastores. Picton himself, with the 45th, 83rd, 88th, and 94th, guarded the direct road from Ciudad Rodrigo; Colville, with three squadrons of V. Alten's Brigade, the 5th and 77th Regiments and 21st Portuguese, and two batteries of Portuguese Artillery under Major Arenschildt, guarded a similar road leading to Fuente Guinaldo, and was posted two miles on Picton's left.

Montbrun, passing Pastores and El Bodon, fell upon Colville. That officer was strongly posted on high ground, but was unable to stop the enemy, who outflanked him. As Montbrun's squadrons reached the brow of the hill they were received with artillery and musketry fire, and charged again and again with the utmost gallantry by Colville's Cavalry, consisting of a squadron of the 11th Light Dragoons and two of the 1st Hussars K.G.L. For an hour Colville thus held the enemy in check. At length Montbrun brought up his guns in support of his Cavalry, which then got in among the Portuguese Artillery. The Artillerymen died at their guns, which fell into the hands of the French. The loss was but momentary. The 5th Fusiliers, who had been lying down behind the crest line, sprang to their feet, charged the astonished horsemen with the bayonet and

IN THE PENINSULA

recovered the guns. The 77th and 21st repelled an attack at the same time. Picton was now coming up, but, entangled among the vineyards at El Bodon, his progress was slow. Wellington, as usual, was at the critical point. He now ordered both Picton and Colville to fall back upon the main position at Fuente Guinaldo. Colville accordingly formed the 5th and 77th in one square, the 21st Portuguese in another. The latter, with the Cavalry and guns, retired first, covered by the British battalions, who were immediately surrounded on the tableland by the French Cavalry, but repelled a vigorous charge made upon three faces of the square; and at two miles in rear of their original position effected a junction with Picton and with a Brigade of the 4th Division which had been sent to their support. The coolness and steady bearing of Colville's Brigade had been magnificent, and was the theme of a most laudatory General Order. The feat was the more remarkable that the 11th Light Dragoons and 77th had only joined the army a few weeks previously.

The three Brigades then made good their retreat for three more miles to Fuente Guinaldo, where they were joined by the Cavalry Brigades of Calcraft, Slade, and Alten, and by Pack; but all the troops collected mustered only 14,000 sabres and bayonets to defend the position. In the retirement of the 3rd Division the 74th and 60th at Pastores were left to their fate, but, keeping their wits about them, they forded the Agueda and, moving up the right bank, not only reached Fuente Guinaldo safely during the night, but captured a French Cavalry patrol on the way. The British losses on this day amounted to about 150 killed, wounded and missing.

Meanwhile Graham, conforming to the movement of the 3rd Division, had fallen back to Nava de Aver; while the Spanish Infantry took post, as ordered, behind the

Coa, and Sanchez, with the Cavalry, moved round to the enemy's rear.

The 7th Division was retired from Alamedilla to Albergueria, ten miles west of Fuente Guinaldo.

While these events were taking place on the left and centre, Crauford on the right had found an opportunity to display his own peculiar idiosyncrasies. The Quartermaster-General had written on the 23rd specially directing him to retire upon Robledo in the event of the enemy advancing in force. A definite order to retire reached Crauford at 3 p.m. on the 25th, but instead of obeying it he merely fell back four miles to Cespedosa.

When morning broke on the 26th the British Army was still widely dispersed. Graham at Nava de Aver and the 7th Division at Albergueria were ten miles distant from Fuente Guinaldo. The 5th Division at San Payo was twelve miles distant; the Light Division, whose most direct line of junction had been intercepted, sixteen miles. Wellington, with a scattered force, was in presence of a concentrated enemy in overwhelming numbers, for by this time Marmont was in front of Fuente Guinaldo with 60,000 men and 120 guns. The earthworks were unfinished, the position was not very strong, and a vigorous attack could hardly fail to drive the Allies out of it, leaving the enemy free to deal with Graham and with the Light Division. To abandon Crauford seemed essential, but what the loss of the Light Division would have meant to the Army it is difficult to exaggerate. In this crisis Wellington's iron nerve once more saved the situation. Despite Marmont's swaggering despatches he had gauged that Marshal's character, and decided to hold his ground. At 3 p.m. Crauford came in. Wellington gave an instance of his marvellous self-control. He merely expressed his pleasure at the safe arrival of the Division. "I was in no danger, I assure you," said

Crauford. "But I was, through your conduct," replied his Commander. Crauford, unable even now to see how unpardonably he had behaved, turned away muttering, "He is d——d crusty to-day."

While Wellington was thus successfully playing the game of "bluff" Marmont was wasting the whole day in an idle demonstration and a reconnaissance of his adversary's position. To the Marshal who had so strongly censured Masséna for not fighting a battle " qu'il aurait evidemment gagnée, et qui aurait fixé le sort de la campagne," the feeble works thrown up at Fuente Guinaldo appeared "an impracticable escarpment"; and the camp was, in his eyes, covered with revetted work and armed with heavy guns. In spite of the protests of Dorsenne, Thiébault, and others, he decided to withdraw the combined armies to Rodrigo, under pretext of conforming to secret instructions given to him by the Emperor, to the effect that it suited him to retain the British Army in the Peninsula. No word of any such policy is, however, to be found in the despatches to Marmont which were intercepted by Wellington. Their tone is, in fact, entirely opposed to such an idea.

The French Army—excepting one Division which formed the rear guard—had actually withdrawn, when it was discovered that Wellington had evacuated his position.

The British Commander rightly decided that to remain at Fuente Guinaldo after the arrival of the Light Division was to tempt fortune. He had therefore given orders for a concentric retirement to be begun three hours after sunset and for the occupation of a new position 12 miles further back behind the Villa Maior river within the Portuguese frontier. Graham's troops occupied Bismula on the left; the 5th Division (which had arrived from

San Payo) Aldea Velha on the right. The 4th and Light Divisions, the Cavalry Brigades of Calcraft, V. Alten and Slade, and the Portuguese Brigades of Pack and McMahon were posted in the centre, about Alfayetes, with Cavalry picquets at Aldea Ponte in front and Furcalhos on the right. The 3rd and 7th Divisions were formed in second line behind Alfayetes. The position, which covered about 10 miles of ground, faced nearly due east, and was in easy communication with Sabugal 10 miles further back, which in its turn was on the direct road to Castello Branco. The distance from Sabugal to Penamacor, where Hill's nearest Brigade was posted, is about 18 miles.

Advancing along two roads on the morning of the 27th, Wathier's Dragoons drove the Cavalry picquets over the Villa Maior stream, and at 10 a.m. occupied the village of Aldea Ponte. The 3rd (Thiébault's) French Division coming up at noon, attacked the heights beyond, but was repelled by Pakenham's and Harvey's Brigades of the 4th Division. Some pretty fighting took place about the village; but Thiébault being unsupported and over-estimating the numbers of the Allies—who, being deployed, covered a comparatively large extent of ground—did not push the attack again beyond it, but retired to the further side. At about 4.30 p.m. Souham brought up his Division and renewed the attack. At dark the firing ceased; Aldea Ponte remaining in the enemy's hands. The British casualties were something over 100. Those of the French, 40 killed and 110 wounded.

During the night Wellington evacuated his position and fell back 4 miles to the Coa, where he posted his army between Rendo and the Sierra de Meras along the chord of a semicircle formed by a bend of the river which protected both his flanks. On this strong position Marmont did not venture to make an attack. His provisions, indeed, were exhausted, and he decided to terminate his operations so pompously begun only a few days since, by which he had gained absolutely nothing but the revictualment of Ciudad Rodrigo. "Parturiunt Montes, &c." Marmont retired to the valley of the Tagus, and Dorsenne to Salamanca. "The opportunity of invading Galicia," observes Napier, "was lost; nothing had been gained in the field, time was wasted, and the English General's plans were forwarded."

While applauding Wellington's firmness at Fuente Guinaldo and in his position on the Coa, Napier criticises his tardy concentration. On the arrival of the French Armies at Ciudad Rodrigo, the whole of the British troops should at once have been collected at Fuente Guinaldo, whereas in consequence of the delay 14,000 men were exposed to the attack of 60,000; and it was only through the magnificent fighting of Colville's Brigade that the enemy did not absolutely sever the right wing from the left.

Wellington now established his Headquarters at Frenada and resumed the nominal blockade of Ciudad Rodrigo. Headquarters of the Cavalry were at Alverca, and the Brigades took monthly turns of outpost duty on the Agueda. The Infantry was cantoned as follows:— 1st Division about Lagiosa; 3rd, Albergueria; 4th, Gallegos; 5th, Guarda; 6th, Freixada; 7th, Penamacor; Light, Fuente Guinaldo.

The Cavalry was reduced to three squadrons per regiment; and under instructions from the Horse Guards, three weak battalions—the 29th, 85th and 97th —returned to England. Although the recent reinforcements raised the Army to a higher strength than heretofore, the newly-arrived regiments were still suffering from fever contracted in the Walcheren marshes. Fourteen thousand men—of whom, however, half were wounded—were in hospital on the 18th of November, and others were unable to stand exposure to the night air. This was particularly the case with the Cavalry, and only the old regiments could be actively employed.

On the retirement of the French Armies, Dorsenne occupied the country between Astorga and the Tamames, while Marmont distributed his Infantry Divisions between Plasencia and Madrid, but posted his Cavalry at Penoranda, 20 miles south-east of Salamanca; while at Aroyo des Molinos, 50 miles south of Plasencia, Girard's Division of the 5th Corps connected Soult with Marmont.

The Armies of the North and of Portugal, connected by a Division at Alba de Tormes, were spread over a front of 150 miles, and their dispersion invited attack; but on the arrival of reinforcements, the Army of the North once more concentrated. Ciudad Rodrigo was again beginning to fall short of provisions, and on the 1st of November General Thiébault cleverly introduced a convoy. By this time the country between the Coa and Agueda was exhausted, and Wellington was compelled to disperse his troops as far as the Mondego, retaining, however, a strong body on the Coa. In the face of Dorsenne's concentrated army dispersion was dangerous; but the rivers were in flood, the enemy at some distance, and Marmont's attention turned to an operation of General Hill against Aroyo des Molinos. By this time the siege train already mentioned had been brought up from Villa de Ponte and placed inside Almeida, the walls of which were now sufficiently repaired to resist a sudden attack.

CHAPTER XXV

Napoleon's instructions to Marmont—Suchet captures Valencia—Operations in Andalusia—Hill surprises Girard at Arroyo des Molinos—Defence of Tarifa.

THE following figures give the "State" of the French Armies in the Peninsula on the 1st of October, 1811 :—

	Under Arms.		Detached.			Effective.	Horses.	
	Men.	Horses.	Men.	H'rses	Hospital.	Men.	Troop	Transport.
Army of the South	66,912	11,757	7,539	2,232	13,398	88,033	9,251	3,393
,, of the Centre	19,125	6,262	511	84	1,685	21,321	5,196	553
,, of Portugal..	50,167	11,662	1,283	858	10,012	61,462	6,909	4,706
,, of Aragon ..	28,966	5,303	6,583	308	4,424	39,953	3,322	1,960
,, of the North	87,913	10,821	6,201	1,069	9,414	103,528	6,769	4,186
,, of Catalonia	26,954	1,365	993	168	11,186	39,241	1,150	289
Total	280,037	47,170	23,110	4,717	50,119	353,538	47,684	
Reinforcements..	9,232	689			1,226	10,458	516	
Grand total ..	289,269	47,859	23,110	4,717	51,345	363,996	48,200	

Writing on the 18th of September to Marmont, Berthier, Napoleon's Chief of the General Staff, observed that towards the end of September the Army of Portugal would comprise 41,700 men and 80 guns. Ciudad

Rodrigo was to receive three months' provisions; and, provided Wellington had no siege train for the attack of that fortress, Marmont — based on Badajoz — was to invade the Alemtejo. To this end Soult was directed to furnish him with 3,000 Cavalry; and, the 5th Corps being also placed under his orders, his total strength would be raised to 57,300 men. Elvas was to be besieged, and its capture might be expected by the middle of November. In the event of Wellington taking advantage of Marmont's absence to march on Salamanca and Valladolid, he would find the former provisioned and fortified. Dorsenne could, however, retire before him as far as Burgos, where he would be able to concentrate 50,000 men. The chances, albeit, were that the British Army would hasten to the defence of Lisbon, in which case Dorsenne would follow it up with 25,000 men. Should Wellington concentrate his entire force on the Tagus, Dorsenne was to detach 15,000 to reinforce Marmont, and by so doing raise the force of the latter to 72,300 men. "This operation," added Berthier, "is the only one which can do honour to our arms, enable us to abandon our present defensive attitude, make the English tremble, and bring on the great objective of the war. . . . The capture of a fortress under the eyes of an English Army; the conquest of a part of Portugal which will cover the Army of the South and your reinforcement by 25,000 men from that Army, will be motives of glory and success. On the other side Suchet will march upon Valencia, which should be taken by the time you have reduced Elvas, whereupon you can be reinforced with another strong Division."

In the event, on the other hand, of Wellington being in a position to attack Ciudad Rodrigo, Marmont was directed to march to its relief, since Dorsenne would not be able to do so unaided. In such a case Marmont was

IN THE PENINSULA

to take command of the Army of the North in addition to his own.

Partly through the indecision of Marmont, partly through Wellington's foresight in providing himself with a siege train, Napoleon's great projects were never even attempted.

VALENCIA.

As a reward for the capture of Tarragona in July, 1811, Suchet had received his bâton as Marshal of France. In the early autumn he was ready with 24,000 men to attempt the conquest of the province of Valencia. His force seemed hardly adequate; but 8,000 men had been left on the line of communication in Catalonia, and 8,000 were in Aragon. It was, however, the system of Napoleon's strategy that his armies in the Peninsula should mutually support one another. Thus, the Armies of the North and of Portugal protected Suchet; for Dorsenne, by menacing Galicia, held Wellington on the Agueda; and an advance on the part of Marmont would equally prevent the British Army taking the offensive. On the other hand, Suchet's advance into Valencia was calculated to take the pressure off Soult on the side of Murcia, and Soult in his turn would be in a position to reinforce Marmont.

On the 20th of September Suchet concentrated his Corps at Castellon de la Planca. On the 28th he laid siege to Saguntum, an old Moorish city built on a mountain rock and extremely difficult of access. The siege, however, made gradual progress. Towards the end of October, the Spanish General Blake, at the head of the Army which had fought at Albuera—and in spite of its shortcomings was the best and most experienced army which Spain had produced—came to the relief of the city, but being defeated under the walls in a battle fought on the 26th, fled with the loss of 6,000 men and 12 guns. Saguntum then surrendered.

Unexpected activity among the "Partidas," aided by the British squadron off the coast, delayed Suchet's progress; and sickness in Macdonald's army prevented that Marshal giving effectual help from Catalonia. At length, however, Suchet advanced to the Guadalaviar, and—although nearly two months later than the Emperor had originally calculated—captured the city of Valencia on the 9th of January, 1812, with the whole of Blake's Army, numbering 18,000 men. Forty thousand muskets, 390 guns, and enormous stores of gunpowder were also taken; and Suchet, rewarded by Napoleon with the title of Duc d'Albufera, set to work to adminster the city and district, a task which he performed with his customary tact and ability, utilising so far as was possible the existing local authorities.

The value of this operation was fully appreciated by Napoleon, who had directed Berthier to inform Marmont that as the capture of Valencia was the most important object in hand, he was to detach 12,000 men to Suchet's support, while Soult was instructed to hold 10,000 in the Despenas Peros Pass to assist that officer in case of need. The Emperor understood that Wellington had 20,000 invalids, and could in consequence undertake nothing on the offensive. But the capture of Valencia would place Portugal at the mercy of the French.

Wellington was equally alive to the importance of Valencia. It was termed the Garden of Spain. Most of the Spanish grandees had estates in the province upon the revenues of which they lived after the loss of everything elsewhere. It was therefore to be expected that its conquest would induce a large number to submit to French rule. The British Commander also observed that the occupation of Valencia would promote the concentration of the enemy's forces. Even if Suchet should be unable to push further southward than Valencia, and Soult should find it impossible to extend his troops so far as to communicate with Suchet through Murcia, the latter would have a shorter line of communication than hitherto with the Armies of the Centre and Portugal, and with the troops in Castille. He would also cut off the supplies of the guerilla chiefs in that neighbourhood.

In pursuance of the Emperor's instructions, Marmont detached Montbrun with a Division of Cavalry and two of Infantry to co-operate with Suchet. Montbrun reached Almanza on the 9th of January—more than a fortnight after time—and then, contrary to Suchet's wishes, advanced against Alicante and summoned it. Napier believes that had Montbrun shown a little more firmness the place would have surrendered; but Montbrun was a man of weak character. The attempt failed. Montbrun withdrew, and as Alicante was immediately fortified, Suchet, instead of receiving aid, was only retarded by his colleague. About this time 6,000 Poles belonging to the Army of Catalonia were recalled by Napoleon to take part in his invasion of Russia. The Marshal had then only 15,000 men remaining. He therefore halted on the Zucar river, and being himself dangerously ill, abandoned the idea of further operations.

Galicia and Asturias.

During the winter of 1811–12 nothing of importance was effected by the Spaniards in Galicia. What little was done was achieved by the Partidas under the supervision of Sir Howard Douglas, R.E.; for the Spanish Commander-in-Chief, General Abadia, was occupying himself in fitting out an expedition, equipped out of British stores, to put down the insurgent colonists in South America!

Asturias was reoccupied by Bonet in November, 1811.

ANDALUSIA.

In Andalusia, Soult—based upon Seville, whence he communicated through Estremadura with Marmont and through La Mancha with the King at Madrid—held his own. Victor, however, having an inadequate force of 20,000 men, made no progress in the blockade of Cadiz; and a Brigade from the British part of the garrison—now commanded in Graham's place by General Cook—was withdrawn by Wellington. The French 4th Corps, 11,000 strong under Leval, guarded the Murcian boundary and the sea-coast. Soult had, in addition, a reserve Corps of 20,000 men, and the Army of the South contained 67,000 men present, exclusive of Spaniards enrolled in the French service.

ESTREMADURA.

The French 9th Corps having been broken up, General Drouet, Count d'Erlon, took command of the 5th, 12,600 strong, in place of Marshal Mortier, who had returned to France.

"Estremadura," observes Napier (book xv. chap. 4), "was the most difficult field of operation. There Badajoz was to be supplied and defended from the most formidable army in the Peninsula; there the communications with Madrid and the Army of Portugal were to be maintained by the way of Truxillo; there the 5th French Corps had to collect its subsistence from a ravaged country, to press its communications over the Sierra Morena with Seville, to protect the march of monthly convoys to Badajoz, to observe Hill, and to oppose Morillo's troops, now becoming numerous and bold. Neither the Spanish nor British Divisions could prevent Drouet from sending convoys to Badajoz, because of the want of bridges on the Guadiana below the fortress; but Morillo incommoded his foraging parties; for being posted at Valencia de Alcantara, and having his retreat on Portugal always secure, he vexed the country about Caceres, and even pushed his incursions to Truxillo. Drouet therefore was compelled to keep a strong detachment beyond the Guadiana, which exposed his troops to Hill's enterprises; and that bold and vigilant commander, well instructed and having 10,000 excellent troops, was a very dangerous neighbour."

In October Soult sent 3,000 men to Fregenal. The 5th Corps then crossed the Guadiana and concentrated at Merida. On the 11th Drouet advanced as if to invade the Alemtejo, and drove Morillo from Caceres. Just at this moment, however, Ballesteros, who had landed at Algesiras in September, made a diversion in the Ronda; and although he was soon repelled by Generals Godinot and Semelé, and driven under the fortifications of Gibraltar, Soult was in the meantime disinclined to continue the advance of the 5th Corps. He therefore recalled Drouet, who retired to Zafra, leaving Girard's Division and Briche's Cavalry Brigade at Caceres.

This abortive movement—of which Wellington took no notice except to return to Hill one of the Brigades of the 2nd Division at Castello Branco—was the only attempt made to carry out Napoleon's instructions for the invasion of Portugal.

The isolated position of Girard's Division of the 5th Corps at Caceres invited attack from Hill on the Portuguese frontier. Girard was quite unsupported; the other Divisions of the Corps, accompanied by Count d'Erlon in person, being 100 miles to the southward at Zafra. On the 23rd of October Hill concentrated at Albuquerque. On the 26th he drove the French Cavalry out of Malpartida and halted there. Girard then abandoned Caceres, which was occupied next morning by the Spanish General Morillo, while Hill advanced on Torre Mocha. During the course of the march information was received to the effect that Girard had halted at Aroyo des Molinos in the belief that the British force had followed the Truxillo road. Hill at once brought up the 2nd Cavalry and 2nd Infantry Divisions by a forced march to Alcuescar, thus heading off Girard's most direct line of retreat upon Merida. "The town of Aroyo Molinos," said Hill in his subsequent despatch, "is situated at the foot of one extremity of the Sierra de Montanches, the mountain running from it to the rear in the form of a crescent, almost everywhere inaccessible, the two points being about two miles asunder. The Truxillo road runs round that to the eastward. The road leading from the town to Merida runs at right angles with that from Alcuescar, and the road to Medellin passes between those to Truxillo and Merida, the grounds over which the troops had to manœuvre being a plain thinly scattered with cork and oak trees. My object, of course, was to place a body of troops so as to cut off the retreat of the enemy by these roads."

At 2 a.m. on the 28th Hill moved upon Aroyo. The 2nd Division was commanded by General Howard. One Brigade, under Colonel Stewart of the 50th with three guns, supported by Morillo's Infantry, advanced straight against the village. Howard himself, with the second Brigade (at present commanded by Colonel Wilson *vice* Lumley), supported by Ashworth with the 6th Portuguese and 6th Caçadores, moved diagonally to the right to intercept the enemy on the Medellin road. The Infantry columns were connected by the Cavalry.

Captain Blaquière of the 60th succeeded in penetrating into the town, and brought back useful information.

Girard had been warned of Hill's proximity by the Spaniards, but did not credit the report. One of his Brigades under General Remond had, however, started for Medellin before daybreak. Two Battalions, a Cavalry Brigade, and half a battery were still in the town. At dawn Stewart charged down the main street. Never was surprise more complete. The French Cavalry were bridling their horses. Dumbrowski's Brigade of Infantry, consisting of a battalion of the 34th and one of the 46th, negligent and unwatchful, crowded the road. Caught as they were in a trap, the French veterans most gallantly attempted to retrieve their error. In spite of the deadly British fire, they formed square to gain time for the withdrawal of Briche's Cavalry Brigade. To some extent they were successful. They got clear of the village. But the road to Merida was already in the possession of Wilson's Brigade. Then Count Penne Villemur cleverly interposed his Brigade of Spanish Cavalry between the enemy's columns, and although Briche's troopers cut to pieces Downie's "harlequin" regiment of Spanish Hussars, yet, charged in their turn by Long's Brigade, they gave way and fled along the Truxillo road. Three guns were shortly afterwards taken by the 13th Dragoons.

Girard's Infantry, thus isolated, continued its retreat in excellent order along the base of the mountain; but just as it approached the Truxillo road and safety seemed assured, it was headed off by the Light Companies of Wilson's Brigade which had successfully seized the second road to Merida and those leading to Medellin and Truxillo. With an enemy on three sides and hemmed in by the almost inaccessible Sierra Montanches on the fourth, surrender appeared inevitable. About 1,000 prisoners were in point of fact taken on the spot. The rest of the hardy veterans, headed by Girard, attempted to scale the heights. The Light Companies followed in pursuit; but the French, throwing off their knapsacks, gained on their heavily laden pursuers. Eventually, Girard, Dumbrowski, and Briche escaped in an easterly direction to Zoita in the Sierra de Guadaloupe. Thence, after crossing the Guadiana at Crellano, they rejoined Count d'Erlon at Zafra, bringing with them, however, only about 600 men.

About 1,300 prisoners were taken, including General Bron and the Prince d'Aremberg, a relative of the Emperor. Morillo reported that he found the bodies of 600 Frenchmen on the mountains, in addition to those lying in the plain; but this statement looks like a piece of Spanish exaggeration. The British losses were slight, amounting only to 7 killed, 64 wounded, and 1 prisoner—Lieutenant Strenowitz of the K.G.L. Hussars, who had so often distinguished himself as a Cavalry officer, and was now acting as A.D.C. to Sir W. Erskine. He was shortly afterwards exchanged.

During the engagement Campbell's Portuguese Brigade and Ashworth's remaining regiment arrived on the scene; and, together with the Brigades of Long, Penne Villemur, and Stewart, were directed on Merida, which they reached on the morning of the 30th.

Girard's error was flagrant, and Soult expressed his annoyance freely. The Marshal at first intended to try him by court-martial; but in consideration of Girard's personal gallantry and resolution, relented and merely deprived him of his Division, the command of which was given to General Barois. Girard had the opportunity at a later date of retrieving his reputation, and was eventually killed at Ligny.

IN THE PENINSULA

After this very successful little enterprise Hill returned to the neighbourhood of Portalégre. He had spread commotion throughout the French armies up to the gates of Seville and Madrid. The 5th Corps was reinforced up to a strength of 3,000 Cavalry and 14,000 Infantry. A detachment from it re-occupied Caceres, and Foy's Division, crossing the Tagus at Almaraz, entered Truxillo. The Governor of Badajoz was directed to use every means to provision the fortress. Soult began to concentrate at Seville, and Marmont at Toledo. On the 5th of December Count d'Erlon occupied Almendralejos, and on the 18th Merida. But any further advance against Hill was stopped by insubordination which had broken out among the troops of the 5th Corps.

Thereupon Hill in his turn advanced, "partly to protect Morillo, partly to save the resources of Estremadura, partly to make a diversion in favour of Ballesteros and Tarifa, and in some sort also for Valencia." On the 27th he crossed the Spanish border at Albuquerque in the hope of effecting another surprise. In this he failed, but forced the enemy to evacuate Merida. Thence on the 1st of January, 1812, following up Count d'Erlon, he moved to Almendralejos, but failing to bring the French to bay, was compelled to halt by stress of weather. He sent forward, however, Colonel Abercrombie of the 28th —a son of Sir Ralph—with a detachment of Cavalry to harass the enemy's rearguard. Count d'Erlon retreated to Monasterio; but on the 13th Marmont began to advance along the valley of the Tagus, whereupon Hill, who had not indeed attained the full object of his movement, but yet had captured 600,000 pounds of wheat and other foodstuffs, returned to Portalégre, and d'Erlon to Llerena. Morillo, who had also crossed the Guadiana, declined to retire, and was promptly attacked and his force routed at Almagro by a detachment of the 5th Corps.

On the retirement of Ballesteros to Gibraltar, a Division of the 4th Corps by Soult's orders occupied San Roque and stopped his further egress. This movement formed part of a political plan which the Marshal had for some time past been revolving. Victor was making no progress in the blockade of Cadiz. His line of investment was too long for his force, yet his flanks were ever liable to be turned by the troops disembarked by the "Mistress of the Seas." Communication with Seville and Grenada was liable to interruption, and the occupation of Tarifa by the Allies deprived him of the supplies of cattle grazing on the plains beneath.

Now, Tarifa is situated at the narrowest point of the Straits of Gibraltar, and its capture by the French would furnish "a dangerous point of offence to the Mediterranean trade." "It affected the supplies of the French before the Isla—it was from its nearness and the run of the current the customary point for trading with Morocco —it menaced the security of Ceuta; and it possessed, from ancient recollections, a species of feudal superiority over the smaller towns and ports along the coast, which would give the French a moral influence of some consequence" (Napier). Soult looked on the capture of Tarifa as the first step in a project for subduing the whole of Andalusia, and eventually of driving the British from the Peninsula. He succeeded in negotiating a treaty with the Emperor of Morocco, by the terms of which British agents were to be forbidden access to his coast, and the Moorish flag was to be allowed to cover the cargoes of all nations, which in future were to supply the French instead of the Allies—provided that the former could occupy Tarifa as a depôt. The capture of Tarifa would, in fact, give Soult command over all the coasting trade; for a favourable current always brought the Moorish vessels thither.

To take it seemed an easy task, for the walls had no ditch, and were not even proof against field-guns. They were also commanded on the east and north sides by high ridges. In fact, so untenable did the town appear that Colonel Skerrett—who by order of General Colin Campbell at Gibraltar, occupied it with a garrison drawn partly thence, partly from Cadiz—resolved to abandon the place, and was deterred only by the remonstrances of Captain Charles Smith, the chief engineer, and the positive orders of Campbell. The quick eye of Smith had detected various local conditions which went far towards counteracting the natural disadvantages of the case. Of these he made the most, and was supported by the ships in the roadstead whose fire would flank the enemy's approach.

The garrison consisted of 700 Spaniards and 1,800 British soldiers—detachments from the 11th, 47th, 82nd, 87th, and 95th Rifles. The Artillery was weak and scanty. On the 20th of December the place was invested by the Divisions of Semelé and Leval, who had left a detachment in observation of Ballesteros and another at Vejer to cover their right flank. On the 22nd they began their approaches against the eastern front. Fortune favoured them, for a gale compelled the British ships to put to sea; and the river which bisected the town being flooded by rain, carried away palisades and injured the interior defence. On the 1st of January, 1812, an assault was gallantly made and as gallantly repulsed. Rain then injured the French batteries, and interfered with their supplies, and though it did equal damage to the defenders, Leval was probably not aware of the fact, and on the 4th he retired.

The projects of Soult were consequently foiled, and his disappointment was great. For he considered it impossible to advance against Badajoz unless his left were secured by the occupation of Tarifa, and he felt that the capture of the latter would be a greater blow to the British and the garrison of Cadiz than that of Alicante or even of Badajoz.

In compelling Skerrett to hold Tarifa, General Campbell showed not only breadth of view and appreciation of the situation, but also moral courage; for he had no definite authority over either the Colonel or the troops drawn from Cadiz, and his opinion was at variance with that of Wellington, who had been misled by inaccurate reports. His reward was an official reprimand by Lord Liverpool.

The ministerial rebuke probably sat lightly on Campbell. Worse things have happened in our own time. We have seen an ex-Commander-in-Chief—one whose services to his country are beyond compute—for the crime of explaining the difficulties of his position (difficulties due chiefly to ministerial incapacity), lectured and insulted in the House of Lords by a Secretary of State in a tone and temper suggestive of an ill-bred schoolmaster.

CHAPTER XXVI

Siege and capture of Ciudad Rodrigo—Siege and capture of Badajoz.

THE following Return—taken from Wellington's Supplementary Despatches (vol. vii. p. 249)—gives the number of casualties in Wellington's Army to date. It would, however, appear not to include those of the Portuguese troops:—

	Number of Men joined.	Number of Men dead.	Discharged.	Deserted.	Transferred.
From April 29 to Dec. 15, 1809	5,277	4,754	42	281	455
,, Jan. 1 to June 15, 1810	2,114	2,715	40	183	545
,, July 1 to Dec. 15, 1810	2,500	1,202	38	253	659
,, Jan. 1 to June 15, 1811	3,190	2,662	44	256	1,309
,, July 1 to Dec. 15, 1811	8,968	3,404	92	277	3,869
General Total	22,049	14,737	256	1,250	6,837

The figures show a net loss of 1,031. It is curious that the number of men "dead" is much the largest in the half-years during which little or no fighting took place. The column showing men "transferred" includes those sent home, either sick or to recruiting service or to the depôt.

The opinion expressed by Napoleon that the ill-health of the British Army precluded it from undertaking anything on the offensive, was encouraged by Wellington, who adopted also other expedients to conceal his designs against Ciudad Rodrigo. Necessity, too, aided the British Commander; for in consequence of the exhaustion of the resources of the country in the neighbourhood of Almeida and the neglect of the Portuguese Government to furnish supplies, he was compelled, in order to keep his troops alive, to occupy extended quarters to an extent dangerous in the face of the enemy. To get supplies from Lisbon to the Agueda took fifteen days. They were brought by sea and river up to Ruiva on the Mondego, and thence by land over more than 100 miles of mountainous country. The British Divisions were consequently spread over a large tract extending as far as the valley of the Douro, and on the cessation of the rainy season rapidly recovered their health.

With great ability Wellington turned the situation in his own favour; for Soult, harassed on one flank by Ballesteros and on the other by Hill, was unable to rid himself permanently of either. Marmont had been obliged to retire up the valley of the Tagus, and Dorsenne, alone, was unable to resume the invasion of Galicia.

On the other hand, the strategical position of the French armies precluded an advance of Wellington into Spain, for an attack on any one would expose his flank to the other two.

The key to the situation lay in the possession of the frontier fortresses of Ciudad Rodrigo and Badajoz. "If a frontier, naturally strong," observes Hamley ("Opera-

IN THE PENINSULA

tions of War," part v. ch. 6), "have few issues, the strong places that guard them become of immense importance. In 1812 the French held Ciudad Rodrigo and Badajoz; they thus closed the doors between Spain and Portugal, and the one fortress would afford a base to Marmont, the other to Soult, in offensive operations against Lisbon.

"If, on the other hand, Wellington, masking Badajoz, were to take the offensive against Soult in Andalusia, Marmont from Ciudad Rodrigo would in a moment recall him by threatening Lisbon; and Soult would in the same way from Badajoz prevent an attack on Marmont.

"The peculiar circumstances in which the French occupied Spain rendered it necessary that they should spread widely in order at once to obtain subsistence and to keep down the hostile population. The scantiness of provisions generally reduced them to the defensive during the winter and early part of the year, till the harvest filled with grain their central depôts of supply. At these seasons they could safely disperse their troops to seek subsistence, as long as the two fortresses kept the English at bay. But Wellington, supplied from the sea, was more independent of the country, and if he could capture the fortresses he might take the offensive at a season when it was most inconvenient for the French to assemble in masses. Hence it was that the possession of these places was so important to either side, and that Wellington rightly considered it worth the risk and certain heavy losses of the famous attacks by storm."

Dorsenne had retired into Navarre. The capture of Ciudad Rodrigo would therefore probably compel Marmont to concentrate his army in Leon. Not only would the strategical situation be then altered in Wellington's favour, but he felt certain that the French could not subsist in large masses.

The political prospect was also brightening. War between France and Russia—a factor on which Wellington had always reckoned—was evidently imminent. Not only was the arrival of Napoleon in person no longer to be dreaded, but 40,000 men were drawn from Spain to reinforce the Grand Army in Germany, while 20,000 others, invalids, were also struck off the strength. Marmont at Toledo was about to be weakened by the detachment of Montbrun into Valencia, and evidently was unsuspicious of any offensive movement on the part of the English.

Wellington was not very sanguine of success, but the attack of Ciudad Rodrigo might have the effect of bringing back Montbrun and of saving Valencia. Consequently the occasion was not to be lost; and though with a view to strengthening the main line of communication with France, Marmont was just at this time directed by Napoleon to Valladolid, his Divisions were still dispersed.

The eternal jealousy between French Commanders also favoured Wellington, for it happened that although the 6th and 7th Governments, including Ciudad Rodrigo and the Divisions of Souham and Bonet, had in a recent redistribution been allotted to the Army of Portugal, they do not seem to have been as yet formally handed over to it. Thus neither General Dorsenne, who had been ordered to give them up, nor Marmont, who was about to take them over, would admit responsibility for the security of the fortress in the interval.

In the first days of January, 1812, a bridge was thrown across the Agueda at its confluence with the Azava, six miles below Ciudad Rodrigo. The fortress was of no great strength, and inadequately garrisoned with two companies of Artillery, and a French, a German, and an Italian battalion, making up about 2,000 men. If only the Armies of the North and of Portugal could be kept at a distance, its capture without any great loss of life was assured. As matters, however, stood, time was all important, and it became essential to accelerate the engineer's art by sacrifice of men. Even so, Wellington calculated that twenty-four days would be required. Large numbers of gabions and fascines had been prepared in advance. In bitter wintry weather, with the ground covered by snow, the 1st, 3rd, 4th, and Light Divisions, with Pack's Portuguese Brigade, broke up their cantonments, and advanced to the attack.

The following orders were issued:—

"INSTRUCTIONS TO GENERAL OFFICERS COMMANDING DIVISIONS EMPLOYED IN THE SIEGE OF CIUDAD RODRIGO.

"GALLEGOS,
"8th January, 1812.

"The Commander of the Forces proposes to attack Ciudad Rodrigo, and in order that the troops may suffer as little as possible from exposure to the weather, he intends that the operations shall be carried on by each of the Divisions of the army employed, alternately, for twenty-four hours.

". . . When a Division is ordered for the duty of the siege, each of the Battalions belonging to it is to march from its cantonments before daylight in the morning. The troops from the several cantonments of the Division separately, by the shortest and most convenient route, which the General Officers commanding Divisions are requested to ascertain. The troops will be able to cross at the fords above La Caridad, and all the fords below the ford of Los Carboneros inclusive. The troops are to have with them a day's provisions (cooked), and they are to be followed by two days' spirits and no other baggage. . . .

"The Chief Engineer will require daily from each Division, 20 miners, 30 artificers, or persons accustomed to work, with a proportion of non-commissioned officers. . . .

"Each regiment is to take along with it the intrenching tools belonging to it.

"There will be orders daily respecting the working parties, covering parties, guards, &c.

"The musket and rifle ammunition attached to the Light Division is to be taken to the ground the first day, and remain there. The nine-pounders attached to the 4th Division will likewise be taken to the ground on the first day, and remain there. The artillerymen are to be relieved daily by those belonging to the Brigades and troops attached to the 1st, 4th, and Light Divisions.

"The Engineers will order to the ground a sufficiency of cutting-tools to enable those men not immediately on duty to supply themselves with firewood, these tools to be handed over from the relieved to the relieving Division.

"Each Division to be attended by the medical staff belonging to it. A place will be fixed upon to which men who may be wounded are to be carried to be dressed, and means will be provided for removing them from thence to their cantonments.

(Signed) "WELLINGTON.

"To the General Officers Commanding
    Divisions in the Siege of Ciudad Rodrigo."

On the north side of the fortress were two parallel ridges, the further termed "the Greater," the nearer, "the Lesser Tesson," at distances of 700 and 150 yards respectively from its parapets. On these ridges only the ground in the neighbourhood of the fortress was not rocky, and the possession of the Lesser Tesson would

IN THE PENINSULA

enable batteries to breach the parapets of the Enceinte over the crest of the glacis.

The Spaniards under Carlos d'Espana and Julian Sanchez were placed in observation along the line of the Tormes, four marches distant.

On the 8th of January the Light Division, with Pack's Portuguese Brigade attached, crossed the Agueda above the fortress, marched round it behind the Greater Tesson, and stormed a redoubt thereon. The rest of the night was not wasted. In spite of a heavy fire a parallel, 600 yards in length, 3 feet in depth, had been formed by daybreak.

A hard frost set in; the troops had a terribly trying time. In order to reach the trenches they had to wade through a river, the water often up to their waist. They were thus almost frozen at the outset, yet no fires could be allowed, and the night was spent in clothes stiff with frost.

On the 9th the investment was completed, and batteries were begun. The work in the trenches was undertaken in rotation by the Light, 1st, 4th, and 3rd Divisions. Weather was fine, but the hardness of the ground and the incessant fire of the garrison prevented any very rapid progress. "The worst obstacle," says Napier, "was the disgraceful badness of the cutting-tools furnished from . . . England. . . . The Engineers eagerly sought for French implements, because the English tools were useless." On the 12th, news—although incorrect, for the Marshal had not yet heard of the siege—arrived that Marmont was concentrating his troops to relieve the place. The remainder of the Army was then brought up to the Coa in readiness for battle.

During the night of the 13th and 14th the batteries on the nearer slopes of the Greater Tesson were armed with twenty-eight 24-pounder guns, and the Convent of

Santa Cruz, between the Lesser Tesson and the Enceinte, was stormed by a Battalion of the King's German Legion.

At the moment, however, of the 1st Division being relieved by the 4th, the garrison made a sortie, and very nearly captured the siege guns. Eventually the enemy was driven back, and in the evening breaching batteries opened fire with great effect, although opposed by double the number of guns in the fortress. After nightfall the 40th Regiment stormed the Convent of San Francisco.

Rapid progress followed, and a breach having been made in the rampart, a summons was sent on the 16th to the Governor, General Barrié, but without effect. Next day a terrible artillery duel took place with varying fortune, but in the evening the fire of the besiegers almost silenced that of the garrison. During the night a second breaching battery on the Lesser Tesson was armed with seven guns; and on the 18th a smaller breach was effected, two hundred yards to the south-east of the other. Although the counterscarp had not been blown in, and the enemy's fire was as vigorous as ever, both breaches were on the 19th reported practicable, and an assault was ordered for the same evening. "Ciudad Rodrigo must be taken to-night" were the words which concluded the order for the assault. The task was committed to the 3rd and Light Divisions, the two most distinguished in the Army. Major Manners, of the 74th, commanded the storming party of 500 men belonging to the 3rd Division, who were to attack the great breach. Major George Napier, of the 52nd, was in charge of that of the Light Division, 300 strong, for the assault of the small breach. Colonel O'Toole, of the Caçadores, was to cross the bridge from the left bank with a few companies, and escalade an outwork in front of the castle, and a false attack was to be made by Pack against the St. Jago Gate on the east side.

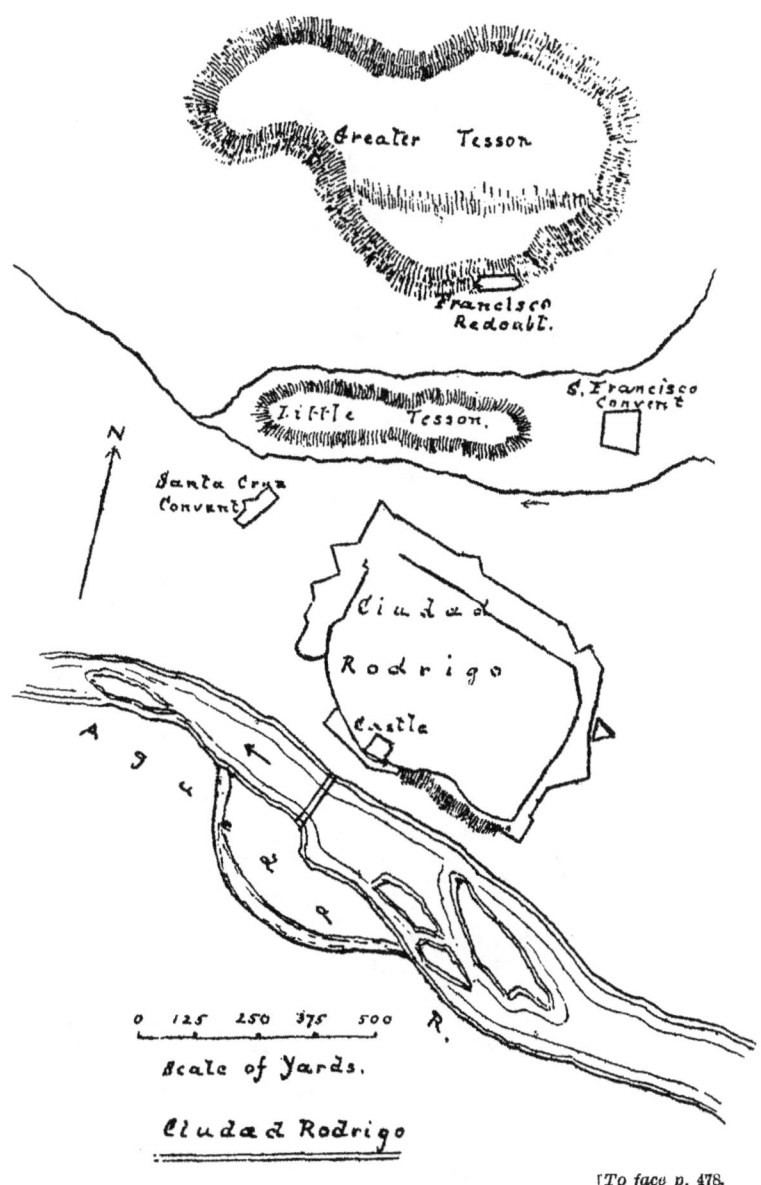

IN THE PENINSULA

The night proved dark. The troops paraded in the parallels, but the preparations were hardly complete when on the extreme right Colville's Brigade—the 5th, 77th, and 94th—anticipating the signal, dashed forward, and in a moment were half-way up the great breach. Here they were checked by a deadly fire from the adjacent houses, for the breach had been retrenched, and so rapid was the advance that Mackinnon's supporting Brigade had not been able to keep pace. But on the left the storming party of the Light Division, with magnificent *élan*, had carried the smaller breach, and the supports coming up spread right and left along the rampart. The advance of the 43rd on the right in the direction of the great breach enfiladed its defenders. Aided by this diversion and by the explosion of the enemy's expense magazines, the 3rd Division, with a renewed effort, carried the breach; but Mackinnon and 150 men lost their lives in the explosion. About the same time O'Toole and Pack entered the place on the opposite side. Little further fighting took place. The Governor surrendered at the Castle, and with him 78 officers and 1,700 men. One hundred and fifty guns, including Marmont's siege train, were found in the fortress. In spite of the explosions—another occurred next day—the actual capture of Ciudad Rodrigo cost Wellington the comparatively small number of 700 officers and men, the casualties during the siege from first to last amounting to 1,300.

But Crauford had been mortally wounded while encouraging his Division at the smaller breach, and died a few days afterwards. That he was a man of great ability is undoubted, for Napier, who is not prejudiced in his favour, and had the best opportunities of forming an opinion, says so. There probably has never been a person in whose character light and shade were more vividly contrasted. He fell, as was fit, at the head of the Light Division, with which his name will ever be associated, and was buried in the rampart which he had captured. Lord Wellington must have received the news of the departure of that wild, perverse, and turbulent spirit with mingled feelings. In his despatch of the 29th he spoke of the dead General in the nicest possible terms.

The other General Officer who had lost his life—Mackinnon, of the Coldstream—had a disposition the exact reverse of Crauford's, and was beloved by all who knew him. Among those who mourned his loss was Napoleon himself, for in their boyhood the two had been intimate friends.

Thus in half the calculated time Ciudad Rodrigo fell. The following extract from "Wellington's Supplementary Despatches," vol. vii. p. 256, gives a comparative statement of the two sieges of the fortress :—

1810.	1812.
"Marshal Masséna took up his ground before the place on April 2, 1810, with the 6th and 8th *corps d'armée*. He invested it completely on the 11th of June; broke ground before it on the 15th of June; and opened fire on the 24th of June. The place surrendered on the 10th of July. "According to the intercepted letter from Berthier to Masséna of May 28, 1810, the latter must have had upwards of 50,000 men under him at the siege, exclusive of 12,000 under Kellermann, destined to keep up his communications, and secure his flanks and rear.	"Lord Wellington's despatch of the 1st of January announces his intention of attacking Ciudad Rodrigo. "On the 8th he invested the place; and finding the difficulty of approach had been increased by the enemy's having constructed a strong redoubt connected with the body of the place by a chain of fortified convents, he caused this work to be stormed early on the same night. It was carried and converted into a part of the first parallel, which was immediately opened. The fortified convents were taken on the nights of the 13th and 14th.

IN THE PENINSULA 481

"Lord Wellington's despatch of July 11, 1810, estimates the force of the 6th and 8th Corps engaged in the siege of Ciudad Rodrigo as follows:—

	Effectives.
6th Corps (Ney's)	31,611
8th Corps (Junot's)	25,956
Total	57,567

Including 9,572 cavalry."

On the 14th the batteries opened against the place, and the second parallel was begun the same night. On the 19th the breaches were practicable, and the place was carried by assault that evening.

"The garrison appears to have consisted of two companies of Artillery, two battalions of the 34th Light Infantry, and one battalion of the 113th regiment of the line commanded by General Barrié."

That Wellington's constant censure in regard to the want of discipline—apart from "fire discipline"—among his troops, and the neglect of duty by the regimental officers, was not ill founded, is shown by the breaking of all restraint when the victorious soldiers entered the town. Intoxication and madness reigned supreme.

For his services up to the capture of Ciudad Rodrigo, Lord Wellington was promoted to an earldom.

News of the siege does not seem to have reached Salamanca till the 13th. Marmont received the first intimation at Valladolid on the 15th. By the 25th, six Divisions, numbering 45,000 men, had concentrated at Salamanca. Next day the fate of the fortress was known. From intelligence received by Wellington, it seemed likely that Marmont would attempt to turn his right by threading the Pass of Perales and interposing between him and Hill. The latter was therefore directed to send the 2nd Division to Castello Branco. Marmont, however, made no such attempt, but dispersed his troops again for purposes of subsistence. Ciudad Rodrigo was committed to the care of Carlos d'Espana with orders to repair the breaches and provision the fortress. He grossly neglected both duties.

Half only of Wellington's task was completed. He at once turned his mind to the capture of Badajoz. "Was the object worth the risk?" asks Napier (bk. xvi. ch. 7), and he answers the question thus: "Suchet had subjugated Aragon by his mildness, Catalonia and Valencia by his vigour. In Andalusia, Soult had tranquillised the mass of the people, and his genius, solid and vast, was laying the deep foundation of a kingdom close to Portugal; he was forming great establishments, and contriving such plans as would, if permitted to become ripe, have enabled him to hold the Peninsula alone should the French armies fail in all other parts. In the centre of Spain the King, true to his plan of raising a Spanish party, was likely to rally round him all those of the patriots whom discontent . . . might induce to seek a plausible excuse for joining the invaders; and on the northern line the French armies, still powerful, were strengthening their hold of the country by fortifying all the important points of Leon and old Castille. The great army which the Emperor was carrying to Russia might or might not be successful, but this was the only moment when an offensive war against his army in Spain could have been carried on with success: and how could any extensive offensive operation have been attempted while Badajoz remained in the enemy's possession? If Wellington had advanced in the north, Soult, making Badajoz his base, would have threatened Lisbon; if Wellington marched against the French centre the same thing would have happened, and the Army of the North would also have acted on the left flank or have retaken Rodrigo. If an attempt had been made against Soult it must have been by the Lower Guadiana, when the French Army of Portugal, coming

IN THE PENINSULA

down to Badajoz, could have either operated against the rear of the Allies or against Lisbon."

"Badajoz was therefore the key to all offensive operations by the Allies, and to take it was an indispensable preliminary. Yet how take it? By regular or by irregular operations? For the first a certain time was required, which from the experience of former sieges it was not to be expected the enemy would allow. What then would have been the result if thus, year after year, the Allies showed they were unable even to give battle to their enemies, much less to chase them from the Peninsula? How was it to be expected that England would bear the expense of a protracted warfare affording no hope of final success? How were the opposition clamours to be replied to in Parliament? How were the secret hopes of the Continental Governments to be upheld if the military power of England, Portugal, and Spain united was unable to meet even a portion of the secondary armies of Napoleon, while with 400,000 men he stalked, a gigantic conqueror, over the wastes of Russia? To strike irregularly, then, was Wellington's only resource. To strike without regard to rules, trusting to the courage of his men and to fortune to bear him through the trial triumphant. Was such a crisis to be neglected by a general who had undertaken on his own judgment to fight the battle of the Peninsula? Was he to give force to the light declamation of the hour, when General Officers in England were heard to say that every defeat of the French was a snare to decoy the British further into Spain! Was he to place the probable loss of a few thousand men, more or less, in opposition to such a conjuncture, and by declining the chance offered show that he despaired of success himself? What if he failed? He would not have been, save the loss of a few men, worse off than if he had not attacked: in either case he would have been a baffled general with a sinking cause. But what if he succeeded? The horizon was bright with the coming glory of England."

The period for operations in the Alemtejo and Andalusia was favourable, for the heavy rains which now flooded the rivers about Rodrigo formed a formidable barrier against an enemy's attack, and would "impede the junction of the French forces in Estremadura"; and in addition, the hay and corn harvest was earlier in the southern than in the more northerly provinces.

In regard to the movements of the Army of Portugal, Wellington noticed that he had to provide against four contingencies—

1. (The most probable) that Marmont might leave Leon and Castille to their fate and march the whole of the eight Divisions now under his command into Estremadura.* In this case Abadia from Galicia and Carlos d'Espana from Ciudad Rodrigo ought to march to the Tormes, attack the enemy's works and do him all the mischief in their power.

2. Marmont's five Divisions in the north might attack Galicia. They would drive Abadia before them, but would be harassed on their flank and rear by Bacellar and Silveira from the Tras os Montes.

3. They might attack Portugal by the north of the Douro, in which case the same plan of defence—*mutatis mutandis*—would hold good.

4. They might penetrate between Ciudad Rodrigo and Almeida. If so, Bacellar was to protect the magazines on the Douro and Mondego, and force the enemy into Lower Beira, while Abadia advanced to the Tormes.

---

* He had been reinforced by the Divisions of Souham and Bonet, hitherto attached to the Army of the North.

Victor Alten was left with a Cavalry Brigade on the Yeltes to observe the Army of Portugal, with orders to retire slowly on Castello Branco if attacked in force. In such case Silveira was directed to cover Oporto, Trant to defend the defiles of the Estrella with his militia, and Le Cor those of Castello Branco. With a view to hindering a junction between Soult and Marmont, Wellington desired Hill to surprise the French posts at Almaraz and destroy the bridge. The result of this would be to compel Marmont to cross the Tagus at Toledo. Circumstances made it, however, necessary to defer the execution of the plan.

The tone of Lord Wellington's letters at this period was hopeful. To Lord Wellesley he wrote (March 12th), "If I should succeed, which I certainly shall, unless those admirably useful institutions, the English newspapers, should have given Bonaparte the alarm and should have induced him to order his Marshals to assemble their troops to oppose me, Spain will have another chance of being saved."

Secret preparations were made, and stores, &c., collected in the neighbourhood of Elvas, to be used against Badajoz. In the beginning of March the Army marched from the Coa. Major (afterwards Sir Alexander) Dickson, R.A., with considerable difficulty collected a siege train of fifty-two guns; of which some were brought down from Rodrigo, but means of transport thence failing, the greater part were a miscellaneous collection picked up anyhow, and brought by the Tagus from Lisbon to Abrantes. Difficulties made by the Portuguese authorities delayed matters for a few days, but on the 15th of March a pontoon bridge was thrown across the Guadiana, four miles from Elvas. On the 17th, after a grand parade of the whole force in Review Order, terminated by the bands of all the regiments playing " St.

Patrick's Day," Beresford, with the 3rd, 4th, and Light Divisions and a Brigade of Hamilton's Division—in all 15,000 bayonets—made a partial investment of the fortress; while Graham, with the Cavalry Brigades of Slade and Le Marchant, and the 1st, 6th, and 7th Divisions, moved in the direction of Llerena, and Hill with the 2nd Cavalry Division, the 2nd Infantry and the remainder of Hamilton's Division, occupied Almendralejos. The 5th Division had not yet arrived from Beira, but the covering force amounted to 5,000 Cavalry and 25,000 Infantry, and the whole number of British and Portuguese sabres and bayonets amounted to 31,000 and 20,000 respectively, making up about 60,000 of all ranks and arms, organised as follows :—

CAVALRY.

1st Division.

Lieut.-General Sir Stapleton Cotton, K.B.

Heavy Brigade.		Major-General Le Marchant.	3rd Dragoons, 4th Dragoons, 5th Dragoon Guards.
,,	,,	Major-General Bock.	1st and 2nd Dragoons, K.G.L.
Light	,,	Major-General Anson.	12th, 14th, and 16th Light Dragoons.
,,	,,	Major-General Victor Alten	11th Light Dragoons, 1st Hussars, K.G.L.

2nd Division.

Major-General Long (temporarily).

Heavy Brigade.	Major-General Slade.	3rd and 4th Dragoon Guards.
Light ,,	Major-General Long.	9th and 13th Light Dragoons, 2nd Hussars, K.G.L.

Each regiment consisted of three Squadrons.

Some Portuguese Cavalry, very weak in numbers, was included in each Division.

IN THE PENINSULA

INFANTRY.

1st Division.

Lieut.-General Sir Thomas Graham, K.B.

Brigade of Guards.	Major-General Stopford.	1st Batt. Coldstream, 1st Batt. 3rd Guards, 1 Company 60th Rifles.
Highland Brigade.	Major-General Wheatley.	1st and 2nd Batts. 42nd, 79th, 1 Company 60th.
K.G.L. ,,	Major-General Lowe.	1st, 2nd, and 5th Batts. K.G.L.

2nd Division.

Lieut.-General Sir Rowland Hill, K.B.

	Major-General Howard.	1st Batt. 50th, 1st Batt. 71st, 1st Batt. 92nd.
	Major-General Chowne (formerly known as Tilson).	2nd Batt. 28th, 2nd Batt 34th, 2nd Batt. 39th, Provisional Batt. 3 Companies 60th, 1 Company 3rd Batt. 95th.
Portuguese Brigade.	Col. Ashworth.	6th and 18th Regts.

3rd Division.

Lieut.-General Picton.

	Major-General Kempt.	1st Batt. 45th, 1st Batt. 74th, 1st and 2nd Batts. 88th, 3 Companies 60th Rifles.
	Col. Campbell.	2nd Batt. 5th, 2nd Batt. 94th, 2nd Batt. 83rd, 77th.
Portuguese Brigade.	Col. Champlemond.	9th and 21st Regts.

4th Division.

Lieut.-Gen. Hon. Lowry Cole (Major-Gen. Colville temporary).

	Major-General Kemmis.	3rd Batt. 27th, 1st Batt. 40th, 1st Batt. 97th, 1 Company 60th.

| | Major-General Bowes. | 1st and 2nd Batt. 7th, 1st Batt. 23rd, 1st Batt. 48th, 1 Company Brunswick Light Infantry. |
| Portuguese Brigade. | Brevet-General Harvey. | 11th and 23rd Regts., 1 Batt. Lusitanian Legion. |

5th Division.
Lieut.-General Leith.

	Major-General Hay.	3rd Batt. 1st, 1st Batt. 9th, 1st Batt. 38th, 1 Company 60th.
	Major-General Walker.	1st Batt. 4th, 2nd Batt. 30th, 2nd Batt. 44th, 1 Company Brunswick Light Infantry.
Portuguese Brigade.	Brigdr.-Gen. Spry.	3rd and 15th Regts.

6th Division.
Major-General Clinton.

	Major-General Hulse.	1st Batt. 11th, 2nd Batt. 53rd, 1st Batt. 61st, 1 Company 60th.
	Major-General Burne.	2nd, 32nd, 1st Batt. 36th.
Portuguese Brigade.	Brigdr.-General Baron Eben.	8th and 12th Regts.

7th Division.
Major-General Charles Alten (temporary).

	Major-General Sontag.	51st, 68th, Chasseurs Britanniques, Brunswick Light Infantry.
	Major-General C. Alten.	1st and 2nd Batts. King's German Legion.
Portuguese Brigade.	Col. Palmerini.	7th and 19th Regts.

Light Division.
Colonel Barnard (temporary).

| | Col. Barnard. | 1st Batt. 43rd, 4 Companies 1st Batt. and 1 Company 2nd Batt. 95th Rifles, 3rd Portuguese Caçadores. |

IN THE PENINSULA 489

Major-General Vandeleur (wounded at Ciudad Rodrigo). — 1st Batt. 52nd, 4 Companies Batt. 95th, 1st Caçadores.

Lieut.-General Hamilton's Portuguese Division.

Major-Gen. Power and ? Col. Fonseca — 4th, 10th, 2nd, and 14th Regts.

Unattached Brigades.

Brig.-General Pack.   1st and 16th Regts.
Brig.-General Bradford.   5th, 13th, 24th Regts.

ARMY STATE.
April 5, 1812.

	Present.	Sick.	Command.	Prisoners.	Total.
Cavalry.					
British	4,299	564	755	3	6,048
Portuguese	347	9	492	—	848
Infantry.					
British	26,897	11,452	2,779	2	40,703
Portuguese	20,224	5,532	1,507	18	27,281
Artillery.	2,880	—	—	—	—
Total	54,647	17,557	5,533	23	74,880

(This return, taken from Napier, vol. iv. app. vi. 1, appears to include sergeants, but not officers or drummers.)

The German Heavy Cavalry Brigade was in rear at Estremoz, and two Portuguese regiments were in Abrantes.

Before the end of March the Anglo-Portuguese Army was distributed as follows :—

WELLINGTON'S OPERATIONS

At the Siege of Badajoz.

	British.	Portuguese.	Total.
3rd Division	2,882	976	3,858
4th ,,	2,579	2,384	4,963
5th ,,	2,896	1,845	4,741
Light ,,	2,679	848	3,527
Hamilton's Division	—	4,685	4685
Total Rank and File	11,036	10,748	21,748

Covering the Siege.

Sir Rowland Hill's Corps.

At Almendralejos.

	British.	Portuguese.	Total.
Cavalry	783	347	1,130
Infantry	6,156	2,385	8,541
Total	6,939	2,732	9,671

Sir Thomas Graham's Corps.

At Zafra.

	British.	Portuguese.	Total.
Cavalry	3,517	—	3,517
Infantry	10,154	5,896	16,050
Total	13,671	5,896	19,567

On the advance of Graham towards Llerena, Barois evacuated Villa Franca with his Division of the 5th Corps, and marched on Medellin with a view to forming a junction with the other Division under Daricau, and opening communication with Marmont by Truxillo.

IN THE PENINSULA

Graham then halted at Zafra, where he took post in anticipation of the approach of Soult, who was at present before Cadiz.

The garrison of Badajoz, under the well-tried and able General Phillipon, consisted of about 5,000 men—French, Germans, and Spaniards. The place was well provisioned and its works had been considerably strengthened of late. It was, however, rather short of ammunition.

Wellington's army was still destitute. Although both in regard to the season of the year and the position of the enemy time was all important, the Portuguese Government would do nothing to find the necessary means of transport. "It was in vain," says Napier, "that Wellington threatened and remonstrated . . . in vain Mr. Stuart worked with equal vigour to give energy to this extraordinary Government . . . disgraceful subterfuges and stolid indifference on the part of all the civil functionaries met them at every turn. . . . The English General was forced to arrange the most trifling details of the service himself, and his iron strength of body and mind were strained until all men wondered how they held, and in truth he did fall sick, but recovered. . . . The critical nature of the war may here be judged of, for no man could have supplied his place at such a moment, no man, however daring or skilful, would have voluntarily plunged into difficulties which were like to drive Wellington from the contest."

"Badajoz," says Napier (bk. xii. ch. 2), "stands at the confluence of the Guadiana with the Rivillas; the first a noble river, 500 yards broad; the second, a trifling stream. A rock, 100 feet high, crowned by an old castle, overhangs the meeting of the waters. The town . . . was protected by eight regular curtains and bastions, from 23 to 30 feet in height, with good counterscarps, covered way and glacis. On the left bank of the Guadiana the outworks were: (1) The Lunette of San Roque, covering a dam and sluce on the Rivillas, by which an inundation could be made; (2) an isolated redoubt, called the Picurina, situated beyond the Rivillas, and 400 yards from the town; (3) the Pardaleras, a defective crown work, central between the Lower Guadiana and the Rivillas, 200 yards from the ramparts. On the right bank of the Guadiana a hill, crowned by the San Christoval fort, 300 feet square, overlooked the interior of the Castle; and a quarter of a mile farther down the stream the bridge, 600 yards in length, was protected by a bridge-head, slightly connected with San Christoval, but commanded on every side."

The attack of Soult in 1811 had been directed against the Picurina and Pardaleras; those of Beresford and Wellington against San Christoval and the Castle.

On the present occasion it was Wellington's desire to attack one of the western fronts; but the powder, most of the shot, and Engineers' stores had not yet reached Elvas; there were not enough of "miners, mortars, or guns" for such an attack; and it was finally decided to operate against the Trinidad bastion on the south-eastern side, "because the counterguard there being unfinished, that bastion could be battered from the hill on which stood the outlying Picurina fort. The difficulties in the way were, however, enormous. Besides the deficiency of stores, there was no organised corps of Sappers and Miners; and to supply the place of skilled workmen, 150 volunteers were called for from the 3rd Division. "It is inconceivable," observed Wellington, in a letter to Lord Liverpool of the 11th of May, "with what disadvantage we undertake anything like a siege for want of assistance of this description. There is not a French *corps d'armée* which has not a battalion of sappers and a company of miners. But we are obliged to depend for assistance of this description upon the regiments of the

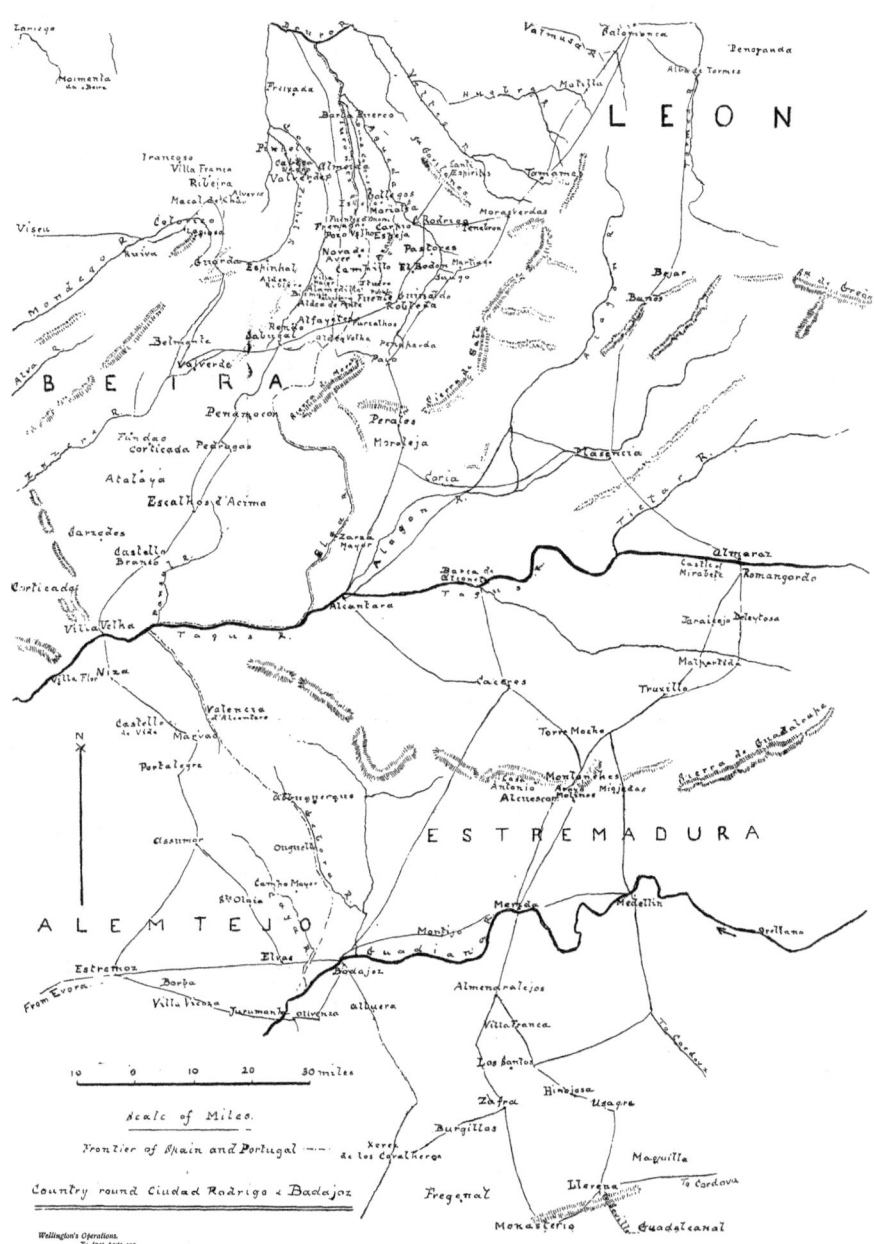

IN THE PENINSULA

line; and although the men are brave and willing they want the knowledge and training which are necessary. Many casualties among them consequently occur, and much valuable time is lost at the most critical period of the siege."

Of the 900 gunners, one third were British, the remainder Portuguese. "Picton had direction of the siege; Colville, Kempt, and Bowes alternately commanded in the trenches; the Engineer officers, Burgoyne and Squire, conducted the attack."

During the night of the 17th, a working party of 1,800 men, protected by a covering party of 2,000, opened a parallel 600 yards long, 3 feet deep, and $3\frac{1}{2}$ feet wide, at a distance of 160 yards from the Picurina. Next night two batteries were traced and the parallel was extended. On the 19th Phillipon made a sortie with both Cavalry and Infantry. A party of the former galloped down to the Engineers' park at San Michel and carried off some of the entrenching tools. The Infantry, 1,300 strong, aided by 100 men from the Picurina, surprised the workmen in the parallel, drove them out and began to destroy it. The relief, however, came up; the trench guard returned to the attack, regained the lost ground, and drove the enemy back into the Castle. In this affair Colonel Fletcher, C.R.E., was wounded, and the British casualties amounted to 150; but the French lost 300 men whom they could ill afford.

For the next few days heavy rains hindered the siege works. With a view to saving labour the fortress had not been invested on the right bank of the Guadiana, and Phillipon cleverly took advantage of the fact to place three guns in battery on that side and enfilade the parallel. On the evening of the 22nd, the flooded river overflowed the pontoon bridge and stopped the flying ones. Had the river not quickly subsided, the siege would have been brought to an end, for neither provisions nor ammunition could be brought across. On the 24th the arrival of the 5th Division enabled Wellington to complete the investment, and his batteries which (partly owing to the marshy nature of the ground, partly from the danger of being rushed from San Roque, which was only 300 yards from the trenches) had been erected in rear of the parallel were armed with ten 24-pounders, eleven 18-pounders, and seven 5½-inch howitzers.

On the 25th San Roque was silenced. The Picurina seemed no better off, and orders were given for its assault after nightfall. The task was entrusted to Kempt—General Officer of the day—with 500 men of the 3rd Division. No great opposition was expected; but on the delivery of the assault at 9 p.m. the redoubt was found to be well garrisoned with 250 men, heavily armed with seven guns, and with its parapets practically uninjured. It was captured, but at a cost of 319 officers and men killed and wounded. Of the garrison, hardly a man escaped, 90 were taken, the rest killed or drowned in the inundation behind.

This lamentable loss of life saved, however, four or five days of valuable time upon which General Phillipon had reckoned. The second parallel was formed. And now, step by step, the besiegers gained ground, although every inch was stoutly contested with the utmost skill, courage, and obstinacy; while Phillipon—like Napoleon before Waterloo—spurred his men to redoubled effort by pointing out the terrible cruelty with which the English nation treated its prisoners by immuring them in hulks.

Up to this time nothing had been heard of Soult. In point of fact that Marshal, relying on the strength of Badajoz and the skill and resource of its commander to stand a six weeks' siege, thought it more important to concentrate a force strong enough to give battle to the

IN THE PENINSULA 495

British Army than to advance at an earlier date with comparatively small numbers. His march was delayed also by the position of a Spanish force about the Ronda which threatened Seville; but at length he was able to make a start, and on the 30th his approach was known in the British camp.

At the same time Marmont, who had been concentrating his Divisions between Valladolid and Salamanca, appeared to menace Ciudad Rodrigo, which, owing to the neglect of Carlos d'Espana, was by no means in a state of defence. Wellington was disquieted. The prey seemed likely to be snatched from him. He consequently brought the 5th Division across the left bank, leaving only Power's Portuguese Brigade on the right, and redoubled his efforts to sap up to the ravelin of San Roque. Forty-eight guns battered the faces of the Trinidad and Santa Maria bastions. On the 1st of April distinct progress had been made. On the night of the 2nd a party made a gallant attempt to destroy the dam of the inundation. The sentry was surprised, the powder barrels placed in position, but the explosion unfortunately did not have the desired effect. Next day, on the approach of Soult, Graham fell back on Albuera, where Lord Wellington had determined to give battle with the whole of his army, excepting two Divisions which were to be left in the trenches. Hill retired at the same time to Talavera Real. On the 5th the breaches on the ramparts of Badajoz were pronounced practicable. Soult had reached Llerena. Time was all important, but Wellington was resolved not to risk a premature assault. He therefore gave orders to open a third breach in the curtain between the Trinidad and Maria bastions. Next morning—the 6th—the guns opened fire with such effect upon the bad masonry that in two hours their task was completed. The respite had, however, given time to Phillipon to retrench the original breaches.

Orders were then issued for the assault the same evening. The 3rd Division was directed to cross the Rivillas and attack the Castle by escalade. On its left a detachment of the 48th was to attempt to storm the San Roque lunette.

The 4th and Light Divisions were to assault the breaches.

The 5th Division was ordered to make a false attack on the Pardeleras, and, if possible, a real one on the San Vincente bastion, although "the glacis was mined, the ditch deep, the scarp 30 feet high."

A Brigade of Hamilton's Portuguese Division under General Power was to make a feint against the bridgehead on the right bank of the Guadiana.

The hour at first selected for the assault was 7.30 p.m., but it was afterwards found impossible to complete the preliminary arrangements so soon, and the time was accordingly changed to 10 o'clock. Unfortunately, however, the siege batteries ceased fire at the earlier hour, and the resourceful General Phillipon took advantage of the interval to crown the breaches with *chevaux de frises* of sword blades and to strew their front with "crows' feet" and harrows.

In the absence of Lowry Cole, General Colville had been temporarily transferred from the 3rd to command the 4th Division. The casualties in the Light Division at Ciudad Rodrigo had been so many that it was now commanded by a Lieutenant-Colonel; but though comparatively junior in rank, it would have been difficult to find a better man than Andrew Barnard.

It had been intended that the various attacks should be made simultaneously, but shortly after 9.30 p.m. a fireball

IN THE PENINSULA 497

from the Castle lit up the 3rd Division and gave warning to the garrison of the approaching assault. Further delay was consequently impossible. Two hundred men of the 48th burst, almost unresisted, into the ravelin of San Roque. The 3rd Division—led in Picton's momentary absence by General Kempt—advanced to the attack; the 4th and Light Division at once conformed. The 5th Division was unfortunately not yet in position, for a delay had occurred in the arrival of the ladder parties.

To attempt an account of the assault of Badajoz after Napier's magnificent description would be ridiculous. The merest outline must now suffice; but no more splendid illustration of the incomparable fighting power of the British soldier has ever been given.

Kempt cleverly crossed the Rivillas by a narrow bridge in single file; and, despite heavy musketry fire from the Castle, without excessive loss. He then fell wounded, and General Picton, who arrived shortly afterwards, was also struck down and incapacitated for twenty minutes. An attempt was made to escalade the Castle walls, 18 to 24 feet high, with the two ladders available. The men "with incredible courage ascended amidst showers of heavy stones, logs of wood, and bursting shells rolled off the parapet, while from the flanks the enemy plied his musketry with fearful rapidity, and in front stabbed the leading assailants or pushed the ladders from the walls; and all this was attended with deafening shouts and the crash of breaking ladders, and the shrieks of the crushed soldiers answering to the sullen stroke of the falling weights" (Napier).

The first attempt was repelled. The troops reformed, and a second effort, headed by Major Ridge of the 5th, who had already distinguished himself so much at El Bodon, proved successful. Picton was not a man to fritter away his troops in driblets. His supports were close at hand. The garrison was driven into the town. A counter attack was repulsed, and before midnight the Castle—whose fate involved that of the fortress—was undeniably won. A magnificent feat of arms, covering Picton and the "Fighting Division" with glory.

That General then gave orders for a sortie to clear the breach—about 300 yards distant; but either that, finding his own position not sufficiently secure to enable him to give aid outside, the orders were revoked, or that through accident or the fact of all the General Officers of the Division being wounded, they were neglected, does not appear. Anyhow no serious attempt was made to carry them out.

Concurrently with the advance of the troops on their right, the storming parties of the 4th and Light Divisions (avoiding the inundation) had assaulted the breaches. As at Ciudad Rodrigo, the counterscarp had not been blown in. In spite of a terrific explosion the ditch was successfully gained. Then the Light Division unfortunately missed the breach of the Santa Maria and assailed those in the curtain and the Trinidad. But the latter were the goal of the 4th Division. The columns consequently became intermingled, and though Barnard succeeded in separating them, they were soon mixed up again. In the confusion, the head of the 4th Division, in crossing the wet ditch, fell into the cunette, and many were drowned. The remainder continued their course. Parties gained the summit of the great breach; but finding it retrenched with *chevaux de frise* which could be neither broken nor surmounted, were obliged to fall back under the terrific fire of the defenders, aided by the bursting of shells and hand grenades and the explosion of powder barrels rolled down the ramparts. The Engineer officer detailed to act as guide had been wounded at the outset.

The weakest breach—that in the curtain, between the two bastions—was protected by deep holes dug in front, and was never seriously assailed.

Again and again did bodies of men, headed by their heroic officers, dart forward and gain the summit of the great breach. Again and again did they fall back baffled by the sword blades. Sir John Jones, the C.R.E., avers that the breaches were practicable and would have been carried without difficulty by the united effort of strong columns. He declares that no formed body of more than fifty men ever attacked the breaches at once. Napier's account differs, and he retorts on Jones by saying that "Engineers, intent upon their own art, sometimes calculate on men as they do on blocks of stone or timber; nevertheless where the bullet strikes the man will fall; the sword blades were fitted into ponderous beams, and these last, chained together, were let deep into the ground; how then was it possible for men to drag or push them from their places when behind them stood resolute combatants, whose fire swept the foremost ranks away?"

At length—apparently a little before midnight—the bugles sounded the recall.

Seated on a mound, at a convenient distance, Lord Wellington watched the scene of carnage. "One of his Staff sat down by his side with a candle to enable the General to read and write all his communications and orders relative to the passing events. . . . Due respect prevented any of us bystanders from approaching so near as to enable us to ascertain the import of the reports which he was continually receiving: yet it was very evident that the information which they contained was far from flattering; and the recall on the bugles was again and again repeated."* At length, somewhat before

* "A Boy in the Peninsular War," p. 267.

midnight, Picton's A.D.C. galloped up with the news that a lodgment had been made in the Castle, but that in order to maintain it the troops had been withdrawn from the trenches. Reinforcements were despatched and orders given that at daybreak the breaches should again be assaulted by the 4th and Light Divisions, aided by a flanking attack on the part of the 3rd.

Meanwhile the 5th Division, which had been delayed by the non-arrival of its scaling ladders, had come into action. The 8th Caçadores, in pursuance of its orders, began a false attack on the Pardaleras outwork; the Brigade commanded by General Walker, of Vimeira fame, succeeded in escalading the San Vincente bastion and pushed along the rampart in the direction of the breach. At the same time a wing of the 4th Regiment succeeded in entering the body of the town and marched through the streets unopposed except for a few shots fired from the windows of some houses. It was well after 11 p.m. and, although the fact was unknown to the troops, the Castle was already in our hands. But the attack on the breaches was still in full force, and the 4th attempted, although without success, to effect a diversion by assailing the defenders in rear. Being repelled with loss, it retired into one of the central squares.

With the remainder of his Brigade General Walker had been advancing along the rampart in the direction of the breaches. Part of the garrison had been withdrawn from this side to aid in a counter attack upon Picton, but it was replaced by men who had successfully repelled the assaults of the 4th and Light Divisions. A fierce combat consequently took place; but the British were not to be denied. Three bastions were gained in succession; and Walker, advancing along the rampart, nearly reached that of Santa Maria. The crisis seemed over, when a portfire, lighted on a sudden by a French gunner, was

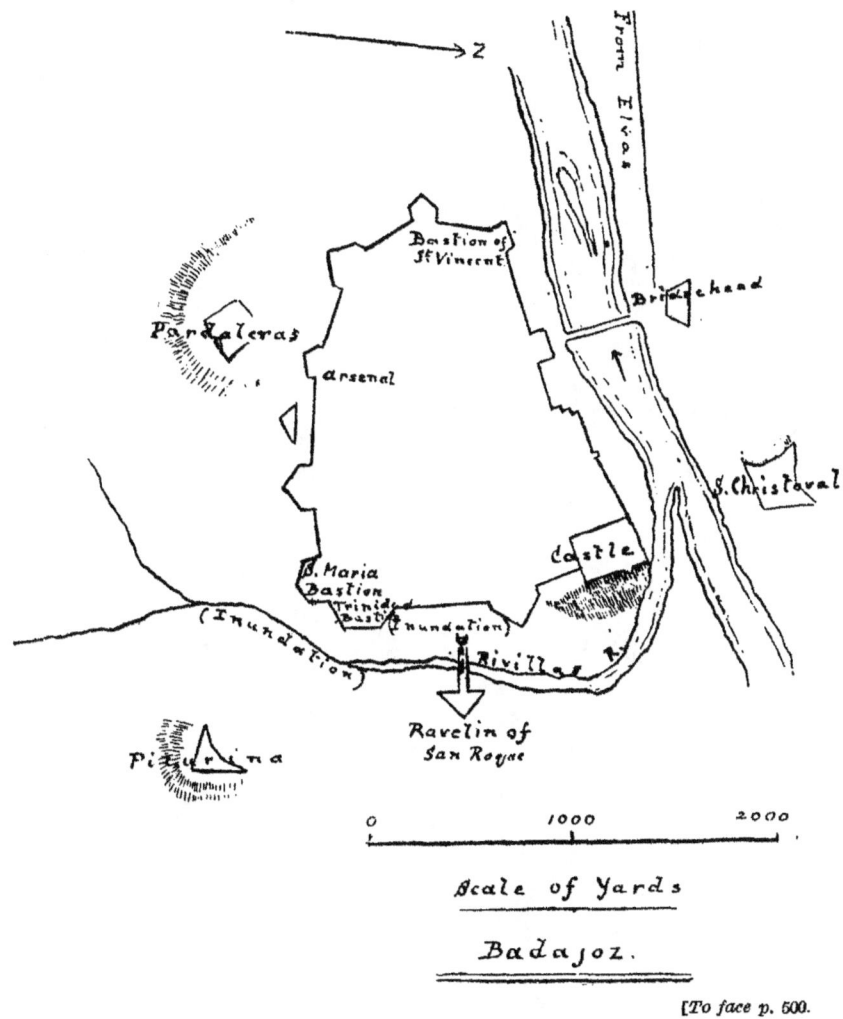

[To face p. 500.

IN THE PENINSULA 501

mistaken for a mine. Thereupon, to use the words of Napier, "those troops who had not been stopped by the strong barrier, the deep ditch, the high walls, and the deadly fire of the enemy, staggered back appalled by a chimæra of their own raising." The French, observing the confusion, seized the occasion; charged and drove Walker's Brigade along the ramparts, back to the San Vincente bastion at which it had entered. At this point the tide turned. Hay's Brigade formed the sole reserve. One of its battalions, the 38th (only 200 strong), had been posted here. It stopped the victorious enemy with a well-directed volley. The Brigade rallied, and in a counter attack pushed him back once more up to the breaches. The attack upon them had by this time ceased, but the 3rd Division had opened fire upon the defenders from the Castle, and Walker did the same from his side.

The advance of the 5th Division and the enfilading fire from both flanks terminated the contest. Towards morning the firing ceased. The breaches were abandoned; the 4th and Light Divisions marched over them unopposed. Phillipon, with a few hundred men, made good his retreat across the Guadiana into San Christoval, where he still hoped to be able to hold out until Soult's arrival. The rest of the garrison surrendered; and at daylight the Governor, having no time to organise further resistance, did the same: Soult being then close to Villa Franca, two marches distant from Albuera.

Thus ended the magnificent attack and no less magnificent defence. Badajoz was taken; but at what a cost! The garrison, composed of five French and two German battalions, was over 5,000 strong. Its losses during the siege amounted to about 1,200 killed and wounded. In the actual assault its casualties were probably about half as many. The British losses were terrific. No less than 651 officers and men were killed, 2,349 wounded—including Generals Picton, Colville, Kempt, Bowes, and Harvey—and 22 missing, at the assault alone. During the siege 838 had been struck. The Portuguese had 235 casualties previous to the assault; 730 during it. On the fatal night of the 6th, the purely British losses by Divisions were as follows: Light Division, 927; 4th, 829; 5th, Walker's Brigade, 466; Hay's, 44. The 3rd Division, whose capture of the Castle would in any case have decided the fate of the town, had comparatively few casualties—580. It was now once more on equal terms with the Light Division; for whereas Ciudad Rodrigo had been won by the latter, at Badajoz the 3rd Division had " saved Lord Wellington's honour." (General Orders.)

The scene on the morning of the 7th was appalling. "As soon as light served," writes an eye-witness, ". . . I bent my way along the ramparts towards the main opening in the Trinidad bastion. . . . The sun rose in majesty and splendour. . . . The country around was clothed in luxuriant verdure, refreshed by recent dew. . . . Proudly and silently the Guadiana flowed. . . . On its fertile banks the forward harvest already promised abundance. . . . The fruit trees opened their rich and perfumed blossoms; . . . birds sang in heaven. . . . When I arrived at the great breach the inundation presented an awful contrast to the silvery Guadiana; it was fairly stained with gore, which, through the vivid reflection of the rising sun . . . gave it the appearance of a fiery lake of smoking blood, in which were seen the bodies of many a gallant soldier. The ditches were strewn with killed and wounded; but the approach to the bottom of the main breach were fairly choked with dead. A row of *chevaux de frise*, armed with sword blades, barred the entrance at the top of the breach, and so firmly fixed that when the 4th and Light Divisions marched through, the greatest exertion was required to make a sufficient opening for their admittance. Boards fastened with ropes to plugs driven into the ground within the ramparts were let down, and covered nearly the whole surface of the breach; these boards were so thickly studded with sharp-pointed spikes that one could not introduce a hand between them; they did not stick out at right angles to the board, but were all slanting upwards. In rear of the *chevaux de frise* the ramparts had deep cuts in all directions, like a tanyard, so that it required light to enable one to move safely through them even were there no opposing enemy. From the number of muskets found close behind the breach, all the men who could possibly be brought together in so small a space must have had at least 20 firelocks each, no doubt kept continually loaded by persons in the rear. Two British soldiers only entered the main breach during the assault; I saw both their bodies. . . . In the Santa Maria breach not one had entered. At the foot of this breach the same sickening sight appeared as at that of Trinidad; numberless dead strewed the place. On looking down these breaches I recognised many old friends whose society I had enjoyed a few hours before, now lying stiff in death."*

"Let it be considered," says Napier "that this frightful carnage took place in a space of less than 100 yards square; that the slain died not all suddenly, nor by one manner of death—that some perished by steel, some by shot, some by water, that some were crushed and mangled by heavy weights, some trampled upon, some dashed to pieces by the fiery explosions; that for hours this destruction was endured without shrinking, and the town was won at last. Let these things be considered, and it

* "A Boy in the Peninsular War," p. 272.

must be admitted a British army bears with it an awful power. And false would it be to say that the French were feeble men; the garrison stood and fought manfully and with good discipline, behaving worthily; shame there was none on any side, . . . but no age, no nation, ever sent forth braver troops to battle than those who stormed Badajoz.

"When the extent of the night's havoc was made known to Lord Wellington, the firmness of his nature gave way for a moment, and the pride of conquest yielded to a passionate burst of grief for the loss of his gallant soldiers."

"And why," asks Napier (bk. xvi. chap. 7), in burning words which should appeal to every Englishman except a certain section of politicians who frequent Westminster Hall to the possible advantage of their party but to the undoubted detriment of their country, "why was all this striving in blood against insurmountable difficulties? Why were men sent thus to slaughter when the application of a just science would have rendered the operation comparatively easy? Because the British Ministers, so ready to plunge into war, were quite ignorant of its exigencies; because the English people are warlike without being military; and, under the pretence of maintaining a liberty which they do not possess, oppose in peace all useful martial establishments. Expatiating in their schools and colleges upon Roman discipline and Roman valour, they are heedless of Roman institutions; they desire, like that ancient republic, to be free at home and conquerors abroad, but start at perfecting their military system, as a thing incompatible with a constitution which they yet suffer to be violated by every minister who trembles at the exposure of corruption. In the beginning of each war England has to seek in blood the knowledge necessary to insure success."

IN THE PENINSULA

Although written seventy years ago, these words are equally true at the present day. There is much talk of War Office reform. But the expression is used in very different senses. To the soldier it means the pursuit of the highest possible degree of efficiency; to the Member of Parliament in general it means the gagging of military opinion.

Terrible scenes, which are mentioned with indescribable horror by eye-witnesses, followed the capture of Badajoz. The fury of our men was excited, not against their gallant opponents but against the inhabitants. The Spaniard, his wife and his daughter got no mercy. To palliate such barbarity is impossible. It may, however, be remarked that the repeated insults of the citizens in past days had sunk deeply into the hearts of our soldiers, who now exacted a fearful vengeance. Their conduct may also have been partly due to a certain natural reaction from the bonds of that discipline which had compelled them to risk their lives so long and to see their comrades so terribly slaughtered the night before. Partly, too, to the fact that the citizens, aware of our addiction to drink, had placed bottles of *aquadente* outside their doors. Had it been beer no great harm would have followed; but the fiery spirit made our men mad in their drunkenness, and in this state they were beyond the control of the officers, and when checked for their conduct frequently fired on them.

PART V

THE SALAMANCA CAMPAIGN

CHAPTER XXVII

Repression of excesses in Badajoz—Approach and retirement of Soult—Lord W. Bentinck from Sicily proposes a diversion on the east coast of Spain—Marmont approaches the Agueda—Retreat of Victor Alten—Able conduct of Colonels Trant, Wilson, and Le Cor—Marmont retires—His plans contrasted with those of the Emperor—Wellington's plans for an advance into Spain—Hill's surprise of Almaraz.

WELLINGTON took prompt measures to restore order in Badajoz. Stringent orders were issued on the 7th, and the Provost Marshal was directed to enter the town and execute any man found in the act of plundering. Unfortunately there were only two British battalions at hand which had not taken part in the assault. Whether they were unable or unwilling to check the excesses of their comrades does not appear; but Power's Portuguese Brigade, which had been sent in to protect the inhabitants, plundered them even more than our own men did. On the 8th, orders were issued for the rolls to be called every hour, and men were forbidden to enter Badajoz unless provided with a pass. "The Commander of the Forces calls upon the Staff Officers of the Army and the Commanding and other officers of regiments, to assist him in putting an end to

IN THE PENINSULA

the disgraceful scenes of drunkenness and plunder which are going on in Badajoz." Yet, in spite of everything, and although officers risked their lives in protecting women from their own soldiers, it was not until the 9th that, partly from physical exhaustion, partly from the sight of the Provost Marshal's gallows, the "tumult rather subsided than was quelled; the wounded men were then looked to, the dead disposed of."

Nearly 4,000 prisoners were taken, 172 guns and 80,000 shot. The retrenchments of the breaches and the general strength of the fortress—to say nothing of the skill and gallantry of the Governor—amply warranted the surprise expressed by Soult at hearing that a place which he had expected to hold out for six weeks, should have been captured in half that time.

That Marshal was at Villa Franca on the 7th. Drafts for the Russian war, and detachments sent to cope with Ballesteros in the Ronda, had reduced his available force to such an extent that it was with difficulty—and, indeed, only by endangering the safety of Seville and the blockade of Cadiz—that he could muster 24,000 men for the relief of Badajoz. He was, however, in no alarm for the fortress, since both Marmont and Foy had assured him that if it were menaced, the three Divisions of the Army of Portugal, then on the Tagus, would cross the river and unite with the 5th Corps.

Thus, on the 8th, Soult was marching to attack the British at Albuera when messengers, despatched with great forethought by Phillipon just before his surrender, having evaded the posts of the Allies, reached him with the news of the catastrophe. At the same time he heard that Marmont was still in the north. It was impossible to pit his 24,000 men against double that number of the Allies, and he therefore fell back at once on Llerena, where his presence was much needed; for Ballesteros with three Divisions of 11,000 men was menacing Seville (which was weakly garrisoned) from the left of the Guadalquivir, while Penne Villemur and Morillo, who had crossed the Lower Guadiana, were approaching it from the other side. Both forces retired on the approach of Soult, the only result of these minor operations being the repulse of one of Ballesteros' Divisions, 3,000 strong, in an attack on Ossuna, whose garrison was composed of 150 Spaniards in the French service. Throughout the war generally the Spaniards fought better when on the side of the French than against them.

On the 11th Soult reached Seville. His movement southward had been followed by Sir Thomas Graham; and on the same day Sir Stapleton Cotton, with Le Marchant's and Anson's Cavalry Brigades—the latter commanded at present by Frederick Ponsonby, of the 12th—came up with and severely handled the Cavalry of the enemy's rearguard at Usagre, driving it into Llerena and being stopped only by the Infantry of the 5th Corps there drawn up.

The capture of Ciudad Rodrigo and Badajoz had given Lord Wellington a new and broad base of operation and had re-opened the gates into Spain. The long period of weary waiting on the defensive was at an end—weary, to some extent, through the mistakes of his lieutenants; still more through the fatuity and lack of confidence shown by the Spanish, Portuguese, and British Governments. There are, at rare intervals in history, persons whose foresight and breadth of view guides them almost invariably to correct conclusions, yet who never receive the credit due to them, for the reason that those very qualities which raise them above the common herd are not generally appreciated. Wellington was such a one. That the ordinary Member of Parliament, absorbed in his worship of the idol of party spirit, should have failed to appreciate the character of the great Commander, is no matter for surprise. But the Ministers by this time had had ample proofs of his prudence and sagacity, yet they still distrusted his ability, even in purely military matters, and always appointed an officer second in command—first Sherbroke, then Spencer, and now Graham—as a sort of dry nurse in whom they placed more confidence than in the Commander-in-Chief. It is perhaps fair to say that the same mistrust was shown even by Generals of Division, and it was chiefly the uncultivated instinct of the private soldier, so seldom at fault, which reposed entire confidence in Lord Wellington.

The proper corollary of the capture of Badajoz should have been the invasion of Andalusia, the seizure of the great Arsenal at Seville, the relief of Cadiz, and the clearance of the enemy out of the province—possibly out of all the southern provinces of Spain. This, indeed, had been Wellington's intention, but the delinquencies of others had as usual robbed him of half the fruits of victory. Ciudad Rodrigo, which had been handed over to the Spaniards, was neither repaired nor provisioned; and Marmont had crossed the Agueda. It was therefore essential to march into the north of Beira. Before starting Lord Wellington wrote to his brother, Sir Henry Wellesley, at Cadiz, pointing out (1) that the Spaniards must either garrison or destroy Badajoz; (2) that Ballesteros, while making use of Gibraltar as a place of arms, should be ready to create a diversion by advancing upon Seville in the event of the French attacking Badajoz; (3) that Penne Villemur and Morillo should return to Estremadura to re-establish the authority of the Spanish Government. "But," he added, "those measures will not be sufficient, as it may be depended upon that, notwithstanding all that I shall do to weaken the enemy as much as may be in my power, they will collect their forces when the harvest will be on the ground, and they will be certain of subsistence for their army . . . ; and it must be expected that they will be too strong for me.

"Under these circumstances it is most desirable that some diversion should, if possible, be made in my favour on the eastern coast. . . . I propose to urge Lord William Bentinck in the strongest manner to undertake the expedition to the coast of Catalonia. I am about to send my battering train to Gibraltar to be put in order for him; and early in the month of June I will likewise send these British and Portuguese artillerymen, engineer officers, and such other assistance as I can afford. . . . If Lord William Bentinck should be made sufficiently strong, it is probable that we shall succeed in opening a communication between the fleet and the patriots in Catalonia, . . . and there is a chance of recovering Valencia. At all events a diversion of the enemy's force must be created for my operations; without which I shall have upon me the armies of Portugal, the South and Centre, and that of Suchet."

In anticipation of the invasion of Andalusia, Marshal Soult prepared to give battle to the Allies as they debouched from the passes of the Morena, but for the reasons given he was not attacked.

When Lord Wellington quitted Ciudad Rodrigo in March he left General Victor Alten, as already mentioned, on the Yeltes with the 1st Hussars K.G.L., directing him to conceal his—Wellington's—departure for Badajoz by spreading a report that the Commander-in-Chief was bringing his hounds to hunt on the Yeltes; but, if pressed, to fall back gradually upon Penamacor and Castello Branco.

Alten, however, disregarded his instructions, and when,

IN THE PENINSULA

on the 30th of March, Marmont approached, he fell back precipitately, first to Castello Branco, afterwards (though the enemy was not within 30 miles of him) across the Tagus. Thereupon Marmont, who had lost his siege train in Ciudad Rodrigo, and was consequently not in a position to besiege that fortress, left a Division to blockade it, and sent two others forward to storm Almeida. By a clever device Colonel Trant induced them to abandon the enterprise. He and John Wilson then concentrated at Guarda on the 9th of April, with a view to protecting the magazines at Celorico; and with only 6,000 Infantry Militia and six guns, held their ground till the 14th; while Le Cor, in spite of Alten's flight, refused to abandon Castello Branco. Early on the 14th Trant was attacked by two Brigades, and being outflanked was forced to quit his position. He retired in the direction of the Mondego —at first in good order, but eventually his men, pursued by the French Cavalry, fell into confusion, and the river was crossed with difficulty and the loss of 200 prisoners. Meanwhile Wilson held on at Celorico, and when the French, hearing of Wellington's approach, retired on the 17th, he re-occupied Guarda.

Silveira, who should have been hanging on the French right with another Division of Militia, never came up at all. Alten, as we have seen, had abandoned the whole region. Wellington's arrangements for the defence of Beira were consequently nullified, and but for Marmont's amazing indecision or lack of enterprise the gallantry and intelligence of Trant, Wilson, and Le Cor would have availed little.

Meanwhile Lord Wellington, on hearing of Soult's retreat, had lost no time in marching northward with the Divisions which had taken Badajoz, leaving directions for Graham to follow with the 1st, 6th, and 7th; while Hill, with Erskine's Cavalry Division, a Brigade of Portuguese Cavalry, the 2nd and Hamilton's Divisions of Infantry, remained in the neighbourhood of Badajoz. Wellington was anxious to fight Marmont on the left bank of the Coa, but the Marshal, who had 7 Divisions 28,000 strong near Penamacor, finding himself in danger of being hemmed in between the Militia and the British troops, and having the Coa and Agueda in full flood behind him, did not think it advisable to await his adversary, but retired into Spain and dispersed his army amid the plains of Leon.

Marmont's own wish had been to relieve Badajoz by marching into Estremadura and co-operating with Soult; but he was expressly ordered by the Emperor to make a diversion in the north of Beira. Napier vindicates the Emperor's judgment. "Suppose Marmont had aided Soult, and the Army of the Centre had also done so. If they made any error in their combinations Wellington would have defeated them separately; if they effected their junction he would have retreated and Badajoz would have been succoured; but 80,000 French would have been assembled by long marches in the winter rains to the great detriment of their affairs elsewhere, and, unless they came prepared to take Elvas, without any adequate object. For Wellington, after the fall of Ciudad Rodrigo, could have repeated this operation as often as he pleased, which, besides the opening made for insurrection in Spain, would have stamped a character of weakness on the French arms.

"Napoleon judged better. He disliked timid operations; he desired that his powerful armies should throw the Allies on the defensive, and he indicated the means of doing so. Wellington, he said, expecting an effort to retake Ciudad Rodrigo, had called Hill across the Tagus, and to prevent that movement Soult was directed to send 20,000 men against the Alemtejo. The fall of

Ciudad, by compelling the Allies to defend it, gave the French choice of ground for a battle, and at a distance from the sea. It was for Marmont to seize the occasion, but not by joining Soult . . .; he at the worst could be only driven from Andalusia upon Valencia or Madrid, whereas if the Army of Portugal or a part of it should be defeated on the Guadiana the blow would be felt in every part of Spain. Marmont's business was, he said, first to strengthen his own position at Salamanca as a base of operations, and then keep the Allies constantly engaged on the Agueda until he was prepared to fight a general battle; meanwhile Soult could take the fortresses of the Alemtejo or draw off Hill from Wellington, who would then be inferior to Marmont, and yet Hill himself would be unequal to fight Soult.

"'Fix your quarters,' said the Emperor, 'at Salamanca, work day and night to fortify that place; organise a new battering-train; form magazines; send strong advanced guards to menace Ciudad and Almeida; harass the Allies' outposts, even daily; threaten the frontier of Portugal in all directions and send parties to ravage the nearest villages; repair the ways to Almeida and Oporto, and keep the bulk of your army at Toro, Zamora, Benevente, and Avila, which are fertile districts, and from whence in four days you can concentrate the whole upon Salamanca; you will thus keep the Allies in check on the Agueda, and your troops will repose while you prepare for great operations. You have nothing to do with the south. Announce the approach of your new battering-train, and if Wellington marches to invest Badajoz with a few Divisions Soult will be able to relieve it; but if Wellington goes with all his forces, unite your army, march straight upon Almeida, push parties to Coimbra, overrun the country in various directions, and be assured he will return. Twenty-four hours after the receipt of this letter you should be on your way to Salamanca and your advanced guards should be in march towards Ciudad Rodrigo and Almeida.'

"If Marmont had thus conceived the war he would have commenced operations before the end of January; but this letter, written on the 18th of February, reached him in the latter end of that month and found him desponding and fearful even in defence. Vacillating between his own wishes and the Emperor's orders, he did nothing; had he, as this despatch recommended, commenced his operations in twenty-four hours, his advanced posts would have been near Rodrigo early in March, when the Allies were, as has been shown, disseminated all over Portugal, and when only the 5th Division was left upon the Coa to oppose him. The works of Almeida were then indefensible and the movement upon Badajoz must have necessarily been suspended. Thus the winter season would have passed away uselessly for the Allies, unless Wellington turned to attack Marmont, a difficult operation and dangerous to the Alemtejo while Soult held Badajoz, for that Marshal had received orders to attack Hill with 20,000 men. Here, then, the errors were in the execution; the Emperor's combination was evidently solid. It remains to test his second combination designed to baffle the siege of Badajoz.

"Marmont was so to dispose his army that he could concentrate in four days; he was to invade Beira when Wellington crossed the Tagus; he was to menace Oporto; to attack Almeida; and Coimbra was to be occupied. These operations would have brought the Allies back, because the fall of Badajoz could not be expected under three weeks, which would have been too long to leave Beira and the fortresses at the mercy of the invader; but Marmont did not reach the Agueda until the 31st of March, when the siege of Badajoz was near its conclu-

IN THE PENINSULA

sion; he did not storm Almeida, nor attack Rodrigo, nor enter Coimbra, nor menace Oporto, yet his feeble operations forced Lord Wellington to relinquish the invasion of Andalusia and return to Beira. Again, therefore, the error was in the execution. And how inferior in hardihood the French General was to his adversary! Wellington, with 18,000 men, escaladed Badajoz, a powerful fortress defended by an excellent governor and 5,000 French veterans; Marmont, with 28,000 men, would not attempt to storm Rodrigo, although its breaches were scarcely healed and its garrison disaffected. Nor did he assail Almeida, which, hardly meriting the name of a fortress, was only occupied by 3,000 Militia scarcely able to handle their arms; yet in Almeida he would have found a battering-train with which to take Ciudad Rodrigo and thus have balanced the campaign."

On the retirement of Marmont it was impossible to follow him, for the magazines at Castello Branco had been lost through Victor Alten's conduct. Lord Wellington then once more contemplated a campaign in Andalusia, but was again baffled by circumstances. For the harvest of 1811 had failed and the means of transport had been dispersed. To replace the magazines Wellington found it necessary to quarter his troops at the highest navigable points of the rivers and to employ the army mules in carrying stores thence to Almeida and Ciudad Rodrigo. The consequence was that his army was extended in groups along pretty nearly the whole length of the Portuguese frontier. A movement on the offensive was at present impossible; and indeed Lord Wellington could only hope for immunity from attack until the ripening of the corn would enable the enemy to concentrate once more. But, as the French very well knew, the British Commander, when once his magazines were replenished and his transport collected, had now the power of assuming the offensive at pleasure. The enemy's forces had been largely reduced by drafts sent to the Grand Army now ready for the invasion of Russia, and it could not be long before the tramp of a British army would be heard on the Upper Douro or Tagus. The only question was whether Wellington could be himself attacked before he was ready to take the offensive. But the British Commander was resolved that it should be through no fault of his own if the question were not decided in his favour. Andalusia being no longer feasible, he turned his thoughts to Castille. From the strategical point of view this line of advance would be equally good. To defeat Marmont in a pitched battle would be to strike a blow at the grand line of communications of the French armies, as Sir John Moore had done; would ensure the capture of Madrid; would probably force Soult to raise the blockade of Cadiz and evacuate Andalusia. The only doubt was whether it would be possible to defeat Marmont before the Army of the North or of the Centre could come to his aid, or Soult menace Portugal from the south.

As to the Army of the Centre, a good deal might be risked in view of its disorganised condition. But to prevent the Army of the South advancing into Portugal by the valley of the Tagus and to obstruct its communications with the other Armies was a matter of the first importance; and as a preliminary to that end Wellington desired Hill to destroy the bridge of boats at Almaraz. The project had been revolved by Wellington before the investment of Badajoz, but perforce abandoned through the failure of the Portuguese Government to find transport. The task was anything but easy, for not only was the bridge defended by three forts and a bridge-head, but an attacking force would be compelled to defile through a fortified pass over the Mirabete mountains. And withal, the assailant would be surrounded by foes, for Foy with his Division of the Army of Portugal was in the valley of the Tagus; a Division of the Army of the Centre, under D'Armagnac, was at Talavera de la Reyna; D'Erlon, at Hinojosa, with his Cavalry on the Medellin road, was in a position to intercept Hill's retreat at Merida; and Erskine with the 2nd Cavalry Division and Hamilton's Portuguese Division, at Almendralejos, was liable to be attacked by Soult from Seville.

Yet the object was worth the trial, for the bridges below Almaraz had been destroyed as far as Villa Velha; and those of Arzobispo and Talavera, upstream, were so much hemmed in by mountains as to be nearly useless. Hence the bridge of boats at Almaraz formed the only practical communication this side of Toledo, between the Armies of Soult and Marmont.

To support Hill, Wellington detached the 1st Cavalry Division, the 1st and 6th Infantry Divisions to Portalégre under Graham; but in order to gain time for the arrival of the latter rumours were spread and demonstrations made, to encourage the enemy to believe that an invasion of Andalusia was in hand.

The moment for action was cleverly chosen at a time when Soult had gone to Cadiz. On the 12th of May, Hill, who had been delayed a fortnight at Merida in repairing the bridge, crossed the Guadiana with 6,000 men and 12 guns, and was joined there by a battery of 24 pounders which had been sent by the right bank. On the 15th he was at Truxillo, 50 miles distant; on the 16th at Jaraceijo, nearly 20 miles further on. After nightfall the advance was continued in three columns which were expected to reach their respective points of attack before dawn. That on the left—under command of General Chowne (formerly known as Tilson, who now commanded the 2nd Division)—consisting of the 28th and 34th belonging to Wilson's Brigade, and the 6th Caçadores, was directed on the tower of Mirabete, a strong work about 4 miles south-west of the bridge of Almaraz. The centre column, made up of Ashworth's Portuguese Brigade—6th and 18th Regiments—the 13th Light Dragoons and the guns—the whole under General Long—advanced along the main road against the fortified pass. The right column, made up of Howard's Brigade—50th, 71st, and 92nd—under Hill in person, had to make a circuitous march by the village of Romangordo through the mountains, in hope of penetrating to the bridge of Almaraz.

The dangers and difficulties inseparable from night operations are often overlooked. Even the brilliant success of Tel el Kebir, when everything combined to favour the night march, was within an ace of proving an utter failure. Distances are hard to judge; points are not recognised; a general feeling of helplessness prevails; and progress is always slow. The present case was no exception to the rule. Chowne alone reached his point before dawn, but made no use of his advantage and did not attack the tower of Mirabete in the darkness. Daylight surprised the other column still on the march, and compelled a halt.

The coup had failed. To attack the Mirabete works and force the pass on the main road by daylight would be too costly; yet reconnaissance showed by this road alone artillery could move. Hill's position was critical in the extreme. Almost hemmed in on the north by Foy and D'Armagnac; on the south by Drouet; his retreat on Merida would be most difficult, and in the event either of victory or defeat he could only hope to escape westwards by way of Caceres or Alcantara. But Sir Rowland was not a man easily discouraged. On the evening of the 18th, in pursuance of a bold plan, he started with Howard's Brigade strengthened by two Companies of the

60th and the 6th Portuguese, to continue the march which his column had begun, in hopes of penetrating into the valley and attacking the forts which protected the bridge itself. The guns were left in charge of General Long on the main road. Chowne was directed to make a demonstration at dawn against Fort Mirabete.

The distance which Hill had to cover was only 6 miles; but the difficulty of making the precipitous descent in the darkness was so great that it was nearly daylight when the 50th, the leading battalion, reached Fort Napoleon— a strongly constructed work armed with guns and garrisoned by 400 or 500 men—which protected the bridge-head on the south bank of the Tagus. At this critical moment, in the very nick of time, the sound of Chowne's guns was heard making the false attack upon Mirabete. Without a moment's hesitation Hill ordered the assault of Fort Napoleon. Three columns, composed of the 50th and a wing of the 71st, formed up under cover of some blind ground within 20 yards of the ditch; then, despite the frontal fire of the garrison and a flanking fire from Fort Ragusa on the further bank of the river, escaladed the ramparts—an operation greatly facilitated by the width of the berm—drove the garrison out of the fort and pursued it through the bridge-head on to the bridge itself. The second line (92nd and other wing of the 71st) and the reserve consisting of the 6th Portuguese and 60th, did not come into action; but, curiously enough, so great was the panic among the fugitives that Fort Ragusa was also abandoned.

The forts and bridge of boats were then destroyed. Many of the French were killed, many drowned, 259 were made prisoners. Hill's casualties amounted only to 33 killed and 144 wounded.

It only remained to capture and destroy the Fort of Mirabete which was now isolated, and this no doubt would shortly have been done had it not been for the advance of Drouet, Count D'Erlon, who reaching the Guadiana with 4,000 men, sent Cavalry patrols on the 18th to the right bank in the direction of Merida and Miajadas; and of Lallemande who at the same time brought his Cavalry Brigade to Zafra. Alarmed by these movements Sir William Erskine reported that Soult—who was in reality before Cadiz—had entered Estremadura with his whole army. Graham consequently came down to Badajoz; and Hill, leaving Mirabete blockaded by the Partidas, retired on Merida which he reached without adventure on the 26th. Count D'Erlon thereupon retired also and Graham returned to Castello de Vide.

Although his success was not complete, Hill deserves every credit for the way in which he carried out Lord Wellington's enterprise—one of those which, in Napier's words, "are regarded with astonishment when achieved and attributed to madness when they fail." Sir W. Erskine was not up to the mark as a General Officer; and Wellington complained of the lack of confidence shown by so many of his lieutenants when in the neighbourhood of the enemy, brave as they undoubtedly were as individuals. Napier acknowledges Wellington's complaint to be well founded in this instance, but his weighty words on the subject generally deserve as much attention at the present day as at the time when they were uttered. " Every British General knew that without powerful interest his future prospects and reputation for past services would wither together under the first blight of misfortune; that a selfish Government would offer him up a victim to a misjudging public and a ribald press with whom success is the only criterion of merit. English Generals are and must be prodigal of their blood to gain reputation, but they are necessarily timid in command when a single failure even without a fault consigns them in age to shame and misery."

CHAPTER XXVIII

The war on the north coast—Formation of the French Army of the Ebro—Catalonia, Valencia and Andalusia—Lord W. Bentinck—Before starting for Russia Napoleon makes overtures to the British Government for peace—United States declare war against England—Lord Wellington devises means to feed the whole population of Portugal—His difficulties increased by the British Government—Comparative strength of the opposing forces.

IN spite of Wellington's successes and the shortcomings of his opponents, the balance of advantage in the Peninsula as a whole still rested with the French. In Galicia the strenuous efforts of Colonel Sir Howard Douglas, the English attaché, failed to spur the Spaniards to useful exertion; and neither Abadia, nor Castanos who succeeded him, made any effectual diversion upon Marmont's flank during the time that Lord Wellington was engaged at Badajoz. The Partidas of the north, however, constantly menaced the grand line of communications with France, and Napoleon in consequence not only fortified Santona and other points on and near the sea coast, but anticipated Lord Kitchener's blockhouse system by converting into a stronghold every church, house, and convent situated at a strategical point.

Bonet, who had evacuated the Asturias during the siege of Ciudad Rodrigo, was directed to re-occupy the province; and did so in May when the mountain passes were cleared of snow, by means of a chain of posts which separated the forces of Galicia from those of Biscay and Castille.

At the same time Marmont fortified the lines of the Tormes and Douro, and, with a view to turning those lines, Sir Home Popham was sent from England with a naval squadron to occupy some point on the neck of the French line of communications; a project the absurdity of which is pointed out by Napier, who remarks that of the 120,000 French soldiers in the Northern provinces, nearly 50,000 were specially set apart to protect this very neck, and were hardly likely to be set aside by the attempts of 1,000 Marines!

During April and May the Guerilla chief Mina was active, and gained some success against convoys until pursued and defeated by General Abbé, now commanding the French forces in Navarre. But the Partidas in general were active throughout Spain at this period, and those on the east coast were so troublesome that an "Army of the Ebro," 20,000 strong, had been formed under General Reille, and was composed of four Divisions commanded respectively by himself, Severoli, Palombini and Frere, whose duty was to suppress the guerilla bands, and to connect Suchet with the Army of the North, the command of which, on the departure of Dorsenne for France, had been given to General Caffarelli. In July, by order of the King, Palombini's Division marched to Madrid, and was transferred to the Army of the Centre.

In Catalonia, Marshal Macdonald was succeeded by General Decaen; but the latter was placed under the orders generally of Suchet. The Catalans were supported by the British fleet, but their operations were desultory. The large number of officers of Irish extraction engaged on this side is rather remarkable. The names of Bourke,

O'Donnell, Blake, Sarsfield, &c., occur, but seem to have brought little accession of military talent. Still, as compared with those of their compatriots, the effort of the Catalans stand out with some prominence.

In Valencia and Andalusia, the administrative talent—so frequently displayed by soldiers—of Suchet and Soult had borne ample fruit. Taxes were fairly and moderately levied. The inhabitants of the towns were content. Industries flourished and, thanks to the ability of Soult, the contest between France and England for commercial supremacy at the Court of Barbary had ended in the exclusion of British trade. The more thoughtful of the Spaniards had begun to realise that the best interests of their country lay rather in accepting the new constitutional monarchy under the superintending genius of Napoleon than in the return of despotism supported by England.

Sir Rowland Hill, after his exploit at Almaraz, marched to Zafra. Count d'Erlon fell back, and Hill despatched Slade's Heavy Brigade to gather the harvest on one side and a Brigade of Spanish Cavalry to do the same on the other. On June 11th, Slade encountered and was badly defeated by Lallemande's Cavalry Brigade at Maquilla with the loss of 166 men. Lord Wellington was intensely annoyed at Slade's escapade. "It is," he said, "occasioned entirely by the trick our officers of Cavalry have acquired of galloping at everything, and then galloping back as fast as they gallop on the enemy. They never consider their situation, never think of manœuvring before an enemy, . . . and when they use their arm as it ought to be used, viz., offensively, they neither keep nor provide for a reserve." In contrast to Slade's clumsiness, Lieutenant Strenowitz, an excellent Austrian officer, moving out next day with 50 troopers defeated a squadron 80 strong and rescued 21 prisoners.

Hill's operations were soon over. Ballesteros, based on Gibraltar, had attacked Conroux on the Guadalete and had been utterly defeated. Soult was in consequence enabled to reinforce d'Erlon with two Divisions of Cavalry and one of Infantry. Hill then fell back and took post at Albuera with about 25,000 men (including the 5th Spanish Army) and 24 guns, but was not attacked.

By this time a new actor had appeared on the scene. In the month of January, 1812, Lord William Bentinck, who now commanded the British forces in Sicily—amounting, inclusive of foreign corps, to some 30,000 men—having deprived the treacherous Queen of power, wrote to the British Government offering the services of 10,000 men to co-operate in the Peninsula. The idea of a diversion upon the Catalonian coast was eagerly taken up by Lord Wellington, who foresaw therein the furtherance of his own projects, since Suchet would be contained and prevented giving assistance to Soult or Marmont. He sent substantial aid to Bentinck in the shape of engineers stores, and a siege train.

Unfortunately Court intrigues still proved too strong, and Lord William found himself unable to spare more than 6,000 men. Then it occurred to him that he could employ a much larger force in Italy and rescue that country from the French. The British Ministers referred the project to Lord Wellington, who at once pointed out that England could not afford to support operations both in Spain and Italy. Italy might in theory be the better theatre, but at all events a solid footing had been established in Spain. In any case the British Government must make up its mind to concentrate its means, which were already strained, upon one field or the other.

Lord Liverpool sensibly adopted Wellington's view, and Bentinck's Italian scheme was stopped. But the

IN THE PENINSULA 525

expedition to Catalonia was delayed and news of it came to Suchet's ears through Paris, which enabled him to make every preparation for its reception. Worse still, Lord Wellington, who was in a state of destitution for lack of specie, and—being restricted by his Government as to the price which he might offer for dollars—had with the greatest difficulty made arrangements for the purchase of a supply at the rate of five shillings and eightpence, was mortified by seeing the markets emptied by Bentinck; for the latter, desirous of forming a military chest and being practically unrestricted as to price, swept off 4,000,000 dollars—including those negotiated for by Wellington—by offering an additional shilling per dollar, and thereby seriously endangered Lord Wellington's prospects of resuming the offensive at all.

But the British Commander was not a man easily deterred from anything which he had a chance of carrying through. Among the advantages gained by the possession of Ciudad Rodrigo and Badajoz was the power of concentrating superior numbers upon any one line of advance, whether the Douro, Tagus, or Guadalquivir. The enemy was perfectly aware of the fact, and as Marmont, Joseph, and Soult all expected to be the object of attack, each wished to strengthen himself at the expense of the others. Napoleon, for his part, was most anxious to terminate the war with England before embarking on his Russian campaign, and once more made overtures for peace, offering as a price the practical renunciation of the Continental System. Portugal was far from being secure; Spain was exhausted; but the efforts of the Emperor proved futile.

It was perhaps too much to expect that British Ministers would foresee the injury which that Continental System was destined to do for England, and that after the lapse of nearly a century we should be confronted in our commerce by the competition of the German industries nourished thereby. Yet for other reasons peace should have been anxiously desired in England. Great distress existed among the labouring classes and we were on the brink of war with the United States. To this we had been brought by our disregard for the rights of neutrals; and although our Government at the last moment offered concessions and repealed the celebrated "Orders in Council" it was too late to prevent hostilities, which broke out in June, and once begun, did not terminate until 1815.

That the United States Government was animated by other ideas than that of mere self-defence is shown by the fact of its continuing the war after the revocation of the obnoxious "Orders"; but whether from the political or economical point of view, the rupture was a gigantic mistake on the part of our Government. America was England's best and surest market for wheat as well as for other things; yet we quarrelled with her at a time when, as Napier observes, "by commerce alone we could hope to sustain the struggle in the Peninsula." By a variety of amazing expedients and the industry of his resourceful mind, the British Commander had also succeeded in importing wheat into Portugal, partly from Brazil, Barbary, and Egypt, but chiefly from the United States. In fact, as already mentioned, he and Sir Charles Stuart engaged personally in trade for the purpose, until forbidden by the Home Government, at the instance of the merchants. In 1808 the importation of bread stuffs from New York amounted to 60,000 barrels. In 1811 it rose to 600,000. It seemed inevitable that this resource would now be cut off, and the war perhaps terminated in consequence. But the genius of Wellington and Stuart succeeded in preserving the neutrality of Portugal during the new contest, and in 1813 the importation actually rose to nearly 800,000 barrels. Thus not only the army, but the whole population of Portugal was being fed by the exertions of the British General and Diplomatist. Yet there are people who say that Lord Wellington was no statesman!

To remedy the lack of specie, a clever expedient was adopted. Portuguese peasants who brought in supplies were paid by bills drawn on the Commissary-General. It was impossible to state the date on which these bills would be met, and no date was mentioned on the face of them; but the class of transaction was one to which the peasants were accustomed, and was popular. Bills were paid, not in turn, but on the equitable principle that original holders—more particularly the holders for the smaller amounts—should have priority of payment before traders who had bought their bills at a discount. (The bills retained their face value until purposely and scandalously depreciated by British merchants in order to enable them to buy the paper at a discount of 20 per cent. The consequence then was that the country people were compelled to raise their prices in order to counteract the heavy discount; and, had they made a practice of turning their bills into cash, the war would have become too costly to be continued.)

Coin was, however, terribly scarce, and instead of being helped, Lord Wellington was thwarted by his own Government. Writing on the 22nd of April to Lord Liverpool, he remarks: "When I say I shall determine upon the line of operations which I shall follow, I ought to add, provided I shall have money to follow any line of operations at all. I wrote to your lordship lately on the subject of the money expected at Cadiz in the *Standard*. That vessel has since arrived at Cadiz; but in consequence of the disapprobation expressed of Sir Henry Wellesley's conduct in appropriating a part of the money received at Cadiz from America on a former occasion, I have not thought it proper to request him to send me any part of this money.

"The Commissary-in-Chief and the Treasury have disapproved of my sanctioning bargains for importing specie from Gibraltar. . . . I have therefore been obliged, within these last three days, to refuse to give my sanction to an offer of 500,000 dollars upon a similar bargain. I can scarcely believe that the Treasury are aware of the distress of this army. . . . The Portuguese troops and establishments are likewise in the greatest distress; and it is my opinion, as well as that of Marshal Beresford, that we must disband part of the Army unless I can increase the money payments of the subsidy. The Commissary-General has this day informed me that he is very apprehensive that he shall not be able to make good his engagements for the payment of meat for the troops; and if we are obliged to stop that payment, your Lordship will do well to prepare to recall the Army, as it will be quite impossible to carry up salt meat, as well as bread, to the troops from the sea coast."

And again on the 6th of May, to Sir C. Stuart : " The British Army have not been paid for nearly three months ; we owe nearly a year's hire to the muleteers of the Army, and we are in debt for supplies in all parts of the country; and we are on the point of failing in our payments for some supplies essentially necessary to both armies, which cannot be procured excepting with ready money."

Yet this was the time when the restrictions placed upon Wellington by his Government enabled Lord William Bentinck to carry off the available specie!

Apart from financial and other difficulties, the forces at the disposal of the British Commander seem at first sight

IN THE PENINSULA 529

quite inadequate for an advance into Spain. The Anglo-Portuguese Army consisted on paper of about 100,000 officers and men. Of these 7,000 were at Cadiz, and although three years had elapsed, the regiments engaged in the Walcheren fiasco were still decimated by fever. Consequently the force under Wellington's personal command amounted only to 4,000 * Cavalry, 40,000 Infantry, and 54 guns, with the addition of 3,500 Spaniards under Carlos d'Espana; and that under Hill to 19,000 * men (of whom 2,200 were Cavalry) and 24 guns, supported by the 5th Spanish Army.

In the extreme north of Portugal General D'Urban occupied the Tras os Montes with 1,200 Portuguese Cavalry.

No great help could be expected from the Spanish forces still in the field. Their Cavalry had been almost destroyed, their guns captured, and their arsenals exhausted. The heavy guns on the Isla at Cadiz were done for, and the foundries utterly neglected.

The French, on the other hand, on paper, were still in overwhelming strength. Their "State" of the 15th of May, 1812, is given on the next page.

But the superiority of the French was rather in appearance than in reality. In the first place, they were extended over nearly the whole of Spain, whereas Wellington and Hill were concentrated and operating on interior lines. In the second, none of the French Commanders would obey the orders of the King, and their insubordination was increased by the fact already noticed, that each expected to be the immediate object of Wellington's attack. This reluctance to obey orders, and the disputes consequent thereon, were made known by

* These figures include all ranks. There were probably about 1,600 Artillerymen with Wellington, and about 600 with Hill.

	Under Arms.		On Detachment.		Hospital.	Gross Total.		
	Men.	Horses.	Men.	Horses.		Men.	Cavalry.	Artillery.
Army of the South	56,031	12,801	2,787	660	4,652	63,470	7,811	4,540
,, ,, Centre	17,395	4,208	158	37	766	19,203	3,332	420
,, ,, Portugal	52,618	7,244	9,750	1,538	8,332	70,700	4,481	3,448
,, ,, Aragon and The Ebro	27,218	4,768	4,458	605	3,701	35,377	2,976	1,980
,, ,, Catalonia	33,667	1,577	1,844	267	6,009	41,580	1,376	279
,, ,, the North	38,771	6,031	2,560	271	7,767	49,098	4,443	1,168
Total	225,700	35,929	21,557	3,378	31,227	279,378	23,919	11,680
Old Reserve at Bayonne	3,894	221	1,642	—	964	6,500	207	—
New ,, ,, ,,	2,598	116	3,176	—	55	5,769	103	—
Grand Total	232,192	36,266	26,375	3,378	32,196	291,647	24,229	11,680

intercepted letters to the British Commander, who took care to confirm each General in his own opinion. Thirdly, the Spanish forces, regular or irregular, still in the field, occupied the attention of large portions of the Armies of the North, of the South, of Aragon, and of Catalonia.

CHAPTER XXIX

Wellington's arrangements for taking the offensive—He concentrates on the Agueda—Counter movements of Marmont—Wellington crosses the Agueda, and enters Salamanca—Siege and capture of the forts—Marmont retires across the Duero.

PREPARATORY to the advance, Graham was recalled to Beira with the 1st Division of Cavalry and the 1st and 6th of Infantry. A shorter line of communication between Hill and Wellington was established by the cleverness of Colonel Sturgeon, R.E., who repaired the bridge at Alcantara on the suspension principle. The valley of the Tagus having been denuded of provisions, and the French pontoon train—indispensable for crossing the numerous confluents of the river—having been destroyed at Almaraz, no great danger was to be feared from that quarter, and Wellington consequently felt his right flank secure. His left might possibly be menaced in the event of Marmont combining with Caffarelli and operating from the north; but even in this case he would be in a position to retire either upon Ciudad Rodrigo or upon Hill in the valley of the Tagus.

"Menace your enemy's flanks, protect your own, and be ready to concentrate upon important points," was Napoleon's advice to his Generals in Spain. Wellington now proceeded to act upon it himself. (1) He directed Silveira and D'Urban, with four Militia battalions and three regiments of Cavalry, to threaten Marmont's right

flank and rear by advancing along the valley of the
Douro, and getting in touch with the Galician Army,
now under Castanos. When Wellington moved forward
Castanos was to undertake the siege of Astorga; and—in
order to draw Caffarelli to the north—Sir Home Popham
was to operate at once with a naval squadron against the
coast of Biscay. (2) Lord Wellington desired the expected force from Sicily to menace the east coast and
prevent Suchet detaching reinforcements to the Army
of the Centre at and about Madrid. (3) Hill had been
sufficiently strengthened to be able to make head against
Soult, who would be deterred by insurrections in Cordova
and minor expeditions from Gibraltar and the garrison of
Cadiz from operating on the side of Badajoz with his
whole force.

In the first days of June Lord Wellington suddenly
concentrated his Army on the Agueda. How far he
could carry out a movement on the offensive was very
doubtful, for water carriage could only be of use to bring
up provisions to a distance of three or four marches
beyond the Agueda, and to feed his troops he therefore had to rely solely on local supplies aided by granaries
which, his friends assured him, had been successfully
hidden from the French. How often at this time must
the mind of Wellington have recurred to the opening of
his Talavera campaign three years previously, and the
fiasco then entailed by reliance on Spanish promises!

Meanwhile Marmont's army had again been spread
over a large extent of country for purposes of supply.
When the Marshal, however, saw that Wellington had
concentrated on the Agueda he lost no time in calling up
Foy from Almaraz and Bonet from the Asturias. In
evacuating the Asturias he was acting contrary to the
wishes of the Emperor, who clearly appreciated the value
of Bonet's position as protecting the main line of retreat.

534 WELLINGTON'S OPERATIONS

The intention of Marmont was to hold the Galicians in check with a Brigade of Dragoons and two battalions; to line the Tormes with two Divisions as an advance guard, and concentrate the main body of his Army about Torro and Valladolid, behind the Douro.

The "State" of the Army of Portugal on the 15th of June is shown on next page.

The total number of combatants, present and under arms, was thus something under 53,000, with 60 guns—mostly 4- or 8-pounders—11 6-inch and 3 4-inch howitzers.

The rains having ceased, Wellington on the 13th of June crossed the Agueda. The Spaniards attached to his Army formed a separate body. The Anglo-Portuguese force marched in three columns, preceded respectively by the 11th Light Dragoons, the 1st Hussars K.G.L., and the 14th Light Dragoons. The columns were organised as follows :—

LEFT COLUMN.	CENTRE COLUMN.	RIGHT COLUMN.
Lieut.-Gen. Picton.	Lord Wellington.	Sir T. Graham.
3rd Division.	Light Division.	1st Division.
Bradford's Portuguese Brigade.	Anson's Cavalry Brigade.	6th Division.
Pack's Portuguese Brigade	5th Division.	7th Division.
Le Marchant's Cavalry Brigade	4th Division.	
	Bock's Cavalry Brigade K.G.L.	
	Reserve Ammunition Column.	
	Headquarters.	
	Military Chest.	

Orders for the march were issued by the Quartermaster-General, Colonel Delancey, in General Murray's absence :—

IN THE PENINSULA

Unit	Commander	Present under Arms. Men.	Present under Arms. Horses.	Detached. Men.	Detached. Horses.	Hospital. Men.	Total. Men.	Total. Cavalry.	Total. Guns.
1st Division	Gen. Foy	5,138	—	319	—	516	5,973	—	—
2nd ,,	,, Clausel	7,405	—	678	—	613	8,696	—	—
3rd ,,	,, Ferey	5,547	—	12	—	926	6,485	—	—
4th ,,	,, Sarrut	5,056	—	214	—	862	6,132	—	—
5th ,,	,, Maucune	5,269	—	588	—	1,513	7,370	—	—
6th ,,	,, Brennier	5,021	—	124	—	720	5,865	—	—
7th ,,	,, Thomières	6,352	61	—	—	1,905	8,257	61	—
8th ,,	,, Bonet	6,681	139	66	—	665	7,482	139	—
Light Cavalry	,, Curto	1,386	1,398	1,073	324	246	2,705	1,722	—
Dragoons	,, Boyer	1,389	1,378	479	358	86	1,954	1,786	—
Artillery		3,612	2,339	513	258	220	4,345	847	74
Engineers		414	9	67	7	84	565	—	—
Army Service Corps		955	1,107	51	44	242	1,251	54	—
Gens d'Armes & Hospital C'rps		325	75	—	—	15	340	—	—
Total		54,550	6,506	4,184	991	8,633	67,370	4,059	74

535

536 WELLINGTON'S OPERATIONS

LEFT COLUMN.	CENTRE COLUMN.	RIGHT COLUMN.
	June 13*th*, 1812.	
To pass the river Agueda and proceed to and bivouac on the river Gavallanes, near the village of Santi Espiritus. (Ciudad Rodrigo to Santi Espiritus 9 miles.)	To pass the Agueda, proceed to and bivouac on the river Tenebron, near to Boca Cara.	To pass the Agueda and proceed to and bivouac on the river Tenebron, near the village of Tenebron. (Ciudad and Santi Espiritus to Tenebron 8 miles.)
	June 14*th*.	
On the river Huebra near the village of Munoz. (Santi Espiritus to Munoz 15 miles.)	On the river Huebra near the village of Munoz. (Boca Cara to Munoz 16 miles.)	On the river Huebra to the left of the road on which it has passed. (Tenebron to Huebra 16 miles.)
	June 15*th*.	
On the rivulet between Aldea Huebra and Robleya. (From Munoz 11 miles.)	On the rivulet near Cayos de Robleya. (8 miles.)	On the rivulet near to Alba de Los Santos. (8 miles.)

On the 16th the 1st Hussars came in touch with the enemy's Cavalry outposts on the Valmusa stream and drove them into Salamanca. Next day the Army forded the Tormes and entered Salamanca. "We were received with shouts and vivas," says an eye-witness. "The inhabitants were out of their senses at having got rid of the French, and nearly pulled Lord Wellington off his horse. The scene in the Plaza was one of the most interesting I ever saw. The troops were there formed, supposed preparatory to an immediate attack. The place was filled with inhabitants, expressing their joy in the most enthusiastic manner. The women were the most violent, many coming up to Lord Wellington and embracing him. He was writing orders on his sabretasche, and was interrupted three or four times by them."*

* "Diary of a Cavalry Officer in the Peninsular War," p. 162.

IN THE PENINSULA

In spite of these manifestations the enthusiasm seems to have pretty quickly cooled, and evidence was given that the Spaniards in reality preferred the French to the British. Perhaps the question of religion had something to do with the preference, although the French officers as a whole would hardly have prided themselves on rigid adherence to dogmatic religion of any kind, and (respected as he was) it was considered an exceptional and remarkable trait in the character of the Engineer General Elbé that he read his Bible. But the whole subject of regard and aversion was curiously complicated in the Peninsula. The British and French troops—although nominally foes—were on the most friendly terms with each other, and both disliked the Spaniards. The Spaniards looked with contempt upon the English and detested the Portuguese. Many, as we have seen, fought well in the French ranks and (even when they deserted the enemy) refused to fight on our side. On the other hand, a few enlisted in the British Army, and were posted to regiments of the Light Division, where, in some respects, they did fairly well. The Portuguese were devoted to the British, but held both French and Spaniards in abhorrence.

Lord Wellington's immediate object was the capture of Marmont's newly-constructed forts. They were believed to be weak, and were invested the same day by General Clinton and the 6th Division. They were three in number: two, Caitana and La Merced, small but well constructed ; the third, San Vincente (contrary to expectation), large and strong, built on a perpendicular cliff overlooking the Tormes, but separated from the others by a deep ravine.

The arrangements for the line of march made it convenient to employ in the attack on the forts one of the

538 WELLINGTON'S OPERATIONS

Divisions of the Right Column. It so happened that the 6th Division had had no experience of siege operations, either at Ciudad Rodrigo or Badajoz. The consequence was that a battery for 8 guns begun at 250 yards distance from San Vincente on the night of the 17th was still incomplete at daybreak on the 18th. During that day a Brigade of the K.G.L. from the 1st Division silenced the greater part of the enemy's fire. The battery was then armed by Colonel Burgoyne, R.E., and two guns placed in the convent of San Bernardo, which overlooked San Vincente. On the 19th fire was opened, but with little effect, and though Colonel Dickson arrived next day with Hill's siege train, consisting of four 18-pounders and six 24-pounder howitzers, no material progress was made. Ammunition then failed and the battery ceased fire.

On the 23rd, Marmont being close at hand, it was resolved to attack the smaller forts. Four 18-pounders opened fire against Caitano, but without much result. An attempt to escalade that fort and La Merced the same night was repulsed with a loss of 120 men out of 300 engaged. Among the killed was General Bowes.

It was not until the 26th that fresh supplies of ammunition arrived from Almeida. San Vincente was then quickly set on fire with red-hot shot. Next day assaults were made on Caitana and La Merced, which surrendered after slight resistance. The garrison of San Vincente was unable to extinguish the flames and defenceless. By the evening it was also in our hands. Seven hundred prisoners and 30 guns were taken in the forts. One hundred of the garrison had fallen in the siege, which had cost the besiegers 90 officers and men killed and 290 wounded. Had San Vincente been provided with bomb-proof cover, Wellington might probably have been compelled to retire again into Portugal. The strength of the

IN THE PENINSULA

fort had been underrated, and the lack of ammunition was a grave oversight.

During the progress of the siege Lord Wellington's anxieties had been multiplied. Hardly had he realised his mistake as to the strength of the forts than he found he had made other miscalculations. Intercepted returns showed that the numbers under Soult and Marmont were much larger than had been supposed; and that Bonet, having evacuated the Asturias, was marching to join the Army of Portugal. Misfortunes never come singly. News arrived of Slade's performance at Maquilla, already noticed, and of the defeat of Ballasteros at Bornos. The latter was not unexpected. But favourable news was not entirely wanting. Castanos had occupied the Asturias on Bonet's departure. Popham had sailed from Corunna on the 18th for the coast of Biscay, and the Partidas were most successful in intercepting Marmont's despatches to the King. It was, however, of course impossible to stop all communication between the two, and by degrees Joseph was able to give Marmont a tolerably clear notion of the general situation.

On the 20th of June, Marmont had concentrated 25,000 men, made up of a Brigade of Cavalry and four Divisions of Infantry, at Fuente Isauco—25 miles north-east of Salamanca on the Toro road—and started to relieve the forts. On his approach Wellington moved his siege train to the left bank of the Tormes, and took up a defensive position astride the road on the Christoval ridge, six miles north of the city, with his right flank resting on the river. The position was about four miles long; strong, well defined, and commanding all the approaches. The only water supply, however, was from the river.

Marmont on arrival threatened the Allied Left with his Light Cavalry; but massed the whole of his Infantry against the Right, and took the village of Morisco immediately in front of the position, driving out the British Brigade of the 7th Division. On the 21st his situation laid him open to counter attack by very superior numbers, and that he was not molested seemed due to a little excess of caution on the part of Lord Wellington. But on the 22nd the Marshal was reinforced by a Brigade of Cavalry and three Divisions of Infantry, and, throwing his weight on the British right, endangered Wellington's whole position. At the critical moment he was, however, attacked by Graham with the 7th Division, and driven back; whereupon he took post on high ground six miles in rear, with his centre resting on Aldea Rubia and his left on the Tormes at Huerta, covering the road to Valladolid.

From his new position Marmont could ford the Tormes at Huerta and advance by the left bank upon the Salamanca Forts. To check such a movement Wellington changed front to the right, posting his left at Morisco, his right at Aldea Lengua, supported by Graham at the fords of Santa Marta.

On the 24th at daybreak, Marmont crossed the Tormes and advanced on Salamanca. Bock's Brigade of Heavy Cavalry K.G.L., who had been watching the Huerta fords, fell back in good order before him. Sir Thomas Graham was at once sent with 14,000 men and 18 guns (made up of the 1st and 7th Divisions and Le Marchant's Cavalry Brigade) across the river; but when the French Marshal observed Graham in his front and Wellington lining the river on his right flank, he halted and retired again to Aldea Rubia. It was not, however, the menacing attitude of the Allies but the news that Caffarelli was advancing to his support which stopped his attack. On the evening of the 26th signals from the Salamanca Forts informed him that they could hold out till the 29th;

but on hearing twenty-four hours afterwards of their capture, and being disappointed of Caffarelli, Marmont retired at 1 a.m. on the 28th in the direction of Toro and Valladolid.

Wellington, following up the French leisurely, reached the Guarena on the 30th and the Trabanços on the 1st of July. He still marched in three columns, headed by an advance guard composed of Victor Alten's Cavalry, the Light Division, and Pack's Brigade; and flanked on the left by Anson's Cavalry Brigade. The Left Column now comprised Le Marchant's Heavy Cavalry, the 3rd Division, and the Spaniards; the Centre, the 1st, 5th, 6th, and 7th Divisions; the Right, Bock's Brigade, and the 4th Division.

On the 2nd of July the Cavalry came into contact with the enemy's rearguard crossing the Douro (or Duero, as it is termed in Spain) at Tordesillas, and inflicted some loss; but the Infantry was not near enough at hand to warrant a general attack.

Marmont, who had destroyed all the bridges excepting that at Tordesillas, now took up a position on the right bank from the Hornijas to Simancas, with fortified posts beyond his right at Toro and Zamora. The Allies concentrated about Pollos and Rueda, with the 1st and 7th Divisions in reserve near Medina de Campo; but an attempt to force the passage would have entailed heavy loss with probable defeat, and Wellington consequently halted to await the development of the movements of Silveira and Castanos.

Silveira and D'Urban had, in accordance with their instructions, marched up the Douro as far as the Esla, severing the communication of the French with Benavente. It was Wellington's earnest hope that they would be joined by a part of the 15,000 men collected in Galicia by Castanos and sent under command of General

Santocildes to besiege Astorga. But the usual procrastination of Spaniards prevailed.

By this time Sir H. Popham was making his presence felt on the Biscay coast. He took one or two places, and alarmed Caffarelli so much that that General, hearing at the same time of Bonet's evacuation of the Asturias, disobeyed the direct orders of the King and declined to reinforce Marmont, thus entailing the retreat of the latter to the Duero. Bonet's retirement from the Asturias was of the greatest advantage to the Allies; for, although on the 8th of July he joined Marmont with 6,000 men, he left Astorga and the whole of Northern Leon open to Santocildes and the Partidas, and laid bare the grand line of communication with France.

In other respects matters were less favourable to Wellington. In fact, an accumulation of misfortunes occurred. Cadiz was being bombarded, and seemed likely to surrender. No diversion was being made in Cordova. Santocildes was short of ammunition, and the siege of Astorga dragged on. The Partidas had been heavily defeated by General Abbé, and showed little inclination to give active aid to the Allies. At this moment it was that Wellington learned also not only that Lord William Bentinck proposed to go to Italy and thus leave Suchet free to reinforce the Armies of the Centre of Portugal, but that the former had swept away the dollars on which he was himself relying. The supply of meat was derived from Galicia, where payment could be made only in cash. It was impossible to see how the supply was to continue, and to make matters worse the British Government took this opportunity to prohibit the circulation of Notes of Hand, based on Treasury credit—a mode of payment which Wellington had found to be popular and adapted to the habits of the country in general. "Bentinck's arrival on the eastern coast at this moment, which would have been certain," wrote he on the 15th of July, "would have relieved me effectually. He would have taken Tarragona, and most probably Valencia, and we should have made a glorious campaign of it altogether. His success in the Peninsula, or even his appearance here, would have had permanent good effects." "Bentinck's decision is fatal to the campaign at least at present. If he should land anywhere in Italy, he will as usual be obliged to re-embark, and we shall have lost a golden opportunity here."

Bad as was Bentinck's defection, his seizure of the specie was even worse. "I have not yet heard of the money expected from England," wrote Wellington on the same day to Stuart. "War cannot be carried on without money.... I have never been in such distress as at present, and some serious misfortune must happen if the Government does not attend seriously to the subject and adopt some measures to supply us regularly with money.... If we do not find means of paying our bills for butcher's meat, there will be an end to the war at once."

To add to Wellington's other difficulties, Graham and Picton were just at this period obliged to quit the army on account of ill-health. General H. F. Campbell took command of the 1st Division: Packenham of the 3rd; Alexander Hope, brother to Sir John, was in temporary command of the 7th. Both the Adjutant-General—C. Stewart—and the Quarter-Master-General—Murray—were absent. Thus it happened that of Wellington's old comrades in arms, only Cotton, Leith, Cole, and Beresford were present; and curiously enough they were all wounded in the ensuing battle.

CHAPTER XXX

Marmont recrosses the Duero and Guarena and turns Wellington's right—Wellington retires on Salamanca—General State of the Allied Army—Battle of Salamanca.

"THE enemy's position," observed Wellington in a despatch to Lord Bathurst—now Secretary of State *vice* Lord Liverpool, who had succeeded Mr. Perceval as Premier—"the enemy's position is very strong, and their army is sufficient to occupy it. On their right they have the strong places of Zamora and Toro, which cannot be taken except by a regular attack.

"Their left rests upon the Pisuerga, which is not fordable anywhere. They have a fortified post at Simancas, where there is a bridge over that river, and they have fortified and have a garrison in Valladolid, where there is another bridge. They occupy with their army and nearly 100 pieces of cannon the bridge of Tordesillas and the heights which command the fords of the Duero from Toro to the Pisuerga." (Toro to Tordesillas, 23 miles.)

"It is obvious that we could not cross the river without sustaining great loss, and could not fight a general action under circumstances of greater disadvantage than those which would attend the attack of the enemy's position on the Duero."

Pending the capture of Astorga and the advance of the Galicians the two armies remained face to face in quiet

IN THE PENINSULA 545

enjoyment of the fine weather and the enormous supplies of wine among the caves of Rueda. Lord Wellington at first expected D'Erlon, in accordance with the King's orders, to march to reinforce the Army of the Centre. In such a case he could himself be more quickly reinforced from Hill's Corps; and he hoped to maintain his ground, even though the Army of the Centre should form a junction with Marmont, for although the French were used to reap the corn and grind it themselves, it would be insufficient for the numbers of the combined armies.

The state of inactivity did not last very long. Between the 15th and 16th of July Marmont concentrated his troops on his right, and made a feint of crossing the Duero at Toro, the bridge of which he had repaired. Wellington replied by concentrating his Left and Centre (3rd, 1st, 6th, and 7th Divisions) at Canizal on the heights above the Guarena. But his opponent, suddenly withdrawing his troops, moved rapidly back to Pollos and Tordesillas, threw his army across the river, and by the evening of the 17th had concentrated at Nava de Rey. The distance from Tordesillas to Nava de Rey was thirteen miles. By this excess of manœuvring Marmont had gained nothing except the massing of his army against Wellington's right wing, now commanded by Sir Stapleton Cotton at Castrejon, and consisting of Anson's Brigade, the 4th and Light Divisions. On the other hand, he had lost forty-eight hours and was further from Salamanca than he had been at Toro.

Next morning Wellington directed the 5th Division on Torecilla, five miles behind Castrejon, and joined Cotton in person with the Cavalry Brigades of Bock, Le Marchant, and Victor Alten. Marmont then crossed the Trabanços, turning Cotton's left by Alaejos, and marched on the Guarena ten miles distant. Wellington retired on a parallel line through Torrecilla. The hostile columns were separated by a space of only about fifty yards. The British moved the faster, crossed the Guarena, and took up a strong position on the further heights. Marmont at once threw Clausel's Division across the river at Castrillo a little lower down. Clausel gained the heights near Canizal, when he was charged with the bayonet by two Brigades of the 4th Division and forced back to the edge of the Guarena.

By this time the whole Allied Army was concentrated between Valleza and Canizal. A general action was expected, for it was still early. But it was not Wellington's object to fight except at great advantage, and the French, who had been marching incessantly for three days, were exhausted. The loss of the Allies on this day amounted to 95 killed, 393 wounded, and 54 missing. That of the enemy was greater—a general officer and 240 men had been captured; but the tactical advantage lay with Marmont, who had, as Napier observes, "taken the initiatory movement, surprised the right wing of the Allies, and pushed it back about ten miles."

The 19th passed quietly, but on the morning of the 20th Marmont marched rapidly upstream, and, crossing the Guarena at Canta la Piedra, turned Wellington's right. The British Commander at once fell back, in hopes of stopping the enemy at Cantalpino; and again the two armies raced westward in parallel columns. This time the French had the best of it, passed Cantalpino and reached the Tormes first. At nightfall Marmont had gained a decided advantage. Not only had he secured his point of junction with the Army of the Centre, but was in a position to sever Wellington's line of communication with Ciudad Rodrigo, and could at his pleasure either fight a battle on ground where victory would entail ruin on the Allies or await the reinforcements which were approaching. His advantage was

IN THE PENINSULA

even greater than his opponent thought, for Carlos d'Espana, without reference to Lord Wellington, had withdrawn the garrison from Alba de Tormes, which was now occupied by the French. It was the knowledge of this fact which regulated Marmont's manœuvres; and ignorance of it which made Wellington at first give little heed to the operations against his right flank. Yet he could not fail to be "deeply disquieted," as Napier says, at the result of the day. He wished to fight a battle, but only at advantage and if likely to prove decisive. A month earlier he could have done so, had he thought the occasion good enough, on this very ground; but now the opportunity seemed to have passed away for ever; for, in addition to his present disadvantageous position, he felt sure of the immediate arrival of the King with the Army of the Centre.

"It might appear," says Hamley ("Operations of War," Part iii. 3), "that Marmont in thus manœuvring to his left was to a certain extent uncovering his own communications. But in reality he ran no risk. For though the great road, the only one back to France, lay through Valladolid, yet French armies occupied both Madrid and Andalusia, and the King was then moving through the mountains to Blasco to co-operate with him. Thus supported, he might feel confident of regaining the Douro.

"In the series of manœuvres just described, one skilful general had sought to assail and the other to defend a line of communication. And the strategical advantage remained entirely with the French leader, who had pressed his antagonist back from the Douro to the Tormes, and now compelled him to form front parallel to his line of retreat. But to gather the fruits of his success he must still defeat his enemy in battle."

The following was the order of battle and General State of the Allied Army, the latter dated July 11th :—

General the Earl of Wellington, K.B., Commander of the Forces.
Lieutenant-Colonel Lord Fitzroy Somerset, Military Secretary.
Marshal Sir W. Carr Beresford, K.B., Commanding the Portuguese Army.
Lieutenant-Colonel Waters, Acting Adjutant-General.
Lieutenant-Colonel de Lancey, Acting Quarter-Master-General.
Mr. Bissett, Commissary-General.
Dr. McGrigor, Principal Medical Officer.
Marischal de Campo Don Miguel Alava, Spanish Military Attaché.
Brigadier Don Josef O'Lalor, Spanish Military Attaché.
Lieutenant-Colonel Framingham, Commanding Royal Artillery.

For further details *vide* pp. 549–553.

The Spaniards under Don Carlos d'Espana are returned as 500 Cavalry and 3,000 Infantry; and, including them, we find a grand total under Lord Wellington of 75,328 officers and men of whom about 53,000 were present. Making allowance for casualties which occurred between the 11th and 22nd of July, and for detachments which joined him, we may estimate his strength on the day of the battle of Salamanca at 46,000 sabres and bayonets with 60 guns; and that of the enemy at 42,000 sabres and bayonets with 74 guns. (*Vide* " Supplementary Despatches," vol. xiv. pp. 59–62.)

The British Army passed the night of the 20th between Vellosa and Aldea Rubia, and on the 21st occupied its old position on the San Christoval heights. A curious piece of good fortune now attended Lord Wellington. He wrote to inform Castanos that he could not hold his ground. The letter was intercepted, and elated Marmont to such a degree that he resolved to decide the issue without waiting any longer for the King. During the

IN THE PENINSULA 549

CAVALRY DIVISION.

Lieutenant-General Sir Stapleton Cotton, K.B.

Divisions and Brigades.	Officers.	N.C.O.	Drummers or Trumpeters.	Rank and File.					Horses.			
				Present.	Sick.	Command.	Prisoners of War.	Total.	Present.	Sick.	Command.	Total.
Major-General Le Marchant...	61	66	15	914	213	294	19	1,440	971	251	67	1,289
Major-General G. Anson ...	59	72	11	942	205	281	1	1,429	941	62	190	1,193
Baron Victor Alten	44	61	9	717	101	166	1	985	700	47	98	845
Baron Bock, K.G.L.	47	49	11	689	77	183	6	955	723	107	25	855
Br.-Gen. D'Urban (Portuguese)	—	—	—	724	—	—	—	724	724	—	—	724
Total of Cavalry ...	211	248	46	3,986	596	924	27	5,533	4,059	467	380	4,906
Royal Artillery and Drivers...	109	45	19	2,043	370	839	—	3,252	2,087	—	—	—
Artillery K.G.L.	17	6	2	220	46	122	—	388	188	—	—	—
Royal Engineers	23	12	9	209	31	—	—	240	—	—	—	—
Royal Waggon Train... ...	32	18	3	188	31	377	—	546	546	—	—	—
Total...	181	76	33	2,610	478	1,338	—	4,425	2,728	—	—	—

These returns include also the Artillery, Engineers, and Waggon Train in Estremadura under Lieut.-General Sir Rowland Hill, K.B.

Return of the Artillery, British and Hanoverian, present at the battle of Salamanca, July 22, 1812:—

	Guns.	Howitzers.	Total.
3 Troops of Royal Horse Artillery	15	3	18
5 Brigades of Royal and K.G.L. Artillery	25	5	30
Total pieces of ordnance			48

N.B.—The heavy brigade of Royal Artillery, under command of Lieutenant-Colonel Dickson, consisting of three 18-pounders and five 5½-inch howitzers (iron), arrived on the field at the conclusion of the battle, but was not in action. There were 12 Portuguese and Spanish guns present in the battle which are not included.

| | | Officers | N.C.O. | Drummers | Rank and File ||||| |
					Present	Sick	Command	Prisoners of War	Total
1st Infantry Division. *Major-General H. F. Campbell.*										
Brigade of Guards.	Colonel Hon. T. Fermor	50	117	32	1,773	416	36	—	2,225
Highland Brigade.	Major-General Wheatley	104	118	46	1,960	750	71	—	2,781
K.G.L. Brigade.	Major-General Baron Low	82	99	36	1,611	513	49	—	2,173
3rd Division. *Major-General Hon. E. Pakenham.*										
	Colonel Wallace	81	99	54	1,568	1,101	127	—	2,799
	Lieutenant-Colonel Campbell	99	106	55	1,606	814	148	3	2,568
Portuguese Brigade.	Brigadier-General Power	90	102	62	1,943	672	139	—	2,754
4th Division. *Lieutenant-General Hon. G. Lowry Cole.*										
Fusilier Brigade.	Major-General W. Anson	45	72	27	1,117	946	27	—	2,090
Portuguese ,,	Lieutenant-Colonel Ellis	66	84	47	1,216	1,164	214	—	2,594
	Colonel Stubbs	127	108	45	2,264	653	101	—	3,018

IN THE PENINSULA

5TH DIVISION.
Lieutenant-General Leith.

		Officers.	N.C.O.	Drummers.	Present.	Sick.	Command.	Prisoners of War.	Total.
						Rank and File.			
	Colonel Greville ...	85	109	47	1,565	855	143	—	2,563
	Major-General Pringle	136	150	71	1,842	1,065	113	—	3,020
Portuguese Brigade.	Brigadier-General Spry	156	119	37	1,993	882	68	—	2,893

8TH DIVISION.
Lieutenant-General Henry Clinton.

		Officers.	N.C.O.	Drummers.	Present.	Sick.	Command.	Prisoners of War.	Total.
	Major-General Hulse ...	87	87	38	1,252	831	133	—	2,216
	Colonel Hinde ...	89	83	42	1,242	713	165	—	2,120
Portuguese Brigade.	Colonel Douglas ...	134	108	33	2,356	610	155	—	3,121

7TH DIVISION.
Major-General Alexander Hope.

		Officers.	N.C.O.	Drummers.	Present.	Sick.	Command.	Prisoners of War.	Total.
	Major-General de Bernewitz	69	90	35	1,463	491	21	1	1,976
		75	77	39	1,167	721	603	1	2,492
Portuguese Brigade.	Br.-Gen. Conde de Rezende	122	90	28	1,918	728	188	—	2,834

LIGHT DIVISION.
Major-General Baron Charles Alten.

	Officers	N.C.O.	Drummers	Present	Sick	Command	Prisoners of War	Total
Colonel Barnard	49	64	24	993	488	47	—	1,478
Major-General Vandeleur	55	75	38	1,178	543	56	—	1,777
Portuguese Brigade, 1st and 3rd Caçadores	30	55	40	942	151	72	—	1,165

PORTUGUESE UNATTACHED BRIGADES.

	Officers	N.C.O.	Drummers	Present	Sick	Command	Prisoners of War	Total
Brigadier-General Pack	87	125	53	2,342	390	156	17	2,905
Brigadier-General Bradford	112	87	20	1,675	482	147	—	2,304
Totals of British, Hanoverian, and Portuguese	2,030	2,224	954	36,986	15,879	2,979		55,866

IN THE PENINSULA

The Corps under Sir Rowland Hill in Estremadura at this time was made up as follows:—

	Officers.	N.C.O.'s.	Drummers and Trumpeters.	Rank and File.					Horses.			
				Present.	Sick.	Command.	Prisoners of War.	Total.	Present.	Sick.	Command.	Total.
Cavalry ...	110	185	24	1,708	876	390	105	2,574	1,697	280	209	2,186
Infantry...	311	351	159	6,601	1,894	375	—	8,880	—	—	—	—
Portuguese	617	588	180	11,448	1,588	1,186	—	14,192	—	—	—	—
Total ...	1,088	1,204	363	19,752	3,358	1,951	105	25,146	1,697	280	209	2,186

Total of all ranks, 27,571.

afternoon the Marshal forded the Tormes between Alba and Huerta, and occupied the further edge of a wood extending from the river to Calvariza de Ariba. One Division was, however, left on the right bank at Babila de Fuente, a little below Huerta; and to guard against possible operations on that side, the 3rd British Division, with D'Urban's Brigade of Portuguese Cavalry, was left entrenched at Cabrerizoz, while, with the rest of his army, Wellington, near sunset, also crossed the Tormes at Santa Marta and Aldea Lengua. At nightfall a terrible storm—" that common precursor of a battle in the Peninsula "—came on. The Light Division crossed the river with difficulty; some men and horses of the 5th Dragoon Guards near Calvariza de Abaxo were struck by lightning, whereupon the rest of the horses stampeded in terror, and 30 were lost.

The position occupied that night by the Allies extended from the fords of Santa Marta on the left, along the high ground held by Graham in June, to within half a mile of the village of Arapiles, fronting E.N.E. and covering Salamanca. But during the night Wellington was informed that General Chauvel, who had been despatched by Caffarelli, had reached Pollos with 2,000 Cavalry and 20 guns. Under these circumstances the British General determined not to await the arrival of Chauvel, but to retire at once into Portugal.

Daybreak on the memorable 22nd of July showed that Marmont had brought the Division from Babila de Fuente to the left bank of the Tormes, and had occupied Calvariza de Ariba with those of Bonet and Maucune. At 8 a.m. he seized a wooded height crowned by a chapel called Nuestra Senora de la Pena, about three-quarters of a mile in front of Wellington's advanced posts. With the remainder of his available troops he was menacing the British right, from which he was separated by two

IN THE PENINSULA 555

steep and rugged hills named the Arapiles, about 1,400 yards due east of the village of that ilk. Napier remarks that by seizing these, Marmont "could have formed across Wellington's right and compelled him to fight on bad ground with his back to the Tormes." The fact that so keen an observer as Wellington should have neglected these hills seems to show that he had no idea that his right would be the point of attack. When their importance was pointed out to him by Colonel Waters shortly after daybreak, he at once ordered the hills to be occupied. The French Tirailleurs were already creeping up to them. They seized the one nearest to themselves. The Allies were in time to take possession of the other. About the same time a detachment of the 7th Division obtained a footing on the Senora height, but was unable to drive the enemy off it.

Aided by the wooded ground, Marmont had been playing a game of brag. He had in reality only two Divisions in hand, but was doing his utmost to bring up his army from the Tormes with a view to concentrating it on Wellington's right flank. But his occupation of one of the Arapile hills—also termed the Hermanito—would enable him to mass his army behind it and attack the Allies to advantage in their retreat. Wellington drew back the 4th, 5th, and 6th Divisions to protect his right, and posted them at right angles to his left wing, facing due south, but concealed from Marmont. William Anson's Brigade of the 4th Division was placed at the angle formed by the two wings and occupied the English Arapile, being connected by Pack's Brigade with the remainder of the Division which was drawn up behind the village of Arapiles. The 5th and 6th Divisions were massed on the interior slope of the Arapile hill. The 3rd Division, with D'Urban's Cavalry Brigade, was brought across the Tormes and posted near Aldea

Tejada, on the road to Ciudad Rodrigo, between three and four miles west of the village of Arapiles.

"The position of the two Armies now embraced an oval basin, formed by ridges enclosing it like an amphitheatre, the Hermanitos being the doorposts. It was about one and a half miles broad from north to south, and more than two miles long from east to west. On the northern and western ridges stood the Allies. . . . The eastern side was held by the French, and their left, under Maucune, was moving along the southern ridges." (Napier, bk. xviii. ch. 3.)

The greater part of the Allied Army was hidden by the broken ground from Marmont on the top of the Hermanito, but the clouds of dust raised by the baggage train moving in the direction of the Ciudad Rodrigo road gave the impression that Wellington had already begun a retreat. The idea was premature; but in order to ensure such retreat the British Commander had in point of fact ordered the 7th Division to attack the Hermanito, when Marmont, bringing up the Divisions of Foy and Ferey to a wooded height between it and the Senora de la Pena, made the hill safe. Lord Wellington thereupon countermanded the attack, resolving to delay his retreat till nightfall.

Five Divisions of Marmont's Army had by this time appeared on the scene. Foy, supported by Ferey, was now posted on the French right; Bonet, at the Hermanito, formed the centre; Maucune and Thomières, who had been edging away from their first position, the left.

The impression formed by Marmont as to his adversary's retirement proved fatal. Determined that Wellington should not escape him, the Marshal directed Maucune, with his own Division and that of Thomières, to extend to his left and get possession of the Ciudad Rodrigo road,

IN THE PENINSULA

covering the movement with the fire of 50 guns. It was the old manœuvre of Frederick the Great, a manœuvre the fallacy of which was, however, conspicuously shown by that able General when used against himself at Rosbach.

Maucune's flank march soon opened a wide gap between him and Bonet, who remained near the Hermanito. It was now 3 p.m. Wellington sat on his horse, intent on the enemy. His Staff were intent on their dinner. To their amazement the Chief suddenly threw down such a rare delicacy as a chicken-bone, with which he was playing, and with the exclamation, "Marmont's good genius has deserted him!" gave a few brief directions to his Divisional Generals. In compliance therewith, the troops behind the Arapile, by a rapid movement beautifully executed, deployed into double lines of Divisions to the right: the front lines composed of the 4th and 5th Divisions, the second, of the 6th and 7th. On the right of the 7th Division, but somewhat refused, was posted Bradford's Portuguese Brigade. The Cavalry Brigade of Le Marchant, supported by that of Anson, was formed on Bradford's right, while D'Espana helped to fill up the two-mile gap between the Cavalry and the 3rd Division. The 1st and Light Divisions, together with the Cavalry Brigades of Bock and Victor Alten—in all, 12,000 men and 30 guns—posted on high ground in rear of the Arapile hill, formed a reserve to the whole in readiness either to repel an attack of Foy and Ferey from the side of Calvarissa, or to support the main body.

As soon as this movement had been executed, Wellington went off to Pakenham, on the extreme right. "Do you see those fellows on the hill?" said he, pointing to Maucune and Thomières. "Take your Division, throw it into column, and drive them to—the devil!" "Yes," replied his brother-in-law, "if you will give me a grasp of that conquering right hand." And Wellington having directed Sir Stapleton Cotton to let Anson and Le Marchant, with Bull's famous Horse Battery, co-operate in the movement of the 3rd Division, Pakenham advanced "round the foot and under cover of a small height which sloped up in the direction of the enemy's left" to attack the head of Maucune's columns. The 3rd Division was formed in four columns, supported on the left flank by 12 guns, and on the right by D'Urban's Brigade of Portuguese Cavalry. It did not come into collision with the enemy till 5 o'clock.

Meanwhile, the sudden deployment of four Divisions whose presence was utterly unknown to him had filled Marmont with amazement. His own right wing—Foy and Ferey—was still skirmishing on the high ground by Senora de la Pena. His left, under Maucune, was, as we have seen, pointing for Miranda de Azan. The two wings thus extended in a semicircle were separated by an interval of over four miles, destitute of troops except for Bonet's Division at the Hermanito. In an instant the French Marshal grasped all the peril of his situation, yet for a time still hoped, by his fire, to stop the threatened advance of the British centre. Then seeing that the hope was vain, he sent off Staff Officers at full gallop: some to hasten up the Reserve Divisions which were still entangled in the forest stretching down towards the Tormes in rear; others in the tardy attempt to countermand Maucune.

The Latin word "securus" would denote the mental condition of that officer. The left wing, headed by Thomières, was advancing in column along a narrow ridge covered with fir trees, leading on and close to the village of Miranda, when on a sudden, to his astonished gaze, appeared the "fighting 3rd Division," deploying as it advanced, and swiftly bearing down upon the head and flanks of his leading sections. In vain the French columns attempted to extend their front. Bull's Horse Artillery battery, posted on the crest of the height under cover of which Pakenham had approached, hurled destruction into their ranks. In vain the French artillerymen died at their guns in the endeavour to stop the glittering line of bayonets. The impact was irresistible. The leading battalions were hurled back, and those in rear, prevented by the folds of the ground from seeing what was passing in their front, and struggling in the woods, were in no condition to give effective support. In spite of an effort on the part of Maucune's Cavalry on the outer flank, which was repelled by the 5th Regiment and D'Urban's Brigade, Pakenham, pursuing his victorious career, drove the enemy to the bottom of the hill, and gained the crest-line of the height beyond.

Meanwhile, in pursuance of Wellington's orders, on the development of Pakenham's attack, the 4th and 5th Divisions, supported by the 6th and 7th, had moved forward, while Pack's Brigade, with one of the 4th Division, assaulted the Hermanito to protect the left flank of the advancing line. Matters seemed desperate for the French. Marmont had been carried off the field badly wounded. In his absence confusion at first appeared worse confounded. But Bonet gallantly held his ground, and at the critical moment was reinforced by the timely arrival of Clausel. Bonet fell terribly hurt, and Clausel—one of the very best of the Imperial Generals—found himself in chief command. He made a grand attempt to retrieve the battle. His own Division filled the gap between the centre and left, and had something in hand for the reinforcement of Maucune. Thus the whole line of heights south of the Arapiles was occupied; but the French troops were blinded by the sun and dust, which rivalled that of the Long Valley, and the various units were without cohesion and formed at haphazard, according to the circumstances of the moment.

Hardly had Clausel realised the situation when a terrible charge of Sir Stapleton Cotton at the head of Le Marchant's Brigade, supported by that of Anson and Bull's Battery, through the lessening interval which separated the 3rd from the 5th Division, broke in pieces the unhappy remnant of the enemy's left wing. Those struck down by Le Marchant were finished off by Pakenham. Thomières was mortally wounded. Five guns and 2,000 prisoners were taken, and the Divisions of Thomières, Maucune, and Clausel "no longer existed as a military body."

Le Marchant was killed, and his Brigade halted from weariness. Anson "took up the running," and passing completely over the ridge, joined hands with D'Urban. But at this terrible moment the calm gallantry of the French Generals was conspicuous. Anson was checked by the artillery. On the other flank, Foy also contained the 1st and Light Divisions by the fire of his guns, while Clausel brought up Ferey in support of Bonet. At the same time the Divisions of Sarrut and Brennier emerged from the forest. With this welcome reinforcement the French Commander made a supreme effort to snatch victory out of defeat. Just at this time Pack's Portuguese Brigade, repulsed in its attack on the Hermanito, was flying in disorder, and the left flank of the 4th Division was laid bare. Assailed in front by Ferey, Brennier and Boyer's Dragoons, and on the left by Bonet, Cole and Leith were unable to maintain their ground. Both Generals fell badly wounded, and though

Beresford—who the next moment shared their fate—wheeled up Spry's Portuguese Brigade and opened a flanking fire upon Brennier, the 4th and 5th Divisions fell back from the southern heights, which they had nearly won, into the valley behind.

Victory hung in the balance, for Maucune was now making head against Pakenham, but at the critical moment Lord Wellington reinforced his centre with the 6th Division. Hulse's Brigade, pressing gallantly forward, was almost annihilated. The 11th and 61st lost so heavily that at the end of the day their numbers were diminished by 80 per cent.; while the 53rd, the left regiment of the Brigade, was overwhelmed by a charge of the enemy's Dragoons. But the remnant closed their ranks, and quickly formed a rallying point for the rest of the Brigade. Maucune was soon forced to give way again before Pakenham, and the whole British line advancing once more carried the enemy's heights. A second charge of Boyer's Dragoons was repelled by Hulse; General Ferey fell mortally wounded, the Hermanito was abandoned, and the victory was won.

Wellington now gave orders for the 1st Division to penetrate between Foy on the Calvarissa height and the rest of the French Army. The order was unfortunately not obeyed, and Foy, evacuating his position, cleverly joined his comrades of the main body. Clausel, who although wounded remained in command, then ordered Foy and Maucune to cover the retreat: the former by disputing the woods leading on Huerta and Encina; the latter by occupying a steep ridge and covering the road to Alba de Tormes.

Wellington, counting on the occupation of Alba—it seems odd that he should not yet have known that its Spanish garrison had abandoned it some days before—believed that the only line of retreat for the enemy lay through the fords of Huerta and the Encinas. If he could cut the French from these fords, their ruin seemed inevitable. He therefore directed the Light Division—supported by the 1st, and protected on its right flank by two Brigades of the 4th—against Foy. This large force, followed by the 7th Division and Spaniards in reserve, seemed ample for the purpose. But the light was rapidly failing. Foy retreated with great skill, and though the 4th Division at one point succeeded in intervening between him and the Centre, he regained touch, and disappeared into the forest at nightfall.

During this time Maucune was standing his ground with the Division of Bonet, which had been sent to reinforce him, and 15 guns; and not only covered the retreat of the Army, but held his own against a premature attack of the 6th Division, until once more outflanked by Pakenham. Then seeing Foy safe, his task was done, and under cover of the darkness he rapidly vanished into the forest. The whole French Army made good its retreat across the Tormes at Alba, for the 6th Division was too much exhausted to pursue.

Meanwhile Lord Wellington had accompanied the Light Division in person, confident of finding the enemy in confusion at Huerta. The Division, deployed in line, marched for several miles across country after Foy, and as Wellington rode behind it he was struck on the thigh by a musket ball whose force had happily been broken by his holster. But Foy cleverly changed direction in the darkness unperceived, and when the Light Division reached Huerta no enemy was to be seen. The left wing of our Army then bivouacked on the banks of the river.

The loss of the Allies proved more severe than was at first supposed, and amounted to 694 officers and men killed, 4,526 wounded and missing. Hulse's Brigade of

IN THE PENINSULA

the 6th Division suffered most, losing about 1,000 men. Among the General Officers, Le Marchant had been killed; Beresford, Cole, Leith, and Alten were badly wounded. Cotton was accidentally hit by a sentry in returning to the lines after the battle. These numerous casualties, coupled with the fact that the Commander had also been struck, and that nearly the whole of his Staff were new-comers, no doubt seriously affected the subsequent operations.

The losses of the French were enormous. Generals Ferey, Bonet, Thomières, and Desgraviers were killed; Marshal Marmont and General Clausel wounded; General Curto captured. For some days after the battle Clausel was unable to collect more than 20,000 men, and he did extremely well in carrying off five-sixths of his artillery. In his despatch Wellington estimated the number of prisoners at nearly 7,000. This number must have included the wounded men left on the field of battle, for the official state of the French Army reckons its losses between July 10th and August 10th at 4,029 officers and men killed or taken, 7,761 wounded, and only 645 missing. It admits the loss of 12 guns and the eagles of the 22nd and 101st Regiments.

The Battle of Salamanca was pithily described by a Frenchman as the "defeat of 40,000 men in forty minutes," and is said to be that on which Wellington would have desired his reputation as a General to rest. The lightning-like rapidity with which (having hitherto been steadily outmanœuvred by Marmont) he seized the opportunity given him by one false step to deal a crushing blow on his enemy, must ever excite the keenest admiration. The attack of the Centre seems indeed to leave something to be desired, but the tactical execution of the advance on our right was not less brilliant than its conception. "Perhaps," writes an eye-witness, "there was never seen a more perfect combination of the three arms than that of the 3rd Division, Bull's troop of Horse Artillery and the Brigade of British Heavy Cavalry." The Cavalry charge was prepared by Wellington in person; but great credit is due to Pakenham, a young General, and unaccustomed to the command of a Division, for the accuracy with which he brought up his men, and the terrible weight of his blow. Throughout the Peninsular War no more brilliant or decisive exploit was performed than this of the "Fighting Division."

Marmont's error was glaring, and no doubt the result of over-confidence engendered by his success of the last few days. He now had leisure to contemplate the reason of Masséna's reluctance to join battle with Lord Wellington. In his anguish of mind and body bitterly must he have recalled the sarcastic remarks made about his predecessor now that to his cost he had discovered that an action against British troops was anything but a synonymous term for victory! It would seem doubtful whether Joseph's orders to await the arrival of the Army of the Centre had ever reached him; but at all events he was aware of the King's approach and of the consequent increase in his strength. It seems probable that his action was influenced by jealousy of Joseph. Napoleon, on receiving his reports in the heart of Russia, tore his excuses into shreds. "Why had Marmont joined battle without the orders of his Commander-in-Chief? Why did he not take orders as to the part which he had to play, subordinate to the general system for my Armies in Spain? It is the crime of insubordination that has been the cause of all the misfortunes of this affair; and, even had it not been his duty to put himself into communication with his Commander-in-Chief for the purpose of carrying out such orders as he might receive, how did he bring himself to advance from his defensive position on the Duero when, without any great effort of imagination, it was easy to see that he might be strengthened by the arrival of the Division of Dragoons, 30 guns, and upwards of 15,000 French troops whom the King had at hand? And how could he change from the defensive to the offensive without awaiting the junction of a Corps of from 15,000 to 17,000 men? The King had ordered the Army of the North to be sent to Marmont's aid. It was on the march, and Marmont could not have been unaware of the fact, since the Cavalry arrived on the evening of the battle. Salamanca is many, many marches from Burgos. Why did he not wait two days for this Cavalry which was so much needed? . . . Taking into consideration the fact of his taking the offensive without the orders of his Commander-in-Chief, with that of not delaying the battle for two days in order to receive 15,000 Infantry which the King was bringing him, and 1,500 Cavalry from the Army of the North, one cannot but feel that the Marshal was afraid lest the King should participate in the success of the battle, and that he has sacrificed his country's glory and the good of the service to personal vanity.

"Give orders to the Generals of Division to send the account of their losses. It is intolerable to have false states rendered, and the truth concealed from me."

On reading Wellington's despatch, the Emperor was, however, in some degree mollified. "I see," he said, "what happened. Well, Marmont has fought a battle and been wounded; and I forgive him." That "Napoleon never forgave" is the common assertion of English writers. It would be more correct to say that he spent his life in doing nothing else. But in writing about the great Emperor veracity is usually the last consideration.

King Joseph, on the other hand, received grave rebuke from his brother. The King's Staff Officer did not reach Moscow till the 18th of October, the very eve of the terrible retreat. After hearing the complaints which he brought, the Emperor pointed out that the movement of the Army of the Centre in support of Marmont had been undertaken a month too late, and that the King should have followed the precedent of 1808 when Napoleon had not hesitated to quit Madrid in order to fall upon the English who had advanced to Valladolid. After the battle the King ought to have marched to the Duero to form a rallying point for the Army of Portugal. The Emperor finally observed that Soult was the only one of his servants in Spain who had a military head on his shoulders, and that he could not remove him nor be bothered with petty quarrels at this crisis.

That Napoleon had for some time past been dissatisfied with the conduct of affairs in Spain is shown by his despatch (not included in his correspondence, but quoted at length by Napier, vol. iv., Appendix 9) to the Minister for War dated Dresden, May 28th. In it he points out the need of holding bridge-heads on the Agueda as the sole means of getting daily intelligence of the Allies, observing that if on the contrary Marmont placed an interval of 30 leagues between himself and the enemy, as he had already done on two occasions, he lost the initiative, left the English General free to move wherever he pleased, and had no weight in the affairs of Spain. Further, he remarked on the exposed position of Biscay and the north in consequence of the evacuation of the Asturias by Bonet, and observed that Santona and St. Sebastian were endangered by the failure to re-occupy that province. General L'Huillier was instructed to keep an eye upon St. Sebastian and to have 3,000 men always in hand for the relief of that fortress if required. "En général," he continues, "pour parer à la mauvaise manœuvre et à la mauvaise direction que le duc de Raguse donne à nos affaires, il est necessaire d'avoir beaucoup de monde à Bayonne. . . . Prescrivez au général L'Huillier de tenir ses troupes dans la vallée de Bastan, à Bayonne, St. Jean de Luz, et Irun, en lès munissant bien, les barraquant, les exerçant, et les formant. Ce sera au moyen de cette resource que si le duc de Raguse continue à faire des bévues on pourra empêcher le mal de devenir extrême."

Thus early did the Emperor foresee that the war might at no distant date be brought to the very gates of France.

"To meet the Emperor's views," says Napier (bk. xviii., ch. 4), "Marmont should, as Soult advised, have left one or two Divisions on the Tormes, have encamped near Banos and on the Upper Agueda to watch the Allies. Caffarelli's Divisions could have joined those on the Tormes, and then Napoleon's plan for 1811 would have been exactly renewed; Madrid would have been covered, a junction with the King secured, and Wellington could scarcely have moved beyond the Agueda. Marmont, apparently because he would not have the King in his camp, ran counter to the Emperor and to Soult. He kept no troops on the Agueda, which might be excusable if to feed them was difficult; but then he did not concentrate behind the Tormes to sustain his forts, neither did he abandon his forts when he abandoned Salamanca; thus 800 men were sacrificed merely to secure his concentration behind the Duero. His line of operations was perpendicular to the Allies' front, instead of lying on their flank; he abandoned 60 miles of country between the Tormes and the Agueda; he suffered Wellington to take the initial movement; he withdrew Bonet from the Asturias, whereby he lost Caffarelli's support and realised the Emperor's fears. He regained the initial, however, by passing the Duero on the 18th, and had he deferred the passage until the King was over the Guadarama, Wellington must have gone back upon Portugal with some show of dishonour. But if Castanos, instead of keeping 15,000 Galicians before Astorga, a weak place with a garrison of only 1,200 men, had blockaded it with 3,000 or 4,000, and detached Santocildes with 11,000 down the Esla to co-operate with Silveira and D'Urban, 16,000 men would have been acting upon Marmont's right flank in June; and as Bonet did not join until the 8th of July he could scarcely have kept the line of the Duero.

"The secret of Wellington's success is to be found in the extent of country occupied by the French armies and the impediments to their military communication, while from Portugal, an impregnable central position, he could rush out unexpectedly against any point. This strong post was, however, of his own making; he had chosen it, had fortified it, had defended it, knew its full value, and availed himself of all its advantages. The battle of Salamanca was accidental in itself, but the tree was planted to bear such fruit, and Wellington's combinations must be estimated from the general result. He had only 60,000 disposable troops, and 100,000 were especially appointed to watch and control him; yet he passed the frontier, defeated 45,000 in a pitched battle, and drove 20,000 others from Madrid in confusion without risking a single strategic point. His campaign up to the conquest of Madrid was therefore strictly in accord with the rules of art, although his means and resources have been shown to be precarious, shifting, and uncertain; want of money alone would have prevented him from following up his victory if he had not persuaded the Spanish authorities in the Salamanca country to yield him the revenues of the government in kind, under a promise of

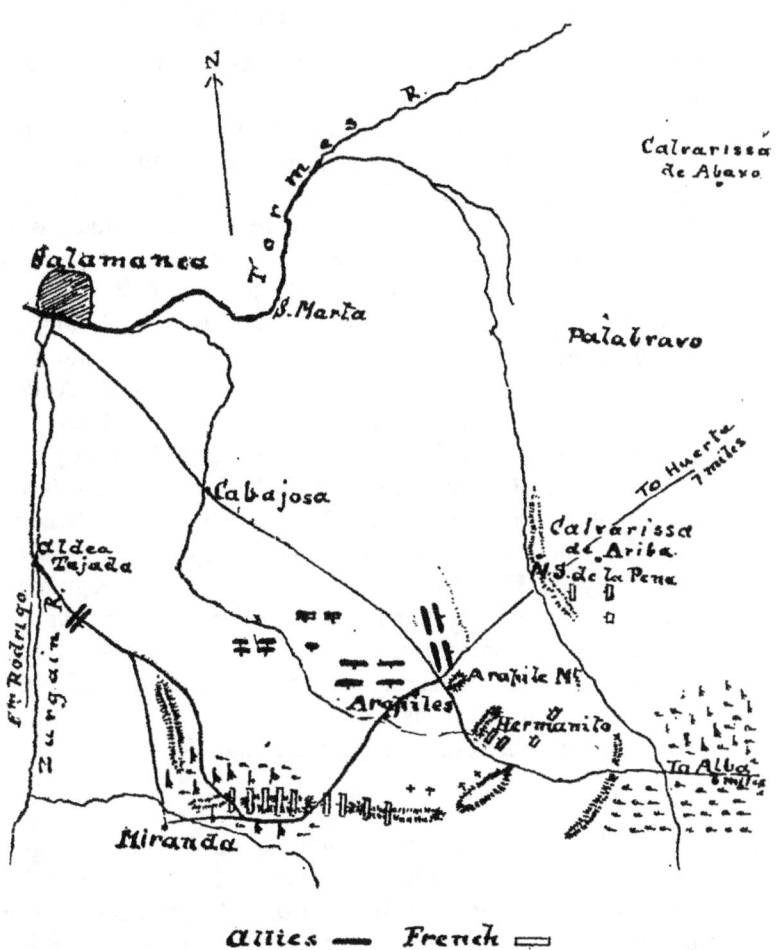

Sketch of the Salamanca position at 4 P.M July 22 1812.

repayment at Cadiz. No General was ever more entitled to the honours of victory.

"The Allies' success indicates a fault in the French plan of invasion. The Army of the South, numerous, of approved valour and well commanded, was of so little weight in this campaign as to prove that Andalusia was a point pushed beyond the true line of operations. Its conquest in 1811 was the King's plan, and it was not liked by Napoleon though he did not absolutely condemn it. The question was indeed a grave one. While the English held Portugal, and Cadiz was unsubdued, Andalusia was a burthen rather than a gain. Had the communication with France been first established by the southern line of invasion, to attack Andalusia would have been methodical; or to have held it partially by detachments for the sake of the resources, keeping the base of the army in Estremadura, would have been regularly within the northern system of invasion. For in Estremadura Soult would have covered the capital, been more connected with the Army of the Centre, and his co-operation with Masséna in 1810 would probably have compelled the English to quit Portugal.

. . . .

"If the King had judged well he would have merged the monarch in the General, exchanged the palace for the tent. Holding only the Retiro and a few posts near Madrid, he would have organised a pontoon train, established magazines at Segovia, Toledo, and Talavera, kept his army constantly united, and employed to open roads through the mountains and chase the Partidas while Wellington remained quiet. Thus acting he would have been ready to succour any menaced point. . . .

"If Marmont and the King were at fault in the general plan of operations, they were not less so in the particular tactics of the campaign. On the 18th of July the Army of Portugal passed the Duero in advance. On the 30th it repassed that river in retreat, having in twelve days marched 200 miles, fought three combats and a general battle. One Marshal, 7 Generals, 12,500 men and officers had been killed, wounded, or taken; . . . In the same period the Allies marched 160 miles, and had 1 Field-Marshal, 4 Generals, and nearly 6,000 officers and soldiers killed or wounded.

"This comparison proves Wellington's sagacity when he determined not to fight except at great advantage. The French Army, although surprised in the midst of an evolution and instantly swept from the field, killed and wounded 6,000 of the Allies—the 11th and 61st Regiments of the 6th Division had not together more than 160 men and officers left standing at the end of the battle; twice six thousand then would have fallen in a more equal contest, and as Chauvel's Cavalry and the King's Army were both at hand, a retreat into Portugal would have followed a less perfect victory. The battle ought not, and would not have been fought but for Marmont's false movement on the 22nd. Yet it is certain, if Wellington had retired, the murmurs of his army, already louder than was seemly, would have been heard in England; and if an accidental shot had terminated his career all would have been terminated. The Cortes, ripe for a change, would have accepted the intrusive King, and the American War just declared against England would have so complicated affairs that no new man could have continued the contest. Then the cries of disappointed politicians would have been raised. It would have been said that Wellington, desponding and distrusting his brave troops, dared not venture a battle on even terms, hence these misfortunes. His name would have been made, as Sir John Moore's was, a butt for the malice and falsehood of faction, and his military genius would have been measured by the ignorance of his detractors.

. . . . . .

"In the description of the battle, Marmont's own account of his views and the time when he was wounded has been adopted; but there are other versions which tend to place his errors in a stronger light. It is affirmed he twice sent orders to Maucune, once by Fabvier, once by Colonel Richemont, his aide-de-camp, to assemble four Divisions and press the English Army, which was, he said, in full retreat by the Ciudad Rodrigo road. Maucune replied that he was more likely to be attacked himself, and in fact Pakenham fell upon him very soon afterwards. That so far from wishing or ordering his left wing to fall back on their centre, Marmont was satisfied the Allies were retiring; that being at dinner and in the act of holding his plate, he was struck by a shell just before Pakenham's attack commenced. That after the battle he had a violent altercation with Maucune, whom he reproached for having extended the left so rashly, and when the latter pleaded the orders received by Fabvier, Marmont exclaimed against that officer, and denied that he had sent any orders to pursue the Allies. However that may be, the battle of Salamanca, remarkable in many points of view, was not least so in this, that it was the first decided victory gained by the Allies in the Peninsula. In former actions the French had been repulsed, here they were driven headlong as it were before a mighty wind without help or stay, and the results were proportionate. Joseph's secret negotiations with the Cortes were crushed, his partisans were everywhere abashed, the sinking spirit of the Catalans revived, the clamours of the opposition in England were checked, the Provisional Government of France was dismayed, the secret plots against the French in Germany were resuscitated, and the shock, reaching even to Moscow, heaved and shook the colossal structure of Napoleon's power to its very base."

Tradition says that on the arrival in England of the news of the battle of Salamanca, it was telegraphed by semaphore to London. The message had got as far as "Wellington defeated at Salamanca . . . " when a fog came on, and for several hours Londoners were kept in an agony of suspense before the message could be completed.

As a reward for the victory Wellington received £100,000 and a Marquisate. "What the devil is the use of making me a Marquis?" was his remark on hearing of his promotion in the Peerage.

CHAPTER XXXI

Joseph abandons Madrid—Wellington enters it—Landing of an Anglo-Sicilian force at Alicante—Soult abandons the blockade of Cadiz and joins the King—Courses open to Wellington.

AT daylight on the 23rd Wellington crossed the Tormes with the Cavalry Brigades of Bock and Anson, 2 Batteries R.H.A., and the 1st, 4th, 7th, and Light Divisions. He moved up the right bank of the river in search of the enemy who had so unexpectedly eluded him the night before.

The Cavalry Brigades, weakened by detachments during the night, mustered barely 800 sabres. At 10 a.m. Bock—senior Cavalry General in Sir Stapleton's absence—came up at La Serna with the French rearguard under Foy, retiring along the valley of the Almar in the direction of Penoranda. Anson drove away the enemy's Cavalry. Bock charged three battalions of Infantry formed in squares, and though the French stood firm on high ground and received the Germans with such a fire that over a hundred were struck down, the latter—in spite of the difficulties of the approach—rode right through their ranks and captured the whole. "I have never witnessed a more gallant charge," wrote Wellington in his despatch.

The Light Division coming up, the pursuit was continued along the Penoranda road, until checked at

Nava de Setraval by the arrival of Chauvel's Brigade of Cavalry from the Army of the North. That night Clausel halted at Flores de Avila, 40 miles from the battlefield. On the 24th he hoped to rest, but the Allied Cavalry was close on his heels; and abandoning all idea of regaining Tordesillas, he marched to Arevalo on the Adaja with a view to forming a junction with the King. On the 25th Lord Wellington halted between the Zapardiel and Adaja rivers to rest his troops and give time for the Commissariat to come up. "This," observes Napier, "was a wonderful retreat . . . the pursuit, however, was somewhat slack. The British left wing, being quite fresh, could have ascended the Tormes on the night of the battle and reached the Almar before daylight, or passing at Huerta, have marched by Ventosa to Penoranda; but the vigorous following of a beaten enemy was not a prominent characteristic of Lord Wellington's warfare." Nevertheless Anson with his Brigade and 12 R.H.A. guns had marched 25 miles on the 24th; and though at Cisla he seems to have missed an opportunity of dealing an effective blow, yet he forced Clausel back to the Adaja, and halted only within 12 miles of Arevalo, which was occupied next day by Victor Alten's Brigade, now commanded by Colonel Arenschildt.

From Arevalo Clausel retired across the Duero at Valladolid to restore his communications with the Army of the North; abandoning the garrisons of Toro, Zamora, and Tordesillas, yet without effecting his junction with the King. The latter, quitting Madrid on the 21st with 14,000 men, reached Blasco Sancho on the 24th. Although in fact within a few miles of Clausel at Arevalo, he was in ignorance of Marmont's defeat. The report came upon him with a shock next day, for he had repeatedly sent to tell Marmont of his approach, and felt confident that the Marshal would not fight pending his arrival. On receipt of the fatal news Joseph might still have joined Clausel, who had promised to halt if possible behind the Duero; but the King's instinct was to retire on his capital, and he therefore made a rapid retrograde march to Espinar.

On the 2nd, Clausel, finding himself unmolested, passed the right wing of his army over the Duero at Bocilla; but, having gained the bridge of Tudela, remained with the left wing on the left bank, and sent word to the King that he was no longer hotly pressed. Joseph consequently moved from the passes of the Guadarama mountains to Segovia, and with his Cavalry pushed forward to Santa Maria. In this position he remained from the 27th to the 31st, hoping to be joined by Clausel, but that General had now been pushed across the Duero (partly by the 1st and Light Divisions, partly by the advance of Santocildes, whom Wellington had brought up from the Esla to the Zapardiel) and retired in three columns up the valleys of the Arlanza, Esquiva, and Duero towards Burgos. On the 30th, Valladolid was entered by Wellington, who there found 800 of the French sick and 17 guns. He then divided his army: Anson's Brigade and the 6th Division, under Clinton, being left at Cuellar to guard the line of the Duero in combination with Silveira, Santocildes, and some of the Partida bands; while the rest of the army marched against the King. But Joseph was in no condition to make a stand alone. He therefore retired over the Guadarama, and Wellington's object of separating him from the Army of Portugal was, rather unexpectedly, attained.

On the 10th of August the Allied Army crossed the Guadarama range, but on the 11th D'Urban's Brigade of Portuguese Cavalry was repulsed at Majadahonda by the

French Cavalry of the rearguard with the loss of half a battery R.H.A. Bock's Brigade restored the fight, but it was not until the arrival of Ponsonby's—late Le Marchant's—Brigade and the 7th Division that the guns were recovered and the enemy fell back. The Portuguese General, Viscount Barbacena, was captured and our casualties amounted to 53 killed, 98 wounded, and 43 missing.

By this time Joseph had resolved to abandon his capital, and intended to march towards the Morena to meet Soult, whom he ordered to give up the blockade of Cadiz and evacuate Andalusia. The Court quitted Madrid, and at Valdemoro met the King and the army. The greatest confusion prevailed. "The military line of march was broken by crowds of weeping women and children and despairing men: courtiers of the highest rank were to be seen in full dress desperately struggling with savage soldiers for the possession of even the animals on which they were endeavouring to save their families."

By the evening of the 13th, Court and Army had crossed the Tagus at Aranjuez, but the sum of the King's misfortunes was not yet complete. A mail arrived. Soult wrote, practically refusing to evacuate Andalusia and relinquish all the fruits of his administration during the last few years. Suchet sent the startling news that the British expedition from Sicily had landed on the 7th at Alicante. The King then altered his course and marched, harassed by the Partidas, towards Valencia. He reached Almanza with his extraordinary *entourage* in great misery, but heard that a Brigade which Suchet had sent to reinforce him at Madrid, had been intercepted near Utiel on the 25th whilst marching to rejoin the Marshal and defeated with the loss of all its guns by the Spaniards under Villa Campa.

WELLINGTON'S OPERATIONS

Meanwhile Lord Wellington had entered Madrid in triumph on the 12th. On the 14th the Retiro, forming the Citadel, surrendered with a garrison of 2,000 men in addition to invalids; 189 guns; 20,000 stand of arms; 900 barrels of powder, besides the eagles of the 13th and 51st Regiments and large stores of all kinds. The garrisons of Tordesillas, Astorga, and Guadalaxara were all in the hands of the Allies shortly afterwards, and the loss of the French at Salamanca was thus doubled.

On the 14th Wellington received news of the landing of the Sicilian Division under General Maitland at Alicante.

The following was the embarkation return of this force, dated June 25th, 1812:—

Lieutenant-General F. Maitland, in command.
Major-General Mackenzie.
Major-General Honstedt.
Major-General J. Campbell. Adjutant-General.
Colonel Adams, 21st Regiment. Deputy-Adjutant-General.
Major-General Donkin, Quartermaster-General.
A. Grant, F. Daniel, Deputy-Commissaries-General.
Surgeon E. Brown, Acting Deputy Inspector of Hospitals.

Corps.	Rank and File.
20th Light Dragoons	180
Foreign Troop	75
Royal Artillery	177
Royal Marine Artillery	30
Royal Engineers	57
Royal Staff Corps	16
10th Regiment, 1st Battalion	958
58th "	902
81st "	1,294
K.G.L., 4th Battalion	1,018
K.G.L., 6th Battalion	1,099
De Roll's Regiment	338
Dillon's Regiment	562
Calabrian Free Corps	360
Total	7,066

IN THE PENINSULA 579

Great importance was attached by Wellington to this expedition. It had been his wish that Lord W. Bentinck should send from Sicily at least 10,000 good British soldiers, who were to be joined by the Spanish Divisions of Whittingham and Roche at Minorca. He desired that the combined force should land in Catalonia, attack Tarragona and afterwards Valencia; thus diverting Suchet's attention from himself. But when it came to the point Bentinck found himself unable to send more than 7,000 men, half British, half foreign regiments, some of the latter being of no very good repute. Then the Spanish authorities declined to let Roche's Division serve under Maitland; and that of Whittingham, 4,000 strong, was composed of raw troops hardly fit for service.

The arrival of the expedition was expected by the French in Catalonia as well as the Catalans themselves; and on the 31st of July the transports did in point of fact make their appearance off Palamos. But on arrival there, the information given by the Spanish Generals showed they could furnish no accurate estimate of the strength of the French army in the field. The Naval Officers stated that the coast was unsafe; and Tarragona would evidently require regular siege operations. After consideration, Maitland decided—it would seem quite rightly, although Wellington was discontented on hearing the news—that his force was not strong enough to reduce Tarragona by a *coup de main;* and, after three days, sailed away, with the intention of attacking Valencia (which would also have suited Wellington); but changed his mind, and on the 7th of August landed at Alicante, where he protected the remains of a Spanish Corps under Joseph O'Donnell which, having advanced towards Valencia, had been decisively beaten at Castalla. Maitland was sick; his army ill-equipped; and finding the usual difficulties as to acting in concert with the Spanish chiefs, he contented himself with fortifying his position at Alicante. But, as already stated, the news of his arrival had made the King relinquish his intention of marching into the Morena, and had brought him instead to Valencia.

When Soult received the King's orders to evacuate Andalusia and thus abandon not only the blockade of Cadiz but the whole fruit of his able administration during the past three years, and of his diplomatic success at the Court of Barbary, he was grievously discontented. Expressions which Joseph had—perhaps loosely—made use of after the battle of Ocana in 1809, and other apparently suspicious circumstances, led Soult to fear that he was not true to the Emperor. The Marshal believed the accounts of the defeat at Salamanca to be exaggerated, for it was not till the 12th that he had official news of the disaster from the King. He observed in reply that the loss of the capital was nothing—a line of communication might be established with France by the sea coast—that the effects of the defeat would be counterbalanced if the King were to concentrate the Armies of Aragon and the Centre—if possible also the Army of Portugal—and bring them into Andalusia; in which case he would be on the border of Portugal and threatening Lisbon with a force of at least 80,000, and, under the most favourable circumstances, of 120,000 men; and would inevitably compel the British Commander to fall back to guard his very base of operations.

Soult's exhortations were vain. The King refused to listen; and Soult, appreciating the value of time, called in his outlying detachments, destroyed his elaborate works opposite at Cadiz, stores and 1,000 guns; broke up the blockade and, on the 25th, began his retreat. His first idea was to retire on La Mancha, and he marched *viâ* Seville upon Cordova; but hearing on the 26th that Joseph had abandoned his plan of forming a junction in that province and had retreated to Valencia, the Marshal changed his own direction and marched *viâ* Grenada for Murcia.

Meanwhile Lord Wellington from Madrid had been closely watching the turn of events. The naval expedition of Sir Home Popham had not only the effect of detaining Caffarelli and the Army of the North, but encouraged the Partidas, who succeeded in occupying Castro, Santander, and Bilbao. Guateria, Santona, and San Sebastian alone remained in the enemy's hands, and the spirit of insurrection spread as far as Aragon. But it was to the south that the British Commander was chiefly looking. He had hoped by vigorous measures to drive the French out of Andalusia and at the same time prevent Soult sending aid to the King. General Cooke at Cadiz was directed to make a general assault upon the lines of investment; Ballesteros from Gibraltar was to operate on the enemy's flank. Hill had hitherto been ordered to remain on the defensive with a view to drawing near Wellington in the event of the 5th Corps marching to join the King. He was now instructed to attack Count d'Erlon, and, if necessary, follow him into Andalusia.

By these measures Wellington hoped to attain his object. Hill had 25,000 men, and the whole Allied forces available seemed adequate for the task. If necessary, however, Wellington was prepared to bring a reinforcement of 20,000 men from Madrid.

His orders were only partially executed. The assault upon the lines of Chiclana was not delivered. But troops from Cadiz landing at the mouth of the Rio Tinto river, drove the enemy out of San Lucar on the 24th, and attacked his rearguard at Seville on the 27th of August.

Ballesteros, flying before Leval and Villatte, by whom he had been defeated in one of his raiding expeditions, was saved by the news of the battle of Salamanca which stopped the French Generals in their pursuit. He now moved by the Rueda mountains to harass Soult's flank.

Hill advanced against Count d'Erlon, who was on the point of retiring on Toledo in pursuance of orders from the King, when urgent representations from Soult induced him to join the Marshal at Grenada. The junction was completed before the middle of September, and on the 15th Soult, who had now concentrated 45,000 men, including 6,000 Cavalry, and 72 guns, evacuated Grenada, which two days later was occupied by Ballesteros. A retreat upon Murcia, which was full of yellow fever, was however impossible. Although encumbered with 9,000 sick and several hundred Spanish families who thought their unhappy country would be better governed by Joseph than by Ferdinand, the Marshal (with his flank protected from Maitland at Alicante by Suchet's advanced troops), took to the mountain roads, marching by Huescar and Hellin upon Almanza, where he came in touch with Suchet, and on the 3rd of October effected a grand junction with the Armies of Aragon and the Centre; having successfully evaded perils which if not as thrilling as those in his retreat from Portugal in 1809, were hardly less substantial.

Hampered by an enormous train, he had traversed a hostile country for upwards of 400 miles mostly by mountain roads; having Ballesteros with nearly 20,000 men on his right flank, Hill with 25,000 on his left, and the detachment from Cadiz in his rear. Had the pursuit been close, and had Wellington been in a position to fall upon him through the Despena Perros pass in the Sierra de Morena, it is difficult to see how Soult could have escaped a terrible disaster.

IN THE PENINSULA 583

Sir Rowland Hill had been directed to follow up Count d'Erlon into Andalusia. Either he did not get his orders, or (deceived perhaps by the magazines which Soult had formed at Cordova to enable himself to move in any direction), he thought the Marshal's intention was to concentrate at that town and move thence to join the King, whom Sir Rowland probably believed to be still in the neighbourhood of Madrid. Hill marched from Zafra on the 27th of August by Medellin and Truxillo; crossed the Tagus at Almaraz, and, in pursuance of fresh orders from Lord Wellington, reached Toledo by the right bank at the end of September.

Before this the following troops, hitherto forming the garrison of Cadiz, were brought by sea to Lisbon and marched thence to join Wellington at Madrid. Detachment 2nd Hussars K.G.L., 3rd Batt. 1st Foot Guards, 2nd Batt. 87th, 20th Portuguese Regiment, and 2 Batteries R.A. A weak Brigade consisting of the 47th and a battalion of the 95th, under Colonel Skerrett, also joined Hill in October.

Napier points out that after the victory at Salamanca, Lord Wellington had choice of four lines of operation:—

1. To pursue the King into Valencia, and by forming a junction with Maitland, cut Soult from Joseph and Suchet.

This was contemplated as a course for a future time, but for the present it was inadmissible. As a reinforcement, Maitland's force was not worth having; it would be necessary to leave three or four Divisions on the Duero to hold Clausel in check, and the army thus weakened would find itself in Valencia, nearly 300 miles distant, hemmed in between Soult and the King. The question also of supply was one of great difficulty, if not insoluble. The sea power of England enabled a new base to be formed at any seaport not occupied by the enemy, but in view of the yellow fever raging in Murcia, the new base would necessarily be confined to Alicante. It may also be incidentally observed that Wellington had at the moment no General Officer fit to take command of the detachment to be left on the Duero, or good enough to stop Clausel by a circuitous march forming a junction with the King in Valencia.

2. To attack Soult with the whole army. This was actually Wellington's intention; but as a preliminary to overcoming the difficulties incidental to the adoption of a new line of operations, it was indispensable to secure his present line of communications by the capture of Burgos. Want of specie also impeded this project.

The evacuation of the south of Spain was, however, secured by the almost accidental circumstance of the arrival of the Anglo-Sicilian force at Alicante, but for which, Joseph, being unmolested in his retreat across the Tagus, would have been in a position to join Soult, and the combined armies could have been further reinforced by Suchet.

3. To follow Clausel and the Army of Portugal. The objections to this course were that Clausel at Burgos could do him no harm, whereas a movement northward would lay Salamanca, and the line of communications, open to attack by the King.

4. The course actually adopted. The expected fall of Astorga would bring Wellington a reinforcement of 8,000 Spaniards. The moral effect of the occupation of the capital would be great, the physical result of destroying the large arsenal at Madrid would be still greater. Clausel could be watched, and Hill could bring up his Corps. The Allies under Wellington would thus be concentrated in a central position with regular lines of supply and ready to operate on interior lines against the

IN THE PENINSULA 585

enemy. The strategical situation thereby gained was consequently sound; but to make it perfect, Joseph would have been struck while crossing the Tagus. "The Cavalry of the Allies," says Napier, "could have driven the whole before them into the Tagus, yet Wellington did not molest them, either from ignorance of their situation, or what is more probable, compassionating their misery; he knew that the troops by abandoning the convoy could easily escape over the river, and he would not strike when the blow could only fall on helpless people without affecting the military operations; perhaps also he thought it wise to leave Joseph the burthen of his Court."

During his stay at Madrid, Wellington had his usual share of vexations. Discipline became relaxed. Outrages—more particularly by the Portuguese—became frequent on the line of communications. The regiments newly arrived from England or the Mediterranean broke down in health; partly from their own irregularities, partly from the neglect of their Commanding Officers to obey the orders given them to supply their men with blankets before leaving Lisbon. Of the wounded, large numbers were unprovided for. Medical equipment was sadly deficient. Ambulances had been introduced into the French Army by the celebrated Surgeon Larrey, and the care of his wounded was ever uppermost in the thoughts of Napoleon. By England they were neglected. Disabled soldiers were carried off the field of battle, some on mules, some in bullock carts, in the three waggons provided per Division, or in any other conveyance that happened to be at hand. The science of surgery was in the British Army almost confined to the practice of amputations, and such was the prevailing ignorance that the encouragement of conservative surgery by the Emperor formed the basis of one of the many ridiculous outcries against him. The exertions of Wellington's Principal Medical Officer, Dr. M'Grigor, were unremitting; but with an inadequate and ill-taught staff he could not do impossibilities; and the wounded officers were at present actually dying of want at Salamanca. To keep body and soul together, some sold their horses, others their very clothing; and though Wellington on hearing of their sad state ordered them to be supplied from the Purveyor's stores, some died literally of hunger.

The old grievance of want of specie now pressed Lord Wellington with redoubled force and was one cause of his failure to reap the full fruits of his victory. "I have been able," wrote he to Lord Bathurst on the 18th of August, "to pay the troops only half their pay for April. . . . The want of money in the army is become a most serious evil. . . . We must be regularly supplied or we cannot get on."

Another annoyance arose from the conduct of the Spaniards, both civil and military. So dilatory was Castanos that it was not till the 19th of August that Astorga fell. Then the Spanish Government made appointments purely, as it would seem, for the purpose of thwarting Wellington's wishes. An Intendant was appointed to the province of Salamanca regarding whom Wellington pithily observed that "Senor . . . is not only the most useless and inefficient of God's creatures, but is an impediment to all business; and he cannot speak one word of truth. . . . At Truxillo, after I had forced him to acknowledge that he had told a falsehood, I turned him out of the house and desired that I might never see his face again." "Another equally inefficient and without character General has been sent to replace Don Carlos in Old Castille; and I learn that they have appointed a

General . . . to command in New Castille, in which situation is included that of Governor of Madrid, which is at present by far the most important post in the country, with duties to be performed which require activity and intelligence; and yet the person selected to fill this office is, I understand, an idiot of between 70 and 80 years of age."

Besides all these annoyances Lord Wellington had difficulty with General Maitland. He wished him to march against Suchet by the sea coast, depending on the fleet for supplies very much as he had done himself in the Vimeira campaign. Maitland would not, however, be persuaded, and was consequently desired to defend his entrenched camp at Alicante. But he had been ordered by Lord William Bentinck to return to Sicily in the second week of September and was anxious to carry out his instructions. Wellington thereupon took the matter into his own hands and forbade him to leave Spain.

CHAPTER XXXII

Clausel resumes the offensive—Wellington marches against him—Reaches Burgos—Siege of Burgos—Wellington's difficulties—Advance of the Armies of Portugal and the North—Retreat from Burgos.

LORD WELLINGTON at Madrid was keeping a keen eye on Soult, and revolving in his mind the difficult combinations necessary for the adoption of a new line of operations in the south. It was impossible for him to move until assured that the Marshal intended to march on Valencia and not La Mancha. But long before he could ascertain this, and indeed as early as the 14th of August—the very day of the surrender of the Retiro—Clausel descended the Pisuerga from Burgos and entered Valladolid at the head of 22,000 men and 50 guns, with a view to co-operating with the King, who would, he hoped, by this time be strong enough to drive the Allies from Madrid. On the approach of Clausel, Santocildes evacuated Valladolid in such haste as to leave behind "400 prisoners and all the guns and stores captured there by the Allies." General Clinton also fell back from Cuellar, not—as directed—on Olmedo, but as far as Arevalo. Wellington's line of communications, amply guarded as he believed by 18,000 men, was thus laid bare. On the 17th General Foy, with a Division of Cavalry and two of Infantry, was despatched to relieve Astorga.

Marching up the Duero, Foy carried off the garrison of

IN THE PENINSULA 589

Toro and advanced to relieve Astorga. But that town capitulated on the 19th, and Foy thereupon moved down the Esla. Silveira, with his Portuguese Militia, had barely time to get out of his way, and on the 25th Foy entered Zamora. From Zamora, Foy was in the act of marching upon Salamanca to sever Wellington's communications with Ciudad Rodrigo, when advices reached him from Clausel stating that the British Army was in movement, and ordering him to rejoin headquarters.

Some such enterprise as that of Foy had been expected by Wellington, who was not sorry that the garrisons of Toro and Zamora had escaped; for so dilatory had Castanos been in the siege of Astorga that the British Commander had feared he would be obliged to employ his own troops in the attack of the other two places. The conduct of Castanos merely reflected the lethargy of the Spanish people which had become positively intolerable. That of Clinton, being unexpected, was more serious; but Wellington faced the crisis with his usual promptitude. Leaving in Madrid—under command of Charles Alten, pending the arrival of Hill—the Cavalry Brigades of D'Urban and Victor Alten, the 3rd, 4th, and Light Divisions, he marched on the 1st September for Arevalo with Bock's, Anson's and Ponsonby's Cavalry Brigades, the 1st, 5th, and 7th Divisions.

His ideas as to the future theatre of operations still held good, his immediate intention being merely to keep Clausel at a respectful distance by the capture and possession of Burgos. Then, returning to Madrid, he meant to operate with his main body strengthened by Maitland and such Spanish bodies as might be available in the south and east of Spain.

Writing on the 8th of September, he ordered Hill with his Corps to cross the Tagus at Almaraz (the bridge of which spanning the very deepest chasm had been repaired by Colonel Sturgeon, R.E.) and march to Madrid. The small British force at Carthagena under General Ross was ordered to join Maitland at Alicante, raising the force of the latter to 7,000 British and 9,000 foreign troops; and Ballesteros was instructed to occupy Alcaraz in support of the strong fortress of Chinchilla—erected at an important junction of roads—where he would connect Hill with Maitland and be in a position to operate on the flank of any French army which might take the initiative and approach Madrid from the east. Lord Wellington expected, however, to return from Burgos before the enemy could be ready to undertake any very serious operation against the capital; for the Army of Portugal was still little more than a wreck, and Burgos seemed unlikely to hold out for long.

Having concentrated about 30,000 men at Arevalo, Wellington marched thence on the 4th of September, crossed the Duero on the 6th and entered Valladolid unopposed next day. His line of advance seems to have been dictated by considerations of supply. Otherwise it is open to criticism. A rapid advance from Valladolid might indeed, as pointed out by Napier, have severed Foy from Clausel, but to effect this the march should have been begun sooner. On the other hand a line of advance by the Somosierra and Aranda upon Burgos, would have threatened Clausel's flank and endangered his retreat. As it was Clausel, having been rejoined by Foy, retired leisurely up the valleys of the Pisuerga and Arlanzan, occupying daily successive positions too strong to be attacked in front, and the turning of which necessitated time and patience on the part of his adversary.

It was not until the 16th that Wellington was joined by 11,000 men and 8 guns under Santocildes, who had

IN THE PENINSULA

been dawdling on the road in the true spirit of Spanish inertness. Clausel was then holding a position to cover Burgos, but on seeing his enemy reinforced, evacuated that town, and retired on Briviesca, leaving General Dubreton to stem the tide by holding the fortress of Burgos.

The place was weak: the garrison only 1,800 strong; but in addition to 6 mortars, 9 heavy and 11 field guns forming the normal armament, Clausel's reserve artillery was stored inside the walls.

Wellington's siege train on the other hand consisted only of three 18-pounder guns and five 24-pounder howitzers; for the train used at Ciudad Rodrigo and Badajoz had been sent to Maitland to enable him to attack either Valencia or Tarragona. That the siege should have been undertaken with means so inadequate appears to have been due to Wellington himself. It is stated that both Sir Howard Douglas, R.E., and General Pakenham, now acting as Adjutant-General, urged the need of a more powerful train, and each offered to supply it: the former by bringing up the guns of two frigates at Santander, the latter by twelve Russian siege guns found in the Retiro at Madrid. But although Pakenham promised to find animals to draw the guns, his chief evidently did not believe he would be able to do so. That Wellington was not over confident of success at the outset is proved by his letters. He seems, however, to have relied chiefly on hopes of cutting off the food and water supplies of the garrison.

Napier considers that his chief's proper course would have been to mask the Castle and follow Clausel; in which case the latter would admittedly have retired behind the Ebro, possibly to Pampeluna and St. Sebastian. The French expense magazines would then have been destroyed and the Army of Portugal placed *hors de combat* for at least another month.

The siege of Burgos was entrusted to the 1st and 6th Divisions, aided by the Portuguese Brigades of Pack and Bradford, forming a force of between 13,000 and 14,000 of all ranks. The 5th and 7th Divisions, about 10,000 strong, and the Spaniards under Santocildes posted near Monasterio and Briviesca, covered the attack against any attempt on the part of Clausel, the main body of whose army occupied the right bank of the Ebro from Miranda to Logrono, with advanced posts at Pancorvo and Briviesca.

On the 19th of September the 1st Division crossed the Arlanzan above the town of Burgos; and the Highland Brigade belonging to it captured the same night the important outlying work of San Michael, 300 yards from the Castle, which commanded the whole of the fortress excepting one work erected on the highest point of the Castle, termed the Napoleon Battery. But the affair was mismanaged, and although success crowned the initial effort, it had been attained only at the cost of 420 men. On the 22nd an attempt was made to escalade the outer defences of the Castle. The assault failed "because Major Lawrie of the 79th, the Field Officer who commanded, did that which is too common in our army. He paid no attention to his orders, notwithstanding the pains I took in writing them, and in reading and explaining them to him twice over. He made none of the dispositions ordered; and instead of regulating the attack as he ought, he rushed on as if he had been the leader of a forlorn hope and fell, together with many of those who went with him. He had my instructions in his pocket; and as the French got possession of his body, and were made acquainted with the plan, the attack could never be repeated. When he fell, nobody having received orders what to do, nobody could give any to the troops. I was in the trenches, however, and ordered

IN THE PENINSULA 593

them to withdraw. Our time and ammunition were then expended, and our guns destroyed in taking this line; than which at former sieges we had taken many stronger by assault." (Wellington to Lord Liverpool, November 25, 1812.)

It soon became evident that in the absence of a regular siege train the two Divisions employed were unequal to the task. The 6th was not in very good order. In the 1st the Brigade of Guards set an example of steady, hard work in the trenches, but it was not followed by the other troops whether British or Portuguese. Bitterly must Wellington have regretted the absence of the tried 3rd, 4th, and Light Divisions. Five assaults were delivered, but little material progress was made, and his losses were great. In one of these assaults fell Lieut.-Colonel Somers Cocks, an officer of exceptional talent and energy. His loss was felt by no one more than Wellington himself, who went so far as to say that he should not have regretted the unfortunate result of the siege had Cocks survived. Colonel Cocks had been recently promoted from the 16th Light Dragoons into the 79th Highlanders, and had been employed confidentially by his Chief on innumerable occasions requiring a cool head and steady nerve.

At a time when his whole attention was demanded for the military situation, Lord Wellington was as usual harassed by a variety of extraneous circumstances. The British Government propounded an absurd scheme for the sale of the Portuguese Crown and Church lands, forgetting not only the opposition which such a proposal must ensure from the parties concerned, but also that it was unlikely that buyers would come forward in a country which within the last eighteen months had been occupied by the French and might be occupied by them again.

It happened also that the newly-arrived Quartermaster-

General, Colonel Willoughby Gordon, was discontented with his position and desirous of being made "Chief of the Staff," an office hitherto unknown in our Army. But of more serious consequence was his habit of acquainting his friends in England—leading politicians on the opposition side—with the contents of Wellington's confidential despatches, and thus enabling them to use the information as the ground for making attacks upon the Government.

Sir Home Popham wrote to express his intention of going home. Wellington remonstrated, pointing out that if Sir Home were to desist from his operations, and the siege of Burgos were to be raised, he would certainly have the Army of the North as well as that of Portugal down upon him.

As some set-off against these annoyances, it was just at this period that Lord Wellington was offered, and with the assent of his Government accepted, the office of Commander-in-Chief of the Spanish forces. It had previously been offered and declined; but circumstances were now to some extent changed. The Spaniards had lost pretty nearly the whole of their Cavalry and Field Artillery, and Wellington was in a position to dictate his terms of acceptance.

The siege of Burgos went on badly. Although Sir Home Popham was sending two 24-pounder naval guns, for which he had improvised mountings, they were still on the road. The three 18-pounder siege guns were injured by the defenders' fire. Small arms ammunition began to run short; and though Popham was forwarding a fresh supply, Wellington could not, pending its arrival, cut the Gordian knot by an assault as at Ciudad Rodrigo and Badajoz.

Meanwhile General Clarke, the French Minister of

War, appreciating the situation after the battle of Salamanca, had met the crisis by calling Marshal Masséna once more to the front and appointing him to command the whole of the French forces in the northern provinces of Spain. Within sixteen months of his supersession time had thus brought the veteran Commander his revenge; but for Masséna active service was a thing of the past. He declined the proffered honour and proposed General Souham for the command of the Army of Portugal. Marmont himself wished to be succeeded by Clausel, and the recent conduct of that officer had proved his talent; but Masséna prevailed. On the 3rd of October Souham arrived on the Ebro with reinforcements from France and justified his selection, for he was the only French General who ever encountered Wellington without meeting defeat.

The Army of Portugal now consisted of 35,000 men. That of the North, to the extent of 9,000 men and 16 guns, was being concentrated by General Caffarelli at Vitoria. The Commanders were keen to relieve Burgos, and had waited only to hear news of events in Valencia; but so active were the Partidas in harassing the lines of communication that direct correspondence with the King was impossible, and letters had to be addressed to the Minister of War at Paris, who forwarded them to their destination. Even so, many were intercepted, and the French Generals would have been almost destitute of information had not the English newspapers—conspicuous among which are to be found the honoured names of the *Times* and *Morning Post*—come gallantly to the rescue by publishing the most minute and confidential details about the Allied Armies, and thus furnishing Clarke with the most reliable intelligence!

The French concentration was at first viewed with little alarm by Wellington, who believed Caffarelli to be too much engaged with Popham and the Guerillas to furnish aid to his colleague. Sir Home, however, after his first success was twice repulsed from Gueteria, and the Partidas received damaging blows at Calatayud, Requena, etc. Caffarelli was therefore set free. But elsewhere the guerilla warfare went on, and the country round Saragossa was for a time in the hands of the chiefs; for General Reille, expecting Wellington to advance on that city, had withdrawn his detachments and concentrated his army.

For a few days Souham, over-estimating Wellington's strength, contented himself with demonstrations; but realising his error, and hearing that the King was about to advance from Madrid, on the 18th of October put in motion his army and that of Caffarelli, suddenly drove in the British picquets, and next day occupied with his centre a position on the heights of Monasterio; his right being posted at Villa Escuso and his left at La Sombria. Souham's intention was to attack the Allies on the 20th; but early that morning arrived a letter from the King forbidding him to enter into a general action, on the ground that his Majesty's proposed operations would of themselves compel Wellington to abandon the siege of Burgos.

Souham obeyed; or rather deferred his attack, for having only provisions till the 26th, he felt it preferable to fight at advantage before that date rather than injure the *morale* of his newly-organised troops by a retrograde movement. Everything favoured his intention. The combined armies under his command mustered 44,000 men, including 5,000 Cavalry—and more than 60 guns, while the whole force of the Allies amounted only to about 25,000 Anglo-Portuguese troops of all ranks and arms with but 24 guns—for the Portuguese artillery had disappeared from lack of animals to draw it—and perhaps

IN THE PENINSULA 597

12,000 Spaniards with 12 guns. The Allied Cavalry was nominally 4,000 strong, but not two-thirds of it was British or K.G.L.

Leaving Pack to blockade the Castle of Burgos with his own Brigade and one from the 6th Division, to which were added two British, two Spanish and a Portuguese battalion—a force of about 5,000 men—Lord Wellington on the 20th took up a position with the rest of his army between Burgos and Monasterio; but the moment was critical; he was unaware of Caffarelli's arrival and of his own great inferiority in numbers, while in his rear was the Castle whose guns commanded the bridges in his line of retreat over the Arlanzan. Nor was this the full extent of his disadvantage. The Spanish contingent could not be reckoned on for great things. The Anglo-Portuguese were discouraged, and though Wellington had gained a tower of strength by the arrival on the 16th of Sir Edward Paget, who came from England as second in command, and had been appointed to the 1st Division, no great reliance could be placed on the other divisional Generals, who were mostly newcomers. Had a battle ensued one hopes that British valour would have prevailed. But in the light of after events, the action, as at Talavera, must have been followed by a retreat and the abandonment of our wounded to the enemy. Happily the King's message caused the crisis to pass away with nothing more serious than a partial attack which was repulsed by the 1st and 5th Divisions under Sir Edward Paget.

But on the 21st, the day following that on which Souham had received the King's letter of the 6th of October, Wellington had one from Sir Rowland Hill at Madrid, dated the 17th, giving rather alarming news. Ballesteros, indignant at Wellington's appointment to the command in chief of the Spanish forces, had refused to comply with his directions, although forwarded by his own Government, to move into La Mancha. The fort of Chinchilla, at the point where the high road from Madrid branches off to Valencia and Alicante respectively, had surrendered on the 9th after a show of resistance ; and the combined armies of Soult and Joseph were marching on the Tagus which in many places was fordable.

On confirmation of this intelligence, Wellington, without hesitation although in bitter disappointment, abandoned all his deep-laid plans. It was essential to form a junction with Hill. Burgos was relinquished. The siege which had cost the enemy 623 men and himself 1,974, was raised. Eight guns captured from the French, and the three damaged British 24-pounders were perforce left behind, for all available draught animals had been sent to draw Sir Home Popham's guns from Santander. Under the very nose of the vigilant Dubreton, Wellington skilfully withdrew his army across the bridge of Burgos, over the Arlanzan, and gained Cellada del Camino during the night.

It was not until the evening of the 22nd that Souham ascertained his opponent's retreat. By a forced march he came up at 7 a.m. next morning with the rearguard of the Allies, consisting of the two Light Battalions K.G.L. forming Colin Halkett's Brigade of the 7th Division, two batteries R.H.A., with the Cavalry Brigades of Bock and Anson flanked by two bodies of Guerillas ; the whole commanded by Sir Stapleton Cotton.

Souham attacked without hesitation. The picquets were driven from the bridge of Baniel on the Pisuerga ; and in spite of a vigorous charge and obstinate resistance for three hours, the rearguard was forced to retire upon Bock's Brigade, formed in support at a house named the Venta de Pozo. The line of retreat ran across two narrow bridges, and while Anson was slowly crossing the defile the Guerillas covering the left came pouring down on the flank in headlong flight, hotly pursued by the French Hussars. Anson's Brigade was thrown into disorder, but succeeded in rallying on Halket's Infantry posted in rear of the second bridge, who with the aid of the guns covered the retirement. In spite of the artillery fire, however, a Brigade of the enemy's Cavalry coming up fresh, crossed the bridge. It was then charged by Bock, but just too late, for the French had time to form ; and getting the better of Bock, drove him and Anson to the rear in confusion. The moment was critical. The British were greatly outnumbered. Anson's Brigade seems to have mustered only 460 sabres, and that of Bock comprised but two squadrons. Happily Wellington was as usual present just when wanted. He made Halket form squares, posting him and the guns to cover the retreat of the beaten Cavalry. This saved the situation. Halket's men standing firm repelled three separate charges, and the French eventually gave up the contest; but the defeat of our Cavalry was a bad omen for the retreat. The rearguard, still covered by Halket, retired to Quintana near the Pisuerga, which had been crossed earlier in the day at Cordovillas and Torquemada by the main body of the army.

Whilst the rearguard was fighting for its existence, a large portion of the main body was spending the day in a state of hopeless intoxication among the wine vaults of Torquemada. The retreat had now continued for fifty miles. The convoys of sick and wounded were still on the right bank of the Duero. Wellington therefore contented himself on the 24th with taking post behind the Carrion, where he halted during the next day and was joined by the 1st Battalion 1st Guards and by drafts. His position between Villa Muriel and Duenas facing nearly due east was strong, resting on high ground with his front and left flank covered by the Carrion, his right by the Pisuerga. Orders were given for the destruction of the bridges over the two rivers. Those at Duenas and Villa Muriel were blown up. At Banos the mine failed, and at Palencia on the 25th, Foy, coming suddenly upon the detachment entrusted with the duty, prevented the demolition and made some prisoners, while Maucune approached the bridges of Banos, Isidro, and Muriel. Foy's movement compelled Wellington to throw back his left, consisting of the 5th Division and Spaniards, and form a new front almost at right angles to that of his right and centre. Maucune by a clever stratagem discovered a ford at Muriel and pushed his troops across the river. The situation was becoming uneasy when Wellington, coming up, directed General Oswald to retake the village with the 5th Division. Oswald, who had only that day joined the army, made an unfortunate beginning by offering an objection. He probably did not do so a second time. The order was carried out; the village retaken; and a dry canal running parallel to the river occupied in force.

But the loss of the bridge over the Pisuerga at Banos had made Wellington's position untenable. Souham could now either mass his troops against the left wing of the Allies and force them to fight with their backs to the Pisuerga, or intercept them on the Duero at Tudela, and, leaving them no other line of retreat than that of Valladolid and Tordesillas, break their communication with Hill at Madrid.

Under these circumstances, Wellington, without hesitation, sent his baggage at nightfall to Valladolid, and, evacuating his position before daybreak on the 26th, marched straight to Cabezon, sixteen miles distant, crossed over to the left bank of the Pisuerga and mined the bridge. At the same time the 7th Division, under

Lord Dalhousie, who had just joined the army, was directed to move to the left and hold the bridges of Valladolid, Simancas, and Tordesillas; while another detachment occupied the bridge of Tudela over the Duero.

Souham followed by the left bank of the Pisuerga, and was in front of Cabezon on the morning of the 27th. He deployed his troops, and for the first time Wellington became aware that, in spite of the continued operations of Popham on the coast, the Army of the North, as well as that of Portugal, was before him, and that in view of his great inferiority in numbers it would be impossible to hold permanently either the line of the Pisuerga or of the Duero, even though the latter was now in full flood.

Matters were critical. The line of communication with Ciudad Rodrigo was in confusion. Mr. Kennedy, the Commissary-General, had been away in England and had only rejoined the Army on the 20th. In his absence mistakes had been made. Hill's line of supply by way of Badajoz and the valley of the Tagus was full; but were he, if overpowered, to retire as arranged upon Wellington, his magazines would admirably serve to provision Soult in an advance on Portugal. On the other hand, Wellington's line of supply by Salamanca and Ciudad Rodrigo was nearly empty, but since this was the intended line of retreat for Hill as well as Wellington, it was absolutely necessary, on all accounts, to transfer the magazines from the southern to the northern line. The operation was anything but easy, and before it was finished Kennedy received orders from Lord Wellington to clear the hospitals at Salamanca. "The means," says Napier, "were, indeed, sufficient, but the negligence of many medical and escorting officers conducting the convoys of sick to the rear, and the consequent bad conduct of the soldiers—for where the officers are careless the soldiers will be licentious—produced the worst effects. Outrages were perpetrated on the inhabitants along the whole line of march, terror was everywhere predominant, the ill-used drivers and muleteers deserted, some with, some without their cattle, and Kennedy's operation was disastrous. The commissariat lost nearly all the animals and carriages employed, the villages were abandoned, and the under commissaries were bewildered or paralysed by the terrible disorder thus spread along the line."

From Cabezon Wellington wrote to Hill to say that he could not hold his ground; and since Sir Rowland's position would be endangered by his withdral, he directed him also to retire, and hoped—although with no great confidence—that the two Corps would be able to effect a junction on the Adaja, at Arevalo, on the 4th of November. Thence, with all the advantage of interior lines, Wellington hoped to contain Souham with a detachment, and intended to give battle to Soult with the bulk of his Corps combined with that of Hill. Decisive success would speedily rectify the misfortunes at Burgos and restore the general situation. Something, however, would have to depend on the movements of Soult, and it was not impossible that Hill might be cut off from Wellington and compelled to retire upon Almaraz. In the hope, however, that the junction might still be made, and at all events to gain time for Hill, Lord Wellington put a bold face on the matter and held his ground on the Pisuerga.

On the 28th General Souham pushed forward down the right bank of the Pisuerga, and with a view to turning Wellington's left, attacked the bridges of Valladolid and Simancas. The assault on the former was repelled by Lord Dalhousie with the main body of the 7th Division. At Simancas, Colonel Halket with his Brigade of the same Division blew up the bridge in self-defence, and sending the Brunswick Oels Regiment to the bridge of Tordesillas still further to the left, destroyed the roadway of that bridge also. But though the enemy was so far baffled, Wellington fully appreciated the importance of his manœuvre, and seeing him extend still further to his right, retired on the 29th to the left bank of the Duero. Scarcely had he, however, crossed when news arrived of a terrible misfortune, destroying the whole ground of his combinations, and involving him in most imminent peril.

Halket, as already stated, had sent the Brunswick Regiment to guard the river at Tordesillas. This regiment is stated by Sir George Napier (brother to the historian) to have been composed principally of deserters and French prisoners of Dupont's army, whose only means of escaping from their horrible suffering on board the Spanish hulks at Cadiz was to accept the offer of the British Government to enlist in our service. By the terms of the capitulation of Baylen these men were entitled to a free passage to France, and it was only by a gross violation of good faith that they were detained as prisoners. It was hardly probable that they would fight with much zeal against their old comrades. In point of fact they deserted by scores; and it is not too much to suspect that on this occasion their conduct was, to some extent, the result of pre-arrangement. Anyhow, when the French arrived on the 29th and found the bridge destroyed, a small party of sixty men swam across the river and drove the whole Regiment of Brunswick Oels away!

The startling news that the enemy was in possession of the remains of the Tordesillas bridge and was rapidly repairing it, reached Wellington the same evening. Not only was his left flank turned but his very line of retreat on Salamanca in jeopardy. He promptly grappled with the crisis. Moving to his left early on the 30th, he succeeded in taking up a new position between the heights of Rueda and Tordesillas, facing the Duero, before Souham could bring up the main body of his army to cross the bridge. Wellington's junction with Hill was now secure; but as Souham continued to extend to his left, orders were given to destroy the bridges at Toro and Zamora. "I assure you," wrote Wellington to Lord Bathurst next day, " that considering the numbers of the enemy, the state of the Spanish troops, the great proportion of foreign troops in the Divisions which I have with me, and their general weakness and the weakness of our Cavalry, I think I have escaped from the worst military situation I was ever in."

The casualties in the Allied Army between the 22nd and 30th of October amounted to 127 killed, 522 wounded, and 243 missing.

CHAPTER XXXIII

Soult and the King advance on Madrid—Hill abandons the line of the Tagus.

WE must now return to Sir Rowland Hill. That officer having crossed the Tagus at Almaraz, reached Toledo in the last days of September with between 25,000 and 30,000 men, made up of the 2nd and Hamilton's Division, the 2nd Cavalry Division, and the Spanish contingents of Morillo and Penne Villemar. He then took over from Charles Alten command of the 3rd, 4th, and Light Divisions, which had been left by Wellington in the neighbourhood of Madrid when he started to operate against Clausel. With this force, amounting to upwards of 40,000 men, 24 English and 6 Portuguese guns, Hill assumed a position on the right bank of the Tagus from Toledo to Aranjuez, to guard against attack from the side of Valencia. The Mercian army, under General Elio — lately our enemy at Buenos Ayres—joined Hill. The guerilla bands of Bassecour, Villa Campa and Juan Martin (nicknamed the Empecinado), came up at Wellington's request to La Mancha; and Bellesteros, as already noted, was desired to occupy the mountain of Alcaraz, with a view to the protection of Chinchilla.

An army of 60,000 men, of whom half were Anglo-Portuguese, formed a barrier against counter-attack on the part of Soult, Suchet, and the King. "By these dispositions," observes Napier (book xix. chap. 3), the Allies had several lines of operation. Ballesteros from the mountains of Alcaraz could harass the flanks of the advancing French, and when they passed could unite with Maitland to overpower Suchet. Hill could retire if pressed by Madrid or by Toledo, and could gain the passes of the Guadarama or the valley of the Tagus. Elio, Villa Campa, Bassecour, and the Empecinado, could act by Cuenca and Requena against Suchet or against Madrid if the French followed Hill obstinately; or they could join Ballesteros. And besides all these forces, there were 10,000 or 12,000 Spanish levies in the Isla waiting for clothing and arms, which under the recent treaty were to come from England. The English Ministers had nominally confided the distribution of these succours to Wellington, but following their usual vicious manner of doing business they also gave Mr. Stuart a control without Wellington's knowledge; hence the stores, expected by the latter at Lisbon or Cadiz, were by Stuart unwittingly directed to Corunna, with which place the English General had no secure communication."

During the first days of October, Bassecour, Villa Campa, and Juan Martin occupied the road leading from Cuenca to Valencia. Other partisan bodies were assembled in the neighbourhood of Sarragossa, and the whole line of the Allies thus extended from Toledo on the right by Cuenca and Calatayud almost to Jaca at the foot of the Pyrenees.

Unfortunately Ballesteros, who should have been at Alcaraz with 30,000 men, on hearing of Wellington's appointment to the command-in-chief of the Spanish armies, took offence thereat, refused to obey his orders, although conveyed to him direct by his own Government, and remained at Grenada. Upon this occasion the Spanish Government behaved well. Ballesteros was

IN THE PENINSULA 607

placed in arrest and deprived of his command; but it was too late to remedy the evil.

We have seen that Soult formed his junction with the King at Almanza on the 3rd of October. High words ensued, and Joseph offered the command-in-chief to Jourdan and Suchet; but as each in turn declined Soult was reinstated. His troops required rest, and the long convoys of sick, wounded, and Spaniards had to be sent to Valencia. Happily for the French the absence of Ballesteros enabled them to occupy extended quarters and thus get food. Time was not wasted. On the 9th Soult attacked and captured Chinchilla with little resistance, and the great outwork of the Allied position was thus lost at a breath. The initiative now lay with the French. The incursions of Bassecour and Villa Campa were repelled, and Hill found himself threatened at the moment that the Tagus was becoming fordable everywhere above Aranjuez. On the 17th he reported the situation to Lord Wellington, and the result of his report was the abandonment of the siege of Burgos.

As early as the 1st of October King Joseph had written to inform Souham of his intended march on Madrid. If Wellington evacuated Burgos, Souham was to harass his rear. If, on the contrary, he remained on the Arlanzan, the King, after capturing Madrid, proposed to threaten the line of communications of the Allies with Salamanca. In order to march on Madrid with the largest available force, the King desired the aid of a large portion of Suchet's army. Suchet did not respond. He observed that in view of the position of the Anglo-Sicilian force at Alicante, and of the fact that, pending the clearance of the Saragossa country, the sole line of communication with France lay through Valencia, it was essential that his army should not be diminished by a single man.

Joseph yielded. On the 19th he advanced with the Army of the Centre—12,000 men with 12 guns, under Count D'Erlon—from Cuenca by Tarancon; while Soult, with 46,000 men and 72 guns, marched simultaneously by the road of San Clemente upon Aranjuez. On their approach Hill, whose advanced posts had been near Belmonte, withdrew his left behind the Tajuina.

On the 29th the Army of the Centre crossed the Tagus unopposed at Fuente Duenas and Villa Maurique, and on the same day Soult pushed his advance guard over the river at Aranjuez. In accordance with Wellington's orders Hill retired before the superior numbers of the enemy. He had two lines of retreat open: one by the valley of the Tagus, where he would not only cover Lisbon, but be in a position to operate on the flank and rear of a force moving against Wellington; the other, by the Guadarama mountains, in which case these advantages would be lost, but a junction with his chief would enable the latter to act with all the advantage of interior lines and superiority of numbers against either of the armies opposed to him. The former course was perhaps the more attractive to Hill—to an ambitious man the continuance in independent command might have been irresistible—the latter, the more sound; and Sir Rowland, with his usual loyalty, followed it. Destroying the stores and the fort of La China in Madrid, on the night of the 30th, he retired and concentrated his columns next morning at Majadahonda.

The evacuation of Madrid was carried out amid the loud lamentations of the citizens; not so much from fear of the enemy, for public opinion seems to have been pretty evenly divided as to the comparative merits of the opposing forces, as from dread of the return of the guerilla bands when no longer kept in order by the British, and the knowledge that an interval must elapse before the arrival of the French army would bring new protection. In other ways also they deplored the departure of the English. Napier tells us that at the time when Wellington entered the capital, "though the markets were full of provisions, there was no money wherewith to buy; and though the houses were full of rich furniture there were neither purchasers nor lenders: even noble families secretly sought charity that they might live. The calm resignation with which these terrible sufferings were borne was a distinctive mark of the national character; not many begged, none complained; there was no violence, no reproaches, very few thefts. . . . But with this patient endurance of calamity the Madrilēnos discovered a deep and unaffected gratitude for kindness received at the hands of the British officers who contributed, not much, for they had it not, but enough of money to form soup charities by which hundreds were succoured. It was in the 3rd Division the example was set, and by the 45th Regiment, and it was not the least of the many honourable distinctions those brave men have earned."

Hill was accompanied in his retreat by Penne Villemur, Morillo, and Carlos d'Espana. With a view to the protection of Lisbon, uncovered as it was by the direction of Hill's march, Wellington had desired that Elio, Bassecour, and Villa Campa might join the army lately commanded by Ballesteros and now by General Virues, and operate from the valley of the Tagus against any French force advancing on the Portuguese capital. But the rapid movement of the enemy separated Elio from Hill, and the former decided to remain near Sacedon, on the Tagus, where he was joined by Villa Campa and Juan Martin.

On the 3rd of November Soult and Joseph entered Madrid and deposited there the numerous Spanish families which had hitherto encumbered their march.

CHAPTER XXXIV

Wellington retires behind the Tormes and is joined by Hill—Junction of the French Armies—Departure of the Army of the North—Soult turns Wellington's flank—Wellington retreats—Capture of Sir E. Paget—The Allies reach the Agueda and go into winter quarters—Wellington's censure—Comments.

THE orders given by Wellington to destroy the bridge over the Duero at Toro were duly carried out; but his whole line was too long to be guarded, and Souham, arriving on the further bank with his right wing, quickly repaired the bridge. The position of the Allies was once more critical. Its left and rear were laid bare, and it was obvious that the idea of standing to fight on the Adaja in conjunction with Hill must be given up. An immediate retirement on Salamanca seemed imperative, but Lord Wellington, hearing of the arrival at Villa Castin of a part of the Army of the Centre which had quitted Madrid on the 4th and had advanced over the Guadarama, merely despatched Ponsonby's Brigade of Cavalry and the 5th Division to Alaejos to guard against any attack from the side of Toro; ordered Hill to march for the Trabanços river by Frontiveros instead of on Arevalo—where he would have been liable to be intercepted by Joseph's advance—and, with a view to covering the movement, held his position at Rueda until the 6th, when he retired by way of Pitrigua in order to protect the road from Toro to Salamanca. On the 8th Hill crossed the Tormes with-

IN THE PENINSULA 611

out molestation and took up a position behind it about Alba de Tormes, while Wellington took post on the heights of San Christoval.

On the same day Joseph came in touch with Souham at Medina del Campo. Thus the forces on each side were united: those of the French amounting to 100,000 men (including 12,000 Cavalry) with 130 guns; while the Allies mustered something over 70,000 men and about 66 guns; but of these 16,000 men and 12 guns formed the not very reliable Spanish contingent. Yet Wellington still hoped to maintain permanently the line of the Tormes and rest his troops. Both he and Hill had marched about 200 miles in retreat. Excepting the 3rd, 4th and Light Divisions, which had had some rest, the Army had been marching and fighting almost incessantly since January. Their discipline was much impaired; their clothing and equipment worn out.

Wellington's position extended over about 15 miles: from San Christoval on the left to the bridge of Alba on the right. The Cavalry remained on the right bank of the river to watch the approaches. The Castle of Alba, also on the right bank, was occupied by General Howard's Brigade of the 2nd Division, supported on the left bank by Hamilton's Portuguese Division. The two other Brigades of the 2nd Division guarded the fords of Encina and Huerta, communicating with the Divisions of Wellington's Corps which was posted between Aldea Lengua and the heights of San Christoval. The Light Division and that of Don Carlos were quartered in the town of Salamanca. The 3rd and 4th Divisions, posted at Calvarissa de Ariba, formed the reserve of Hill's Corps.

"While desirous to fight," says Napier. (bk. xix. ch. 5), "the English General looked also to retreat; sending his sick to the rear, he brought up small magazines from

Rodrigo to intermediate points, caused the surplus ammunition at Salamanca to be destroyed by small explosions, and delivered large stores of clothing, arms and equipments to the Spaniards, who were thus completely furnished; but in an hour they were selling their accoutrements under his very windows! . . . The Spaniards (at Salamanca) civil and military evinced hatred for the British. Daily did they attempt or perpetrate murder . . . and no redress could be had for this or other crimes, save by counter violence which was not long withheld. . . . The civil authorities, not less savage, were more insolent than the military, treating every English person with an intolerable arrogance. . . . The exasperation caused by these things was leading to serious mischief when the enemy's movements gave another direction to the soldiers' passions." In one case at least bread was refused to British stragglers dying of hunger, which was being baked for the approaching French! Such was the people for whom we were shedding our blood! It is only fair to say that the Spanish women formed an honourable exception.

It was at this moment of anxiety, with his men somewhat out of hand and the enemy in hot pursuit, that Wellington received a letter from Lord Bathurst discussing the question what was to be done when the French had been expelled the Peninsula, and—with that mania for frittering away the resources of the nation so characteristic of the day—proposing half a dozen plans for expeditions to Holland, Italy, Germany, &c. Wellington in reply briefly exposed Bathurst's fallacies, and with a touch of sarcasm dismissed the subject.

The fords over the Tormes, although the river was beginning to fall, were impassable. On the 9th Soult, with a view to seizing the bridge of Alba, made a demonstration against the Castle, but was eventually repelled after firing 1,500 shells. On the 11th Joseph made him Commander-in-Chief of the combined Armies of the South and Centre (with the exception of his own Guards and Spaniards) and superseded Souham by Count d'Erlon. The reason of Souham's supersession is not clear. His campaign had been one of unbroken success, and his successor was not a great General. At the same time Caffarelli returned to Burgos, and his departure reduced the enemy's numbers to 90,000 men and 120 guns. Nevertheless the question of supply was becoming serious, and Wellington was surprised that the French had remained concentrated for so long. Inaction was obviously impossible. So Marshal Jourdan, Chief of the Staff, proposed that advantage should be taken of Wellington's extended position to concentrate at night, force the fords of the Tormes between Villa Gonzala and Huerta at daybreak, and penetrate the Allied centre at Calvarissa de Ariba. Soult, on the contrary, strongly advocated a turning movement by the fords 7 or 8 miles above Alba; an operation which, with a little care, should be invisible to the Allies and would place the French Army on their flank and rear, threatening their communications with Ciudad Rodrigo, and forcing them at pleasure either to fight in a situation where defeat would mean little less than ruin, or to beat a hasty retreat involving the abandonment of a part of their forces. The reply to this was that Wellington would discern the enveloping movement in time to retire quietly, and that even should his communication with Ciudad Rodrigo be severed, his line of retreat by a more northerly route upon Almeida would still be open. Clausel, the ablest of many good officers present, whose conduct at Salamanca had earned for his opinions a title to respect, supported Soult. The other Generals sided with Jourdan, and Napier observes that although each had reason on his side, in view of the strength and confidence of the French Armies, the adoption of that Marshal's plan would probably have secured the better results. Still it must be remembered that Wellington, even if attacked at disadvantage, was unequalled at fighting a battle, and though Jourdan might have surprised and cut off Hamilton and the Alba garrison, it is by no means certain that he would have done so; and the Division guarding the fords of the Tormes ought to have been able to hold him at bay long enough to enable the whole Army to assemble on the heights of Calvarissa de Ariba.

Eventually Soult gained his point. Early on the 14th he crossed the Tormes at Galisancho, two leagues above Alba, with the Armies of the South and Centre, and took up a position on the road leading from Alba to Tamames facing north-east, with his right at Nostra Senora de Otrero and his left at Mozarbes.

During the last few days Sir Rowland Hill had expressed some anxiety as to his position, and seems to have desired to destroy the bridge at Alba, the castle of which was occupied by 300 Spaniards under Colonel Miranda. Wellington belittled the danger, and even on hearing of Soult's flank march kept his Corps at San Christoval and contented himself with ordering Hill's Cavalry and the 2nd Division to attack the head of the enemy's column as Pakenham had done at Salamanca. Hamilton's and the 4th Division remained at Alba; the 3rd Division occupied the Arapizes. But the French Army was already in position. The 2nd Division was then withdrawn, the Alba bridge blown up, and the Spanish garrison directed to retire as best it could. Under these rather difficult circumstances Miranda behaved well. He held his post until the 27th, and then cleverly carried off his men at night.

By the morning of the 15th Wellington had concentrated his whole Army on the Arapiles, but Soult showed no disposition to attack. Having been joined by the Army of Portugal, which on the day previous had been left to make demonstrations against San Christoval and draw attention off Soult, that Marshal extended his left towards Val Buena, threatening the Salamanca-Tamames-Ciudad Rodrigo road. His movement was out of Wellington's reach, and the British Commander now found that in under-rating his enemy he had waited too long. Seeing the danger to his communications, and being unable to attack with advantage, at 2 p.m. he crossed the Zunguen stream in three columns near Aldea Tejada, covering the flank march with his Cavalry and Artillery, but marching with his Infantry so well closed up that if attacked they could at any moment have fronted in order of battle. Favoured by fog and rain the Allies, although within a mile of the French, marched unmolested; and gaining the Valmusa river at nightfall were clear of the toils and had regained their communications with Ciudad Rodrigo.

On the 16th Wellington continued his retreat by three roads through thick forest and bivouacked behind the Matilla. To say that his Army retained no semblance of order would be an exaggeration, but—no doubt owing to the failure to complete the arrangements for transferring the magazines from the valley of the Tagus to the more northerly line—few or no rations were issued, and the men, dying of hunger and reduced to subsist on the sweet acorns of the country, began firing on the herds of pigs frequenting the woods. Great confusion was naturally caused. Two men were hanged, but the pangs of hunger overcame the fear of death and the practice was not stopped. The weather was terrible, the roads in places knee-deep in mud. The Staff Officers did not show intelligence, the regimental either neglected their duty or, more probably, found it impossible to keep men in the ranks. Stragglers were so numerous that 2,000 were captured. Happily the march was short—only 12 miles —and unmolested by the enemy until just at the close.

The Quartermaster-General, Colonel Willoughby Gordon, was in bad health, and his performance of his duty was unsatisfactory. During the night the Cavalry was withdrawn without notice from the rear, leaving the Infantry to its fate. When day broke on the 17th, the Light Division, which formed the rearmost of the central column, found itself confronted by a body of 8,000 French Cavalry. Fortunately the enemy did not realise the position, and was momentarily checked by a clever demonstration which gave time to our men to retire. The remaining Divisions of this column were the 1st, 5th, and 7th. Marching through the thick wood they seem to have lost connection. Intervals occurred between them, and through those intervals pressed the enemy's squadrons. "As opportunity offered they galloped from side to side sweeping away the baggage, and sabring the conductors and guides." Sir Edward Paget, commanding the column, rode up to see what was the matter, and being very short-sighted, was captured. His loss was much felt by Wellington.

After crossing the Huebra the Allied Army took post on the left bank, extending from Tamames on the right to Boadilla on the left. Soult, who had hoped to intercept it at Tamames, and had consequently marched by the Salamanca-Vecuis road, was close at hand with his Infantry, and opened a heavy fire. Nevertheless Alten halted the rearguard on the left bank and, for reasons best known to himself, threw it into squares. Happily Wellington, who had a most astonishing knack of being on the spot when wanted, came up. According to custom

IN THE PENINSULA

he said nothing to the General, but reprimanding the regimental officers for Alten's errors, ordered an immediate retirement over the river, which was successfully effected.

During the evening sharp skirmishing took place on the British right. To carry off the army next morning —the 18th—was a difficult task, although the baggage had been sent off to Ciudad Rodrigo during the night. A mile in rear of the bivouac the main road was flooded. It was therefore necessary to retire by a by-path. The Generals of Division, Stewart, Lord Dalhousie and Clinton, surprised at getting orders to march by a circuitous route, and unaware of the reason, resolved to disobey. They retired accordingly by the high road. Presently they were brought to a standstill by the flood. Before they could find a way out of the difficulty up came Lord Wellington in person. "What are you going to do now?" They did not know. "Very well, gentlemen, if you do not know, perhaps you will be good enough to obey my orders in future." Then, without another word, he led the way, followed by his insubordinate Generals looking like whipped hounds, back to the right path. Soult happily never crossed the Huebra, and the whole army, with the exception of the men wounded the previous night, was withdrawn in safety. But the fate of the wounded was terrible. Being left to the mercy of the enemy, who, as already noted, never came up, they died in lingering agony.

Along the marshy plains straggled the weary army, its patience exhausted, its discipline almost non-existent. As an organised body it seemed likely to dissolve altogether. Many a gallant fellow was lying on the road dying of hunger, fatigue, and the inclemency of the weather; for although the marches were only 12 or 14 miles in length, the stiff clay made progress slow and painful, and the men had to carry their packs from morning to night. On one spot lay dead about 100 English and Portuguese soldiers after the halt. A heart-rending case was that of a Rifleman of the 95th. "Having marched as long as strength allowed, at last he sank from exhaustion, and crawled upon his hands and knees until he expired."

But on this day the sufferings of the army in general came to an end. The rain ceased. Rations were distributed. Next day (the 19th) the troops were billeted in and about Ciudad Rodrigo, and the retreat from Burgos was over.

Our losses were never accurately known, chiefly because the Spaniards made no returns, but they were certainly very heavy. Between Burgos and the Duero the casualties amounted to 892. Between the Duero and Tormes they were small, but the attack of Soult on Alba cost us 113 men. Hill lost 400 between the Tagus and the Tormes. Up to this point, therefore, the losses of the Anglo-Portuguese, including those at the siege of Burgos, may be taken at 3,400, and Napier estimates those of the Spaniards during the same period at 1,000. For the last phase of the retreat, from the Tormes to the Agueda, Wellington returned his losses at 50 killed, 139 wounded, and 178 missing. Marshal Jourdan, however, positively asserts that the number of prisoners, British, Portuguese, and Spanish, brought into the Spanish headquarters at Salamanca, amounted on the 20th of November to 3,520, and Napier estimates the total loss from the first attack on Burgos at not less than 9,000 men. There is therefore a great discrepancy between the actual loss and that officially returned, which is said to be accounted for by the fact that the official returns included only the men lost in action.

Had the French Cavalry belonging to the Army of the

South, commanded by Generals Pierre Soult and Tilley, shown a little more enterprise, it is difficult to estimate the disaster which it might have caused. Joseph complained with reason to the Emperor of the inertness of these officers.

Both armies now went into winter quarters, for both sorely needed repose after the prolonged toils of the campaign. On the French side the Army of Portugal established its headquarters at Valladolid; the Army of the South at Toledo; the former being designed to guard the lines of the Esla and Tormes, the latter to cover Madrid by occupying the district from Avila in Old Castille on the north, to La Mancha in the south. The two armies were connected by that of the Centre with the King's Guards at Segovia.

On the part of the Allies, the 5th Spanish Army occupied Estremadura. Sir Rowland Hill, with Erskine's Cavalry Division, the 2nd and Hamilton's Divisions, was quartered at Coria and Plasencia with an advanced post at Bejar to watch the Pass of Banos. Two Divisions in the neighbourhood of Castello Branco supported Hill. The Portuguese Cavalry was posted at Moncorvo. Victor Alten's Cavalry Brigade and the Light Division lined the Agueda. The remainder of Wellington's Corps went into cantonments; the Cavalry along the valley of the Mondego, and the Infantry in that of the Douro; the improvement effected in the navigation of those rivers making food supply an easy task. Headquarters were at Freneda. Two lines of communication connected the flanks of the army and enabled it to concentrate upon any point at short notice. The first ran by the bridge of Alcantara, Moraleja and the Pass of Perales to the Agueda; the second in rear, by Penamacor and Guinaldo.

On the French side the extremities of their line were connected by the Roman road leading over the Gredos mountains from the Upper Tormes by Puerto de Pico to Talavera, and by a second road from Avila to Toledo by Escalona. But in comparing the lateral communications of the opposing forces, it will be noticed that the distance between Alcantara and the Douro was not much above 130 miles, whereas that from Zamora to Ciudad Real is twice as great; and in addition, the roads on which the French depended were practically impassable in winter.

The Allies thus had the advantage of position; and, what was of even greater importance, were able to recruit in the winter by a long period of rest; whereas the French had to maintain an incessant warfare under terrible hardships against the Partidas in order to recover ground which had been perforce abandoned during the concentration against Wellington and Hill.

On the 23rd of November Lord Wellington, in a letter to the Prime Minister, Lord Liverpool, summed up the results of the campaign: "From what I see in the newspapers I am afraid that the public will be disappointed at the result of the last campaign, notwithstanding that it is in fact the most successful in all its circumstances, and has produced for the cause more important results than any campaign in which a British Army has been engaged for the last century. We have taken by siege Ciudad Rodrigo, Badajoz and Salamanca; and the Retiro surrendered. In the meantime the Allies have taken Astorga, Guadalaxara and Consuegra, besides other places taken by Duran and Sir H. Popham. In the months elapsed since January this army has sent to England little short of 20,000 prisoners, and they have taken and destroyed, or have themselves the use of the enemy's arsenals in Ciudad Rodrigo, Badajoz, Salamanca,

Valladolid, Madrid, Astorga, Seville, lines before Cadiz, &c.; and upon the whole we have taken and destroyed, or we now possess, little short of 3,000 pieces of cannon. The siege of Cadiz has been raised, and all the countries south of the Tagus have been cleared of the enemy."

Embittered, however, at the disappointing termination of a campaign the greater part of which had been so brilliant; stung no doubt also by finding that an army under his command should fall so utterly to pieces, Wellington now issued a Circular to the General Officers commanding Brigades and Divisions in which he reflected in strong terms on the conduct of the regimental officers and the men. The circular was intended to be confidential, and read in this light it is not much open to criticism. Unfortunately it was mistaken for a General Order, and being published, raised a storm of anger which some aver cost Lord Wellington his popularity among the troops under his command for ever.

"*To Officers Commanding Divisions and Brigades.*
FRENEDA, 28*th Nov.*, 1812.

"GENTLEMEN,—I have ordered the Army into cantonments, in which I hope that circumstances will enable me to keep them for some time, during which the troops will receive their clothing, necessaries, &c., which are already in progress by different lines of communication to the several Divisions of Brigades.

"But besides these objects, I must draw your attention in a very particular manner to the state of discipline of the troops. The discipline of every army, after a long and active campaign, becomes in some degree relaxed, and requires the utmost attention on the part of the general and other officers to bring it back to the state in which it ought to be for service; but I am concerned to have to observe that the Army under my command has fallen off in this respect in the late campaign to a greater degree than any army with which I have ever served, or of which I have ever read. Yet this Army has met with no disaster; it has suffered no privations which but trifling attention on the part of the officers could not have prevented, and for which there existed no reason whatever in the nature of the service; nor has it suffered any hardships excepting those resulting from the necessity of being exposed to the inclemencies of the weather at a moment when they were most severe.

"It must be obvious, however, to every officer, that from the moment the troops commenced their retreat from the neighbourhood of Burgos on the one hand, and from Madrid on the other, the officers lost all command over their men. Irregularities and outrages of all descriptions were committed with impunity, and losses have been sustained which ought never to have occurred. Yet the necessity for retreat existing, none was ever made on which the troops had such short marches; none on which they made such long and repeated halts; and none on which the retreating armies were so little pressed on their rear by the enemy.

"We must therefore look for the existing evils, and for the situation in which we now find the Army, to some cause besides those resulting from the operations in which we have been engaged.

"I have no hesitation in attributing these evils to the habitual inattention of the officers of the regiments to their duty, as prescribed by the standing regulations of the Service, and by the orders of this Army.

"I am far from questioning the zeal, still less the gallantry and spirit of the officers of the Army; and I am quite certain that if their minds can be convinced of the necessity of minute and constant attention to understand, recollect, and carry into execution the orders which have been issued for the performance of their duty, and that the strict performance of this duty is necessary to enable the Army to serve the country as it ought to be served, they will in future give their attention to these points.

"Unfortunately the inexperience of the officers of the Army has induced many to consider that the period during which an army is on service is one of relaxation from all rule, instead of being, as it is, the period during which of all others every rule for the regulation and control of the conduct of the soldier, for the inspection and care of his arms, ammunition, accoutrements, necessaries, and field equipments, and his horse and horse appointments; for the receipt and issue and care of his provisions; and the regulation of all that belongs to his food and the forage for his horse, must be most strictly attended to by the officers of his company or troop, if it is intended that an army, a British Army in particular, shall be brought into the field of battle in a state of efficiency to meet the enemy on the day of trial.

"These are the points, then, to which I most earnestly entreat you to turn your attention, and the attention of the officers of the regiments under your command, Portuguese as well as English, during the period in which it may be in my power to leave the troops in their cantonments. The commanding officers of regiments must enforce the orders of the Army regarding the constant inspection and superintendence of the officers over the conduct of the men of their companies in their cantonments; and they must endeavour to inspire the non-commissioned officers with a sense of their situation and authority; and the non-commissioned officers must be forced to do their duty by being constantly under the view and superintendence of the officers. By these means the frequent and discreditable recourse to the authority of the provost, and to punishments by the sentence of the courts martial, will be prevented, and the soldiers will not dare to commit the offences and outrages of which there are too many complaints, when they well know that their officers and their non-commissioned officers have their eyes and their attention turned towards them.

"The commanding officers of regiments must likewise enforce the orders of the Army regarding the constant, real inspection of the soldiers' arms, ammunition, accoutrements, and necessaries, in order to prevent at all times the shameful waste of ammunition, and the sale of that article and of the soldiers' necessaries. With this view both should be inspected daily.

"In regard to the food of the soldier, I have frequently observed and lamented in the late campaign the facility and celerity with which the French soldiers cooked in comparison with those of our Army.

"The cause of this disadvantage is the same with that of every other description, the want of attention of the officers to the orders of the Army, and the conduct of their men, and the consequent want of authority over their conduct. Certain men of each company should be appointed to cut and bring in wood, others to fetch water, and others to get the meat, &c., to be cooked; and it would soon be found that if this practice were daily enforced, and a particular hour for seeing the dinners, and for the men dining, named, as it ought to be equally as for parade, that cooking would no longer require the inconvenient length of time which it has lately been found to take, and that the soldiers would not be exposed to the privation of their food at the moment at which the Army may be engaged in operations with the enemy.

"You will of course give your attention to the field exercise and discipline of the troops. It is very desirable

IN THE PENINSULA 625

that the troops should not lose the habits of marching, and the Division should march ten or twelve miles twice in each week, if the weather should permit, and the roads in the neighbourhood of the cantonments of the Division be dry.

"But I repeat that the great object of the attention of the General and Field Officers must be to get the captains and subalterns of the regiments to understand and perform the duties required from them, as the only mode by which the discipline and efficiency of the Army can be restored and maintained during the next campaign.

"I have the honour to be, &c.,
"(Signed)   WELLINGTON.
"To Officers commanding Divisions and Brigades."

Wellington undoubtedly hit the right nail on the head in saying that active service was the occasion of all others in which every regulation for the care of man and horse should be most strictly observed; and neglect of these regulations had been the theme of his censure, times innumerable, since 1809. On the other hand, much of the evil in the present case arose from causes far beyond the control of regimental officers. It was the failure to complete the transfer of the magazines of supply from the Tagus to the Rodrigo-Salamanca line which caused the troops to feel so bitterly the pangs of hunger during the last phase of the retreat.

That the French soldiers could adapt themselves to circumstances with greater facility than could the English was true. A French army was a very complete organisation. It habitually not only reaped the corn, but threshed and ground it in the mills which formed part of its equipment. In regard to cooking, also, the French were far superior to ourselves. But it must be remembered that the French soldier required much less solid meat than did our own men, and that in obtaining his food he was not, as a rule, hampered by ultra consideration for the people of the country. He had no difficulty in making a fire when he could help himself to the doors and beams of the nearest house. The first British soldier doing so would have received 1,000 lashes; the second would have been hanged on the spot.

Much of the disorder was due to the neglect or inefficiency of the Staff Officers, although they were not named in Wellington's censure. Colonel Willoughby Gordon, at the head of them, as his Chief openly admitted, "had not turned his mind to the duties to be performed by the Quartermaster-General of such an Army as this, actively employed in the field, and . . . he has, in fact, never performed them." The duties of a Q.M.G. during a retreat must always be most difficult, and Gordon's incapacity was daily evident. But his case was not solitary. Napier remarks " the discontent of the veteran troops with the Staff Officers. The assembling of the sick men at the time and place prescribed to form the convoys was punctually attended to by the regimental officers—not so by the others, nor by the Commissaries who had charge to provide the means of transport —hence delay and great suffering to the sick, and the wearing out of healthy men's strength by waiting with their knapsacks on for the negligent. When the Light Division was left on the right bank of the Tormes to cover the passage at Alba, a prudent order that all baggage or other impedimenta should pass rapidly over the narrow bridge at that place without halting on the enemy's side was, by those charged with the execution, so rigorously interpreted as to deprive the troops of their ration bullocks and flour mules at the very moment of distribution, and the tired soldiers, thus absurdly denied food, had the further mortification to see a string of commissariat carts deliberately passing their post many hours afterwards. All regimental officers know that discontent thus created is most hurtful to discipline, and it is in these particulars the value of a good and experienced staff is found."

All said and done, however, there was much foundation for Wellington's censure. The wine vaults of Torquemada intoxicated his men during the first days of the retreat before any hardships had been felt; and even previously great want of discipline had been shown by the Divisions engaged in the siege of Burgos. Officers—other than those of the Guards—had deserted their working parties in the trenches; men had wasted their ammunition; and a bad spirit had in general prevailed. Nor had Sir Rowland Hill any greater success in maintaining discipline. He had under him the best Divisions of the Army, and his men had had on the whole a fair period of rest; yet on the very first day of his retirement 500 men of the 4th Division broke their ranks and plundered the roadside houses, and, although not pressed by Soult—who throughout the operations appeared very chary of coming to close quarters with the British—had lost 400 stragglers before reaching the Tormes. Hill's system was based on the personal affection of his men; Wellington's on severity; that of Moore appealed to the moral force of the individual. The last was certainly the correct one, yet each alike broke down under the strain of retreat. It is, however, noticeable that the men of the Light Division, Moore's own pupils, were in private excepted by Wellington from his censure, as, also, greatly to their credit, were the Guards.

The mention of Sir John Moore recalls the many resemblances between his retreat and that of Wellington, enumerated by Napier. Each General saved Andalusia, but was overwhelmed by the concentration of greatly superior numbers. Each was impeded by his Spanish allies. Each retreated for little less than 300 miles. Discipline failed with Moore as with Wellington, and in 1809, as in 1812, the last few marches were the most disastrous.

The difficulties encountered by Moore were, however, much greater than those of Wellington. The retreat of the former was conducted in the depth of winter over rugged and barren mountains. He was opposed by a force three times the size of his own. He had not Joseph, but Napoleon pitted against him. Finally it may be noticed that the extreme caution shown by Soult during the whole of Wellington's retreat seems to prove that he had a vivid recollection of and respect for the way in which a British Army at bay may turn on and rend its pursuers, as happened at Corunna.

CHAPTER XXXV

Position of the French Armies—The Anglo-Sicilian contingent at Alicante—Wellington's reinforcements—He goes to Cadiz—Reorganises the Spanish Army—Returns viâ Lisbon—Affairs of Portugal.

ON the retirement of the Allies behind the Agueda, General Reille was given command of the Army of Portugal, and Count d'Erlon resumed that of the Centre. The former reoccupied Leon and Old Castille, and seized the fortress of Astorga, but not before it had been rendered incapable of defence.

Caffarelli, on returning to the north, had his time pretty fully occupied by the Partidas and the warfare on the sea-coast; but Sir H. Popham had gone away, leaving only a few ships to maintain the blockade; and Santona was relieved by the French.

In Aragon and Navarre the Partidas under Mina were most active, and demanded the unremitting attention of the French Commanders. In Valencia, Villa Campa, from the neighbourhood of Segorbé, operated against Suchet's communications.

After Soult and Joseph had passed through Madrid in pursuit of Hill, Generals Elio and Bassecour, with regular troops and Partidas, entered the capital to the terror of its citizens, and committed great excesses. This exploit should have been stopped by Suchet, who had been asked both by Soult and the King to protect

Madrid; but Suchet, hearing nothing of their progress
and unaware even in November that they had crossed the
Tagus, hesitated, left the capital to its fate, and in consequence found himself in a hornet's nest. Del Parque,
the successor of Virues, crossed the Morena into La
Mancha and came up to Villa Nueva. Bassecour and
Elio, leaving Madrid to the tender mercies of Juan
Martin and his guerillas, came to Albacete and communicated with the Anglo-Sicilian force at Alicante. Suchet
did nothing, and thus it happened that 20,000 Spanish
regular troops were massed on his flank, the contingent
at Alicante was in his front, and Villa Campa menacing
his rear. The Marshal was in a dangerous situation,
which was relieved only by the return of Soult and the
King. On the 3rd of December the latter reoccupied
Madrid and Guadalaxara, while the advance of Soult
upon Toledo made Del Parque retire once more behind
the Morena.

Although Suchet had been burdened with the care of
the sick men belonging to the Armies of the South and
Centre, yet with a disposable force of about 20,000 men
he ought not to have permitted the concentration of the
Spaniards. His inaction was chiefly due to the presence
of the Anglo-Sicilian force, whose numbers and efficiency
he greatly overrated. This unfortunate army had been
afflicted with a succession of incompetent generals, and
was now commanded by William Clinton. While still
before Burgos, Wellington had suggested to Clinton an
attack upon Valencia, but the latter refused to move until
he should be given possession of the citadel of Alicante.
This the Spanish governor at first declined to do, and did
not give way till the 22nd of November. Even then, however, nothing was done although Clinton had 13,000 men
and Elio nearly as many, while the co-operation of the
fleet was ensured. Elio strongly advocated an attack

upon Suchet, but was unable to persuade either Clinton or his successor, William Campbell, who arrived from Sicily on the 2nd of December with a reinforcement of 4,000 men; and at length, not unreasonably disgusted, marched away into Murcia.

Suchet, finding himself to his surprise unmolested, then assumed the offensive in a variety of minor operations; surprised several Spanish detachments, and advanced even to Alicante, where numbers of the Italian soldiers in the British service deserted to him. The pressure of the Partidas upon his communication about Tortosa was still, however, a constant source of annoyance and even of loss.

"As Aragon was now unquiet," observes Napier in summing up the situation (bk. xix. ch. 6), "Navarre and Biscay in a state of insurrection, the French in the interior of Spain were absolutely invested. Their front was opposed by regular armies, their flanks annoyed by the British squadrons; their rear, from the Bay of Biscay to the Mediterranean, plagued and stung by Partidas and insurrections. And England was the cause of all this. England was the real deliverer of the Peninsula. It was her succours thrown into Biscay that had excited the new insurrection in the northern provinces, and enabled Mina and the other chiefs to enter Aragon while Wellington drew the great masses of the French towards Portugal. It was that great insurrection, so forced on, which, notwithstanding the cessation of the regular warfare in Catalonia, gave life and activity to the Partidas of the south. It was the Army from Sicily which induced Suchet to keep his forces together instead of hunting down the bands on his communications. In fine, it was the troops of England who had shocked the enemy's front of battle, the fleets of England which had menaced his flanks with disembarkations, the money and stores of England which had supported his Partidas. Every part of the Peninsula was pervaded by her influence or her warriors, and a trembling sense of insecurity was communicated to the French wherever their armies were not united in masses."

Napier by no means exaggerates the case. Even though driven from Corunna, Lisbon, or Cadiz, every seaport in the Peninsula was, thanks to the naval power of England, at her disposal for the formation of a new base of operations. But the historian might indeed have gone further. He might have pointed out that in the war as a whole (not only in that part of which Spain and Portugal were the theatre), England and France were the principals, the other European powers being little more than puppets compelled, whether they liked it or not, to join in the contest, sometimes on one side, sometimes on the other, as the scale turned in favour of France or England. France fought England for commercial supremacy. But by her commerce England was victorious. France denied the trade of her foe to the continental nations. But the continent could not do without it, and using her commerce as a lever England compelled Prussia, Austria, and Russia again and again—at last successfully—to take up arms against her own enemy. Long before his downfall Napoleon, even when he had arrayed all the Powers against England, saw that he was not strong enough for his object, and attempted reconciliation; but, rightly or wrongly, England refused his repeated overtures.

"Such were the various military events of the year 1812, and the English General, taking a general view of the whole, judged that however anxious the French might be to invade Portugal, they would be content during the winter to gather provisions and wait reinforcements from France wherewith to strike a decisive blow at his army. But these reinforcements never came. Napoleon, unconquered of man, had been vanquished by the elements. The fires and snows of Moscow combined had shattered his strength, and in confessed madness, nations and rulers rejoiced that an enterprise, at once the grandest, the most provident, the most beneficial, ever attempted by a warrior statesman had been foiled—they rejoiced that Napoleon had failed to re-establish unhappy Poland as a barrier against the most formidable and brutal . . . tyranny that has ever menaced European civilisation."

"The catastrophe of Napoleon's Russian campaign was absolutely necessary to the final success of the British arms in the Peninsula. . . . If Russia owed her safety in some degree to that contest, the fate of the Peninsula was in return decided on the plains of Russia; for had the French veterans who there perished returned victorious, the war could have been maintained for years in Spain, with all its waste of treasure and of blood, to the absolute ruin of England, even though her army had been victorious in every battle" (bk. xx. ch. 1).

As Lord Wellington expected, the termination of the campaign caused great disappointment in England and an outcry against himself; for his difficulties were not realised, and the British civilian, careless and ignorant as he is of military matters, has never hesitated to pass harsh judgments upon soldiers who, possibly amid unexampled obstacles, are risking life and reputation to maintain the honour of their country's arms.

The British Ministers also deservedly came in for a share of blame, and were attacked by no one more vigorously than by their late colleague, Lord Wellesley, who, remarking that the administration of the late Mr. Perceval had in it "nothing regular but confusion,"

634 WELLINGTON'S OPERATIONS

accused his successors of gross remissness in supplying their General either with men or money, and maintained that his brother's failure to derive the most decisive results from the late campaign was due solely to this inertness.

The reinforcements received by Wellington during 1812 had been as follows :—

> 5th Dragoon Guards.
> 1st and 2nd Heavy Dragoons K.G.L.
> 1st and 2nd Life Guards.
> Royal Horse Guards.
> 1st Battalion 1st Guards.
> 6th Regiment.
> 20th   ,,
> 91st   ,,
> 42nd   ,,
> 38th   ,,
> 82nd   ,,
>
> *Drafts.*
> Cavalry and Infantry, 6,000.
> Artillery (not more than), 600.

The Cavalry regiments were all weak, averaging hardly 400 sabres. The total of the reinforcements, including the drafts, amounted probably to something over 15,000 of all ranks. But of this number only one fifth part, viz., the 5th D.G., the Dragoons K.G.L., the 38th and 42nd, joined Wellington before the battle of Salamanca. The 82nd joined in August; the Guards on the 24th of October. The Household Cavalry, the 6th, 20th, and 91st Regiments did not come up till the end of the year. The drafts had been sent from England late; and thus it happened that hardly more than a third part of these reinforcements arrived in time to take any part in the campaign. Yet during this period there had been in Great Britain 16 regiments of Cavalry and 45 battalions of Infantry, in addition to foreign regiments, doing nothing but police work in Ireland.

Having seen his troops comfortably settled in cantonments, Lord Wellington paid a visit to Cadiz, where he arrived on the 24th of December, and met the Cortes as well as the leading men of the Spanish Government. "He was received," says Napier, "without enthusiasm, yet with honour." He did his best to induce the Spaniards to put away their private quarrels and devote their whole attention to the prosecution of the war. Incidentally he found it necessary to conciliate the clergy by upholding the Inquisition; and no better instance of the irony of fate could be found than the fact that whereas this institution, abhorrent to the majority of Englishmen, had been abolished by Napoleon, it was now being supported by the representatives of Britain.

In accordance with Wellington's wishes the Spanish Armies were re-organised as follows: The Army of Catalonia, commanded by General Copons, was called the 1st Army. The 2nd was made up of the Divisions of Sarsfield, Duran, Bassecour, Roche and Villa Campa, with Juan Martin's Partidas. It was commanded by General Elio. The 3rd Army, under Del Parque in the Morena, comprised that formerly commanded by Ballesteros. The 4th Army under Castanos, included the troops and Partidas on the west side of Spain between Galicia and Estremadura. Two Reserve Corps were also formed: one under O'Donnell in Andalusia, the other under Lacy, about the Lines of San Roque.

In regard to his own position as Commander-in-Chief of the Spanish forces, Wellington made certain stipulations. They were not faithfully observed, but the following powers were promised him:—1. To have the sole recommendation of officers to be appointed to a chief or divisional command. 2. To suspend and dismiss any

636 WELLINGTON'S OPERATIONS

officer guilty of misconduct. It was also arranged that the Chief of the Staff and the Inspectors General of Cavalry and Infantry should in future be attached to his Staff instead of remaining at the seat of Government.

Wellington's exhortations had little effect on the politicians of Cadiz. A violent struggle was being waged between the Clerical and anti-Clerical parties. The latter was inclined to side with the French, and Napier states—on the authority of a work compiled from the King's correspondence—that not only were many members of the Cortes in correspondence with Joseph, but that early in 1813 a part of Elio's Army, and the whole of that of Del Parque, made proposals to pass over to the French, and that the negotiations were only broken off by reason of the weakness of the French forces in Spain, which, being by this time depleted to fill up the gaps in the Grand Army caused by its disasters in Russia, were being directed by Napoleon to abandon the Peninsula south of the Duero.

On his return journey Lord Wellington spent a few days at Lisbon. Portuguese affairs as conducted by the Regency were going from bad to worse. The Army, owing to gross neglect, had well nigh disappeared; for the Government, believing the country safe from invasion, took little interest in the war. The peasantry was robbed and oppressed by the rulers, and ill used by the detachments of British soldiers marching through the country. Wellington was unremitting in his efforts to bring the guilty parties to trial, but neither magistrates nor peasants would attend the courts martial in person; and though the British Commander made some attempt to get the admission of written evidence legalised in accordance with the practice of Portuguese law, the law officers of the Crown in England refused consent; and indeed the

IN THE PENINSULA

remedy might easily have been worse than the disease.

Another matter of concern was the distress suffered by the poorer Portuguese and Spaniards who had sold supplies to the British Army and had been paid with bills drawn upon the Commissariat Department. When the bills fell due and were presented for payment, it often happened that Wellington had no cash to meet them. At first, however, the bills retained their face value, but British merchants at Oporto, seeing an opportunity for making profit, depreciated their value, and induced the holders to part with them at a discount which amounted to 15 per cent. in Portugal, and 40 per cent in Spain. Although Wellington did his utmost to give priority of payment, when specie came in, to the most needy and deserving, his credit fell and the poor people were almost ruined. To meet the crisis Mr.—by this time Sir Charles —Stuart, guaranteed payment of the bills in full with interest; but even so, the cost of supplies rose and Lord Wellington's financial difficulties were proportionately increased.

The Portuguese Army required thorough re-organisation, and Beresford had been obliged to come away from Burgos for the purpose. Under his energetic management a force of 27,000 men was brought into line in time for the approaching campaign.

In addition to their ordinary duties, Wellington and Stuart set themselves to reform the civil administration of the kingdom. The incidence of taxation was unfair, and its mode of collection extremely faulty. An amelioration and increase of revenue was produced by the efforts of the two Englishmen; but the Regency set itself so strongly against reform that in April, 1813, Wellington found himself compelled to make a personal appeal to the Prince Regent at Rio de Janeiro, calling attention to the state of the Portuguese troops and establishments in consequence of the heavy arrears of pay due to them. The active Army had received no pay since September; the troops in garrison, since June; the Militia, since February, 1812. Yet the British subsidy had been regularly remitted, and the revenues of the State were by nearly 30 per cent. greater than they had been during the last five years. They would have been still larger had Wellington's recommendations as to collection been carried out, for it was not denied that the taxes were evaded, or that his proposals if vigorously executed would have furnished the necessary funds, but "the uniform refusal of the Government of the kingdom to attend to any one of the measures" which he had suggested was his apology for addressing the Prince in person. But this earnest appeal produced little or no effect.

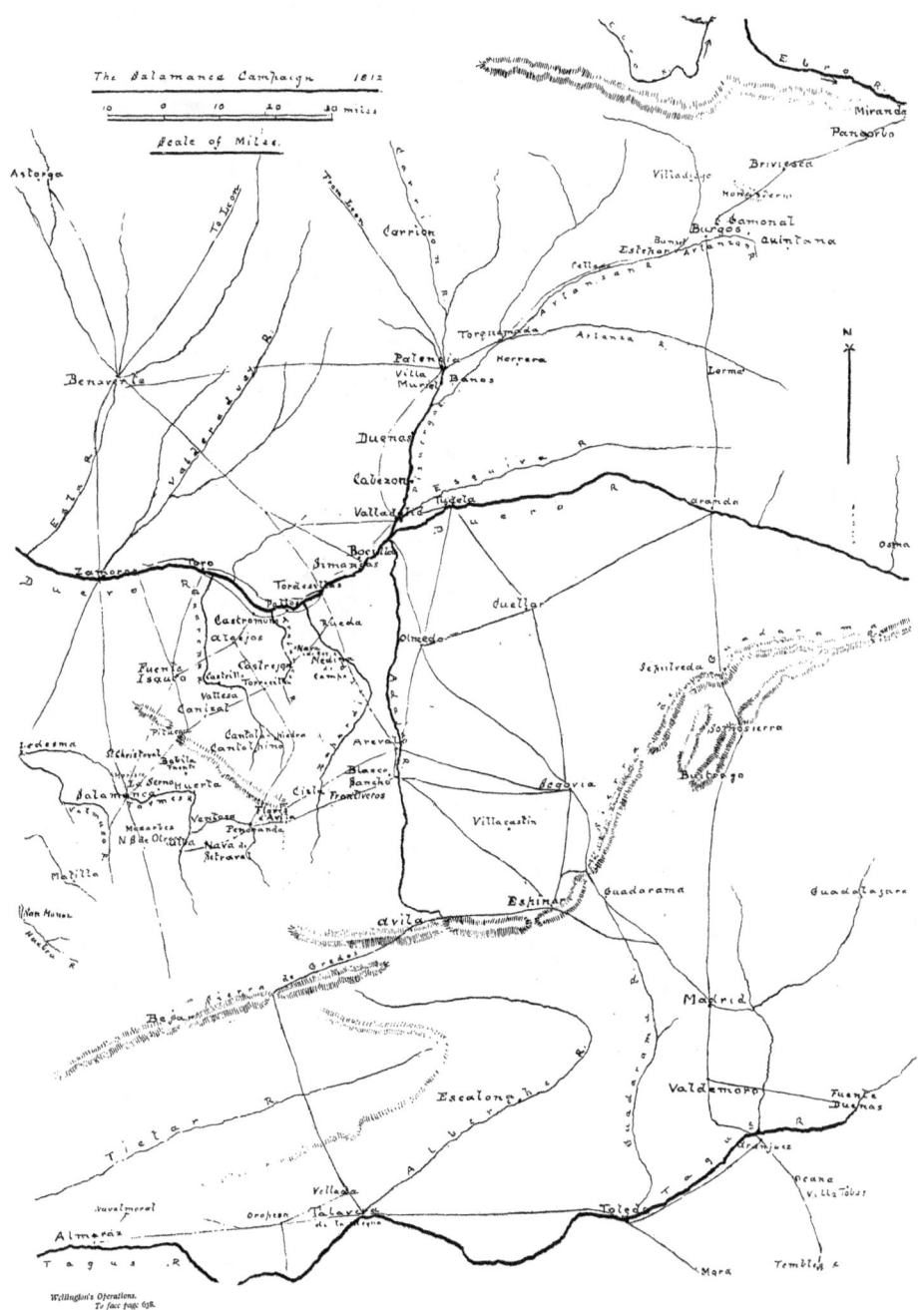

PART VI

THE VITORIA CAMPAIGN AND INVASION OF FRANCE

CHAPTER XXXVI

Position of the French forces at the beginning of 1813—Insurrections in the Northern Provinces—Sir J. Murray takes command of the Anglo-Sicilian force at Alicante—His action at Castalla—Plans suggested to him by Wellington—His failure at Tarragona—Lord W. Bentinck arrives and takes command.

DURING the winter of 1812–13 the French Armies "occupied a line stretching from Valencia to the foot of the Galician mountains." On the extreme right, General Reille held the lines of the Tormes and Esla with the Army of Portugal, occupying Leon and Benavente on the former river, Ledesma, Salamanca and Alba on the latter; with supporting posts at Toro, Tordesillas and Valladolid. A Division under General Foy, posted at Avila to keep an eye on Bejar, marked the left of this Army.

The headquarters of the Army of the South under Soult were at Toledo. A detachment on the Tietar, communicating with Foy by the passes of the Gredos mountains, watched Hill at Coria. A second detachment ocupied Talavera de la Reyna in observation of Morillo and Penne Villemur in Estremadura. A third guarded the issues of the Morena against Del Parque.

The Army of the Centre occupied the Madrid district from the Guadarama range to Cuenca, forming a support to Soult and connecting him with Suchet, who was holding the line of the Zucar in face of the Anglo-Sicilian contingent at Alicante.

The task of Caffarelli and the Army of the North was to guard the line of communication with France. Caffarelli was, however, in dire straits on account of the Partida bands of Biscay and Navarre, composed at this period not only of freebooters, but of men belonging to the best families in Spain. Their operations became serious and impeded the communication with Bayonne to such an extent that, says Napier, "The Minister of War (at Paris) only heard of Joseph receiving his despatches of the 4th of January on the 18th of March, and then through the medium of Suchet. The contributions could not be collected, the magazines could not be filled, the fortresses were endangered, the Armies had no base of operations, the insurrection was spreading through Aragon. . . . the troops, sorely pressed for provisions, were widely disseminated and everywhere occupied, and each General was averse to concentrate his own force or aid his neighbour."

On hearing from Caffarelli the state of affairs Napoleon, whose first care was always for the safety of his line of communications, directed the King to fix his headquarters at Valladolid—holding Madrid merely as a post of observation—to concentrate the Armies of the South, Centre and Portugal, re-establish free communication with France, and put down the Partidas of Biscay and Navarre even if it should be necessary to reinforce Caffarelli with the whole Army of Portugal for the purpose. But Joseph was warned that his attitude towards the Allies was not to be one of passive defence. The available forces were to be held in such a position as to menace Portugal and deter Wellington from embarking any considerable portion of his Army and landing it on the French coast.

King Joseph was an estimable person, most anxious for the welfare of his subjects. He had many difficulties to contend with and many reasonable grounds for complaint. His revenues were seized by the General Officers for the supply of their troops. When he resented their action they said truly enough that they could not see their men die of hunger. In such distress was he for money that the members of his Court were starving; and even his Chief of the Staff, Marshal Jourdan, was reduced to penury. Joseph had very good abilities, but he was no soldier. He utterly failed to realise the critical nature of the situation, occupied himself in negociations with Del Parque; and, not comprehending the danger, delayed until too late to carry out the Emperor's instructions. He quarrelled with all his Army Commanders except Count d'Erlon; and Napoleon finding that in his brother's present frame of mind Soult could do no good, recalled in February, 1813, "the only military head in Spain." The Marshal was succeeded by his Chief of Staff, Count Gazan.

In Catalonia little took place, but in Aragon 40,000 French soldiers were kept employed by the bands of Mina, Villa Campa, Duran and others, while 10,000 more occupied fortified posts. Suchet's line of communications was not less harassed than the Royal Road, and the Partidas severed connection between Valencia and Madrid except by the circuitous route of Saragossa. With such large deductions from his effective strength Suchet could muster only 2,000 Cavalry, 16,000 Infantry and 30 guns on the Zucar. In his front were the Anglo-Sicilian force at Alicante 14,000 to 15,000 strong, and the Spanish Divisions commanded by Whittingham and

Roche; while the Armies under Del Parque and Elio respectively were at Jaen and Hellin, making up a grand total of 50,000 men with 50 guns. But these forces were formidable in appearance rather than reality. They were of indifferent material and badly commanded. Del Parque was closely watched by the French Army of the South at Toledo, and the good faith both of him and Elio was open to grave suspicion.

At the end of February, 1813, Sir John Murray—an officer of whom Wellington had a good opinion (though he afterwards characterised him as wanting in common sense), and of whom Napier remarks that he was good in council but feeble in execution—assumed command at Alicante and at once took the offensive, although in a very half-hearted manner. On the 6th of March he advanced from Alicante, and after a few skirmishes occupied Alcoy and the pass of Albayda. But vacillation followed. Murray decided that he was not strong enough to force Suchet's entrenched camp at Xativa St. Felippe on the right bank of the Zucar, and determined to make himself master of the city of Valencia by means of a maritime expedition.

But before his preparations were complete, orders from Lord William Bentinck recalled 2,000 of his men to Sicily. Among the number was a grenadier battalion detailed for the expedition, which was in consequence abandoned. Meanwhile Suchet was taking the initiative. With a force of 12,000 to 14,000 men and 12 guns he marched in the night of the 11th of April upon Caudete, while another Division under Harispe surprised between 3,000 and 4,000 Spanish troops under General Mijares at Yecla, and defeated them with the loss of 1,700 men.

Murray now took post at Castalla on strong ground three miles behind the pass of Biar. Here, during the afternoon of the 13th, he was attacked—contrary to the Marshal's intentions—by Suchet's advance guard which

IN THE PENINSULA

had captured the Biar pass the day before. The main body of the French joined in. For a time they gained ground, but were at length so strongly encountered and repelled by the 27th Regiment—veterans of Maida—in the centre of the British line, that Suchet abandoned the contest and retired unmolested through the pass of Biar to Fuente de la Higuera. Murray's loss in this partial and unskilful engagement amounted to 400 men and two guns. That of the enemy would seem to have been rather more than double that number of men. Elio took no part in these operations. After the action the Allies advanced to Alcoy, but for the present nothing further occurred.

Sir John Murray now received from Lord Wellington a memorandum of instructions. The objects prescribed were—(1) The possession of the open portion of the kingdom of Valencia. (2) The establishment of a place of arms. (3) The expulsion of the enemy from the Lower Ebro.

Should Murray be able to embark not less than 10,000 Infantry and Artillery, he was directed to attack Tarragona with the largest force available, including the Divisions of Whittingham and Roche. It was calculated that this operation would induce Suchet to weaken his Army in Valencia to such an extent as to enable Elio and Del Parque to occupy a great part if not the whole of the open country. Thus, even should Murray fail at Tarragona, the first of the three objects would be gained and would be secured by Murray's return. If on the other hand Murray succeeded, the second object would be achieved and the attainment of the third would not be far distant.

In a private letter Wellington warned Murray of the inefficiency of his allies. "If," he added, "I had to form a plan for the operations of half the numbers, real soldiers, well equipped and prepared for the field, it would have been of a very different description; but such a plan would not suit, and could not be executed by the instruments with which you have to work." The alternative plan alluded to was to drive Suchet out of Valencia by continually turning his right flank.

On the 24th of April, Del Parque got orders to join Elio; but was persuaded by the latter to make a series of circuitous marches, and the junction of the two was not effected till the 25th of May. Sir John Murray, who had waited to protect Del Parque's march, then at once embarked and sailed on the 31st. His force consisted of about 17,000 men, of whom rather more than half were either British or belonged to the K.G.L., and with him he took the time-honoured siege train with which Wellington had battered the walls of Ciudad Rodrigo and Badajoz.

On the 2nd of June the fleet anchored in Tarragona Bay and the troops disembarked next morning. A detachment under Colonel Prevôt, supported by a Brigade of the 1st Spanish Army, attacked and on the 6th captured the small but important fort of San Felippe de Balaguer, built on a steep rock which commanded the only carriage road from Tarragona to Tortoza.

The siege of Tarragona was begun simultaneously. "The town," says Napier (bk. xiii. ch. 5), "was built upon rocks, steep on the north-east and south, but sinking gently on the south-west and west into low ground. The mole harbour could receive ships of the line, and beyond that there was a roadstead. The upper town, surrounded by ancient walls, crowned the rocks which were again enclosed by a second rampart with irregular bastions running round the whole city. On the east, across the road to Barcelona, was a chain of redoubts connected by curtains, with ditch and covered way; and behind this line

IN THE PENINSULA 645

was a rocky space called the Milagro, opening between the body of the place and the sea. The lower town on the west, separated from the upper by the ramparts of the latter, was protected by three regular and some irregular bastions with a ditch. A square work, called Fort Royal, formed a species of citadel between the two towns, and the whole offered an irregular oblong figure, whose length, lying parallel to the sea, was about 1,200 yards. On the west beyond the walls, a newly constructed line, carried along the coast to the mouth of the Francoli, ended in a large redoubt built to secure access to that river when the ancient aqueducts which furnished the city with water should be cut by the French. . . . On the Francoli side the approach was level, and exposed to the fire of the Olivo, a very large outwork which on the north crowned a rocky tableland, equalling the upper town in height, but divided from it by a ravine nearly half a mile wide, yet united by a double aqueduct. Of irregular construction, the Olivo was 400 yards long with a ditch 24 feet deep and 40 wide."

The garrison consisted of only 1,600 men and the place was at the present time weak, for the rampart of the lower town had been destroyed by Suchet, and Fort Royal was as yet incomplete and unarmed. The issues of the mountain roads from Tortoza, Lerida and Barcelona by which alone the French troops could approach, were blocked by Copons; and their only point of concentration, the open country about Tarragona, was occupied by the Allies, whose numbers were increased by reinforcements from the 1st Spanish Army to 25,000 men. Batteries were erected, and opened fire on the 6th. Although the range—900 yards—was considered too great for the guns of that day, a breach was made in Fort Royal on the 8th. The advantage was, however, not followed up, and the breach was repaired. Rumours began to be circulated of the approach of Suchet, and Murray hesitated. At one moment he decided to go on with the attack. On the 11th his batteries on the Olivo heights again opened fire in concert with the ships in the harbour. He ordered the outworks to be assaulted the same night; but at 10 p.m., when the storming party had paraded and was merely awaiting the signal, he changed his mind, and ordered the guns to be at once removed from the batteries and the siege to be raised.

The cause of this vacillation was the report of Suchet's march from the south and of the approach of a Division under General Maurice Mathieu from Barcelona. Marshal Suchet, having seen Murray's fleet sailing northward past Valencia, quickly concluded that the expedition was intended for Catalonia. Leaving Harispe on the Zucar with 7,000 men and the prospect of being reinforced by Severoli's Division from Teruel, the Marshal marched rapidly northward with a force of 9,000 picked troops, sending word to General Pannetier to join him with his Brigade at Tortosa. He had, however, 160 miles before him, and could hardly expect to reach Tarragona before the 12th or 13th, even by the direct road, but the fact that San Felippe had fallen into the hands of the Allies necessitated a circuitous route. From Barcelona, 70 miles north of Tarragona, Maurice Mathieu could bring 7,000 men in aid, but Mathieu's troops were not concentrated, and it was impossible for him to march on Tarragona until assured that Barcelona would not be the point of attack. A similar force under General Decaen might also be expected, but this officer was at present in the Ampurdam, 130 miles north-east of Tarragona.

Sir John Murray's decision caused so great an outcry in his army that he changed his mind. A few hours later, however, he changed it again and renewed the order to embark. By the night of the 12th his troops were on board ship, and next day stores and horses were embarked without hindrance. No effort was made to save the siege train, and the guns to the number of 18 or 19—dear to Wellington's army from old associations—were spiked and abandoned. Yet on the 13th, at the time of the conclusion of this precipitate retreat, Suchet and Mathieu were respectively 36 and 34 miles distant, the former being behind Perillo, while the latter was actually retracing his steps and marching back towards Barcelona; for, having reached Vendril on the 11th and hearing no sound of guns, he concluded that Tarragona had fallen. He had no news of Suchet, and his force was not strong enough to cope with the Allies singlehanded. Decaen had got no nearer than Rosas, where some British marines had been landed.

Meanwhile Murray's Cavalry and 14 guns under Lord Frederick Bentinck had started for the Col de Balaguer, apparently to get away from their General! In order to recover them Murray sailed to Balaguer and successfully embarked both guns and horsemen. But hearing that Tarragona had after all not been reached by the relieving forces, he sprang from despair to elation. On the 15th he landed his whole army in hopes of striking a blow at Suchet's advance guard, which had got as far as Monroig. But by this time it had been already withdrawn, and Sir John, hearing that Maurice Mathieu (who had learnt that the siege had been raised), having again turned southward, had reached Tarragona and was advancing thence on the Allies, gave orders to re-embark the army on the 17th. At this moment Suchet, alarmed for Valencia, was in full march for that province, and Mathieu, with Murray in his front and Copons on his right flank and rear, should have been annihilated!

But just now Lord William Bentinck appeared in

person and assumed command to the satisfaction of the whole force.

Making all allowance for Murray's inexperience in command, his performance was disgraceful. The curious thing is that he was appointed with the full approval of Lord Wellington, whose combinations he had spoilt at the passage of the Duero in 1809. The expedition to Tarragona was foredoomed to failure. Even before it started the General had lost the confidence of his Staff, of whom General Donkin was the brain and backbone. A man more unfitted for command never existed. Whitelocke's failure at Buenos Ayres was nothing in comparison to that of Murray. The former was indeed cowed and gave in, but not till after a desperate fight and the loss of a fourth of his army. Murray gave in without losing a man. More fortunate than Whitelocke, he was tried by court martial in 1815, when the British public was disposed to leniency; or, to put it in a more complimentary way, when the victories of Wellington had made it strong enough to pardon failure.

What disgusted the Army was the light-hearted way in which he spoke of the loss of his guns. "They were of small value, old iron." But, as Napier truly says, "Great commanders have risked their own lives and sacrificed their bravest men, charging desperately in person to retrieve even a single piece of cannon in a battle. They knew the value of moral force in war. . . ." The feeling is held as strongly at the present day, sometimes even in an exaggerated degree. The abandonment of the guns at Colenso was more sharply criticised than any other episode of the Boer war, although on that occasion the decision of the General was undoubtedly correct and marked his strength of character. "I can certainly recover the guns," he said, "but it would cost me 1,000 men, and I prefer to have the men."

CHAPTER XXXVII

News of the French disasters in Russia—Forces on either side in Spain—Views of the Emperor—The French harassed by Partida warfare during the winter—Wellington's plans—State of his army—Positions of the French forces.

BEFORE leaving Cadiz Lord Wellington had heard of the preliminary misfortunes of the French Army in Russia, and it was not long before the full extent of their terrible losses was realised. Although he had not expected such a *debâcle,* the news did not surprise the British Commander as much as it did other people. He had long foreseen the war between France and Russia and had based upon it his principal hopes of success in the Peninsular contest. In a letter to Lord Bathurst on the 25th of July, 1812, he remarked that if the Czar had any resources and if his men would fight Napoleon would not succeed.

In the first days of 1813 Prussia took up arms against France, and the attitude of Austria became doubtful, but Russia was almost as much exhausted as her enemy by the campaign of 1812. Napoleon was assembling an army even more gigantic than that of the previous year, and the result of the approaching contest could not but be doubtful. So far, however, as Wellington was concerned prospects were bright. He was receiving considerable reinforcements, while the Emperor was no longer able to replace his casualties in Spain.

On the 15th of March, 1813, the General State of the French forces in Spain was as follows:—

	Present under arms.		On Detachment.		Hospital.	Total.		
	Men.	Horses.	Men.	Horses	Men.	Men.	Horses.	Artillery.
Army of the South	36,605	6,602	2,060	1,617	7,144	45,809	8,650	2,601
,, the Centre	16,227	1,966	940	76	2,401	19,568	2,790	451
,, Portugal	34,825	3,654	157	—	7,731	42,713	6,726	2,149
,, Aragon	36,315	3,852	55	—	2,442	38,812	6,123	1,799
,, Catalonia	27,323	1,109	110	—	2,013	29,446	1,884	635
,, the North	40,476	1,978	41	—	8,030	48,547	3,171	830
Reserve of Bayonne	5,877	55	80	—	634	6,591	78	321
Total	197,648	19,216	3,443	1,693	30,395	231,486	29,422	8,786

On the side of the Allies, Wellington had been ordered, much to his annoyance, to send home three weak but experienced regiments of Cavalry, viz., the 4th Dragoon Guards, the 9th and 11th Light Dragoons; and though in their stead he received the Hussar Brigade—10th, 15th, and 18th—counting over 1,500 sabres, it failed to add much to the reputation which it had gained under Sir John Moore.

Three or four Infantry battalions also went home, and were replaced partly by regiments from Cadiz, partly by those from England who had come too late to share in the campaign of 1812.

The military forces of Great Britain had been greatly augmented during the last few years. A return of the Adjutant-General, dated June 8, 1812, gives the following figures for the effective strength of the troops, Regular and Militia, on the dates named:—

	Regular					
	Cavalry.	Foot Guards.	Infantry.	Total.	Militia.	Grand Total.
January 1, 1807	26,261	8,090	144,155	178,506	76,159	254,665
April 25, 1812	27,925	6,873	188,222	223,020	78,489	301,509

Under these circumstances Lord Wellington was surely justified in hoping to receive additional battalions of Infantry. "It will be stated," observes the writer of a Memorandum—apparently Lord Wellesley—printed in Wellington's "Supplementary Despatches," vol. vii. p. 561, "that every disposable man was sent. But why was there not a larger disposable force—Militia, local Militia, &c., &c. ? The Mediterranean, Gibraltar, Sicily, the Cape of Good Hope, &c., might have furnished 30,000 men. . . . The public expectation of an early and a brilliant campaign has been very injudiciously raised, and most unfairly towards Lord Wellington ; for it is very improbable that he should be enabled to realise those expectations. He will probably open the campaign with 75,000 British and Portuguese troops, and will probably find the French forces, as hitherto he has always found them, much stronger than they have been represented or supposed to be." The fact is that even at this period it was not realised that the principal effort of the British nation must be made in the Peninsula. Certain members of the Royal Family and some of the Ministers, unable to concentrate their ideas on one object, had a hankering after operations in the north of Germany. Again and again was the notion combated by Lord Wellington, who showed that many months must elapse before a substantial force could be put in the field on the Elbe or Weser, and that in comparison with the Continental Armies such a force could only be insignificant, and must infallibly play but a subsidiary part. For the moment the project was dropped, but never finally abandoned ; and British troops were eventually employed in Germany, Holland, and Italy, although urgently required by Wellington, then in the south of France.

WELLINGTON'S OPERATIONS

During the early months of 1813 the partisan warfare was kept up in Estremadura, Leon, and Old Castile. In February General Foy failed in an attempt to surprise Hill's advanced post at Bejar; while the success of Sir Rowland at Aroyo des Molinos and Almaraz had made so great an impression on the French Generals that they were in constant dread of some similar exploit; and Napier tells us that the very appearance of a man of the 2nd Division beyond the line of cantonments was enough to make the enemy concentrate! But in March Foy was called away to stem the tide of insurrection in the northern provinces.

In regard to the general position of the French Armies, the Emperor repeatedly expressed the view that the occupation of Madrid (useful for the purpose of watching the Tagus and ensuring a retreat, in case of need, upon Saragossa) was a secondary matter which should be left to a single Division. He declared that Valladolid should be held as the central point, and that troops should be concentrated on the line of the Tormes, thus assuming an attitude of menace towards Portugal, and at the same time covering the line of communications and the Royal Road through Valladolid. Although hardly appreciating the spirit of his brother's instructions, Joseph, in deference to Napoleon's wishes, quitted his capital on the 18th of March for the last time. The Army of the Centre — comprising the Divisions of D'Armagnac, Barrois, and Palombini, Joseph's Guards, Treilhard's Dragoons, and a body of Spanish Infantry — then marched to Burgos; the Army of the South (Conroux, Villatte, Rey, Darricau, and Leval) evacuated La Mancha and took up its quarters between the Duero, Tormes, and Adaja, leaving Leval to hold Madrid, with posts at Toledo and on the Alberche, in case of attack on that flank.

In the north, matters were going badly for the French. The Army of Caffarelli—described by Thiébault as a pandemonium—was unceasingly engaged with the Partidas, but with so little success that towards the end of February Napoleon relieved Caffarelli of his command, replacing him by Clausel, who, with the aid of two Divisions of the Army of Portugal under Foy and Sarrut, defeated the guerilla chief Mina in Navarre, relieved Santona and Bilbao on the sea-coast, and on the 11th of May captured the town of Castro. During this period the main line of communications on the Royal Road was infested by guerilla bands, which captured convoys and intercepted despatches; for at this critical moment the roads were choked with sick men who, had Napoleon's directions been followed, should have been in hospital at Burgos, Pampeluna, &c. At length, after the successive arrival of three other Divisions of the Army of Portugal, the insurrectionary movement, if not quelled, was scotched; and by the end of May Guipuscoa and Biscay were tolerably tranquil. But the Partidas had done their work. Clausel's troops were exhausted by the harassing, ignoble, and wearisome warfare; and before they could be recruited Wellington was in the field and menacing the very existence of the French power in Spain.

During the early winter and spring, the Anglo-Portuguese Army had been enjoying a long period of repose. Early in March an opportunity had presented itself for resuming the offensive and striking a swift and heavy blow, but Wellington was determined not to mar his great combinations by premature action, and with self-restraint refused to embark on an enterprise the result of which, however brilliant, could only be temporary. "French writers," says Napier (bk. xx. ch. 5), misconceiving the character of his warfare, have attributed to slowness in the man what was really the long-reaching policy of a great commander. The Allied Army was not so lithe as the French Army. The latter carried on occasion 10 days' provisions on the soldiers' backs, or it lived upon the country, and was, in respect of its organisation and customs, a superior military machine; the former never carried more than three days' provisions, never lived upon the country, avoided the principle of making the war support the war, paid or promised to pay for everything, and often carried in its marches even the corn for its Cavalry. The difference of this organisation, resulting from the difference of policy between the two nations, was a complete bar to any great and sudden excursion on the part of the British General, and must always be considered in judging his operations.

"If Wellington had passed the Upper Tormes with a considerable force, drawing Hill to him through Bejar and moving rapidly by Avila, he might have broken in upon the defensive system of the King and beat his armies in detail; and much the French feared such a blow, which would have been quite in the manner of Napoleon. But his views were directed by other than mere military principles. Thus striking, he was not certain his blow would be decisive, his Portuguese forces would have been ruined, his British soldiers seriously injured in the attempt; and the resources of France would have repaired the loss of the enemy sooner than he could have recovered the weakness which must necessarily have followed such an unseasonable exertion. His plan was to bring a great and enduring power early into the field, for like Phocion he desired to have an army fitted for a long race, and would not start on the short course."

But as the spring wore on the season approached for

IN THE PENINSULA

the resumption of the offensive on a permanent system. Strategy permitted several lines of operation. (1) Wellington might advance, as in the previous year, by the valley of the Duero. (2) He might do so either by Avila, or, as in 1809, by the valley of the Tagus, and march upon Madrid. (3) Having taken the capital, he might further advance against Saragossa, or join hands with the Anglo-Sicilian Army.

But to each of these alternatives there was an objection. Most of the bridges over the Duero had been destroyed, and the enemy's lines of defence fortified or strengthened. The central provinces of Spain were denuded of supplies; and though by an advance across the Upper Tormes the army would be operating on a single line, and the left flank of the French on the Lower Duero could be turned, the effect of the stroke would be much less than of that which Wellington actually contemplated.

His plan was this: To cross the Duero within the Portuguese frontier, traverse the Tras os Montes, cross the Esla, and, after uniting with the Galicians, advance across the head waters of the Carrion, Pisuerga, and Ebro, keeping up communication with the naval squadron off the coast, and turning not only the positions on the Duero, but the Castle of Burgos itself, while operating directly against the enemy's main line of communications.

To carry out this combination successfully was, however, a most difficult task. Every resource had to be used to deceive the enemy, who, nervous and excited at the suspense, and wearied out by the guerilla warfare, conjured up a thousand fears and, to use a common expression, trembled in his shoes at the blow which was obviously impending, and the more to be dreaded that its direction was inscrutable. The advanced position occupied by Sir Rowland Hill, and the demonstrations of the Partida bands on the Tagus, indicated an invasion either by that line or by Avila. But though the occupation of Coria and Bejar tended to deceive the French, it had this disadvantage, that it prevented Wellington crossing the Duero with his whole force inside Portuguese territory, "for a concentration on his left would have exposed the country on his right to incursions and disclosed his real design." Lord Wellington therefore modified his scheme. Sir Thomas Graham, who had rejoined the Army, was entrusted with six Divisions, and directed to move up the right bank of the Duero and Esla to form a junction with the Galicians; while Wellington himself, calling up Hill, intended with the remainder of the army to advance from the line of the Agueda and force the passage of the Tormes.

The Andalusian Army of Reserve under O'Donnell, now Count de la Bispal, was to co-operate in the movement by crossing the Tagus at Almaraz and marching on Valladolid; for Wellington, unaware that the bulk of the Army of Portugal was across the Ebro, expected vigorous resistance in Leon. The danger of interference on the part of Suchet was guarded against by the arrangements already described for the Anglo-Sicilian force and the 2nd and 3rd Spanish Armies.

Wellington's plans were greatly facilitated by the fact that the Douro, by dint of unremitting labour, was now navigable up to the confluence of the Agueda. A pontoon train of 33 boats had been constructed. Mule transport was supplemented by carts. Tents—three per Company—were carried for the first time, and, strange as it may seem, Wellington and his Principal Medical Officer, Dr. McGrigor, thought in consequence that a blanket would be the sole extra covering necessary for the men. Great coats were therefore by order left behind. The Corps of

Guides (a body hitherto composed entirely of Portuguese), whose duties were partly those of a military police, partly those of escorting despatch riders and keeping up interior communication between columns on the march, was strengthened by troopers from regiments in England to an establishment of 13 officers and 190 non-commissioned officers and men, and placed under command of the celebrated Colonel Sturgeon. Unfortunately it proved a *damnosa hereditas*, and within a twelvemonth the cause of the tragic ending to his brilliant career.

The following abstract of the latest intelligence from Germany is taken from Supplementary Despatches, vol. vii., p. 593 :—

"London, 31st March, 1813.

" Colonel Tettenborn, with 2,000 cavalry of Count Wittgenstein's corps, entered Hamburg on the 18th March. The Russians were received with the most enthusiastic joy.

"Great part of Hanover is in insurrection, and Cuxhaven, Bremen, &c., are open. The advance of the Swedish army has landed in Rügen. . . .

" The enthusiasm in Russia exceeds description. Every class of society is pressing forward to offer service. Very large bodies are organising in the vicinity of Colberg, Berlin, Breslau, and Konigsberg.

" The main Russian army was marching upon Dresden. The King of Prussia and a Prussian corps upon the Oder. General D'Yorell's army near Berlin; Count Wittgenstein's upon the Lower Elbe. . . ."

On the 26th of April the following was the "State" of the Anglo-Portuguese Army. " I never saw the British Army so healthy or so strong, wrote Wellington on the 5th May. . . . We have gained in strength 25,000 men since we went into cantonments in the beginning of December, and infinitely more in efficiency" :—

658 WELLINGTON'S OPERATIONS

Lieut.-General (local General) The Marquis of Wellington, K.G., K.B.
Military Secretary Lieut.-Colonel Lord F. Somerset.
Adjutant-General (Major-General Hon. E. Pakenham.)
 Colonel Lord Aylmer, acting.
Quartermaster-General Brigdr.-General G. Murray.
Commanding Royal Artillery Lieut.-Colonel A. Dickson.
Commanding Portuguese Army Lieut.-General (local Marshal) Sir W. Beresford, K.B.

				Effective Rank and File.	
Cavalry Division Lieut.-Gen. Sir S. Cotton, K.B.	Maj.-Gen. O'Loghlan	1st Life Guards 2nd ,, ,, Royal Horse Guards	... ...	208 224 293	725
	Br.-Gen. Hon. W. Ponsonby	5th Dragoon Guards 3rd Dragoons 4th ,,	... ...	361 353 371	1,085
	Maj.-Gen. Slade	3rd Dragoon Guards Royal Dragoons	... ...	330 366	696
	Maj.-Gen. Long	13th Light Dragoons	... ...	320	320
	Maj.-Gen. G. Anson	12th ,, ,, 16th ,, ,,	... ...	335 390	725
	Maj.-Gen. V. Alten	14th ,, ,, 1st Hussars, K.G.L. 2nd ,, ,,	... ...	380 387 231	998
	Maj.-Gen. Bock	1st Dragoons ,, 2nd ,, ,,	... ...	258 254	512
	Col. Grant	10th Hussars 15th ,, 18th ,,	... ...	505 521 504	1,530
	Colonel Campbell	4th Portuguese 6th ,,	... ...	282 373	655
	Br.-Gen. D'Urban	1st ,, 11th ,, 12th ,,	... ...	298 197 256	746
					7,992

IN THE PENINSULA

The effective numbers of the Cavalry are taken from those of the horses available.

			Effective Rank and File.	
1st Infantry Division. Major-General Howard (temporary)	Maj.-Gen. Howard	1st Foot Guards, 1st Batt. " " " 3rd Batt. 1 Company 60th Rifles ...	355 430 44	829
	Maj.-Gen. Hon. E. Stopford	Coldstream Guards, 1st 3rd Guards, 1st Batt. ... 1 Company 60th... ...	574 746 43	1,363
	Maj.-Gen. Baron Lowe	1st Line Batt. K.G.L. ... 2nd " " " 5th " " "	544 499 476	1,519
	Colonel Halkett	1st Light Batt. " 2nd " " "	584 638	1,222
				4,933
2nd Division. Lieut.-General Hon. W. Stewart	Colonel O'Callaghan	50th Regiment, 1st Batt. 71st " " " 92nd " " " 1 Company 60th... ...	675 873 776 65	2,389
	Br.-Gen. Byng	3rd Buffs, 1st Batt. ... 57th Regiment, 1st Batt. 31st ⎫ 1st Provisional 66th ⎭ Battalion 1 Company 60th... ...	738 679 359 407 56	2,239
		28th Regiment, 1st Batt. 34th " 2nd Batt. 39th " 1st Batt. 1 Company 60th... ...	818 596 768 70	2,252
	Colonel Ashworth	6th Portuguese ... 18th " ... 6th Caçadores ...	1,017 1,216 438	2,671
				9,851

VOL. II.   44

				Effective Rank and File.	
3rd Division. Lt.-Gen. Sir T. Picton, K.B.	Br.-Gen. Brisbane	{	45th Regiment, 1st Batt. 74th ,, 3 Companies 60th Rifles	447 433 194	1,806
	Maj.-Gen. Hon. C. Colville	{	5th Regiment, 1st Batt. 83rd ,, 2nd ,, 87th ,, ,, ,, 94th ,, ...	510 410 501 361	1,782
	Br.-Gen. Power	{	11th Caçadores ... ... 9th Portuguese ... ... 21st ,, ...	277 908 943	2,128
					5,716
4th Division. Lieut.-General Hon. Sir G. L. Cole, K.B.	Maj.-Gen. W. Anson	{	27th Regiment, 3rd Batt. 40th ,, 1st ,, 48th ,, 1st ,, 2nd } 2nd Provisional 53rd } Battalion 1 Company 60th... ...	622 607 449 326 269 56	2,329
	Colonel Skerrett	{	7th Fusiliers, 1st Batt. ... 20th Regiment, ,, 23rd Fusiliers, ,, 1 Compy. Brunswick Oels	639 584 360 39	1,622
		{	11th Portuguese ... ... 1,018 23rd ,, ... 1,094 7th Caçadores 425		2,537
					6,488
5th Division. (Major-General Oswald comdg. temporarily pending arrival of Sir J. Leith)	Maj.-Gen. Hay	{	1st Royals, 3rd Batt. ... 9th Regiment, 1st Batt. 38th ,, ,, ,, 1 Compy. Brunswick Oels	587 633 442 32	1,694
	Br.-Gen. Robinson	{	4th Regiment, 1st Batt. 30th } 4th Provisional 44th } Battalion 47th Regiment, 2nd Batt. 59th ,, ,, ,, 1 Compy. Brunswick Oels	581 250 153 406 759 34	2,183
	Br.-Gen. Spry	{	3rd Portuguese ... ... 15th ,, ... 8th Caçadores	850 875 357	2,082
					5,959

IN THE PENINSULA

			Effective Rank and File.	
6th Division. Maj.-Gen. Hon. *E. Pakenham, afterwards Sir H. Clinton	Colonel Stirling	11th Regiment, 1st Batt. 42nd Highland, ,, 61st Regiment, ,, 79th Highland, ,, 91st Regiment, ,, 1 Company 60th...	609 493 541 602 851 51	3,147
	Colonel Hinde	32nd Regiment, 1st Batt. 36th ,, ,,	511 389	900
	Br.-Gen. Madden	8th Portuguese ... 12th ,, ... 9th Caçadores ...	942 1,095 432	2,469
				6,516
7th Division. Lieut.-General Lord Dalhousie	Br.-Gen. Barnes	6th Regiment ... 24th } 3rd Provisional 58th } Battalion 9 Coys. Brunswick Oels...	944 293 245 378	1,860
		51st Regiment ... 68th ,, ... 82nd ,, ... Chasseurs Britanniques .	374 419 470 768	2,031
	Br.-Gen. Le Cor	7th Portuguese ... 19th ,, ... 2nd Caçadores ...	784 890 428	2,102
				5,993
Light Division Major-General Baron C. Alten	Maj.-Gen. Kempt	43rd Regiment, 1st Batt. 95th Rifles, 1st Batt. ... ,, ,, 3rd ,, ...	895 532 349	1,776
	Maj.-Gen. Vandeleur	52nd Regiment, 1st Batt. 95th Rifles, 2nd Batt. ...	819 398	1,217
		1st Caçadores ... 3rd ,, ... 17th Portuguese ...	602 453 928	1,983
				4,976

* General Pakenham did not take up his duties as Adjutant-General until after the battle of Vitoria. Lord Aylmer was at the head of the A.-G. department in the meanwhile.

662 WELLINGTON'S OPERATIONS

			Effective Rank and File.	
Portuguese Division.	2nd Portuguese	...	... 1,115	
	14th ,,	...	... 986	
				2,101
Lieut.-General Silveira	4th ,,	...	... 1,106	
	10th ,,	...	... 1,174	
	10th Caçadores	...	... 279	
				2,559
				4,660
Brigadier-Gen. Pack	4th Caçadores	...	... 471	
	1st Portuguese	...	... 699	
	16th ,,	...	... 809	
				1,979
				1,979
Brigadier-Gen. Bradford	5th ,,	...	... 469	
	13th ,,	...	... 786	
	24th ,,	...	... 1,074	
				2,329
				2,329
GRAND TOTAL	...	... ...	67,892.	

Making the usual allowance for officers, sergeants, artillery, dismounted troopers, &c., we get a grand total of 81,000 of all ranks and arms. Of this about one half belonged to British regiments. It will be noticed that nearly all the 2nd Battalions—of which Wellington's Army had in the first instance been mainly composed, and which in those days were intended for little else than recruiting depôts filled up with Militiamen—had been replaced by 1st Battalions.

The 4th Spanish Army, 40,000 strong, under Castanos was destined to act in conjunction with Wellington. It included the Divisions of Morillo, Penne Villemur, Downie and Carlos D'Espana, who were to come up with Hill from the Agueda, Giron's Galicians, Porlier's

IN THE PENINSULA

Asturians, and the Partidas of Julian Sanchez, Longa and Mina.

The remainder of the Allied forces in Spain comprised Murray's Army, of about 18,000 men, at Alicante; the 1st Spanish Army, 10,000 men, under Copons in Catalonia; the 2nd (made up of the Divisions of Villa Campa, Bassecour, Duran and Juan Martin), 20,000 strong, under Elio in Murcia; the 3rd Army, comprising 12,000 men under Del Parque in the Morena; and the 1st Army of Reserve under the Count de la Bispal, 15,000 strong, in Andalusia.

The combined armies with which the Allies were about to begin the campaign thus made up a grand total of roughly 200,000 men.

The numbers of the French, on the other hand, amounted, as we have seen, in the middle of March to nearly 230,000 men, exclusive of the King's Guards. In view of the little reliance to be placed on the Spanish troops, the balance appears, at first sight, still more in favour of the French. But of their forces a very heavy proportion was employed in guarding either the main roads to France or the interior communications, and large drafts were being made by Napoleon to strengthen his young levies in Germany, where with a prodigious army of 700,000 men and 1,200 guns he was once more taking the field.

Making allowance for these drafts and for losses in the Partida warfare, Napier reckons the "sabres and bayonets" of the French in Spain at 160,000, of whom 110,000 comprised the Armies of the North, South, Centre, and Portugal. Making the usual allowance for officers, artillerymen, &c., &c., the numbers of the French would thus be about equal to those of the Allies, but the latter were in a position to bring the larger force on to the field of battle.

At the beginning of May Reille had sent a 5th Division to strengthen Clausel, and making Valladolid his headquarters, remained there with his sole remaining Division and the Artillery. His Cavalry guarded the line of the Esla. The headquarters of the Armies of the South and Centre were respectively at Arevalo and Segovia. King Joseph himself was at Valladolid, and had, in the valley of the Duero, 9,000 Cavalry, 35,000 Infantry, and over 100 guns, but, in disregard of his brother's instructions, the troops were scattered over a length of 180 miles, rapid concentration was impossible, and every circumstance presaged disaster.

Just as the campaign was about to begin some slight changes of position were made. On the 11th of May, D'Armagnac's Division of the Army of the Centre came up to Valladolid, while that of Villatte, belonging to the Army of the South, advanced to the line of the Tormes and occupied it from Ledesma on the north to Alba on the south, a distance of about forty miles. The front of the French was thus marked by the Esla and Tormes. Three other Divisions were posted in the valley of the Duero, about Zamora and Toro. Five Divisions of the Army of Portugal were, as stated, helping to repress the insurrection in the north, while those of Conroux at Avila, and Leval at Madrid, from the Army of the South, were too far distant to be available at the outset.

CHAPTER XXXVIII

Wellington's administrative difficulties—He assumes the offensive—The enemy retires—The wings of the Allied Army unite at Toro—Destruction of the Castle of Burgos—Wellington crosses the Ebro and marches down the left bank—Joseph retires into the basin of Vitoria.

THE spring was dry and the season late, but towards the end of April the green forage was sufficiently grown to admit of the opening of the campaign. The Anglo-Portuguese Army was in good health and in a high state of efficiency. Some of the unreliable General Officers had been sent home; discipline had been restored.

But money was very scarce, for the British Government had failed to supply the specie essential to the requirements of the Army. It was impossible to pay the time-expired men the bounty to which they were entitled on re-engagement; and more important still, the Spanish muleteers, who had waited months and months for their pay, at length lost patience and many deserted, while the Portuguese troops applied in thousands for the discharge which they could now legally claim. It required all Wellington's tact and energy to cope with the emergency and pacify the discontent.

But other annoyances arose. The Admiralty, which throughout the war was a hindrance rather than a help to Wellington, did not take the trouble to guard the Portuguese coast, but allowed French or American privateers to cut off the supplies of wheat imported from South America or Egypt; while to make matters worse, the British Ministers took this opportunity to interfere with Lord Wellington's trade in corn, and, at the instance of British merchants at Lisbon, vetoed the rules which he had laid down for the negotiation of the bills drawn on the Commissariat in payment of supplies.

The various difficulties and obstacles having been at last disposed of, Lord Wellington was ready to begin that astonishing campaign which at the outset found the enemy close to the Portuguese frontier and ended by hurling him beyond the Pyrenees.

On the 18th of May, Sir Thomas Graham was entrusted with the left wing of the army comprising the Cavalry Brigades of Anson, Ponsonby, Bock, Grant, and D'Urban (Portuguese), the 1st, 3rd, 4th, 5th, 6th and 7th Infantry Divisions and the unattached Portuguese Brigades of Pack and Bradford. To this wing, which mustered about 45,000 sabres and bayonets, was added the pontoon train, a battery of reserve artillery, an 18-pounder battery, and the reserve ammunition.

Wellington in person took command of the right wing, about 30,000 strong. It consisted of the Household Cavalry, the Cavalry Brigades of Fane (who had just come out again from England, *vice* Slade), Victor Alten and Long; the 2nd and Light Divisions; the 6th Portuguese Cavalry of Campbell's Brigade, Silveira's (late Hamilton's) Portuguese Infantry Division, and 3 batteries Portuguese Artillery; Julian Sanchez' regiment of Spanish Cavalry and Morillo's Division of Infantry. Of these the units composing Hill's Corps were at a distance, but were ordered up without delay.

Towards the end of April Anson, Ponsonby, and Bock, who were occupying winter quarters on the Lower Douro and Vouga, had received a route to traverse the Tras os Montes. The Infantry of the left wing followed suit, and by the 24th of May, after trying marches over nearly impassable mountain tracks, Graham's wing was occupying a line on a front of forty miles extending from Braganza on the left to Miranda de Douro on the right. The force was formed in three columns. On the left, the Cavalry Brigades of Anson and Ponsonby, the 1st Division and Pack's Brigade held Braganza. In the centre, Bock, D'Urban, the 5th Division and Bradford were at Outeiro; the 3rd Division at Vimioso. On the right, the 6th and 7th Divisions, with the 18-pounder Battery, occupied Malhada and Miranda de Douro, which the Hussar Brigade and 4th Division, who formed a link between the two wings, were rapidly approaching.

On receipt of further orders Graham crossed the Portuguese frontier. On the 29th, the three columns, covered by their Cavalry, were at Tabara, Losilla and Carvalajes overlooking the Esla, the front being now contracted to twelve miles, for resistance in force was expected. Magazines were formed at Braganza and Miranda. General Giron had been ordered simultaneously to Benavente with his Galicians.

The campaign had now begun in earnest throughout the Peninsula. Del Parque was putting the 3rd Spanish Army in motion to join Elio. De la Bispal, in Andalusia, was marching to cross the Tagus at Almaraz. Hill, with Long's Cavalry Brigade, a Battery R.H.A., the 2nd Division and Morillo's Spanish Division, was at Bejar on the 20th and had orders to be at Fuenteroble, on the road to Salamanca, on the 24th. Silveira's Division, coming up from Payo and Penaparda by way of Saugo and Morasverdas, was at Moraleja with two batteries of Artillery on the 23rd.

668 WELLINGTON'S OPERATIONS

Graham's line of advance had turned the right flank of the French at Salamanca. The next object was to re-unite the two wings of the British Army. To this end Wellington, on the 22nd, broke up his quarters at Freneda and reached Ciudad Rodrigo the same day. On the 23rd he was at Tamames; on the 25th at Matilla. Next day, Wellington, Hill, and Morillo, "in admirable concert," converged on Salamanca from Matilla, the Moraleja road and Alba de Tormes respectively. Villatte, determined to force the Allies to display their force, held on to the town, but only to find Fane crossing the Tormes in his rear at the ford of Santa Marta and threatening his line of retreat. A hasty retirement on Babila Fuente was inevitable, but effected only with a loss of 400 men and 7 guns.

During the 27th and 28th Wellington advanced northward in the direction of Zamora and Toro, which were occupied respectively by Digeon's Brigade of Dragoons and Darricau's Division. On the 29th his lordship crossed the Duero at Miranda "in a basket slung on a rope stretched from rock to rock, the river foaming hundreds of feet below," and went off to join Graham, leaving Hill in command of his own wing, with orders in case of need to abandon the connection with Salamanca, and move on the Duero at Barca de Villa Campo, which was to be the point of communication between the two wings. On the 30th Wellington reached Carvajales and joined Sir Thomas, who was in difficulty, for the Esla was swollen by heavy rains. However, next day the Cavalry successfully forded the river, and the Infantry crossed by the pontoon bridge.

In the meantime Gazan had called up Conroux from Arevalo to the Trabanços, intending to hold the line of that river; but finding no good position, concentrated the Divisions of Conroux, Rey, and Villatte on the 28th behind the Zapardiel. Digeon at the same time assembled his Dragoons at Zamora, and Darricau his Division at Toro. On the 30th Gazan retired across the Duero at Tordesillas, destroying the bridges. But his Army was still incomplete, for Leval, who had quitted Madrid on the 27th, had not as yet arrived. Of the Army of the Centre, D'Armagnac's Division was on the 2nd of June at Rio Seco, the remainder on the march from Segovia and Sepulveda to Puente Duero; while of the Army of Portugal one Division only was at Rio Seco, for the others were still with Clausel.

The idea of Joseph was to oppose Hill with the Army of the South, and Graham with that of the Centre, holding Reille as a support to either, according to circumstances.

On the 1st of June Graham's advance guard entered Zamora unopposed, for Darricau had destroyed the bridge and retired beyond Toro. After breaking the bridge at that town also, Darricau's rearguard was overtaken on the 2nd at the village of Morales by the Hussars, and broken in a vigorous charge.

The junction of Wellington's two wings was now assured, but the loss of two days on the Esla marred his combination. Had Graham effected the passage on the 29th, and moved at once on Palencia, while Hill moved by the left bank of the Duero upon Valladolid, the enemy's Divisions might well have been attacked and destroyed in detail.

On the 3rd of June Lord Wellington brought his right wing across the Duero at Toro, and halted to close up his rear and give time for Giron with his Galicians (who had reached Benavente on the 31st) to come up into line. The halt is an instance of the extreme caution habitual to the British Commander. Napier considers it justified, but thinks that as a matter of fact more would have been gained by a rapid advance, for the parks of the Armies of Portugal and the South, and large convoys retiring northward from Madrid were crowded together at the confluence of the Duero and Pisuerga near Valladolid, while D'Erlon's Divisions and that of Leval were in no condition to resist an attack.

While Wellington halted the enemy completed his concentration, but the King, fearing for his right, resolved to withdraw. Gazan, in consequence, retired on Torre-Lobaton and Penaflor; D'Erlon on Dunas, at the confluence of the Pisuerga and Carrion; Reille on Palencis.

Wellington had now achieved the initial object of his combination, which, as he afterwards observed, "required more arrangement and more art than anything he had ever done before," and to which the delay of even an additional day might have been fatal.

"Thus," remarks Napier (bk. xx. ch. 7), "the line of the Duero was mastered, and those who understand war may say if it was an effort worthy of the man and his Army. Trace the combinations, follow Graham's columns, some of which marched 150, some 250 miles through the wild Tras os Montes. Through these regions, held to be nearly impracticable even for small corps, 40,000 men, infantry, cavalry, artillery, and pontoons, had been carried and placed, as if by a supernatural power, upon the Esla before the enemy knew even that they were in movement! . . . Had the French even been concentrated the 31st, behind the Esla, the Galicians were then at Benavente . . . and the Asturians were at Leon, where the Esla was fordable, and the passage of that river could have been effected by similar combinations on a smaller scale; for the French had not numbers simultaneously to defend the Duero against Hill, the Lower Esla against Graham, and the Upper Esla against the Spaniards. . . .

IN THE PENINSULA 671

But if Napoleon's instructions had been worked out by the King during the winter, this great movement could not have succeeded, for the insurrection in the north would have been crushed, or so far quelled that 60,000 French Infantry and 10,000 Cavalry, with 120 pieces of artillery, would have been disposable. Such a force held in an offensive position on the Tormes would have compelled Wellington to adopt a different plan of campaign. If concentrated between the Duero and the Esla it would have baffled him on these rivers, because operations effected against 35,000 Infantry would have been powerless against 60,000."

"In the meantime," says another commentator, "the French had been completely deceived as to Wellington's real intentions. At one time, on the 7th of May, they suspected an advance along the valley of the Tagus, Leval, at Madrid, reporting that 25,000 men were moving in that direction. Towards the end of the month Reille thought the whole of the Allied Army was on the Esla, but Graham's delay after reaching Carvajales made him doubt the strength of the Allies and their inclination to cross the river, and he thought the main attack would take place on the Tormes. Gazan at first expected the whole force would operate by the Esla; on the 14th he believed that Hill was to move to Avila to cut off Leval from Madrid, while Wellington attacked by Salamanca. On the 24th he grasped the real situation; on the 26th he was again in doubt. On the 27th, hearing of the capture of Salamanca, he retired, intending to cross the river near Tordesillas, with a view to concentrate the whole Army of the South on the right bank, but Leval had not yet come up, being hampered by the large convoy he had to protect. (Leval quitted Madrid on the 27th of May . . . made a rapid march across the Guadarama Pass, and, moving by Segovia and Cuallar, passed the Duero at

Puente de Duero, and joined the main army at Valladolid on the 3rd of June.)

"Thus the French right extended along the Esla and the Carrion, while their left reached nearly to Segovia and Sepulveda, at a time when their right was practically turned by Graham, and their main body threatened by Hill.

"When Reille fell back his two Divisions * took post at Medina de Rio Seco. Gazan, who had been at Arevalo when he heard of the passage of the Tormes, fell gradually back and eventually crossed the Duero, reaching Tordesillas on the 31st. During these movements D'Erlon's troops were partly between Puente Duero and Valladolid; a Division was at Tudela, and large convoys were on the Lower Pisuerga. Had Graham's movements been as rapid as Wellington intended, *i.e.*, had he been able to cross on the 29th of May, Hill might have pierced the French left centre and destroyed D'Erlon's troops in detail. Graham, who was moving on Palencia, would have cut the French line of communications; then turning against the Armies of Portugal and the South, these would have been caught between himself and Hill, and the disaster of Vitoria would have taken place three weeks earlier.

"On the 30th of May Joseph's idea was to oppose Wellington's main body by Gazan while D'Erlon held the rest in check, Reille being used to support one or the other wing.

"Wellington's halt of the 3rd gave time to the French to rally on the northern side of the Duero, and on the same date Gazan moved on Torrelobaton, D'Erlon upon Duenas, Reille upon Palencia. The bridges at Tudela and Puente Duero were destroyed, and those at Cabezon

* The 2nd Division was that of D'Armagnac, of which for the moment he took command.

IN THE PENINSULA 673

and Simancas on the Pisuerga" (unpublished Précis of the Vitoria Campaign, by Lieutenant-Colonel W. H. James).

On the 4th of June Lord Wellington resumed his advance in four columns. Vide next page.

The right flank of the Allies in their advance was guarded by the Cavalry of Julian Sanchez and supported by the reserve of the Count de la Bispal, who had crossed the Tagus at Almaraz on the 30th of May, and conformed to the general movement of the Army.

Meanwhile the French had found themselves in no condition to stem the flowing tide. On the 6th they were behind the Carrion; next day behind the Pisuerga. The King still cherished hopes of fighting a battle in defence of his crown near Burgos. He had by this time collected 55,000 men, and, ten days previously, had summoned to his aid the Army of the North and the Divisions of Foy and Sarrut, and called up Suchet to Saragossa. But all in vain. The Castle of Burgos was reported untenable. Nothing was heard of Foy and Clausel, who were engaged respectively in Guipuscoa and Aragon. Sarrut was pursuing Longa in the Montana. Suchet was occupied with Del Parque and Sir John Murray.

Under these circumstances the King had no alternative but to abandon Burgos and retire beyond the Ebro. The Royal Road was choked up with the contents of the magazines at Madrid, Burgos, and Valladolid; with the impedimenta of the Armies of the South, Centre, and Portugal, and with the baggage of the Spanish families who had adhered to Joseph and were now fleeing to France for refuge. To add to the confusion, a convoy of treasure sent from Bayonne for the King was met on the road.

Continuously pushing forward his left, Wellington

Date	Giron's Spanish Corps. (Three Divisions.)	Left Column. Sir T. Graham. (Cavalry Brigades of Bock and Anson; 1st and 5th Divisions; Portuguese Brigades of Pack and Bradford.)	Centre Column. Headquarters. (Household Cavalry; Cavalry Brigades of Ponsonby & D'Urban; Light, 3rd, and 4th Divisions; Reserve Artillery, 2 Batteries.)	Right Column. Sir R. Hill. (Hussar Brigade; Cavalry Brigades of Long, Fane, and V. Alten; 6th Portuguese Cavalry; 2nd, 6th, 7th, Silveira's and Morillo's Divisions.)
June 4		Villar de Frades (? Freches)	La Mota	Morales
,, 5		Rio Seco	Castro-monte	Torre-lobaton
,, 6	Gaton and Villaramiel	Vellarias and Torre de Marmajon	Ampudia	Mucientes
,, 7	Becerril	Grixota	Palencia	Duenas
,, 8	Valloldo	San Cebrian and Pena de Campos	Amusco	Torquemada
,, 9	Villasarracino	Santillana and Osorno	,,	Villalaco
,, 10	Herrera	Zarzosa	Melgar de Fernamental	Pedrosa del Principe
,, 11		Sotresgudo	Castro Xerez	Barrio de Santa Maria
,, 12		La Piedra	,,	Bilviestre
,, 13		San Martin de Helines, on the Ebro	Villadiego	Villarejo
,, 14	Polientes, on the Ebro		Masa	Montorio
,, 15	Soncillo	Villarcayo	Quintana, near Puente de Arenas on the Ebro	Villaescusa de Butron
,, 16	Quintanilla de Pienza	La Cerca	Medina de Pomar	Villalain
,, 17	Villasana de Mena	San Martin de Loza and Lastras de Teza	Quincoces	La Cerca
,, 18	Valmaseda	Near Berberana	Berberana	Membligo

IN THE PENINSULA

crossed the Upper Pisuerga on the 8th, 9th, and 10th, and outflanked Reille—whose troops formed the left wing of the enemy in his retreat—at Castro Xerez, while Hill advanced by the direct road to Burgos. Reille, however, succeeded in gaining the Royal Road, and on the 9th took up a position behind the Hormanza to defend the fortress. Here he remained for three days, with D'Erlon and Gazan in support; and as the French had concentrated 50,000 men, while Hill had only 30,000, and Wellington's left and centre were a day's march distant at Villa Diego and Castro Xerez, the enemy had a good opportunity of making a counter-attack which might have driven Hill back to the Pisuerga, and ought to have gained time for the arrival of Clausel and Foy. The King, however, did nothing, and on the 12th, Reille was attacked in front and flank by the advance guard of the Allies, but made good his retreat, with little loss, by the Baniel bridge over the Arlanzan. The retirement was continued in the night to Pancorbo, where a strong position was taken up by the combined Armies. The fortress of Burgos was in no condition for defence, and the Castle was blown up at daybreak on the 13th with such haste as to cause the death of 300 French soldiers passing underneath in column of route.

The report of the explosion is said to have been audible at a distance of fifty miles. On hearing it, Lord Wellington took instant resolution. News had reached him that the victories of Napoleon at Lutzen and Bautzen had been followed by an armistice. As a matter of politics it was everything to prevent the armistice being followed by peace between France, Russia, and Prussia. From the military point of view, the present was a grand opportunity to drive the French out of Spain before they could be reinforced, whatever might be the outcome of the truce; and in order that that outcome should be favourable, a decisive victory was essential. Disregarding, therefore, the remonstrances of his Staff, who urged that enough had been done for the present campaign, Wellington, inclining to the left, marched towards the sources of the Ebro, crossed it on the 14th with his left, and was followed next day by the centre, while Hill with the right wing crossed simultaneously at Puente Arenas, lower down.

A result of this flank march was to cut off the French from the sea-coast; and of the ports west of San Sebastian, Santona and Bilbao in a short time alone remained in the hands of the enemy. Lord Wellington was now able to abandon the old and cumbrous line of communications with Portugal and form a new base of operations at Santander, on the Bay of Biscay, whence his line was not only short, but descended almost perpendicularly on that of the French.

Taking advantage of this fact, the British Commander determined to roll up the enemy's line. Bringing his left round, he poured his troops through mountain pass and defile into the main road leading from Bilbao to Frias, directly on the flank of the French.

"One while," says the author of "The Bivouac," "the columns moved through luxurious valleys intersprinkled with hamlets, vineyards, and flower-gardens; at another they struggled up mountain ridges or poured through Alpine passes overhung with topping cliffs. . . . If the eye turned downwards, there lay sparkling rivers and sunny dells; above rose naked rocks and splintered precipices; while moving masses of glittering soldiery, now lost, now seen, amid the windings of the route, gave a panoramic character to the whole that can never fade from the memory of him who saw it." Yet through this almost impassable country, furnishing most formidable positions for defence, the Allies marched unopposed. "Neither the winter gullies," to quote Napier's vivid description, "nor the ravines, nor the precipitate passes among the rocks, retarded even the march of the artillery; where horses could not draw, men hauled; when the wheels would not roll, the guns were let down or lifted with ropes; and strongly did the rough veteran infantry work their way through those wild but beautiful regions. Six days they toiled unceasingly; on the seventh, swelled by the junction of Longa's Division and all the smaller bands which came trickling from the mountains, they burst like raging streams from every defile and went foaming into the basin of Vitoria."

Meanwhile the King, thinking himself secure among "the impregnable rocks, the defile and forts of Pancorbo," had extended his line for convenience of supply, retaining outposts in advance of the Pancorbo defile, in the hope of resuming the offensive on the arrival of Clausel and Foy. Gazan occupied the centre, supported on his right by Reille at Espejo, and on his left by D'Erlon, whose flank guards reached as far as the Burgos-Logrono road. Reille, having been joined by Sarrut, had now three Divisions in hand. That of Maucune was posted at Frias, where he was in touch with the Army of the South; while on his right La Martinière and Sarrut occupied Espejo and Osma respectively.

On the 15th Clausel received the King's first letter. He at once stopped the pursuit of Mina, called in his flying columns, and made ready to march *via* Logrono to the Ebro. But after providing the necessary garrisons he found the Army of the North reduced to 5,000 men, while the addition of the two Divisions under Taupin and

Barbout, lent temporarily by Reille, raised his available force only to 14,000.

The King continued to hold his position while the enormous mass of "impedimenta" was concentrated in the "basin of Vitoria." He was reinforced by a few small garrisons from the north, and still hoped for success. But Marshal Jourdan, Chief of the Staff, warned him that Wellington was probably manœuvring to turn his right, and Joseph so far deferred to his opinion that he directed Reille to concentrate at Osma, north of Espejo, on the morning of the 18th, and if possible to occupy Valmaceda; but if this should be impracticable, to march on Bilbao and collect Foy's Division and the garrisons in Biscay.

In compliance with his orders, Reille started with the Divisions of Sarrut and La Martinière, but on arrival at Osma found himself already forestalled by Graham with the 1st, 3rd, and 5th Divisions. A skirmish ensued, but at 2.30 p.m. Maucune had not appeared from Frias, and Reille, hearing musketry in his rear, retired towards Espejo, where he met the beaten masses of Maucune, who had been surprised on the march and defeated with the loss of 450 men by the British Light Division. Reille then made good his retreat behind Salinas de Anara.

It was now obvious that a large portion, if not the whole of the Allied Army was already in rear of the French line. An instant retirement was inevitable. The Armies of the South and Centre fell back during the night on Arminon, behind the Ebro. Thence it was necessary to move by the left bank of the Zadorra, shut in on the right hand by the rugged heights of Puebla and on the left by those of Morillas, threading for two miles the defile of La Puebla de Arganzon.

"Here," observes Napier (bk. xx. ch. 7), "was a noble army driven like sheep before prowling wolves, yet in every action the inferior Generals had been prompt and skilful; the soldiers brave, ready, and daring, firm and obedient in the most trying circumstances of battle. Infantry, artillery, and cavalry, all were excellent and numerous, and the country strong and favourable for defence, but that soul of armies, the mind of a great commander, was wanting, and the Esla, the Tormes, the Duero, the Carrion, the Pisuerga, the Arlanzan, seemed to be dried up; the rocks, the mountains to be levelled; Clausel's strong positions, Dubreton's thundering castle, had disappeared like a dream, and 60,000 veteran soldiers, though willing to fight at every step, were hurried with all the tumult and confusion of defeat across the Ebro."

But Wellington's centre, approaching the right bank of the Bayas at Morillas, was nearer the northern issues of the Puebla defile than were D'Erlon and Gazan. Reille was consequently ordered to take post at Subijana de Morillos, on the left bank of the Bayas, and cover the movement of his colleagues. On his steadfastness depended the fate of the French Armies. Wellington had a grand opportunity of inflicting a terrible disaster upon the enemy. Had Reille been at once driven from his position, the British centre would have overtaken Gazan and D'Erlon while entangled in the defile, and a detachment of Hill's Corps should have attacked their rear simultaneously from the direction of Miranda. But the Allied troops were exhausted by a long march, and the 4th Division did not reach Espejo before nightfall. Next morning Cole attacked Reille in front while the Light Division turned his right flank. He fell back for four miles and crossed the Zadorra. But by this time Gazan and D'Erlon had issued from the defile, and the crisis was past.

CHAPTER XXXIX

Position taken up by Joseph—Movements of the Allied Army—Wellington's orders for the 21st—Battle of Vitoria—Retreat of the French.

THAT part of the valley of the Zadorra, termed by Napier "the basin of Vitoria," enclosed by high and rugged mountains, is about eight miles in breadth, and has a length of about ten miles from the defile of Puebla, on the south-west, to a point two miles beyond the town of Vitoria on the north-east. The upper part of the "basin" was at this time thronged with innumerable vehicles forming the trains of the three armies, the stores emptied out of the various depôts, and an enormous quantity of private baggage and belongings—some of it of the most outrageous character. "Vous avez une armée," said a French officer, taken prisoner, to Wellington. "Nous sommes un bordel ambulant." To relieve the congestion a large convoy set out for France on the 19th, and was followed on the 21st by another escorted by Maucune's Division of the Army of Portugal.

Meanwhile the King had taken up a position, not so much for the purpose of fighting a general action as of gaining time for the arrival of Clausel and Foy and the gradual despatch of the trains and baggage.

On the Upper Zadorra, opposite the town of Vitoria, on a line parallel to the Royal Road, was posted the Army of

IN THE PENINSULA

Portugal (now reduced to two Divisions, supported by two Cavalry Brigades under Digeon) with orders to defend the bridges of Gamara Mayor and Ariaga, on the roads leading to Vitoria from Durango and Orduna respectively.

Four miles lower down the river, at right angles to Reille's position—for the Zadorra made a bend—the Army of the South had its centre drawn up astride the Royal Road upon high ground in advance of the village of Arinez. Its right rested on the Zadorra; its left was drawn up at a point immediately in rear of the village of Subijana de Alava, which was occupied by Maransin with his Brigade. Fifty guns commanded the bridges over the Zadorra at Mendoza, Tres Puentes, Villodas, and Nanclares; but some were imprudently pushed forward to within musket shot of the further bank.

D'Erlon formed a second line in rear of Gazan; and the bulk of the Cavalry, the King's Guards, and several batteries of Artillery were posted in reserve at various points between Vitoria and Arinez.

The King's dispositions were more than faulty. He had neither fortified nor destroyed the bridges over the Zadorra, a river for the most part unfordable. A gap of four miles was left between the two wings. Worst of all, the principal line of retreat by the Royal Road, choked as it was with innumerable vehicles, was already imperilled by the direction of Graham's advance; and though Joseph had also the option of retiring by inferior roads upon Pampeluna, by so doing he would abandon his line of communication with Bayonne. A third course, however, still open to him was to retreat *viâ* Logrono and Tudela upon Saragossa, in which case he might expect to form a junction with Suchet as well as Clausel, he would recover a base by Perpignan, and would be able to operate in Aragon, than which—thanks to the good administration of Suchet—there was no province better disposed towards the French. But even had Joseph realised his peril, it is more than doubtful whether he would have made up his mind to a course which in view of the relative position of the opposing armies, he could hardly hope to execute without great moral and material loss, and which could not but involve the abandonment of all his trains and baggage.

On the 19th Sir Thomas Graham reached Zuazo. Hill occupied the Puente Larra on the Ebro. The centre was about Espejo and Subijana de Morillas, the 3rd and 7th Divisions, under Lord Dalhousie, being at Carcamo and Berberana. The 6th Division had been left at Medina del Pomar to guard the stores.

On the 20th Hill marched to Pobes. Dalhousie came up to the Bayas river. Graham occupied Murguia. On this day Wellington realised that the enemy, contrary to his previous expectation, meant to contest the line of the Zadorra, and accordingly issued the following orders for the 21st :—

"ARRANGEMENT FOR THE MOVEMENT OF THE ARMY ON THE 21ST OF JUNE, 1813."

(Extracted from Supplementary Despatches, vol. vii. p. 652.)

" Sir R. Hill will move the troops under his orders at daybreak by the communications ascertained for that purpose into the great road of Vitoria near La Puebla.

"The Divisions of this column to move right in front, and in the following order :—

" Major-General Morillo's Corps.
" The 2nd Division.

"The Condé D'Amaranthe's (Silveira) Division.

"Major-General V. Alten's Brigade to be in rear of General Morillo's Corps, and the remainder of the Cavalry of the right column in rear of the 2nd Division. As the country opens on the advance of the troops, the Cavalry will move out of the column to act as circumstances may require.

"General Morillo's Corps is to move into the high ground on the right of the great road to turn the enemy's left flank. It should never lose its connection with the right column.

"The baggage of the right column not to move beyond La Puebla until an order is sent for it to follow the column.

"The Light Division will move at daybreak, and proceed by the road along the river Bayas through the pass leading to Subijana, and thence by Montevite and the camp of the 4th Division to the village of Nunclares.

"One squadron of the 15th Hussars will act with the advance guard of this Division. The remainder of the 15th Hussars and Major Gardiner's troop of Horse Artillery will follow in rear of the Light Division.

"The 4th Division will move in rear of the 15th Hussars.

"The 18th and 10th Hussars will follow the 4th Division.

"The reserve Artillery will follow the 10th Hussars, but the spare carriages of these brigades to move in rear of the whole of the troops of this column.

"General Ponsonby's Brigade to follow the reserve Artillery, and the Household Cavalry to follow General Ponsonby's Brigade.

"The Divisions and Brigades of this column to march

by their left. The head of the column will receive further orders on approaching the village of Nanclares.

"Brigadier-General D'Urban will place his Brigade of Cavalry in column at some distance to the right of the road, and will move forward to the river Zadorra in a parallel direction to the Light Division, whilst it continues to advance to Nanclares.

"The whole of the baggage of the column is to be in rear of all the troops.

"The 3rd Division, followed by the 7th Division, will move ... at daybreak, and will proceed by the village of Anda, and thence (turning to the right) towards the village of Los Guetos, on the road from Anda to Vitoria.

"On approaching Los Guetos this column will throw out detachments to the right towards Nanclares, to put itself in communication with the detachments of the column marching upon that village.

"Lieutenant-General Lord Dalhousie will have the immediate command of the column composed of the 3rd and 7th Divisions.

"The left column of the Army (Divisions moving by their left) will move from Murguia towards Vitoria.

"Sir T. Graham will put himself in communication as soon as possible with the column of the 3rd and 7th Divisions at Los Guetos, and these Divisions will throw out parties when near Los Guetos towards Murguia to facilitate their communication.

"The movements of the Earl of Dalhousie and Sir Thomas Graham's columns are to be regulated from the right; and although these columns are to make such movements in advance as may be evidently necessary to favour the progress of the two columns on their right, they are not, however, to descend into the low grounds towards Vitoria or the great road, nor give up the advantage of turning the enemy's position and the town of Vitoria by a movement to their left.

"The mules with ammunition to move with the reserve Artillery as far as Nanclares.

"All communications intended for the Commander of the Forces to be sent to the column composed of the Light Division, &c.

"General Giron's Corps to move to Murguia, and to receive further instructions."

For the impending battle Wellington had concentrated an Anglo-Portuguese force—excluding the 6th Division—of 72,000 men of all ranks and arms, with 90 guns. He was aided also by about 20,000 Spaniards, without counting Carlos D'Espana's force of 4,000, which had been left at Miranda, or the 8,000 under De la Bispal who was still a few marches distant. The French are possibly somewhat over-estimated by Napier at 70,000 men, but they had 153 guns.

The memorable 21st of June dawned in mist and rain, amid which the Allied troops broke up from their respective bivouacs. Wellington himself in the right centre (with the Household Cavalry, the Cavalry Brigades of Ponsonby, Grant, and D'Urban, the 4th and Light Divisions) advanced to the Zadorra: the 4th Division directed upon the bridge of Nanclares, the Light upon that of Villodas. The left centre column (3rd and 7th Divisions under Lord Dalhousie) moved simultaneously upon Mendoza, but the wooded and mountainous country hid it from Wellington and impeded its progress. The

4th and Light Divisions, therefore, on reaching the bank of the Zadorra, confined themselves at first to opening fire upon the enemy's skirmishers, while awaiting the appearance of Hill and Dalhousie on their right and left. During this skirmishing Lord Wellington heard that the bridge of Tres Puentes next to that of Villodas, up-stream, was unoccupied by the enemy, and at once detached Kempt's Brigade of the Light Division to seize it. Kempt carried out his orders and took post on the high ground beyond the further bank where he remained undisturbed, although only about 1,200 yards distant from Gazan's flank, and indeed, in rear of part of that officer's line. It was now 1 p.m.

Meanwhile Sir Rowland Hill, pursuant to order, had advanced upon and crossed the Zadorra at the bridge of La Puebla de Arganzon, and at 10 a.m. had occupied that village. The 2nd and Silveira's Division then began to thread the defile of La Puebla; but that of Morillo was directed to move by a road on the right leading at first through a valley but afterwards on to the crest of the Puebla heights. Morillo gained the crest-line but was immediately attacked by Maransin's Brigade, which had been despatched from Subijana de Alava, but just failed to anticipate him. Maransin was repelled, and the 2nd Division issuing from the defile captured the village of Subijana de Alava. A fierce counter attack, however, drove the British out of it again; and Villatte, supported by Daricau, having reinforced Maransin, pushed Morillo back to the very last ridge, where, although supported by battalions from the 2nd Division, he was barely able to maintain his ground. Hill received an order from Lord Wellington to advance no further pending the arrival of Dalhousie in the centre, and the fight consequently languished.

The 4th Division had, however, crossed the bridge of Nanclares on seeing Hill's first advance, and Joseph, hearing of the loss of the bridge at Tres Puentes and seeing that Gazan's flank was laid bare, ordered the Armies of the South and Centre to retire in the direction of Vitoria. At this moment Lord Dalhousie—who does not seem to have shown any great intelligence in realising the spirit of his chief's instructions, or alacrity in carrying them out—made his appearance on the left of the Light Division; and Picton—fuming, no doubt, at being placed under the orders of the dilatory Dalhousie and showing greater command of the King's English than even his intimate friends had credited him with—led the leading Brigades of the 3rd Division over the bridge of Mendoza, while that of Colville, followed by the 7th Division and Vandeleur's Brigade of the Light, crossed by a ford higher up, engaged the enemy's right, captured the village of Margarita, and took therein twelve guns.

Wellington, noticing that the French centre had been weakened to reinforce their left, directed Picton to advance rapidly and seize the "Hill of the English" in front of the village of Arinez. By this movement the whole of the enemy's line south of the Royal Road was outflanked. But Gazan, holding on for a time to Arinez, covered the retreat with his guns and skirmishers; and although the village and that of Hermandad were eventually captured by the 3rd Division, while the rearguard was pursued by Sir R. Hill, the French—unmolested by the British Cavalry, which should have destroyed them —made good their retirement with all the steadiness of veterans for several miles, until at 6 p.m. they "reached the last defensible height one mile in front of Vitoria," and here for a while held their assailants in check.

Meanwhile, Sir Thomas Graham, advancing along the Orduna-Vitoria road with a force of about 24,000 men and 18 guns, encountered a Brigade of Sarrut's Division of the Army of Portugal in occupation of the village of Aranjuis in advance of the Ariaga bridge over the Zadorra. A little after midday Graham captured the village and drove one of Sarrut's Brigades across the river, while Longa's Spanish Division seized Durana on the Royal Road, and thus at the very outset gained possession of the enemy's principal line of retreat. With his other Brigade Sarrut took post at the village of Abechucho to defend the Ariaga bridge; and La Martinière, a mile to the right, held that of Gamara Mayor. Two Divisions of Dragoons and one of Light Cavalry formed a reserve.

Robinson's Brigade of the 5th Division captured the bridge of Gamara Mayor but lost it in a counter attack; and though on the arrival of another Brigade the bridge was again taken, it was a second time lost. Halkett's Brigade of the 1st Division carried Abechucho, but was repulsed at the bridge of Ariaga. Thus at a critical time both bridges remained in the hands of the French, and though there seems to have been a third bridge at Goveo, two miles below that of Ariaga, which was unguarded except, perhaps, by the videttes of a Cavalry Brigade in the vicinity, the fact may probably have been unknown, for the passage was not attempted.

We left Gazan defending the last position in front of Vitoria. To quote Napier's magnificent piece of word painting: " Behind the French was the plain in which the city stands, and beyond the city thousands of carriages and animals and non-combatants, women and children, were crowding together in all the madness of terror; and as the English shot went booming overhead the vast

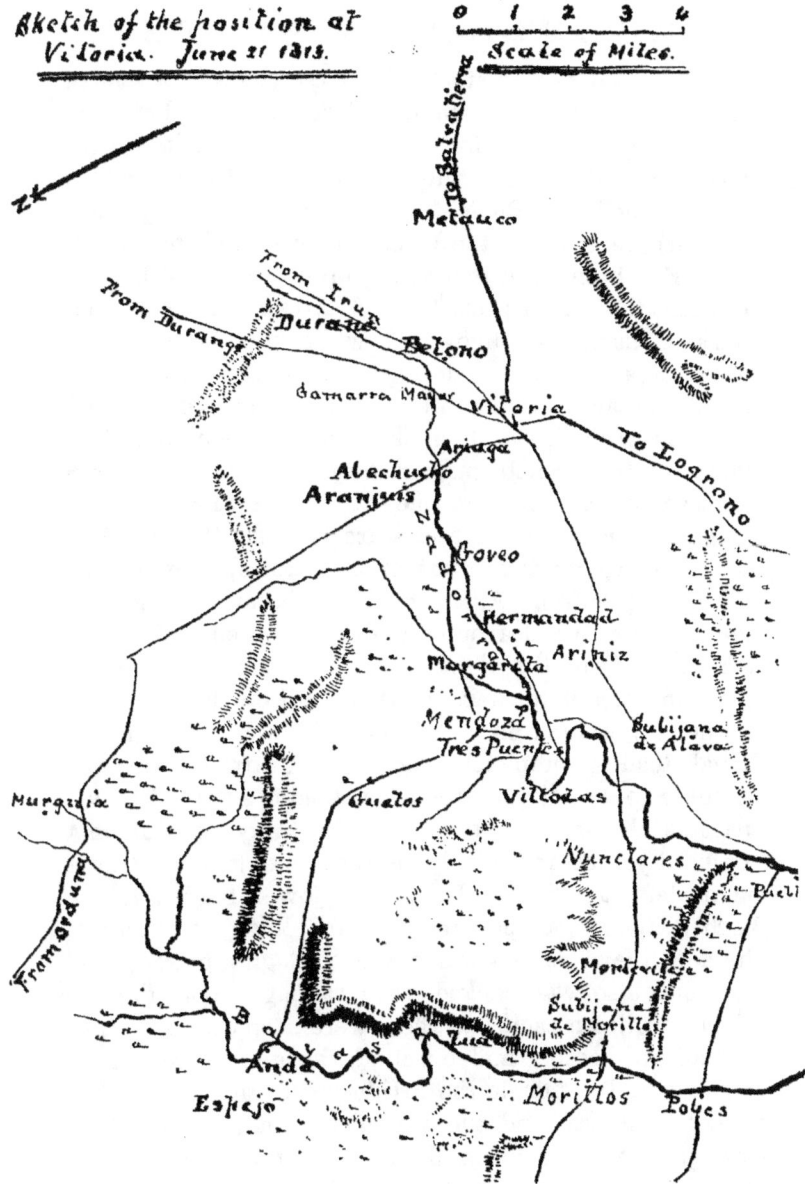

crowd started and swerved with a convulsive movement while a dull and horrid sound of distress arose; but there was no hope, no stay for army or multitude; it was the wreck of a nation. Still the courage of the French soldier was unquelled. Reille, on whom everything now depended, maintained the Upper Zadorra, and the Armies of the South and Centre drawing up on their last heights between the villages of Ali and Armentia, made their muskets flash like lightning, while more than eighty pieces of artillery, massed together, pealed with such a horrid uproar that the hills laboured and shook and streamed with fire and smoke, amid which the dark figures of the French gunners were seen bounding with frantic energy. This terrible cannonade and musketry kept the Allies in check, and scarcely could the 3rd Division, which bore the brunt of this storm, maintain its advanced position. Again the battle became stationary, and the French endeavoured to draw off their Infantry in succession from the right wing; but suddenly the 4th Division rushing forward carried a hill on their left, and the heights were at once abandoned. Joseph, finding the Royal Road so completely blocked with carriages that the Artillery could not pass, then indicated the road of Salvatierra as the line of retreat, and the Army went off in a confused yet compact body on that side, leaving Vitoria on its left; the British Infantry followed hard, and the Light Cavalry galloped through the town to intercept the new line of retreat which was through a marsh; and the road also was choked with carriages and fugitive people, while on each side there were deep drains. Thus all became disorder and mischief, the guns were left on the edge of the marsh, the artillerymen and drivers fled with the horses, and the vanquished Infantry breaking through the miserable multitude, went off by Metauco towards Salvatierra; the Cavalry, however, still covered

IN THE PENINSULA

the retreat, and many of the generous horsemen were seen taking up children and women to carry off from the dreadful scene."

The orders given, as we have seen, to Sir Thomas Graham, directed him to make his attack coincident with and dependent on that of the right and centre. But the time had come when an advance upon Vitoria from his side would have completed the destruction of the French armies. Graham does not seem to have risen to the occasion. It is true that he was unaware of Maucune's departure and that he credited Reille with two Divisions more than that officer actually had; but a forward movement on the part of Longa from Durana, or the advance of a British Brigade from Goveo would at once have made the bridges untenable. Even if he confined himself to hammering away in a frontal attack, he ought at all events to have made use of the whole force at his command, whereas the Brigade of Guards was never brought into action. On the other hand, Reille, holding his position with 13,000 men against nearly double that number, saved the French armies by a splendid instance of skill and valour. When at length Vitoria had been captured and the British Cavalry was assailing his rear while Longa advanced from Durana to cut off his retreat, Reille cleverly withdrew from his perilous situation, holding the Cavalry at bay with Digeon's Dragoons and containing the Spaniards with a small force posted beforehand at Betono. On this force he rallied the whole of his troops, and then retired with the utmost steadiness along the Salvatierra road as far as Metauco, forming a rearguard for the beaten armies of Gazan and D'Erlon. The nature of the country, which was intersected by deep ditches, and the approach of night tended to check pursuit; and it was said that part of the Hussar Brigade fell upon the spoil more vigorously than upon the French. At all events, comparatively few prisoners were made, and Napier states—correctly, no doubt—that the whole loss of the enemy did not exceed 6,000 men. But, of his 153 guns all but one and a howitzer were taken; and "all the parcs and depôts from Valladolid and Burgos, carriages, ammunition, treasure, everything fell into the hands of the victors." The King himself had a most narrow escape. Marshal Jourdan lost his bâton of office. The colours of the 6th and 100th Regiments were captured. General Sarrut was killed.

The loss of the Allies was decidedly heavy. Hill's Corps was knocked about a great deal in the attack on Subijana de Alava. The 5th Division lost heavily at Gamara Mayor. The 3rd Division, which had covered itself with glory, had many casualties in the last struggle on the heights in front of Vitoria.

The losses were divided as follows:—

	British.	Spaniards.	Portuguese.
Killed	501	89	150
Wounded	2,807	464	899

Two hundred and sixty-six men were in addition returned as "missing"; making up a grand total of 5,180 casualties, of which about 1,800 were sustained by the 3rd Division.

The results of Vitoria were so great that it has claims to be considered one of "the decisive battles of the world." Not only was its effect seen in the dethronement of Joseph and the expulsion of the French to all intents and purposes from Spain, but it turned the scale in the wavering councils of the allied sovereigns in Germany, induced Austria to join in the contest, and led directly to the overthrow of the Emperor.

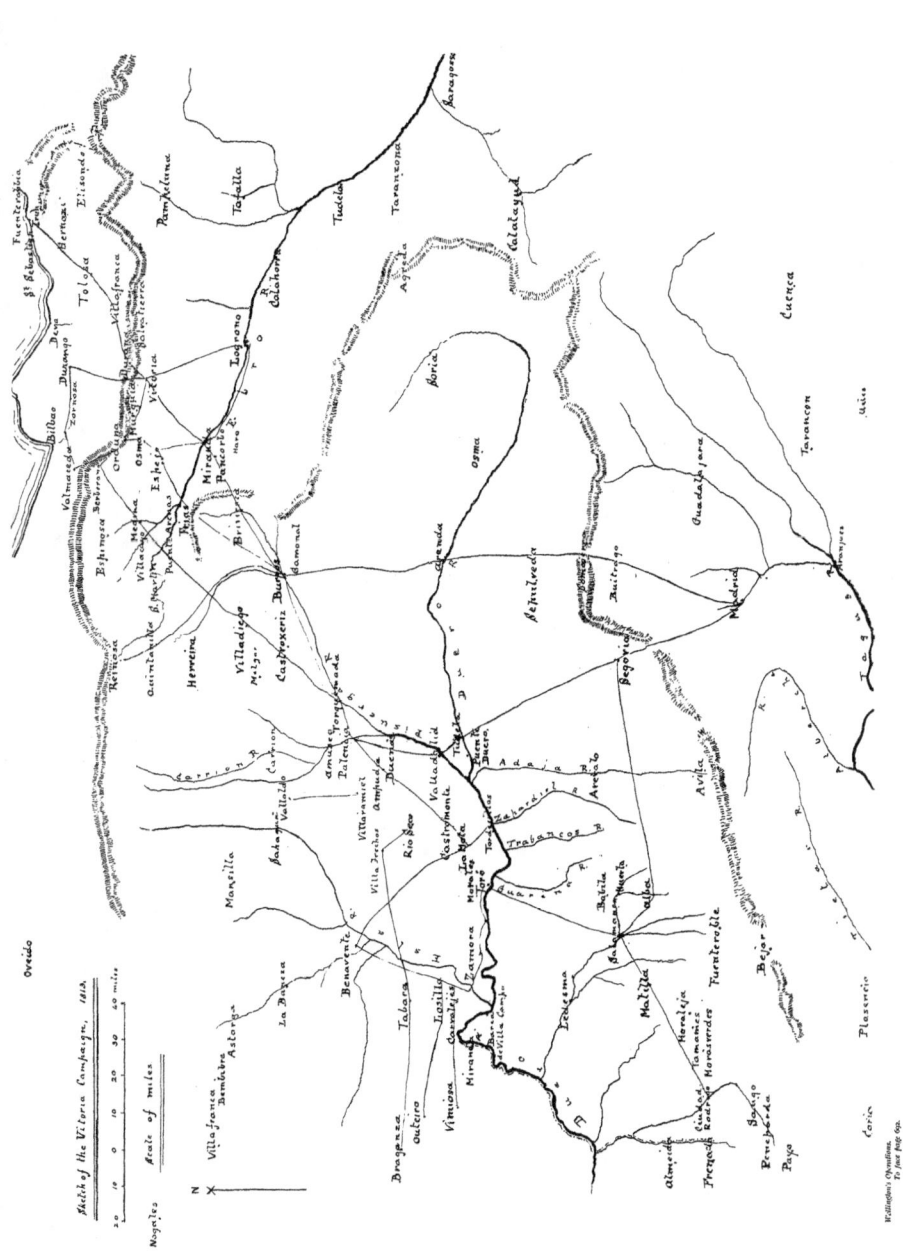

News of the victory was received in England with transports of delight; and Lord Wellington, although still on the list of Lieutenant-Generals, was presented by the Prince Regent with the bâton of a Field Marshal.

CHAPTER XL.

Wellington follows up the enemy—Movements of Foy; and of Clausel—The French retire into France—Misconduct of Wellington's troops—Case of Captain Ramsay—Appointment of Marshal Soult as Lieutenant of the Emperor—Retirement of Joseph—State of the French Army of Spain—Dispositions on either side—The theatre of operations—Soult's plan of attack—His movements—Difficulties of the Allies on the defensive—Soult attacks—Defence of the Passes and the retreat of the right wing of the Allies.

ON the evening of the battle Wellington issued orders for his troops to march in pursuit of the enemy at 10 a.m. next day. The Army consequently moved on the 22nd by three roads to Salvatierra, while Giron was pushed forward by the Royal Road in the hope of overtaking Maucune and his convoy. The Household Cavalry remained at Vitoria. The 6th Division arrived there from Medina del Pomar and its command was resumed by Sir H. Clinton, who had just rejoined the Army from England, while Pakenham took up his duties as Adjutant-General.

Meanwhile Joseph had continued his retreat through the night. Reille halted on reaching Salvatierra at 5 a.m., prepared if necessary to dispute the advance of the Allies. But having made sure that all the French troops had now passed on, he continued his march to Huerta, 30 miles from the field of battle. The King in person went on till he reached Yrursun, at the junction of the roads leading to Pampeluna and Tolosa, where he halted during the 23rd. Reille with his two Divisions was then directed to the Bidassoa, while Gazan and D'Erlon marched on to Pampeluna, where they arrived on the 24th in a terrible state of disorganisation, with their rearguard harassed by Victor and Charles Alten, who captured the only gun saved at Vitoria, and followed up the French next day as they retired up the valley of Roncevalles after reinforcing the Pampeluna garrison.

On the 21st, General Foy had come up to Bergara, 20 miles from Vitoria; and the Division of Palombini— now commanded by St. Paul—with the garrison of Bilbao reached Durango (about 25 miles from the battlefield) on its way to join the King. The news of the disaster led to the immediate abandonment of a number of forts in the neighbourhood; and, on the evacuation of Gueteria, Santona and San Sebastian were the only strongholds on the north coast remaining in the hands of the French.

With a view to saving the two convoys which had left Vitoria before the battle, Foy rallied all outlying detachments and garrisons at Tolosa, recalled Maucune, concentrated his own and St. Paul's Division at Bergara and gave battle at Montdragon to Giron and Longa. Attacked, however, by three times his own numbers, Foy was compelled to retreat with the loss of 6 guns; but he had gained time and saved the convoys. Retiring then to Tolosa, he with difficulty evaded the head of Graham's Corps advancing on Villa Franca; and being attacked by Graham and Giron on the 25th, was forced along the Royal Road almost to Ernani, where he took up a defensive position and found his force increased by reinforcements from the smaller garrisons to about 19,000 men with 10 guns. Then, having entrusted San Sebastian to General Rey and a garrison of 2,600 men, he crossed the

Bidassoa and entered France on the 1st of July, where he formed a junction with Reille; and the two Generals, with a combined force of 25,000 men, took up a line extending from Vera to the bridge over the Bidassoa at Behobie. Sir Thomas Graham invested San Sebastian.

It is now time to glance at Clausel. This officer reached the vicinity of Vitoria with 14,000 men on the evening of the 22nd, but on hearing what had happened retired again to Logrono, where he halted till the 25th. Wellington, who had believed him to be at Tudela, left Hill to invest Pampeluna, and marched at once in person with the Cavalry Brigades of Grant and Ponsonby, the 3rd, 4th, 7th and Light Divisions by Tafalla to intercept Clausel; while the 5th and 6th Divisions, with the Household Cavalry and D'Urban's Portuguese Brigade, moved from Salvatierra and Vitoria direct upon Logrono.

Clausel at once retired, pursued by Mina and Julian Sanchez, upon Tudela, which he reached on the evening of the 27th after a forced march of 60 miles. Unaware of Wellington's occupation of Tafalla, he now believed that his retreat into France was secured; but being warned of his danger, descended the Ebro to Saragossa, whence—with the loss of 300 men and part of his artillery—he succeeded in gaining Jaca in the Pyrenees.

Joseph had in the meanwhile reached France at St. Jean Pied de Port with the Armies of the South and Centre, but finding himself unpursued, directed Gazan to cross the frontier and occupy the valley of Bastan. By this time, however, the Condé de la Bispal, who had been ordered to take the Pancorbo forts, had done so and was marching to join Hill. That officer was consequently enabled, without abandoning the blockade of Pampeluna, to detach the 2nd and Silveira's Division which between the 4th and 7th of July drove Gazan back over the frontier, the line of which from the Pass of Roncevalles in the Pyrenees to the mouth of the Bidassoa was now occupied by the victorious Allies.

That the pursuit of the French Armies was not attended with more brilliant results was largely due to the misconduct of the soldiers, who, in Lord Wellington's words, "were plundering the country in all directions." "We started," wrote he to Lord Bathurst on the 29th of June, "with the army in the highest order, and up to the day of the battle nothing could get on better; but that event has as usual annihilated all good order and discipline. The soldiers of the Army have got among them about a million sterling in money, with the exception of about 100,000 dollars which were got for the military chest. The night of the battle, instead of being passed in getting rest and food to prepare them for the pursuit of the following day, was passed by the soldiers in looking for plunder. The consequence was that they were incapable of marching in pursuit of the enemy, and were totally knocked up. . . . I am convinced that we have now out of the ranks double the amount of our loss in the battle. . . ." And again on the 9th of July, "By the state of yesterday we had 12,500 men less under arms than we had on the day before the battle." Even on the 19th, four weeks after the action, the decrease was 9,633.

The Duke of York, as Commander-in-Chief, did not fail to take serious notice of these complaints. He observed that the stigma did not attach to the privates alone, but "much the greatest share lay with the officers for their inattention to the discipline of their men," and he desired Lord Wellington to make examples among the higher ranks by sending home officers guilty of neglect of duty, from "the Senior General to the lowest Ensign."

It was during this period that the well-known incident of the arrest of Captain Norman Ramsay, R.H.A., took place. Ramsay was a most gallant and brilliant officer, and it is generally, and perhaps rightly, thought that Lord Wellington acted towards him with harshness and injustice. The following letter gives Wellington's account of the affair, and shows that his annoyance was caused by the disobedience of orders habitual to his officers :—" I am sorry that I cannot recommend Captain Ramsay for promotion, because I have had him in arrest since the battle for disobeying an order given to him by me verbally. The fact is, that, if discipline means habits of obedience to orders, as well as military instruction, we have but little of it in the Army. Nobody ever thinks of obeying an order. It is, however, an unrivalled Army for fighting, if the soldiers can only be kept in their ranks during the battle; but it wants some of those qualities which are indispensable . . . to take all the advantage to be derived from a victory; and the cause of these defects is the want of habits of obedience and attention to orders by the inferior officers, and indeed, I might add, by all. They never attend to an order with an intention to obey it, or sufficiently to understand it, be it ever so clear, and therefore never obey it when obedience become troublesome, or difficult, or important. . . . When we were in pursuit of the French in the valley of Araquil, Captain Ramsay was ordered to the front with his troop. Returning from the front I met him, and having thought it would be better to send Sir Thomas Graham with the left of the Army by the high road to Irun, . . . I determined that Captain Ramsay's troop, which has been with Sir Thomas before, should accompany him again if he was attached. But it was necessary to make some inquiries about roads before I should determine to detach him. I desired Captain Ramsay to halt and canton in the village

IN THE PENINSULA

at which I met him, and not to move from it till he should received farther orders from myself, knowing that he would be sent to from the advanced posts. Notwithstanding these orders, he left the village in the morning, before the orders reached him to join Sir Thomas; and he got forward into the defile, and it was not possible to bring him back till the whole column had passed. I consequently put him in arrest, and had determined to make an example of him; but I have since released him, but cannot recommend him for promotion."

News of the terrible defeat at Vitoria reached Napoleon at Dresden on the 30th of June, in the midst of his negotiations with the Continental Powers. Although the full extent of the disaster was not revealed in the first despatches, and it was supposed that Vitoria might possibly be re-occupied, the Emperor at once realised that his brother Joseph could not be allowed to exercise any further military command. Strong measures and the ablest available Commander were essential. Marshal Davoust was not at hand. Besides he had had no experience in the Peninsula. Masséna had declined active service the year before. St. Cyr, second to none in ability, had shown a certain lack of energy in Catalonia. The choice fell on Soult; and without a moment's hesitation, Napoleon despatched him to Bayonne armed with the fullest powers as Lieutenant of the Emperor. Travelling night and day, Soult reached Bayonne on the 12th of July, and Joseph at once retired from the scene.

A new organisation was adopted. The Armies of the North, South, Centre, and Portugal, were amalgamated under the designation of "The Army of Spain." The following figures gives the "State" at the time when Soult assumed command :—

WELLINGTON'S OPERATIONS

Chief of the Staff—Count Gazan.

RIGHT WING.

General Count Reille.

					Present under Arms Men. Horses.		Men effective and non-effective.
1st Division	General	Foy		9 Batt.	5,922	189	6,784
7th	,,	,,	Maucune	7 ,,	4,186	110	5,676
9th	,,	,,	La Martinière	11 ,,	7,127	151	8,906
			Total	... ...	17,235	450	21,366

CENTRE.

General Count D'Erlon.

2nd	,,	,,	D'Armagnac	8 Batt.	6,961	116	8,580
3rd	,,	,,	Abbé	9 ,,	8,030	285	8,728
6th	,,	,,	Darricau	8 ,,	5,966	223	6,627
					20,957	624	23,935

LEFT WING.

General Clausel.

4th	,,	,,	Conroux	9 Batt.	7,056	150	7,477
5th	,,	,,	Vandermaesen	7 ,,	4,181	141	5,201
8th	,,	,,	Taupin	10 ,,	5,981	141	7,587
					17,218	432	20,265

RESERVE.

General Villatte.

French 14,959 2,091 17,929
Foreign 4 Batts. of the Rhine ⎫
    General St. Paul 4 ,, of Italians ⎬ Strength not given
        ,, Casabianca 4 ,, of Spaniards ⎭

CAVALRY.

	,,	Pierre Soult	4,723	4,416	5,098
	,,	Treilhand	2,358	2,275	2,523
		Total	7,081	6,691	7,621

IN THE PENINSULA

	Present under Arms. Men. Horses.	Men effective and non-effective.
Other troops (apparently National Guards, &c.)	14,938	16,946
Second Reserve	5,595	6,105
Total of Field Army	97,983	114,137

GARRISONS.

San Sebastian.	General Rey	2,731	3,086
Pampeluna		2,951	3,121
Santona		1,465	1,674

Suchet had about 70,000 men. The fact that Napoleon should still have been able to hold the Spanish border with nearly 200,000 men, is a proof of the wonderful resources of France. But this force is not to be estimated by mere numbers. It consisted of veteran troops, worth probably nearly as much as the whole mass of 700,000 in Germany; while among its Commanders were several of the very ablest Generals in the French Army. It was the retention of these veterans by Wellington which proved the Emperor's ruin. With their aid Napoleon would have beaten the Continental Powers twenty times over.

Soult at once set himself to clear the situation. Bayonne was strengthened, and an entrenched camp drawn round it. Discipline was restored among the troops; the Spanish families were removed into the interior of France; a system of supply was organised.

The Army of Spain was posted as follows: The left wing, under Clausel, occupied St. Jean Pied de Port, with an outlying detachment under General Paris, 60 miles away at Jaca in Spanish territory. Count D'Erlon with the centre, held the heights about Espellette and Ainhoa, with an outpost near Urdax. Reille, on the right, occupied the Puerto de Vera. Villatte's Reserve held the line of the Bidassoa from Irun to the mouth of the river. A

Cavalry Division was on the Nive; the other, on the Adour. The distance from St. Jean Pied de Port to the mouth of the Bidassoa is something over 30 miles.

On the side of the Allies, Hill's Corps formed the right of the line and was posted thus. On the outer flank, Byng's Brigade of the 2nd Division—about 1,800 officers and men—and Morillo's Division (about 4,000) occupied the Spanish ends of the Passes of Roncevalles and Ibaneta, fronting north-east. On their left, a Brigade of Silveira's Portuguese Division—something over 2,000 strong—under Campbell, was posted on the mountain above Alduides, in French territory.

Sir R. Hill carried the line westward from Campbell by occupying the valley of Bastan with 10,000 men forming the remainder of the 2nd and Silveira's Division. Of this force, Silveira was at Erazu, while two British Brigades under General W. Stewart guarded the Pass of Maya. The line of retreat ran directly in rear to Elisondo, 8 miles distant, which was fixed as the point of concentration. The 4th Division, about 7,000 of all ranks, at Viscarret, about 12 miles south of Alduides, supported Byng and Campbell. Picton, with 5,000 men at Olague, about 18 miles south of the Maya Pass, and 10 or 12 west of Viscarret, formed a general reserve to Hill.

The 7th Division, 5,000 officers and men under Lord Dalhousie, was at Echallar, about 12 miles due west of Stewart at the Maya Pass. The 82nd Regiment maintained the connection between Stewart and Dalhousie. Six miles further to the left the Light Division (4,500) occupied the village of Vera. The 6th Division, nearly 7,000 strong—at present commanded by Pack, for Sir H. Clinton, who had relieved Pakenham after the battle of Vitoria, held the command for only a few days—formed

IN THE PENINSULA 703

at Estevan a central reserve either to Hill or Dalhousie, being in easy communication with either.

Giron's Corps and Longa's Division, supported by the 1st Division, lined the Bidassoa from Vera to the sea. Castanos had been succeeded in command of the 4th Spanish Army by Mendizabel without reference to Wellington.

Wellington's headquarters were established at Lesaca, 3 miles south of Vera. The 5th Division and the Portuguese Brigades of Graham's Corps besieged San Sebastian. The Division of the Count de la Bispal, 8,000 strong, blockaded Pampeluna. When reinforced shortly afterwards by 3,000 men under Carlos d'Espana, de la Bispal was able to maintain the blockade and spare 7,000 men to act with Wellington.

The Partida bands of Mina, Julian Sanchez, Juan Martin, &c., in the neighbourhood of Saragossa, severed the direct communication between Soult and Suchet.

The opposing forces were not unequal in numbers. The Anglo-Portuguese Army mustered 70,000 of all ranks; the Spaniards about 25,000. From these figures must be deducted at least 10,000 men required for the operations against San Sebastian and Pampeluna. Against the net total of 85,000, Soult could bring, as we have seen, 77,500 French regular troops; and with the addition of 12 foreign battalions and the local National Guards his available force probably somewhat exceeded that of the Allies. He had 86 field guns.

"The theatre of operations," observes Napier (bk. xxi. ch. 4), "was a trapezoid, with sides from 40 to 50 miles in length, and having Bayonne, St. Jean Pied de Port, San Sebastian and Pampeluna, all fortresses in possession of the French, at the angles. The interior, broken and tormented by savage mountains, narrow craggy passes, deep water-courses, precipices and forests, appeared a wilderness, which no military combinations could embrace, and susceptible only of irregular and partisan operations. But the great spinal ridge of the Pyrenees furnished a clue to the labyrinth. Running diagonally across the quadrilateral, it separated Bayonne, St. Jean Pied de Port, and San Sebastian from Pampeluna; thus the portion of the Allied Army which more especially belonged to the blockade of Pampeluna was in a manner cut off from that which belonged to the siege of San Sebastian. They were distinct armies, each having its own particular object, and the only direct communication between them was the great road running behind the mountains from Toloza and Irurzun to Pampeluna. The centre of the Allies was indeed an army of succour and connection; but of necessity very much scattered, and with lateral communications so few, difficult, and indirect as to prevent any unity of movement; nor could Hill move at all until an attack was decidedly pronounced against one of the extremities, lest the most direct gun-road to Pampeluna, which he covered, should be unwarily opened to the enemy. The French Generals, taking the offensive, could therefore by beaten roads concentrate against any part of the English General's line, which, necessarily a passively defensive one, followed an irregular trace of more than 50 miles of mountains.

"Wellington having his battering train and stores about San Sebastian, which was also nearer and more accessible to the enemy than Pampeluna, made his Army lean towards that side. His left wing, including the army of siege, was 21,000, with singularly strong positions of defence; his centre, 24,000, could in two marches unite with the left wing to cover the siege or fall upon the flank of an enemy advancing by the high road of Irun; but three days more were required by those troops to concentrate for the security of the blockade on the right. Soult, however, judged that no decisive result would attend a direct movement upon San Sebastian, because Guipuscoa was exhausted of provisions; and the centre of the Allies could fall on his flank before he reached Ernani, which, his attack failing him, would place him in a dangerous position. Moreover, by means of his sea communication, he knew San Sebastian was not in extremity; but he had no communication with Pampeluna, and feared its fall. Wherefore he resolved to operate by his left.

"Profiting by the French roads leading to St. Jean Pied de Port, covering his movement by the Nivelle and Nive rivers, and by the position of his centre, he hoped to gather on Wellington's right quicker than that General could gather to oppose him; and thus compensating by numbers the disadvantage of assailing mountain positions, force a way to Pampeluna. That fortress once succoured, he designed to seize the road of Irurzun, to fall upon the separated Divisions of the centre as they descended from the hills, or operate on the rear of the force besieging San Sebastian, while a Corps of observation, which he proposed to leave on the Lower Bidassoa, menaced it in front and followed it in retreat. The siege of San Sebastian, the blockade of Pampeluna, and probably that of Santona would be thus raised; the French Army united in an abundant country, and its communication with Suchet secured, would be free to co-operate with that Marshal or to press its own attack.

"In this view and to mislead Wellington by vexing his right simultaneously with the construction of the bridges against his left, Soult wrote to Paris, desiring him to march when time suited, from Jaca by the higher valleys towards Aviz or Sanguessa, to drive the partisans from that side, and join the left of the Army when it should have reached Pampeluna. Clausel was directed to repair the roads in his own front, and push the heads of his columns toward the passes of Roncevalles; then to send a strong detachment into the Val de Baygorry, near the lateral pass of Yspegui, to menace Hill's flank which was at that pass, and the front of Campbell's Brigade in the Alduides.

". . . Villatte . . . remained in observation on the Bidassoa. If threatened by superior forces he was to retire slowly and in mass upon the entrenched camp commenced at Bayonne. . . . But if the Allies should in consequence of Soult's operations against their right retire, Villatte was to relieve San Sebastian and follow them briskly by Tolosa."

The only roads leading over the Pyrenees within this area were that from St. Jean Pied de Port to Pampeluna, which was not suited for wheeled carriage, and a still inferior one from Espelette to Urdax. There were also a few mountain tracks. A pretty good road led from Bayonne to St. Jean Pied de Port, and a lateral one from Pampeluna by Yrurzun to Tolosa, which was connected with San Sebastian by the Royal Road.

On the 20th of July the movement began. Reille, having been relieved at Puente de Vera and Sarre by Villatte, marched to St. Jean Pied de Port. D'Erlon retained his position at Espelette and Urdax, covering the march of his colleague. Reille was timed to reach his goal on the 22nd, and the two Cavalry Divisions and the Reserve Artillery were expected to arrive simultaneously. Speed was essential, but rains delayed the march which was not completed till the 24th, when a force of 60,000 men with 66 guns was concentrated in readiness to force the passes of Maya and Roncevalles.

The whole of the Cavalry and Artillery, and Clausel's Corps were formed in two columns in advance of St. Jean;

one, on the heights of Arnegui, overlooking Val Carlos; the other at Vente de Orisson.

On the west side of Val Carlos, Reille, at Arola, was ordered to advance at daybreak and force the passes of Roncevalles and Alduides.

D'Erlon was directed to wait until the operations of Clausel and Reille had compelled the British to abandon the Maya Pass, and then to advance into the valley of Zubiri; taking care, however, to occupy all the lateral passes by which he maintained connection with the left wing of the Army.

Wellington's position was anything but comfortable, and gives a good example of the disadvantage at which a force defending a mountain chain is placed. "Roads across mountains," remarks Lieut.-Col. W. H. James, "are as a rule perpendicular to the general direction of the chain, rarely connected by cross-roads, because they would have to be made across the valleys between the spurs jutting out from the main ridge. Hence it follows that (as Wellington admits with regard to his own dispositions in the present case), the various bodies told off to defend particular passages cannot support one another, and depend for help on troops immediately in their rear. In this case the right wing told off to defend the Roncevalles Pass was separated by the main line of the Pyrenees from the centre detailed to hold back an irruption from the Pass of Maya, and this again by a considerable range of hills from the left wing on the Royal Road. The distances from the advanced points held to the supports were also considerable, due, no doubt, to questions of supply. Thus from Olague to Bentarte was 28 miles. From St. Esteban to Maya, 19 miles."

"As the French," says Napier, "were almost in contact with the Allies' position at Roncevalles, the point of defence nearest to Pampeluna, it followed that on the rapidity or slowness with which Soult overcame resistance in that quarter depended his success; and a comparative estimate of numbers and distances will give the measure of his chances. Clausel had 16,000 bayonets, besides Cavalry, Artillery, and National Guards, the last menacing the valley of Orbaiceta. Byng and Morillo were therefore with 5,000 Infantry to sustain the assault of 16,000 until Cole could reinforce them; but Cole, 12 miles off, could not come up under four or five hours. And as Reille's Division of equal strength with Clausel's could before that time seize the Lindouz and turn the left, the Allies must finally abandon their ground for a new field, where Picton could join them from Olague and Campbell from the Alduides. Then with 17,000 or 18,000 bayonets and some guns they might oppose Clausel and Reille's 30,000. But Picton at Olague was more than a day's march from Byng at Altobiscar; their junction could only be effected in the Zubiri valley not far from Pampeluna; and they could only be reinforced there by 7,000 Spaniards from the blockade, and 3,000 Cavalry from the Ebro.

"Hill, menaced by D'Erlon with a superior force, and having the Pass of Maya, half a day's march further from Pampeluna than the Pass of Roncevalles, to defend, could not give ready help. If he retreated rapidly D'Erlon could follow as rapidly; and though Picton and Cole would thus be reinforced with 10,000 men, Soult would gain 18,000; but Hill could not move until he knew that Byng and Cole were driven from the Roncevalles passes: in fine, he could not avoid a dilemma. For if he held Col de Maya and affairs went wrong near Pampeluna his own situation would be imminently dangerous; if he held Irrueta, his next position, the same danger was to be dreaded; and, Maya once abandoned, D'Erlon, moving by his own left towards the

IN THE PENINSULA 709

Alduides, could join Soult in the Valley of Zubiri before Hill could join Cole and Picton by the valley of the Lanz. But if Hill did not maintain the position of Irrueta, D'Erlon could follow and cut the 6th and 7th Divisions off from the valley of Lanz. The extent and power of Soult's combinations are thus evinced. Hill, forced to await orders and hampered by D'Erlon, required it might be three days to get into line near Pampeluna; but D'Erlon after gaining Maya could in one day and a half, by the passes of Berderez and Urtiaga, join Soult in the valley of Zubiri. Meanwhile Byng, Morillo, Cole, Campbell and Picton would be exposed to the attack of double their own numbers; and however firm and able those Generals might be, they could not, when thus suddenly brought together, be expected to seize the whole system of operations and act with that nicety of judgment which the occasion demanded. It was clear therefore that Hill must in some measure be paralysed at first, and finally be thrown, together with the 6th, 7th and Light Divisions, upon an external line of operations while the French moved upon internal lines.

"On the other hand, Byng, Morillo, Campbell, Cole, Picton and Hill were only pieces of resistance on Wellington's board; the 6th, 7th and Light Divisions were those with which he meant to win his game. There was, however, a great difference in their value. The Light Division and the 7th, especially the former, being furthest from Pampeluna, having enemies in front and points to guard, were, the 7th a day, the Light Division two days behind the 6th Division which was free, and, the drag of D'Erlon's Corps considered, a day nearer to Pampeluna than Hill. Upon the rapid handling of this well-placed body the fate of the Allies therefore depended; if it arrived in time, 30,000 Infantry with sufficient Cavalry and Artillery would be established under the immediate command of Wellington, on a position of strength, checking the enemy until the rest of the Army arrived."

At daylight on the 25th, Clausel (with Soult present in person) attacked Byng at Altobiscar. On Byng's left Reille simultaneously attacked Morillo, and, forcing him back through the Val Carlos, threatened to cut Byng from the Passes of Ibaneta and Atalosti. Byng's right was at the same time turned on the side of Orbaiceta; and his position had become precarious when, at the critical moment, General Ross (afterwards of Bladensburg) came up with a Brigade of the 4th Division, and with the four companies composing its advance guard, vigorously charged the head of Reille's column and secured the communication with Campbell by the Atalosti Pass.

Cole, whose whole Division had by this time arrived from Viscarret, now directed Byng to fall back to the end of the Altobiscar ridge. The Allied force, outnumbered as it was by three to one, held its own throughout the day; but after dark abandoned the crest line of the Pyrenees and made good its retreat down the valley of Urros, while Campbell on the left retired along a parallel valley.

During the retirement a curious but very discreditable incident occurred, showing the amazing lack of discipline among some of our troops. An officer with a party of the 14th Light Dragoons found some Infantry soldiers in a wine house. He ordered them to join their regiments. They not only refused, but fired on and beat off the Dragoons. They deserved execution at the hands of the Provost Marshal, but were unfortunately soon afterwards captured by the enemy.

On the morning of the 26th, Clausel followed Cole, while Reille was ordered to move to his right and menace the rear of the 2nd Division which would then be hemmed

IN THE PENINSULA

in between him and D'Erlon. Happily Reille was stopped by a mountain fog, and finding it impossible to proceed, changed direction and followed Clausel.

Clausel came up with W. Anson's Brigade of the 4th Division, which formed Cole's rearguard, in front of Viscarret, but failed to make any impression. Picton arrived, bringing news of the approach of the 3rd Division, and Cole halting, took up a position on the Linzoain ridge which separated the valley of Zubiri from that of Urroz. Soult resolved not to attack until the next day. The delay should have been fatal, for it gave time for the arrival of the 3rd Division and Campbell's Brigade as well as for the removal of the wounded and incumbrances to the rear; while the Allies, reinforced to nearly 20,000 men, should have been able to hold its new position long enough to enable Wellington to concentrate his reserves and cover Pampeluna.

Picton, however, decided that the heights of Linzoain were untenable and evacuated his position before daybreak. Whether he sent at all to inform Lord Wellington of his decision seems doubtful; but at any rate he failed to send a sufficient number of messengers to ensure the information reaching his Chief; and Wellington remained for many critical hours in ignorance of the retirement. Picton seems to have believed that the maintenance of the blockade of Pampeluna was hopeless; but at the very last moment he changed his mind, halted, and took up a position from Zabaldica to Sorauren, covering the fortress. Soult at once prepared to attack; but at the critical moment a terrific cheer, taken up from regiment to regiment along the British line, announced the sudden and unexpected arrival of Lord Wellington.

Meanwhile, the 2nd Division had been involved in heavy fighting. One Brigade, as already noticed, was detached under General Byng at Altobiscar. Stewart had two British Brigades and one Portuguese remaining. Of the British, that hitherto commanded by Colonel O'Callaghan, but now by Cameron, consisting of the 50th, 71st, and 92nd, was posted to defend the adjacent passes of Maya and Lessassa; while on Cameron's right, that under General Pringle—made up of the 28th, 34th, and 39th—guarded the Pass of Aristacum. Stewart himself, in fancied security, had gone off to Elisondo, ten or twelve miles distant, when on the morning of the 25th his Division was suddenly attacked by the Corps of D'Erlon. The Divisions of D'Armagnac and Abbé assailed the Aristacum; that of Maransin, the Maya Pass. After desperate fighting both passes were forced and 4 Portuguese guns captured. Stewart, who had now arrived, then took up a position on the Achiola ridge, but was gradually pushed back. At 6 p.m. his ammunition failed, and he was on the point of abandoning the mountain when Barnes' Brigade of the 7th Division most opportunely came up from Echallar and drove the enemy back to the Col de Maya. In this sanguinary engagement the losses amounted on either side to 1,400 or 1,500; but the French had gained their point by isolating the 2nd Division from Cole and Picton. Sir Rowland Hill now concentrated his forces, and with Barnes' Brigade, the 2nd, and Silveira's Division, prepared to make a counter attack next day. But during the night news arrived of Cole's retreat; and Hill, leaving a Portuguese Brigade at Elisondo at the junction of the St. Estevan road, fell back on Irrueta, 15 miles from the scene of the engagement. D'Erlon made no attempt to follow up his advantage.

CHAPTER XLI

Wellington joins his troops at Sorauren—Battle of Sorauren—Combat at Buenza—Second battle of Sorauren—Pursuit of the enemy who narrowly escapes into French territory—Cessation of the pursuit.

LORD WELLINGTON was superintending matters at San Sebastian when he became aware that Soult was about to take the offensive in force; but whereas his opponent believed that Pampeluna was hard pressed and that San Sebastian could easily hold out, Wellington had formed precisely the contrary opinion. He was therefore convinced (and his conviction seemed confirmed by various circumstances) that the relief of San Sebastian would be Soult's first object. During the night of the 25–26th, when on his way to headquarters, news reached him of the combats of Maya and Roncevalles. The Cavalry were thereupon ordered to Pampeluna; while Graham was directed to turn the siege of San Sebastian into a blockade and prepare to join Giron on the Bidassoa. On the 26th Wellington reached Irrueta, and realising the true meaning of Soult's movement, ordered the 6th, 7th, and Light Divisions upon Pampeluna. To cover the march of these Divisions, Hill remained at Irrueta till the evening of the 27th, and then marched upon Lanz *viâ* Velate.

The change of front could not fail to cause the greatest confusion. The passes and valleys were choked with encumbrances, and the most alarming reports were rife.

Wellington quitted Hill's camp early on the 27th. At Ostiz, in the valley of the Lanz, he met General Long and heard of Picton's retreat. He at once galloped into Sorauren—hardly two minutes before the road was intercepted by Clausel's troops—and hastily dictated to the only Staff Officer with him orders diverting the approaching Divisions from the valley of the Lanz to the Marcalain road which led to the rear of Cole's position at Oricain. Then, riding conspicuously and alone up to the heights on which the troops of Cole and Picton were drawn up, he was greeted by the thunder of cheers already noticed. The shouts reached the ears of Soult on the opposite heights. The Marshal, as Wellington expected, delayed his attack till he could ascertain their cause, and lost thereby not only the whole day but an opportunity which never recurred.

The Allied troops were drawn up in two lines: the first, along a ridge flanked by the Lanz and Guy rivers; the second, two miles in rear, extending from Gorvaiz to San Cristoval, covering Pampeluna. The first line was occupied from left to right by the 4th Division, Campbell's Portuguese Brigade and two Spanish battalions detached from the blockade of the fortress, with the Brigade of Byng in support. The second line was formed by De la Bispal, Morillo and the 3rd Division. The Cavalry under Cotton were retained about Huarte, guarding the right flank.

On the side of the French, Clausel was posted at Sorauren opposite Cole's left. Reille, with two Divisions, was at Zabaldica on low ground facing the Spaniards; while his remaining Division (that of La Martinière) with one of Cavalry was pushed forward across the Guy river to menace Picton's right and, if possible, communicate with the Pampeluna garrison.

Although Soult knew that the Allies were expecting

IN THE PENINSULA 715

large reinforcements, and time was in consequence an object, it was not till a little before 11 a.m. on the 28th that he began his attack. Clausel was directed to assail Cole in front and flank while Reille advanced against the Spaniards. The former had hardly formed for attack when his right Division was taken in flank by Madden's Portuguese Brigade of the 6th Division, the main body of which, emerging from the village of Oricain, encountered it simultaneously in front. The Brigades of Ross and Stubbs, belonging to the 4th Division, struck it at the same time on the left flank. Clausel at once sent a Division in support, but the attack had been premature; neither Clausel's 3rd Division nor Reille's troops being ready to co-operate. Although the latter came into action as quickly as possible, and some of their columns for the moment actually gained the crest, the assaults were not made simultaneously, and after most desperate hand-to-hand fighting, Reille and Clausel were hurled back into the valley. " I never saw the troops behave so well," wrote Wellington. His second line had not been engaged; the first had repelled double its own numbers, though at a cost of 2,600 officers and men; 20 per cent. of its strength. The losses of the French were stated at only 1,800, a figure believed to be much under the mark. In view of the noted marksmanship of the British troops, it seems surprisingly small, but their ammunition gave out and our men were reduced to that taken from the enemy which, though it could be used, was much too small for the bore of their muskets.

Without acquaintance either with the ground or with a variety of circumstances which may have influenced Lord Wellington, it is impossible to make any positive criticism; but judging superficially it certainly looks as if he lost this day a great opportunity of crushing Soult. Had he allowed the 6th and 7th Divisions to descend the valley of the Lanz upon Clausel's rear, and had he manœuvred with the 3rd Division and the available Cavalry to menace the left flank and rear of Reille at Zabaldica, the French would apparently have been in imminent peril of annihilation.

The 29th passed without renewal of the struggle. D'Erlon, who had hitherto shown a painful lack of energy, marched to join Soult by the valley of the Lanz, and reached Ostiz at midday on the 29th. But the situation was growing hourly more critical for the French. Soult had brought supplies for only four days. (To eke them out, he had, immediately after the fight, sent back his Cavalry and Artillery to France with orders to join Villatte on the Lower Bidassoa.) Hill's Corps, posted between Lizasso and Arestegui, and connected with Wellington by the 7th Division on the Marcalain-Oricain road, was intended to keep D'Erlon at bay or, by assuming the offensive, to menace the rear of Soult by the Lizasso-Olague road.

Under the circumstances the French Marshal abandoned all hope of relieving Pampeluna, but resolved to draw off his Army to the right and place himself between the Allies and the Bastan. By this manœuvre he would be in a position to regain his base by the Dona Maria Pass, and to concentrate for the relief of San Sebastian. To effect the operation it would be necessary to get Hill out of the way. Count D'Erlon, who had more than 20,000 men supported by La Martinière's Division from Reille's Corps, was ordered to attack him. D'Erlon, reinforced by a Cavalry Division, accordingly moved up the Ulzemea valley to Latano, and found Hill with the 2nd Division (minus Byng) and Da Costa's Brigade of Silveira's Division, posted on the Cerro de Mocho near Buenza. Soult came up in person. The attack was made without delay, and

IN THE PENINSULA 717

Hill, outnumbered by two to one and outflanked on his left, fell back with the loss of 400 men to the heights of Ygueras between Arestegui and Berasain where, after being reinforced by the remainder of his Army Corps under Campbell and Morillo, he again offered battle. But Soult had achieved his object, for he had regained touch with Villatte by the Dona Maria Pass, and now believed himself to be in a position to join that officer and succour San Sebastian.

It was not long before he found himself deceived in his calculations. At daylight on the 30th, Lord Wellington having noticed that the mountains of Elcano and the village of Zabaldica were evacuated, had directed Picton and Dalhousie to sweep round with the 3rd and 7th Divisions and encircle respectively the enemy's left and right. Both Generals were successful. La Martinière indeed was already out of the way, and Clausel was retiring up the valley of the Lanz; but by a rapid movement General Inglis, with a Brigade of the 7th Division, followed up and attacked Conroux with decisive effect. On seeing the result of his flanking movements, Wellington pushed forward the 6th Division and Byng's Brigade against the Division of Maucune, while Cole in front and Picton on the flank attacked Foy beyond Zabaldica. Maucune's men broke in headlong rout; 1,400 were captured. Foy found himself severed from his colleague and forced to retreat by a separate line through the Pass of Urtiaga on the frontier to Alduides. Clausel and La Martinière, with the remnant of Maucune's Division, were pursued to Olague; but Wellington, hearing of Hill's fight, halted at Ostiz. The casualties of the Allies this day amounted to 1,900, the Portuguese being the chief sufferers. The fate of Soult's operations was sealed. His losses exceeded 2,000 killed and wounded, as well as 3,000 prisoners.

The Divisions of Conroux and Maucune hardly existed

as a military body. Foy was completely cut off from his comrades, and so many men were dispersed among the mountains that the two Corps of Reille and Clausel could only muster 15,000 men. Soult had still D'Erlon's 20,000, but his position was rapidly becoming precarious. Hill, with 17,000 men, was in his front. The 3rd, 4th, 6th, and 7th Divisions threatened his flank and rear. In a few hours he would be surrounded by 50,000 men.

Lord Wellington made the following dispositions. Picton was directed upon Linzoain, where he was to be joined by the 13th Dragoons and the 6th Division, which were ordered to the valley of Zubiri from Eugui. Cole, with the 4th Division, was to descend from the high ground into the valley of the Lanz. Hill's Corps, supported by De la Bispal, was to march upon Lanz, following up D'Erlon and manœuvring to turn his right flank. The 7th Division was directed upon the Dona Maria Pass.

These orders were issued in the belief that Soult would direct D'Erlon to join Clausel; but in point of fact the Marshal, who (as we have seen) was present in person with D'Erlon, found himself hemmed in by his advanced position to such an extent as to have no alternative but to retire upon the Dona Maria Pass. Calling up Clausel to him from Olague, he began his retreat at midnight on the 30th. At 10 a.m. on the 31st Hill came up with D'Erlon's Corps forming the rearguard. The 7th Division appeared by the valley of the Lanz on Hill's right; but the enemy, assisted by a mountain fog, got away without any great loss, and Hill marched across the ridges dividing the Dona Maria Pass from that of Velate to join Wellington at Almandroz. The latter was making rapid progress. Byng, with the advance guard, had reached Elizondo early in the day, captured a convoy and many prisoners, and occupied the Col de Maya.

Soult reached St. Estevan in safety. Two roads led thence into France; one by Elizondo and the Col de Maya, the other down the Bidassoa by Sumbilla and Yanzi to Vera. The former was the better of the two, but was already in the hands of the Allies. Although aware of the fact, Soult, strange to say, halted at St. Estevan "in a deep, narrow valley." His situation was one of imminent peril. The 2nd, 4th, and Morillo's Division were close at hand. The 7th had occupied the Dona Maria Pass. Sir Thomas Graham was sending a Spanish Division to block the northern issues of the valley at Vera and Yanzi. In a few hours Soult would be surrounded and forced either to surrender or make a desperate attempt to escape by tracks leading over the mountain to Urdax. Wellington came up in person and overlooked the French camp. What followed can best be told in Napier's words. "Soult seemed tranquil, and four of his *gens d'armes* were seen to ride up the valley in a careless manner. Some of the Staff proposed to cut them off; the English General, anxious to hide his own presence, forbade this, but the next moment three marauding English soldiers entered the valley and were instantly carried off by the *gens d'armes;* half an hour afterwards the drums beat to arms; and their columns began to move out of St. Estevan towards Sumbilla. Thus the disobedience of three plundering knaves unworthy of the name of soldiers, deprived one consummate commander of the most splendid success, and saved another from the most terrible disaster."

There was still a chance that the catastrophe had been only postponed for twenty-four hours, and the prospect brightened when it was seen that Soult, instead of taking to the mountains, was still marching down the valley of the Bidassoa. In the narrow cleft at Yanzi he might easily be stopped by Longa's Spaniards, and messengers had been sent in all directions to the Light Division which was known to be on the march, but whose whereabouts was not ascertained, to intercept the retiring enemy at any possible point.

Early on the 1st of August the advance guard of the 4th Division and De la Bispal's troops, arriving at St. Estevan, found the French rearguard, now under Clausel, still at hand. The narrow road and the long procession of wounded men and baggage had prevented an earlier retirement. The Allied troops crowned the heights on either side of the defile and opened fire. A panic ensued; baggage was captured, many of the French fled by the mountains; and it was with difficulty that Soult, as conspicuous in personal exertion as in his retreat through the Tras os Montes in 1809, stopped a "general dispersion."

Meanwhile the advance guard under Count D'Erlon, about two miles south of Beryzaan, near Yanzi, found its progress stopped by a mountain torrent spanned by a narrow bridge in possession of two companies of Spanish Caçadores. Although the Caçadores were reinforced, the bridge was taken and a height on the further side won and held. D'Erlon now turned eastward along a track leading to Echallar, but before the Corps of Reille could clear the defile the Light Division suddenly appeared on the heights overlooking the left bank of the Bidassoa.

On the concentration of the army to resist Soult's incursion, the Light Division had been ordered down from its post at Vera to join the main body. Marching on exterior lines it wandered about for three days on the Pampeluna-Tolosa road, at times within sound of the firing, but without apparently receiving any definite instructions. It was not till the evening of the 31st that Wellington's order to intercept the enemy in his retreat came to hand. General Alten at once marched from

IN THE PENINSULA

Lecumberri, and at midnight on the 1st of August reached Elgorriaga, twenty-four miles distant. He was now about two miles from St. Estevan and rather further from Sumbilla. Although in a position to harass the enemy's flank he had been too late to intercept his retreat, but with a supreme effort to carry out his instructions Alten scaled the steep Santa Cruz mountain and marched another ten miles in the hope of still overtaking the French and cutting them off near Yanzi. The task was hopeless. In the terrific heat the strain was too great. Men laid down and died.

The head of Alten's column reached at length a precipice overlooking the road which the French were traversing, near the Yanzi bridge. Napier quotes from Cooke's Memoirs—the author of which was present—the following account of the scene which ensued: "We overlooked the enemy at stone's throw and from the summit of a tremendous precipice. The river separated us, but the French were wedged in a narrow road with inaccessible rocks on one side and the river on the other. Confusion impossible to describe followed; the wounded were thrown down in the rush and trampled upon, the Cavalry drew their swords and endeavoured to charge up the pass of Echallar, but the Infantry beat them back, and several, horses and all, were precipitated into the river. Some fired vertically at us, while the wounded called out for quarter, and others pointed to them, supported as they were on branches of trees on which were suspended greatcoats clotted with gore and bloodstained sheets taken from different habitations to aid the sufferers."

Yet even in these dire straits French gallantry and discipline were conspicuous. Some men even tried to make a counter attack; and ultimately, although many prisoners and the whole of the baggage was captured by the Allies, the great bulk of the army crossed the bridge and made good its retreat by mountain paths to Echallar.

Lord Wellington was naturally disappointed at the escape of Soult's army. Alten had made prodigious exertions, and it seems hard to impute blame to him; but Longa ought unquestionably to have brought his whole Division from Vera and to have barred not only the Bidassoa road, but the mountain tracks leading to Echallar. The capture of Soult and his army would then have been ensured. Once more Wellington had proof of the futility of placing reliance on a Spanish officer.

On the 2nd, Soult was discovered in position, with his left at Zagaramundi, about two miles from Urdax, and his right on the rock of Ivantelly in touch with Villatte who occupied the spurs of La Rhune mountain. Clausel, with but 6,000 men remaining, was posted in advance between the town and pass of Echallar, inviting attack.

On the British side, Byng was at Urdax; Hill, at the Col de Maya. Picton with the 3rd and 6th Divisions—the latter commanded once more by Pakenham, for Pack had been wounded at Sorauren—had reoccupied the passes of Roncevalles and Alduides. The 4th, 7th, and Light Divisions were available for offensive operations. The last named was directed to turn Clausel's right by the San Barbara mountain, while the 7th Division from Sumbilla attacked his left, and the 4th his front.

General Barnes, at the head of a Brigade of the 7th Division, 1,500 strong, came in contact with the enemy before the combination was complete. Yet without hesitation he attacked the whole of Clausel's Corps, which was occupying what appeared to be an almost impregnable position, and actually drove it off. "In my life I never saw such an attack," said Wellington. It was indeed an astounding exploit, rivalled only by the Boers in 1881 when they captured the Majuba mountain. The feelings of the cautious Dalhousie at being blest with two such dashing Brigadiers as Barnes and Inglis, who crowned him with laurels which he probably would never have gained by himself, can be better imagined than described!

The fact is that after his recent terrible experiences, the French soldier was but a shadow of himself. Clausel now retired upon Soult, who took up a new line within French territory. D'Erlon occupied the high ground at Ainhoue; Clausel, that to the south of Sarré. Reille, with two Divisions, took post at St. Jean de Luz, behind Villatte, his third Division under Foy being at St. Jean Pied de Port. For the moment Wellington contemplated crossing the Bidassoa and establishing himself in France, but abandoned the idea almost as soon as he had formed it, being influenced by a variety of reasons, partly political, partly military. For the attitude of the Allies in Germany was still doubtful, San Sebastian and Pampeluna were intact, and the configuration of the frontier lent itself to a flank attack upon an army holding the line of the Bidassoa and Nivelle. Consequently the troops, fatigued by the incessant marching and fighting of the last nine days, were allowed to halt very much in the positions which they had occupied previous to Soult's inroad. The enemy was left unmolested, an omission for which Wellington is criticised by Napier, who, while approving of the decision against the invasion of France, considers that a golden opportunity of effecting the dispersion of the whole French Army was lost by the cessation of the pursuit at this particular moment. For admitting Villatte to be by this time within the sphere of operations, Wellington, on the other hand, could count on the stronger Corps of Graham; and though the Allies

724 WELLINGTON'S OPERATIONS

were in want of shoes and ammunition, the French were in worse plight, and were in addition so much scattered and disorganised by defeat that Maucune had only 1,000 men remaining, and other Divisions were but little better off, while Foy with 8,000 men was for the time being cut off from his colleagues.

During this series of operations for the relief of the besieged garrisons, ten actions had been fought in nine days. The loss of the Allies amounted to about 8,000; that of the French to double that figure.

CHAPTER XLII

Lord W. Bentinck returns to Alicante—Suchet follows, but on hearing of the Battle of Vitoria retires across the Ebro—Bentinck advances and invests Tarragona—Detaches Del Parque to join Wellington—Is defeated at Ordal—Relinquishes his command—Is succeeded by General William Clinton—Clinton's measures—Occupies the country about Villa Franca.

LORD WILLIAM BENTINCK, on assuming command of the Anglo-Sicilian Army immediately after Murray's failure at Tarragona, embarked his troops and sailed southward in the hope of finding the city of Valencia unprepared against attack. By seizing it he would interpose between Suchet and Harispe, who had been left on the Zucar to oppose the Spaniards under Del Parque and Elio. But on arrival he found himself forestalled by Suchet, who had marched from Tortosa with such speed as to anticipate his opponent, and Bentinck consequently went on to Alicante, where he landed.

During his absence Del Parque had been defeated by Harispe, and Suchet was preparing to resume the offensive in force when news arrived of the decisive battle of Vitoria. The French Marshal at once evacuated the city of Valencia, which was occupied four days later (on the 9th of July) by the Allies.

Suchet, who had under his command a force of 32,000 men, was now in a position to form a junction with

Clausel, who had retired as already noticed upon Saragossa, and to operate thence against Wellington's flank with a combined force of 45,000. He was, however, reluctant to entirely abandon the province of Valencia; and leaving 2,000 men as garrisons in various places, and 5,000 in Tortosa, marched with diminished numbers upon Saragossa. News, however, came of Clausel's retreat to Jaca, and of the loss of Aragon; whereupon Suchet, crossing the Ebro, retired to Tarragona. Had he continued his march on Saragossa he would, in all probability, have recovered the province, and would also have been in time to co-operate—possibly with decisive effect—in Soult's effort to relieve Pampeluna, which ended with the battle of Sorauren.

Lord W. Bentinck received orders from Wellington to get possession of the open country in Valencia and to establish himself on the Ebro, in accordance with the memorandum of April 14th. "This position," wrote Wellington to Lord William on the 1st of July, "would at least have the effect of diverting the attention of Suchet from this Army; and if it should not succeed in that object, the Allies would gain ground on the eastern coast in proportion as our difficulties would be increased on this side by the increase of the force opposed to us."

On the 9th of July Bentinck entered the city of Valencia unopposed. On the 20th he was at Vinaroz, on the border of Catalonia. On the 27th he crossed the Ebro and occupied the heights beyond. But although his progress had been slow, his position was insecure. He had only 10,000 or 12,000 men, and lay open to the attack of double that number. Del Parque was several marches in rear. Elio was at Valencia. Bentinck, however, was full of confidence; and although Lord Wellington desired him to besiege Tortosa, he advanced at once

IN THE PENINSULA 727

to Tarragona, which he invested on the 30th in the belief that Suchet was intent on evacuating Catalonia, and the expectation that his own army would be raised at an early date to 40,000 men by the junction of the 1st, 2nd, and 3rd Spanish Armies. But Suchet, having been joined by General Decaen from Upper Catalonia, was now in command of an army of 67,000 men, of whom 32,000 could be used in active operations. He pushed forward, and Bentinck, hitherto so confident, felt constrained to abandon the blockade of Tarragona and fell back to the Col de Balaguer. Suchet did not, however, molest him, but after destroying the defences of Tarragona, withdrew behind the Llobregat.

At the end of August Lord William detached Del Parque to join Lord Wellington by the Ebro. Soon afterwards he advanced to Villa Franca, pushing forward an advance guard under Colonel Adam to the Pass of Ordal. During the night of the 12th of September, Adam was attacked suddenly by Suchet and driven from the Pass on to the main body, which in its turn was compelled to fall back on Arbos with the loss of 4 guns and 1,000 men.

Lord William had no heart in the Peninsular contest. He seems to have thought it beneath his dignity to serve under Wellington, notwithstanding the large degree of independence which he in reality enjoyed. His mind was full of schemes for the invasion of Italy, and on the 23rd of September he quitted his troops and embarked for Sicily.

The command was then again assumed in virtue of seniority by General William Clinton, elder brother to Sir Henry. But Clinton, feeling himself unequal to the task, begged Wellington to send some one to relieve him. The command was then offered to Sir T. Picton and others, but being declined by all ultimately remained with

Clinton, whose diffidence proved unwarranted, for he did very well. The force entrusted to him comprised about 15,300 officers and men of the Sicilian contingent, of whom something over 12,000 were present and fit for duty. The addition of the 4,000 available men of Whittingham's Spanish Division and of detachments from other corps raised this number in round figures to 20,000 men. The 1st Army of Spain mustered 13,200 men present, but provision for garrisons and blockades reduced the field force of Copons to 9,000. Elio, with 25,000 men, blockaded Tortosa and the French fortresses south of the Ebro. "The courage and discipline of the British and Germans set aside," observes Napier, "it would be difficult to find armies less efficient for an offensive campaign than those of the Allies in Catalonia. Clinton's command over the Spaniards was restricted to Whittingham's and Sarsfield's troops; and though he strove to conciliate Copons, that General's indolence and incapacity impeded or baffled all useful measures."

Clinton was based on Tarragona; Copons, on the Montserrat mountains, and in addition to these disadvantages the former had little or no transport, for Murray in embarking for Tarragona had most foolishly discharged nearly all his mules and carts. Clinton was consequently dependent for food on the vessels off the coast; and his Spaniards were on the point of starving. He set himself to repair the fortifications of Tarragona; a work of time, for the enemy in his retreat had made nineteen breaches in the walls. The necessary escorts for the labourers so diminished his available force that he and Copons combined could only have mustered 18,000 men to resist the 30,000 of Suchet. Under the circumstances Wellington advised a defensive attitude, and suggested that "the two armies should harass the enemy's flanks and rear alternately if he attacked either, but together if he moved upon Tortosa."

IN THE PENINSULA

General Clinton nevertheless assumed a confident bearing. With a view to increasing his supplies, he occupied towards the end of October the country about Villa Franca, and held on to his advanced position in spite, not only of several demonstrations on the part of Suchet, but of Wellington's suggestion that he was not strong enough to do more than hold the line of the Ebro.

By the end of the year Clinton's position had greatly improved. Tarragona was once more in a state of defence, while the force under Suchet had been reduced by 7,000 men, partly Germans whose fidelity was suspected, partly drafts for other parts of the theatre of war.

The operations of the Allies on the east coast had carried no meed of glory, but nevertheless had attained the desired object of retaining Suchet in Catalonia. The presence of that officer in Navarre would have made an unwelcome addition to the strength of Wellington's opponents.

CHAPTER XLIII

Siege of San Sebastian—Its capture—Attempt of Soult to relieve the fortress—Battle of San Marcial—Advance of Hill—Soult withdraws behind the Bidassoa.

ON the day after the battle of Vitoria, General Rey, who had been detained to conduct the convoy despatched by Joseph on the 19th of June, entered San Sebastian and assumed command of the fortress. The garrison, inclusive of reinforcements hastily thrown in, mustered about 3,000 men, but the place had been almost dismantled, and was in no condition to stand a siege. Towards the end of the month the Spaniards appeared and shortly afterwards cut off the aqueduct, reducing the water supply to a few foul wells. On the 2nd of July a small British squadron entered the harbour, but its efforts at a naval blockade were a farce, and Rey received constant supplies from St. Jean de Luz by sea. On the 9th Sir Thomas Graham relieved the Spaniards and undertook the siege.

Graham's force consisted of the 5th Division, the Portuguese Brigade of Bradford and that commanded formerly by Pack, but now by Wilson: in all about 10,000 men. The 1st Division and that of Longa acted as a covering force on the Lower Bidassoa. A new and powerful siege train had been prepared and was supplemented by ships' guns, which raised the number of its pieces to 40. A siege depot was formed at Passages

IN THE PENINSULA

in the interval between the besieging and covering armies; but the base of operations was at Bilbao.

The town of San Sebastian, built on a sandy spit of land, is flanked on one side by the sea, on the other by the river Urumea. Behind it "rose the Monte Orgullo, a rugged cone 400 feet high, washed by the ocean; and its southern face, covered with batteries and overlooking the town, was cut off from the latter by defensive walls. It was crowned by the small castle of La Mota, which was itself commanded at a distance of 1,300 yards by the Monte Olia which rose behind the Urumea. The land front was 350 yards wide, stretching quite across the isthmus. It consisted of a high curtain or rampart, very solid, strengthened by a lofty casemated flat bastion or cavalier placed in the centre, and by half bastions at either end. A regular hornwork was pushed out from this front; and 600 yards beyond the hornwork, the isthmus was closed by the bridge of San Bartolomeo, at the foot of which stood the suburb of San Martin.

"On the opposite side of the Uremea were certain sandy hills called the Chofres, through which the road from Passages passed to the wooden bridge over the river, and thence, by the suburb of Santa Catalina, along the top of a sea-wall which formed a *fausse braye* for the hornwork. The flanks of the town were protected by simple ramparts; one washed by the water of the harbour, the other by the Uremea, which at high tide covered four of the twenty-seven feet comprised in its elevation. This was the weak side of the fortress, for though covered by the river there was only a single wall ill-flanked by the old towers and the half bastion of the Elma, which was situated at the extremity of the rampart close under the Monte Orgullo. There was no ditch, no counterscarp, no glacis; the wall could be seen to its base from the

Chofre hills, at distances varying from 500 to 1,000 yards, and when the tide was out the Urumea left a dry strand under the rampart as far as St. Elma. However, the batteries from Mount Orgullo could see this strand. The other flank was secured by the harbour, in the mouth of which was a rocky island called Santa Clara, where the French had established a post of twenty-five men."

Batteries were to be erected on the Chofre hills with a view to breaching the weak eastern wall. The approaches were divided into a right and left attack. The former, from the Chofres, was carried on by the Portuguese Brigades; the latter, of a subsidiary character, by the 5th Division, whose object was only to dislodge the enemy from the convent of San Bartolomeo which was held as an advanced post, and from a circular cask redoubt which guarded the road leading along the isthmus into the town.

"Two batteries were begun on the night of the 11th of July for six guns to fire against San Bartolomeo, and on the night of the 13th, four others were commenced, three on the Chofre heights and one on the Monte Olia, at ranges of 600 to 1,300 yards, to breach the eastern wall and bombard the town. Fire from the first two batteries was continued until the 17th, on which day the convent and the works connected with it were carried by assault, and two batteries were commenced there to fire against the place. On the 20th, the four batteries on the east side of the river and the two on San Bartolomeo ridge opened fire against the town, and during the night the garrison abandoned the cask redoubt, while the troops of the left attack commenced the first parallel, the left of which rested on the redoubt, the right on the river. The fire was continued during the next three days, and by the 23rd the breaches . . . were considered practicable, and the troops told off for the assault lined the trenches.

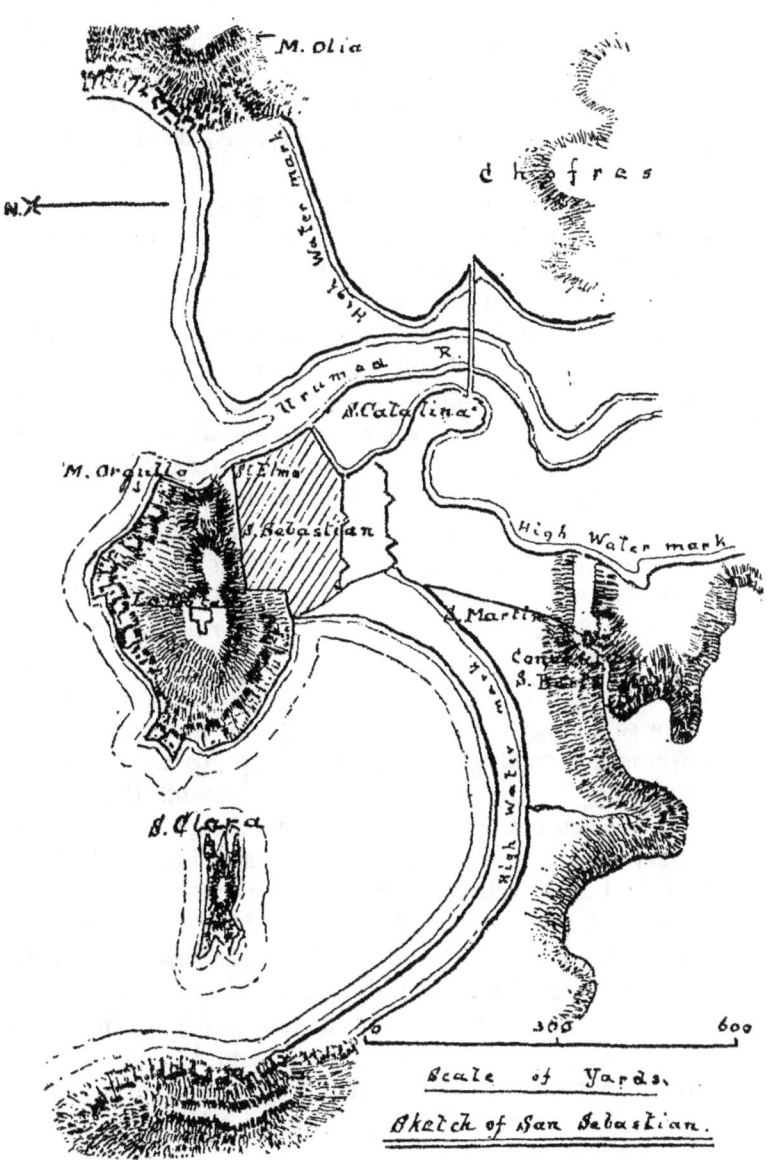

But some houses having been set on fire near the breach, and which it appeared could form an obstacle to the troops after they had carried it, it was determined to postpone the attack to the next day, *i.e.*, until daybreak on the 25th.

"The troops told off for this purpose were furnished by the 5th Division. Major-General Hay's Brigade was told off to assault the principal breach, and another battalion the smaller breach. A mine had been run from the first parallel towards the counterscarp, and its explosion was to be the signal for the assault, to which the troops moved out from the trenches on the isthmus. It had been intended that the advance should be covered by fire from the right attack, but it was so dark when the troops started that the gunners were unable to see to direct their pieces. The ground was rugged and difficult; the troops had 300 yards to go, for part of the distance over rocks slippery with seaweed; but the explosion of the mine diverted the attention of the besieged, and the front of the column reached the main breach without difficulty. Then the French, recovering from their surprise, brought such a fire to bear on the English as to effectually stop all progress, and the troops retired to the trenches. The battalion intended to assault the further breach, seeing the retreat of their comrades from the main one, fell back without making any effort. The total loss in killed, wounded, and prisoners was 425, and the supply of ammunition falling short, active operations ceased for a time, though the blockade was continued.

"The reasons for the failure are not far to seek; the fire of the place had not been sufficiently reduced, the troops made no persistent efforts, and the attack was carried out in the dark, which effectually prevented the artillery supporting it" (Lieut.-Col. W. H. James. Unpublished Précis).

IN THE PENINSULA 735

Soult's inroad into Spain at the end of July caused Wellington to embark the siege train and turn the siege into a blockade; but on the 5th of August the guns were re-landed and the siege was resumed. No great progress was, however, made as the ammunition of the besiegers fell short. Strange to say, Wellington was able to secure very little naval co-operation. Not only did the garrison get all it required by sea, but Lord Wellington's operations were hindered and sometimes entirely stopped by the failure of the fleet to convey either his reinforcements or the daily supplies essential to him. Indeed, the grievance went even further, for French and American privateers carried off many vessels which were attempting to reach the ports of Santander or Bilbao.

For this state of things Napier censures the Admiralty, but it is only fair to say that in view of the American war and its multifarious tasks in other ways, the British navy (in regard to frigates and cruisers) was not strong enough for the work expected of it. This excuse was not, however, pleaded by Lord Melville, the First Lord of the Admiralty, on behalf of the squadron off the west coast of Portugal. The Admiral, George Martin, was confined to the 43rd degree of latitude, and was consequently debarred from the northern coast of Spain; but the disability did not prevent him sending off ships to Bordeaux and other places outside his station; and one suspects if he did not aid the operations on land by escorting convoys and guarding the coast, the reason lay partly in the monotony of such duty. Throughout the Peninsular War comparatively little aid was received either from the Admiralty or the Navy. The former made vexatious regulations, the latter intercepted Wellington's corn ships, gave him inaccurate information, and was rarely in evidence except when opportunity occurred to claim a share in the prize money which had in reality been won solely by the troops.

On the 19th of August a new siege train came out from England. Another arrived on the 23rd, but with ammunition enough only for one day's consumption. During the night of the 25th the batteries on both banks of the Urumea were armed, and opened fire next day, but with a somewhat disappointing result. On the 27th the adjacent island of Santa Clara was occupied after a sharp resistance, and a battery established therein to take in reverse the defences of Monte Orgullo at a range of about 1,000 yards.

An assault was ordered for the 31st; but the enemy's defences were not yet destroyed, and General Officers openly expressed their expectation of failure. Wellington therefore called for 750 volunteers from the 1st, 4th, and Light Divisions—" men who could show other troops how to mount a breach."

This appeal was felt by Sir James Leith, who had just rejoined the army, as a slur upon his Division. He therefore held the volunteers in reserve with two of his Brigades, and confided the assault to the remaining one under General Robinson. A lodgment was with the utmost difficulty effected on the great breach; but only by using up the whole of the reserve. Bradford's Portuguese Brigade co-operated by a gallant attack from the Chofres, but in face of the deadly fire from the fortress no further progress could be made. Leith had lost 2,500 men, and the tide was rising; but just at the moment when retreat seemed inevitable, a terrible explosion of shells killed many of the garrison and ruined their defences. The town was then abandoned and General Rey retired to Monte Orgullo. On the 9th of September, after a defence of 63 days, the gallant old Governor, whose service dated from the Seven Years' War, being overwhelmed with shell fire, had no alternative but to surrender the Castle; and the remnant of

IN THE PENINSULA

the garrison, consisting of 1,300 effective officers and men (537 others being in Hospital), marched out with the honours of war which they had so magnificently earned. The loss of the Allies during the siege had amounted to 967 killed, 2,471 wounded, and 375 missing. Among the killed was Sir R. Fletcher, the C.R.E. It is deeply to be regretted that the outrages committed by a small number of the British troops on getting possession of the town seem to have exceeded even those at Ciudad Rodrigo and Badajoz.

San Sebastian did not fall without an effort of Soult to relieve it. After his retreat into France on the 2nd of August the French troops were disposed as follows:— Reille, with two Divisions, was posted in rear of Villatte; his 3rd, under Foy, strengthened by National Guards and detachments, at St. Jean Pied de Port. D'Erlon and Clausel took up ground in advance of Ainhoa and Sarre respectively.

The design of Soult was to cross the Lower Bidassoa and attack the Allies on the Royal Road. He brought up Foy from St. Jean Pied de Port and concentrated on his right. On the morning of the 30th of August Clausel with 20,000 men was concealed in the woods behind the Bayonette mountains above Vera, and Reille with 18,000, including Villatte's Reserve, behind the mountains near Biriatu, supported by 7,000 men under Foy and 36 guns. D'Erlon held the camps at Serre and Ainhoa.

On the side of the Allies the Galicians—now commanded by General Freyre—and the Division of Longa occupied the steep San Marcial mountain overlooking the Bidassoa opposite Biriatu, supported on the left flank at Yrun by the 1st Division, reinforced by two battalions of the 1st Guards from Oporto and a new Brigade under Lord Aylmer, made up of the newly arrived 76th, 84th, and 85th; and on their right by the two British Brigades of the 4th Division at San Antonio. The Portuguese Brigade of that Division and that of Inglis from the 7th were posted a mile and a half south of the Bidassoa opposite Vera. The Light Division occupied the Santa Barbara mountain on the right bank. The rest of the 7th Division and that of De la Bispal were at Echallar. Hill was about Maya, and Picton (3rd and 6th Divisions) in the neighbourhood of the Alduides, outside the sphere of the present operations. The Allies were occupying positions too extensive for their numbers and were consequently open to be attacked in detail.

At dawn on the 31st Reille forded the Bidassoa above Biriatu and attacked Freyre, but was repulsed after heavy fighting. Clausel had simultaneously crossed the river at Vera, assailed the Portuguese Brigade of the 4th Division under Colonel Stubbs and had driven him and Inglis back to a further ridge, where they came in touch with Cole. Clausel's success proved but momentary. On observing his advance Hill, pursuant to Wellington's orders, made a demonstration towards St. Jean Pied de Port, while the troops at Echallar attacked and drove D'Erlon from his camp. D'Erlon sent word to Soult that the Allies were advancing in force upon Bayonne; and although Hill halted at noon, the Marshal, who had prepared a grand attack on the San Marcial position, withdrew Reille on receipt of the message across the Bidassoa, sent Foy to support D'Erlon at Serres behind the Nivelle, and directed Clausel to do the same at nightfall.

In accordance with these instructions Clausel re-crossed the Bidassoa in person with two Brigades at dusk, but General Vandermaesen, who then took command of the Divisions still on the right bank, found the fords impracticable and was forced to march up-stream to the bridge of Vera. The bridge was occupied by a Company

IN THE PENINSULA 739

of the 95th Rifles, who held it with the utmost gallantry till daybreak, when the passage was at length forced, though with the loss of Vandermaesen himself and 200 men. Had the Riflemen been reinforced from the heights of Santa Barbara the whole French force on the left bank of the Bidassoa should have been taken. The omission was due to the incapacity of General Skerrett, who unfortunately was for the moment in command of the 2nd Brigade of the Light Division.

On the 1st of September Soult again made up his mind to attack the San Marcial position, but on hearing of the loss of the town of San Sebastian gave up all further attempt. During these brief operations the casualties on either side had been heavy. The French had lost 3,600 men, including Generals Vandermaesen and La Martinière killed, Menne, Remond, and Guy wounded. The casualties of the Allies amounted to 2,600, shared as follows: Spanish, 1,680; Portuguese, 530; British, 400.

CHAPTER XLIV

Passage of the Bidassoa—The Allies established within French territory—Sir T. Graham quits the Army and is succeeded by Sir John Hope.

ON the expulsion of the French field forces after the battle of Vitoria from all but the eastern provinces of Spain the first idea of the British Government was to leave 20,000 or 30,000 men to take up a defensive position in the Pyrenees, supported by the Spaniards, and to transfer Wellington and the rest of his British troops to the seat of war in Germany. Upon Lord Wellington's representations the Ministers gave up the idea and were then anxious that he should invade the south of France. But, to say nothing of San Sebastian, Santona, and Pampeluna, four fortresses in Aragon, seven in Catalonia, and four in Valencia were still held by the French. Affairs on the east coast looked indeed so menacing that Wellington made up his mind to go there in person, but on the fall of San Sebastian decided in the first instance to fall in with the political views of the Government to the extent of crossing the Bidassoa and assuming "a menacing position within French territory."

Reille's Corps, forming the right of the French Army, was holding two lines of defence—the first extending from the mouth of the Bidassoa to the Mandale mountain, the second from St. Jean de Luz to Ascain on the Nivelle, where Villatte connected Reille with Clausel,

IN THE PENINSULA 741

whose Corps occupied the Mandale, Bayonette, Commissari, and Great Rhune mountains up to Amotz. From Amotz D'Erlon took up the line along a ridge behind Ainhoa. Finally Foy, with 15,000 men, including National Guards, was at St. Jean Pied de Port, communicating by Cambo with D'Erlon, and the Division of General Paris was at Oleron.

The outpost sentries of the opposing armies were in friendly contact for weeks together. But no fighting took place. The French were intent on fortifying their mountain positions, and though, on the fall of San Sebastian, Wellington wished to effect the passage of the Bidassoa forthwith, the pontoons on which he relied were delayed and the project had to be postponed till the return of favourable tides. "The plan," says Napier, "involved as dangerous and daring an enterprise as any undertaken by him during the whole war. This was to seize the Great Rhune mountain and its dependents, and at the same time force the passage of the Lower Bidassoa and establish his left wing in France."

Early in October Lord Wellington made a feint with his right and deceived Soult, who was expecting the principal attack on that, the obvious side. The demonstrations were continued till the 7th, the day fixed for the grand operation. At dawn on that day Giron (who had succeeded De la Bispal) descended from the Ivantelly rocks, and the Light Division from Santa Barbara, to attack the Great La Rhune. Longa co-operated. The 4th Division was in support at Santa Barbara.

The Light Division, manœuvring by Brigades under Colborne—*vice* Skerrett, who had gone to England—and Kempt, who mutually supported one another, attacked Taupin and nearly gained the crest of the Bayonette mountain. At this point the French General held his assailants at bay until threatened on the left by Kempt and on the right by the Spaniards, who had crossed the Lower Bidassoa. He then retreated in haste to Olette, where he rallied under cover of Villatte.

Giron had simultaneously attacked Conroux, and his men, fighting well, gained the spurs of the Great La Rhune, but failed to drive the enemy from the crest line. The right and front of the position were indeed impregnable; the left was more accessible, and Wellington ordered it to be attacked from this side next day by the Spaniards, supported by the 7th Division. Partly by skill and valour, partly by good fortune, he then succeeded in inducing the French to evacuate the terrible mountain.

Demonstrations by the 6th Division had retained D'Erlon in his position about Urdax. But meanwhile the main object, the passage of the Bidassoa, had been successfully effected. Before daybreak on the 7th the troops assigned for the purpose had been posted in their respective stations overlooking the river. The 4th Spanish Army under Freyre, a Brigade of Guards, and that of Wilson were hidden behind the spurs of San Marcial, on the crest of which Bradford remained in reserve. The rest of the 1st Division was posted opposite fords a little lower down. The British Brigades of the 5th Division, now commanded by General Hay, were opposite Andaya; the Portuguese Brigade, with that of Lord Aylmer, was at Fuenterabia.

Tents were left standing at 7 a.m.; the advance began from the left. Hay and Aylmer crossed the channel and half a mile of sands at low tide without receiving a shot from Maucune, whose Division of Reille's Corps guarded the opposite bank. The 1st Division and Freyre followed. The French were completely taken by surprise, and though Boyer—*vice* La Martinière, killed—brought up the 9th Division from Urogne, Andaya and the Caffé Republicain were captured and the Allies pierced the

French line between the Sans Culottes and the Croix des Bouquets entrenchments. The latter were then attacked and the French expelled after a hard struggle. Higher up the river Freyre captured the Mandale mountain without difficulty and thus turned the left of Reille and the right of Clausel. The former retired in disorder to Urogne, three miles distant, where Soult, arriving in person with part of Villatte's reserve, rallied the fugitives.

The passage of the Bidassoa was won and the Allies were established on French soil. The operation had been a magnificent illustration of the art of war, for " Wellington had with overmastering combinations overwhelmed each point of attack. Taupin's and Maucune's Divisions, each less than 5,000 strong, were separately assailed, the first by 18,000, the second by 15,000 men; and at neither point were Reille and Clausel able to bring their reserves into action before the positions were won " (Napier). In this fight the loss of Reille amounted to 390 men and 8 guns, that of Taupin to 898 men, of whom 536 were prisoners; and the total number of casualties was admittedly 1,387. Those of the Anglo-Portuguese reached 814 and the Spaniards lost about 1,000 men.

During the advance of his Brigade Colonel Colborne, probably the best man in the Army except Lord Wellington himself, did a marvellous feat of arms. Having pressed on in advance of his troops, and with only about 25 men at hand, he so successfully imposed on a French column whom he unexpectedly overtook in a ravine as to induce the whole number—22 officers and 400 men—to surrender at discretion!

The passage of the Bidassoa was the occasion of the last appearance of Sir Thomas Graham in the Peninsular War. He was troubled with an affection of the eyes which had temporarily incapacitated him on previous occasions. Next year he was again called to active service in Holland, but did not add greatly to his reputation.

Concurrently with Graham's departure the old trouble of shortage of General Officers revived in full force. Leith and Oswald had been wounded; Clinton and Skerrett (neither of them of any great use) were sick; Dalhousie and Picton went home. But Graham was succeeded by Sir John Hope, who had commanded the Army at Corunna after Moore had been struck. Senior as a general officer, he volunteered to serve under Wellington as soon as the latter had been awarded Field Marshal's rank. Sir John Hope joined the Army in Spain on the 6th of October and brought a great accession of strength, for Wellington spoke of him as being "certainly the ablest man in the Army," and henceforward, in the event of an accident happening to the Commander-in-Chief, his place would be worthily filled.

CHAPTER XLV

Wellington takes measures to restore discipline—He organises his troops in three Army Corps—Strength of the Allies—Position and strength of the enemy—Soult's plan of combined action is declined by Suchet—Pampeluna surrenders—Battle of the Nivelle—Retreat of the French to the Nive—Wellington forces the passage—The five days' fighting called the Battle of the Nive.

WELLINGTON'S first care on setting foot within French soil was for the discipline of his troops. "The Commander of the Forces is concerned to be under the necessity of publishing over again his orders of the 9th of July last, as they have been unattended to by the officers and troops which entered France yesterday. According to all the information which the Commander of the Forces has received, outrages of all descriptions were committed by the troops in presence even of their officers, who took no pains whatever to prevent them. The Commander of the Forces has already determined that some officers, so grossly negligent of their duty, shall be sent to England, that their names may be brought under the attention of the Prince Regent, and that his Royal Highness may give such directions respecting them as he may think proper, as the Commander of the Forces is determined not to command officers who will not obey his orders."

The forces under Wellington's command were now

746 WELLINGTON'S OPERATIONS

organised in three Army Corps. That on the right of the line was commanded by Sir Rowland Hill. It comprised the 2nd, 6th, Hamilton's (formerly Silveira's), and Morillo's Divisions, as well as Mina's irregulars, and occupied Roncevalles and the valley of Bastan. The Central Corps under Beresford, who for the first time since Albuera, held an executive command of British troops, included the troops under Giron and Longa, with the 3rd, 4th, 7th, and Light Divisions, and was posted about Maya, Echallar, the Bayonette, and Rhune mountains. The Corps on the left was commanded by Sir John Hope, and consisted of the 1st and 5th Divisions, Lord Aylmer's, and the unattached Portuguese Brigades, and the Galician Army.

The State of the 22nd of October showed 63,630 British and K.G.L., and 33,721 Portuguese as the gross strength, including officers; but 20,000 were sick, others were detached or prisoners of war, and the N.Co's. and men actually present amounted only to 41,885 British and 23,470 Portuguese cavalry and infantry. The artillerymen were an additional 3,000 to 4,000, and the Spaniards were about 30,000 strong.

After the British passage of the Bidassoa, Soult was able to hold a less extended line, and from the purely military point of view, his position was improved. Villatte held St. Jean de Luz. Reille occupied a position in advance with two entrenched lines, one extending from Sans Culottes to Urogne, the other at Bordegain and Belchena. Clausel, in the centre, was posted with both flanks resting on the Nivelle—the right at Ascain, the left at Amotz. D'Erlon on the left reached down to the Mondarrin mountain overlooking the Nive. Foy was at Bidarray, higher up that river. Paris was at St. Jean Pied de Port. In rear of the general line, Soult formed

IN THE PENINSULA 747

vast entrenched camps extending from Cambo on the Nive to St. Jean de Luz, a distance of sixteen miles.

But the Marshal's plan rested on the resumption of the offensive in conjunction with Suchet.

On the 16th of September the "State" of his Army was as follows:—

	Present under Arms.		Detached.		Hosptl.	Total.	
	Men.	Horses.	Men.	Horses.	Men.	Men.	Horses.
Army of Spain	81,351	11,159	4,004	1,438	22,488	107,843	11,272
,, ,, Aragon	32,476	4,447	2,721	320	3,616	38,813	6,305
,, ,, Catalonia	24,026	1,670	120	—	2,137	26,283	3,497
Grand Total	137,853	17,276	6,845	1,758	28,241	172,939	20,074

"STATE" OF THE ARMY OF SPAIN IN DETAIL.

Present under Arms.

Reille	Foy	5,002	
	Maucune	4,166	
	Menne	5,707	14,875
D'Erlon	D'Armagnac	4,353	
	Abbé	5,903	
	Maransin	4,842	15,098
Clausel	Conroux	4,736	
	Roguet	5,982	
	Taupin	5,071	15,789
Villatte	Field troops	8,256	
	Garrison ,,	2,168	10,424
Cavalry	Pierre Soult	4,456	
	Theilhard	2,368	
Gens d'armes	Mounted	291	
	Dismounted	1,210	
Parc		895	
Engineers		504	
Garrisons	Pampeluna	3,805	
	San Sebastian	2,366	
	Santona	1,633	
	Bayonne	4,631	
	St. Jean Pied de Port	1,786	
	Navarrens	842	
	Castle of Lourdes	107	

748 WELLINGTON'S OPERATIONS

From the gross total of 81,064 large deductions must, however, be made. The garrison of San Sebastian was already captured. The Cavalry was of little use in the mountains. The Italian Brigade, 2,000 strong, was under orders for Milan. After its departure Soult had only 52,000 men available for field operations, exclusive of Paris and the National Guards, whose numbers may have been 10,000.

Soult was bent upon resuming the offensive in accordance with the traditions of the French Army. He therefore desired to leave the defence of the south-western frontier to the National Guards from the southern districts—a very efficient body—and to about 30,000 conscripts about to be incorporated, by entrusting them with the charge of the entrenched camps at Bayonne and St. Jean Pied de Port; and proposed to Suchet a combined movement by which 90,000 men and 200 guns would have formed a junction at Saragossa with a view to attacking the right flank of the Allies. It was a great scheme. But Suchet refused to co-operate, and by the middle of October any such combination was rendered impossible by the snow which began to fall in the Pyrenees.

On the last day of that month General Cassan and the garrison of Pampeluna after a most gallant defence were starved out and forced to surrender; and as matters were evidently going ill for Napoleon in Germany, and Soult could hope for no reinforcements other than conscripts, Wellington resolved to make another forward movement and drive the enemy from the Nivelle.

Both sides were suffering from great hardships, but the Allies were the worse off. Hill was knee deep in snow; Beresford and Hope were exposed to torrents of rain. Their troops were soaked and shivering without greatcoats, which, thanks to the naval delay, had not yet been

IN THE PENINSULA 749

brought up from Portugal. The Spaniards were terribly neglected by their Government; and Wellington, aware that they could hardly subsist without plunder, hesitated to take them into France. Desertion was rife throughout the Army; 1,200 men, English, Germans, or Spaniards went over to the enemy within four months. The Portuguese also deserted in large numbers, but invariably went home. To remain for the winter in the present positions was obviously impossible. More congenial quarters had to be found.

The forward movement was delayed for several days by heavy rain. On the 7th of November the weather cleared, and on the 10th Wellington having concentrated 90,000 men of all arms and ranks—74,000 of whom were Anglo-Portuguese—and 95 guns, resolved to force the passage of the Nivelle at San Pé. The position at Roncevalles was held by part of Mina's men. The rest of Hill's Corps, with Grant's Brigade of Cavalry—26,000 men and 9 guns—were assembled in the valley of Bastan to attack D'Erlon. Beresford with the bulk of his Corps occupied the valley between the Aitchubia and La Rhune mountains, holding the latter with Longa's and the Light Division and six mountain guns under Charles Alten. The Cavalry Brigade of Victor Alten and three Batteries R.A. followed along the road to Sarré. A body of 36,000 men and 24 guns were thus in readiness to assail Clausel.

The Galician Army, 9,000 men with 6 guns under Freyre, was posted on Charles Alten's left to check any reinforcements which might be sent from Serre to Clausel. Hope's Corps with the Cavalry Brigades of Vandeleur (*vice* Anson) and Bock—in all, 19,000 men and 54 guns—watched Reille and Villatte. The naval squadron under Sir G. Collier came close inshore to aid the operation.

Soult had spared no pains to fortify his positions, which bristled with the most formidable stone "sangars." But his weak point lay in the fact that the line held was too great in extent for the 60,000 men, who (in the absence of Foy and of the Cavalry) defended it. D'Erlon, from the Mondarrin mountain to the bridge of Amotz, occupied a frontage of six miles. Clausel, from Amotz to Ascain, and Reille from Ascain to St. Jean de Luz, extended each over five miles, making a total length of sixteen miles.

During the night of the 9th the columns of attack had in places been pushed forward without detection to within eighty yards of the enemy's posts. As the morning of the 10th dawned brilliantly, three guns from the Aitchubia gave the signal for attack, and the Light Division assailed the right of the French occupying the little La Rhune mountain. The Spaniards on the left were intended to outflank the position but failed to do much in aid. The rush of the 43rd from Kempt's Brigade on the La Rhune proved, however, irresistible; and thanks to the able dispositions of Major William Napier —historian of the Peninsular War—who commanded the regiment, the apparently impregnable strongholds were captured in succession at comparatively small cost.

The 4th and 7th Divisions, who had moved forward simultaneously, captured the enemy's outworks and the village of Sarré. They then prepared to advance against Clausel's main position.

"It was now," says Napier, "eight o'clock, and from the smaller Rhune a splendid spectacle opened upon the view. On the left the ships of war slowly sailing to and fro, were exchanging shot with the fort of Socoa; and Hope, menacing all the French lines in the low ground, sent the sound of 100 pieces of Artillery bellowing up the rocks, to be answered by nearly as many from the tops of the mountains. On the right the summit of the great Aitchubia was just lighted by the rising sun, and 50,000 men, rushing down its enormous slopes with ringing shouts, seemed to chase the receding shadows into the deep valley. The plains of France, so long overlooked from the towering crags of the Pyrenees, were to be the prize of battle, and the half-famished soldiers in their fury broke through the iron barrier erected by Soult as if it were but a screen of reeds."

On the right, Hill had been equally successful. After a toilsome night march, he had attacked the left of D'Erlon and driven the enemy from his advanced posts. Morillo and Mina demonstrated against Abbé who occupied a detached post on the Mondarrin. Urdax and Ainhoa were captured by the 2nd Division, on the left of which the 6th and Hamilton's Division crossed the Nivelle and threatened the bridge of Amotz in reverse. But the rugged rocks hindered their advance, and it was not till 11 a.m. that they could assail the line of redoubts constructed along a ridge behind a ravine extending from the bridge half way to Espellette which formed D'Erlon's main position and was held by the Division of D'Armagnac.

Clinton—once more in command of the 6th Division which within the last few weeks had been commanded by himself and Pakenham twice, as well as by Pack and Colville—cleverly turned the redoubt nearest the Nivelle which was unfinished. It was abandoned by its garrison, and the chain being thus broken, the second and third redoubts were captured by Hamilton and Stewart. D'Armagnac then fell back in the direction of Bayonne to Helbacen and Abbé retired on Cambo. "The deadly strife," says an eye-witness, "was surprisingly grand; yet the sublimity of the scene defied all attempt at description. . . . The fierce and continued charge of the

752 WELLINGTON'S OPERATIONS

British was irresistible; ... onward they bore, nor stopped to breathe, rushing forward through glen, dale, and forest. ... Yet they seemed to chase only the startled red deer, prowling wolf or savage wild boar, until they arrive at the steel bristling stronghold of the foe."

Meanwhile on Hill's left Beresford had carried the heights above Sarré. In spite of the gallant defence of Conroux against overwhelming numbers, that officer was driven back to the Nivelle where he fell mortally wounded. The bridge of Amotz was then seized by the 3rd Division at 11 a.m.; and it was, in fact, this advance of Beresford which paved the way for Hill, and not only ensured D'Erlon's retirement but cut him off from Clausel. The latter, however, with the Divisions of Taupin and Maransin, still made head against the Allies and covered the retreat of Conroux. But Maransin, overwhelmed in his turn by the 3rd, 4th, and 7th Divisions, was driven from his entrenchments; and on his right, Taupin, attacked in front by the victorious Light Division and threatened in flank by Freyre and Longa, gave way in confusion. By order of Clausel a counter attack was attempted with a view to rescuing the 88th Regiment which had been cut off in a redoubt. But Taupin, with only two regiments available for the purpose, was instantly charged by the 95th Rifles and menaced in flank by the 4th Division. Clausel bringing up another regiment, found himself equally assailed. The French broke and fled to the Nivelle which they crossed by the bridges between Ascain and St. Pé. The 88th, left to its fate, surrendered after a gallant resistance, to Colborne with the 52nd. It was now past two o'clock. Conroux' Division pushed along the Bayonne road and was joined at Helbacen by Taupin and D'Armagnac, the retreat being covered by Maransin who held on to the height

IN THE PENINSULA 753

overlooking the right bank of the Nivelle at St. Pé. That village was seized by the 3rd and 7th Divisions.

Matters were now very critical for the French. Two British Divisions were in rear of their right wing. Three others were at hand. Thus the Corps of Reille and Villatte with the reserve Artillery and Darricau's Division of Clausel's Corps were in imminent peril of being cut off. Hitherto the troops in the Sarré camp, only a mile or two beyond Ascain, had taken no part in aid of Clausel. At the beginning of the action Soult himself was at St. Jean de Luz. He seems to have been over confident in the strength of his lines; and though Napier says he hurried up on the first alarm, it was only now that he reached the scene of action at Ascain, accompanied by Darricau, the Reserve Artillery, and all other troops that he could collect. His approach menaced the left flank of Beresford's Corps; and to meet the threatened attack Wellington formed front to the left with the 4th, Light, and Giron's Division. The attack was, in consequence, not pushed home; but Soult had gained his object, for Wellington, who had only the 3rd and 7th Divisions remaining at hand, waited for the arrival of Clinton before driving Maransin from his position and descending into the low ground to encircle Reille and Villatte. Then on the approach of the 6th Division he crossed the Nivelle with the 3rd and 7th (commanded in the absence of Picton and Dalhousie, by Colville and the Portuguese General Le Cor) and after a severe struggle captured the height occupied by Maransin.

By this time, however, the shades of night were rapidly drawing on and stopped any further movement. Soult, realising the perilous position of his right wing (which being contained all day by Sir John Hope was unable to aid Clausel or D'Erlon), withdrew it during the night to Bidart on the Royal Road, halfway between St. Jean de Luz and Bayonne, and thus escaped the impending catastrophe.

On the extreme right of the Allies, Foy, from St. Jean Pied de Port, had in the morning successfully attacked part of the force under Mina and Morillo; but his action was isolated and his force too small to gain any permanent advantage. Finding that D'Erlon was being forced from his position, Foy retired in the direction of Bayonne, and early on the 11th occupied Cambo and Ustaritz on the Nive.

The loss of the Allies is stated in Wellington's despatch at 2,694 killed, wounded, and missing. The figure cannot be considered large, and the proportion of killed to wounded was only one to seven. Among those hurt were Generals Inglis, Kempt, and Byng.

Soult lost 4,265 men, of whom 3,000 were killed or wounded, and 51 guns, as well as the whole of his field magazines at St. Jean de Luz and Espelette. In the course of a winter's day he had been driven from a line of positions which had been carefully prepared during the last three months and might have rivalled those of Torres Vedras. The masterly skill and secrecy with which Lord Wellington brought up his columns of attack in such difficult country and massed overwhelming numbers at the crucial points could not have been exceeded by Napoleon himself. With 20,000 men, Hill assailed the 5,000 under D'Armagnac. Clausel, with 10,000 under Conroux and Maransin, was driven from his position by Beresford with 24,000. Taupin had only 3,000 to oppose to the 8,000 of Alten and Longa. On the other hand Hope, with 19,000 men occupied the attention of 25,000, and on the right of the Allies 6,000 indifferent Spanish troops contained double that number under Foy and Abbé. In short, Wellington was seen at his best, while Soult's conception of a defensive action even on such

IN THE PENINSULA

strong ground was very defective. The result was a "heavy blow and great discouragement" to the French, and those writers who have asserted that the British soldier could only fight on the defensive must be puzzled to account for the victory.

The battle of the Nivelle seems to mark the culminating point of Wellington's genius. He subsequently performed very remarkable strategical manœuvres and gained several victories, but at none of his later battles do we find the happy combination of conception and execution so notable at that of the Nivelle.

On the morning after the action Wellington advanced in heavy rain. Hope occupied St. Jean de Luz and marched towards Bidart; Beresford towards Arbonne. Hill wheeled to the right and halted with his centre at Souraide and Espelette, facing the Nive at Cambo, while his left connected him with Beresford, and his right with Morillo at Mondarrain. Meanwhile Soult had taken up another position with his left at Ustaritz on the Nive, and his right resting on the sea at Bidart, on a front contracted to about eight miles. Feeling himself still insecure, he retired once more, and on the 12th took post with six Divisions; his right being at Anglet and his left resting on the entrenched camp at Bayonne. His remaining three Divisions reinforced Foy at Cambo. A fog stopped the Allies, but Hope eventually occupied Bidart on this day; Beresford, Arbonne and Ste. Barbe. Hill attempted to force the passage of the Nive, but the fords proved impassable; the bridge at Ustaritz had been destroyed, and that at Cambo was successfully defended by Foy.

Fortune now favoured the French. In their demoralised state they could have little hope of withstanding Wellington's victorious advance, but heavy rain intervened; the roads—indifferent at their best—became impassable; it was found impracticable to cross the Nive, and the enemy was saved from the consequences of his defeat. The Allies went into cantonments; Hope occupying a ridge in advance of Bidart as far as Pouy; Beresford, a continuation of the ridge beyond Arcangues, and stretching by the hill of Ste. Barbe to Ustaritz, whence Hill continued the line along the Nive to Itsassu; the whole position from left to right extending over fourteen miles. The villages in rear, Espelette, Sarré, Ascain, &c., were filled with the Infantry. Vandeleur's Cavalry Brigade was partly at Bidart, partly at Urogne. That of V. Alten was at St. Pé. The rest of the Cavalry remained in Spain. Headquarters were fixed at St. Jean de Luz.

The establishment of the Allied troops in the lowlands was the signal for pillage, in which the Spaniards, though pre-eminent, were assisted by some of the English and Portuguese belonging to Hope's Corps. But the marauding was nipped in the bud. Several men were hanged, and the whole of the Spaniards except Morillo's Division were sent back into Spain. The consequence of these vigorous measures was that the French returned to the homes from which they had fled, and soon established a friendly trade with the invaders!

On the side of the enemy, Reille and Villatte were posted between Anglet, in front of Bayonne on the Royal Road, and the mouth of the Adour; their front being covered by an inundation. Bayonne, at the confluence of the Nive and Adour, was a weak fortress, but formidable on account of the entrenched camp covered by swamps and inundations on its south front. Clausel carried the line from Anglet to the Nive, on the right bank of which D'Erlon held an entrenched camp extend-

IN THE PENINSULA 757

ing from Villefranque to St. Jean le vieux Moguerre. D'Armagnac and Foy held the line of the Nive as far as Cambo; while General Paris took post at Lahoussoa, about four miles higher up the river, which was navigable only as far as Ustaritz.

A quiet interval followed the battle of the Nivelle. The opposing outposts were in contact, but by a mutual understanding no unnecessary bloodshed occurred, and the most friendly relations existed between French and English, who indeed carried their good fellowship to the pitch of "plundering in harmony."

Wellington now found himself pent up between the Nive and the sea, in a barren country whose deep clay soil made the movement of Cavalry and Artillery impossible. The enemy, on the other hand, was holding a position supported by the entrenched camp at Bayonne, which, if not impregnable, could at all events not be captured without heavy loss. The best way to dislodge Soult appeared to be to pass the Nive and place the Allied right upon the Adour, "by which operation the enemy, already distressed for provisions, would lose the means of communication afforded by that river, and would become still more distressed" (Wellington's Despatch of 14th December). The British Commander was therefore anxious to force the passage of the Nive. "Yet to place troops on both sides of a navigable river, where the communication, bad at all times, was subject to entire interruption from rain—to do this in the face of an army possessing short communications, good roads, and entrenched camps for retreat, was a delicate and dangerous operation" (Napier).

Early in December the weather cleared and orders were issued for the passage of the river at daybreak on the 9th. Hill, with the Hussar Brigade—now commanded by Colonel Vivian—and that of Victor Alten, the 2nd, and the Portuguese Division (now under Le Cor), with fourteen guns, forded the Nive in three columns above and below Cambo without much opposition, and advanced in the direction of Bayonne. Morillo crossed simultaneously at Itsassu, to protect Hill's right from Paris at Lahoussoa, but that officer retired to Hellette. On the other side, Beresford pushed the 6th Division across the river on pontoons at Ustaritz, and not only drove back D'Armagnac, but so greatly alarmed Foy for his communications that the latter, retiring in haste, left a Brigade under General Berlier at Halsou to its fate, and Berlier escaped with difficulty to Hasparren.

Hill, having sent his Cavalry to watch Paris and the roads leading to St. Jean Pied de Port and Hasparren, left Barnes's Brigade at Urcuray to cover the Cambo bridge, and advanced by the main road towards Bayonne. On reaching the heights of Lormenthoa, within three miles of the fortress, he found D'Erlon in position. The 6th Division coming up drove the enemy out of Villefranque, but the main body of the Allies was still in rear struggling with the deep roads. The fighting was therefore broken off, but the moral advantage lay with Hill, who, with less than three Divisions, had hemmed in four of the enemy. Wellington had, however, not trusted only to the troops actually engaged. Beresford had in hand if needed the 3rd and a Brigade of the 7th Division, while on the left Hope and Alten made a demonstration directly against Bayonne, which had the effect of containing Reille, Villatte, and Clausel. At sundown Hope and Alten retired to Bidart.

Wellington had attained his primary object, but his Divisions, separated as they were by the formidable Nive, were in a position of some danger. Soult was quick to see the weak spot and to take advantage of his own interior lines. Bringing D'Erlon and his four Divisions over to the left bank of the river in support of Clausel and Villatte, he concentrated 60,000 men and 40 guns against the Allied centre, consisting of only half that number of men with 24 guns. Wellington seems to have been to some extent taken unawares. He was himself with Hill. The village of Anglet was held only by a line of outposts. The 1st Division was at St. Jean de Luz, six miles in rear of the main position, which ran along the ridge of Barrouilhet; the 5th was posted about Guéthary. Alten with the Light Division held an extended line at Arcangues. The 7th continued the line of defence by St. Barbe to the Nive.

Soult's first intention was to throw the whole of his force against Arcangues, and such an attack could not have been resisted, for Alten had no support, the 4th Division being several miles in rear. Happily the French Commander changed his mind. Reille, supported by Villatte and Foy—the whole under Soult—moved by the Royal Road against Sir John Hope. Clausel alone attacked Alten at Arcangues; and his attack being little more than a demonstration, the Light Division was able to hold its own.

Reille's attack upon the British left was more serious. At 9 a.m. the picquets were driven in; but Hope was present in person, and held the main position at Barrouilhet until the arrival of the Brigades of Bradford and Wilson (the latter now commanded by Archibald Campbell) and the 5th Division. At 11 a.m. Lord Aylmer's Division came up. Reille was repelled, but Villatte and Foy continued to menace Hope's right when, about 2 p.m., a message reached Soult from Clausel to the effect that large masses of fresh troops were appearing from the side of the Nive. The report was correct. Wellington was bringing up the 3rd, 4th, 6th, and 7th Divisions to reinforce his left and centre; the 1st Division was also approaching from St. Jean de Luz. Soult therefore ceased firing and fell back at nightfall; leaving behind him three German Regiments, who deserted to the Allies. Villatte was wounded, and 2,000 men killed or hurt. Wellington lost 1,500.

On the 11th sharp fighting took place at Barrouilhet without decisive result; each side losing about 600 men. The combat was chiefly notable from the fact that the officers of the Guards incurred Wellington's displeasure by putting up their umbrellas! On the 12th, skirmishing was renewed—apparently by accident—and both French and Allies sustained between 300 and 400 casualties.

Wellington strongly suspected that Soult's operations were a blind, and that his principal effort would be made against Hill. The suspicion proved to be correct, although for reasons other than those contemplated by the British Commander. Leaving Reille and Villatte to guard the entrenched camp before Bayonne, Soult, on the evening of the 12th, concentrated seven Divisions at Mousseroles, on the right bank of the Nive, in hopes of overwhelming Hill next day. The operation should have been in the nature of a surprise. But Soult had put his troops in motion too early, and at sunset Sir Rowland detected the French crossing the Lower Nive by a bridge of boats. Profiting by his observations, he brought up from Urcuray a Brigade under Barnes (who had been transferred to the 2nd Division), leaving Morillo in charge of that post.

On Soult's previous evacuation of the right bank of the Nive, Hill, by orders of Wellington, had occupied a chain of parallel heights about two miles south of Bayonne. The 2nd Division, under Sir W. Stewart, formed the first line. Its centre, consisting of Ashworth's Portuguese Brigade, supported by Barnes, was astride the Bayonne-

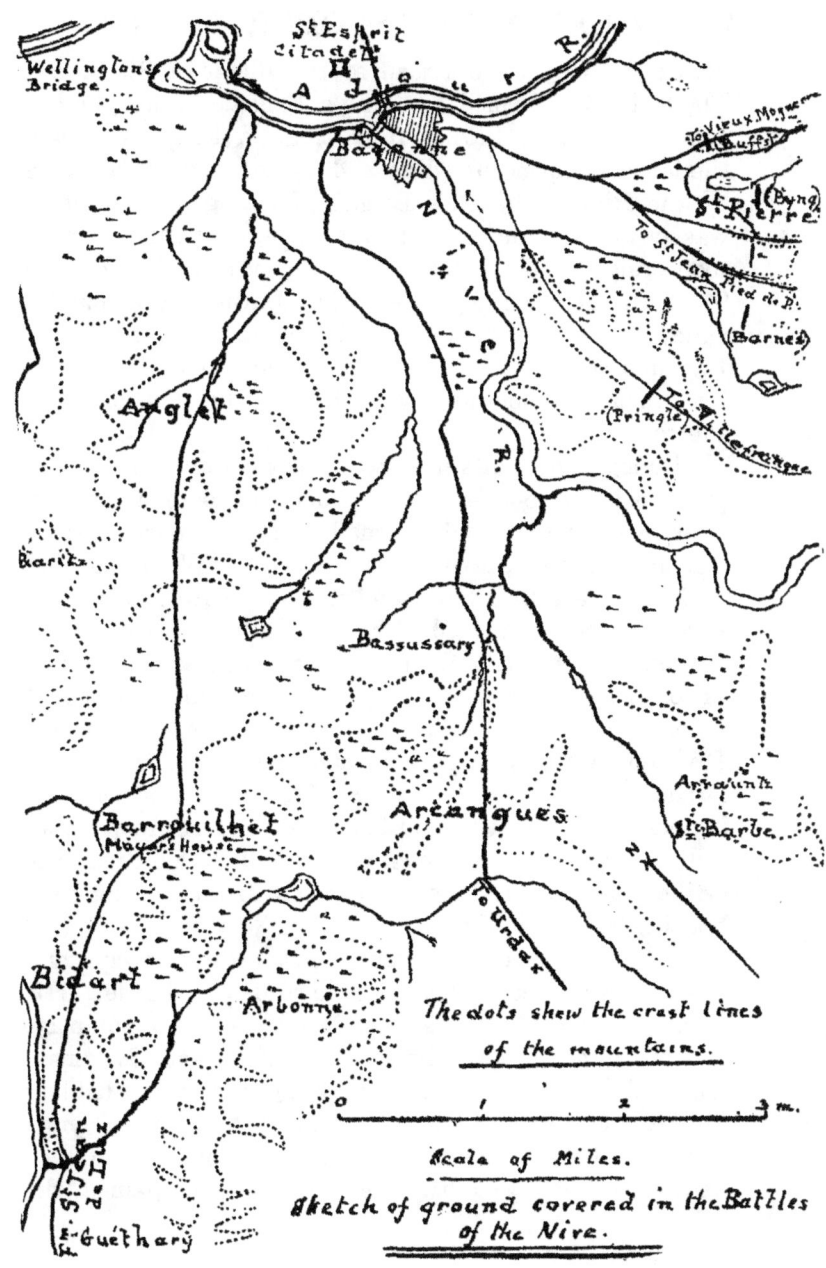

St. Jean Pied de Port road at the village of St. Pierre. The right was formed by Byng's Brigade, posted in the valley separating Barnes from the Old Moguerre ridge, the latter being occupied as a detached post in advance by the Buffs. Pringle's Brigade, forming the left wing, was posted on the Villefranque ridge, covering the pontoon bridge which had been thrown by Beresford on the 9th. Pringle was separated from Barnes by a marshy valley. Two batteries in the centre enfiladed the Bayonne road. Le Cor's Portuguese Divisions with two guns was held in reserve behind the village of St. Pierre.

Although the units were to a great extent isolated, the position was strong and commanded the enemy's sole line of approach, which could be made only on a narrow front. Fortune, however, favoured the French. When morning broke on the 13th it was found that the pontoon bridge at Ustaritz had been washed away. Hill was completely cut off. In his front, Soult had concentrated 35,000 men in seven Divisions, while Paris was menacing his rear at Urcuray. To oppose Paris, Hill had only Morillo's Division, 4,000 strong, supported by Vivian's Cavalry Brigade. On the position of St. Pierre, the 2nd Division included 6,173 British and 2,608 Portuguese troops of all ranks, and Le Cor mustered 4,670. Counting the artillerymen for his 14 guns in action, Hill could not have had 14,000 men in line.

At 8.30 a.m. the morning mist cleared away, and D'Erlon was seen advancing in order of battle. His force consisted of a Division of Cavalry, three of Infantry, and 22 guns. The Divisions of Foy and Maransin followed in support; the remaining two were held in reserve. Darricau attacked Pringle; D'Armagnac, Byng; Abbé assailed the centre; and though Barnes reinforced Ashworth with two battalions, the enemy gained the crest of the position. Barnes, charging with the 92nd (his remaining battalion), for the moment stemmed the tide and gave time to Ashworth and the 50th to rally; but Maransin and Foy came up in support of Abbé, attacking Stewart's flank and centre; and though the last named ordered up two battalions from Byng's Brigade, the position seemed lost. The moment was more than critical; for while on the left Pringle held Darricau at bay, on the right Byng's outer flank had been completely turned by a Brigade of D'Armagnac. Hill, watching the battle from a height in rear, had only the two Brigades of Le Cor in hand. He despatched one in support of Byng, the other to reinforce the centre. Ashworth and Barnes had maintained the losing battle with desperate gallantry. Both fell, terribly wounded; but the 92nd re-formed and advanced at once with fixed bayonets upon the enemy's approaching column. The newly arrived Portuguese Brigade followed in support. The French column turned and retired. Soult, resolute to break Hill's centre, called up D'Armagnac's reserve Brigade. With it, aided by Foy, Maransin, and Abbé, he prepared a fresh assault. Success seemed assured; but by this time—noon—Beresford's pontoon bridge had been restored, and the 6th Division, followed by the 4th, 3rd, and 7th, were descried approaching. The crisis was over; and on the right, Byng, reinforced by Buchan's Brigade of Le Cor's Division, drove D'Armagnac "headlong" off the ridge and captured two H.A. guns. "The day is your own," exclaimed Wellington, as he galloped up with the foremost of the reinforcements and grasped Sir Rowland warmly by the hand.

Soult now gave up all further attempt, and retired under cover of a demonstration; but Wellington at once ordered Byng to advance, and at 2 p.m., assumed the offensive all along the line, following the enemy back to

Bayonne. On reaching his entrenchments Soult sent Clausel back over the Nive, occupied the ground between that river and the Adour with D'Erlon's Corps, and crossing the Adour in person, extended Foy's Division along the right bank. Thus ended the battle of St. Pierre, one of the most desperate during the whole war, and of which Wellington remarked that he had never seen a field so thickly strewn with dead. Happily the nature of the ground, as already noted, prevented Soult using the whole of his force simultaneously. In spite of this he had great superiority in numbers, and it was only by sheer pluck and hard fighting that Hill maintained his position.

During the five days' fighting, in what was officially termed the battle of the Nive, Soult returned his losses at 513 killed, 4,835 wounded, 290 prisoners, and 276 missing. These figures would not include the three German battalions which came over to the Allies after the action of the 10th. Putting them aside the French casualties amounted to 5,914, of which about 3,000 occurred on the 13th. Generals Villatte, Mocquery, and Maucomble were among the wounded.

Wellington lost 5,061 officers and men, 650 being killed, 3,907 wounded, and 504 missing. Five General Officers—Hope, Robinson, Barnes, Ashworth, and Le Cor were wounded.

During the action of the 13th, Paris had merely skirmished with Morillo at Urcuray. At its close he retired to Bonloc.

Although his success had not been very decisive, Wellington had gained his object. His right was established on the Adour, " thus cutting off the enemy's communication by that river," he had access to a fertile country for the Cavalry, and was in a position to gain secret intelligence from a part of the interior of France

IN THE PENINSULA

where the inhabitants were believed to be hostile to the Emperor.

But though successful, the conduct of the British Commander is open to criticism in regard to the arrangement of his right. No better critic could be found than Lord Seaton—better known perhaps as Colonel Colborne—who remarked, " Wellington committed a great error. Hill's Division was quite isolated. Soult passed the bridge and attacked it with his whole army, yet such was the goodness of the British troops, he was repulsed. Soult said himself afterwards, ' Well, if one Division of your troops can stand against seventy or eighty thousand of ours, there's nothing more to be said; but it is an error.' " (Moore Smith's "Life of John Colborne," p. 198.)

It will be noticed that Colborne makes no allowance for the destruction of the pontoon bridge. Perhaps he considered that Wellington was not justified in relying on it. Wellington, in his despatch, slurs the matter over, and his account does not seem to be quite in accordance with the actual facts.

CHAPTER XLVI

Wellington's administration of the country occupied—Causes of friction with his Allies—Is urged from home to advance more rapidly—His reply—His financial distress—Casualties of the British Army in 1813—State of the Allied Army in January, 1814—Position and objects of the opposing forces—Wellington advances against Soult—Passage of the Adour by Sir J. Hope—Investment of Bayonne—Battle of Orthez—Retreat of Soult—Foils his pursuers.

"I NEVER saw such weather, such roads, or such a country," wrote Wellington, two days after the battle of the Nive; and the consequence was that during the remainder of the year little could be done in the way of military operations. Thus the memorable year 1813—begun in Portugal, ended in France—passed quietly away. The civil administration of the country occupied by the Allies was carried on by officials provisionally appointed by Lord Wellington. Trade flourished, and the only interruption of the calm was caused by the excesses of the savage Morillo, who was thereupon attacked by the Basque peasants.

Wellington, dreading a guerilla warfare, at once issued a proclamation giving the peasantry the alternatives either of joining Soult, staying peaceably at home, or being hanged and having their villages burned. But by this time the French peasants had gained confidence in him. Morillo was sternly reprimanded, and though General Harispe, a native of these parts, was brought

IN THE PENINSULA

across from Suchet's army to head the insurgents, the insurrection quickly subsided. " The English General's policy and the good discipline he maintains," said an official letter from Bayonne, " does us more harm than ten battles; every peasant wishes to be under his protection."

Lord Wellington was still beset with difficulties enough to overwhelm an ordinary person. " The country was a vast quagmire." The rivulets swelled to such an extent that the transport mules could not ford them, and a Portuguese brigade on the right bank of the Nive was in danger of dying of hunger.

Equally great were the annoyances in his relations to our so-called Allies. All danger of invasion having passed away from Portugal, the Regency took little further interest in the war. Wellington had less than 20,000 Portuguese soldiers in his army. Although the British subsidy provided for 30,000, and 9,000 men were waiting at the depôts, trained and ready for service, the Portuguese Government declined to embark them before the month of March, and then only to the extent of 3,000.

In Spain matters were even worse. The insubordination of the Spanish troops, the neglect of those troops by their Government, the hostility towards the British of the Regency and of the local authorities, evinced in countless instances, reached such a pitch that Wellington felt himself dealing with an enemy rather than an ally, and foresaw the time when the British Ministers might consequently decide to withdraw their troops from the contest. In such a case the hostility of the Spaniards might make it difficult—perhaps impossible—for our Army to retire into Portugal, and Lord Wellington therefore advised Lord Bathurst to demand from the Spanish Government as security for the embarkation of his Army, the admission of a British garrison into San Sebastian. Such admission would, he felt pretty sure, enable him to embark his Army there and at the neighbouring port of Passages. "I recommend to you," continued Wellington in his letter of November 27, 1813, "to withdraw the troops if this demand be not complied with, be the consequences what they may, and to be prepared accordingly. You may rely on this, that if you take a firm, decided line, you will have the Spanish nation with you, you will bring the Government to their senses, and you will put an end at once to all the petty cabals and counteraction existing at the present moment, and you will not be under the necessity of bringing matters to extremities. If you take any other than a decided line, and one which in its consequences will involve them in ruin, you may depend upon it you will gain nothing, and will only make matters worse. . . . The truth is that a crisis is approaching in our connection with Spain ; and if you do not bring the Government and the nation to their senses before they go too far, you will inevitably lose all the advantages which you might expect from the services rendered to them." On second thoughts, however, aversion to a public display of recriminatory discussion between the Allied Powers at a critical moment caused Lord Wellington to ask the British Ministers to hold his suggestions in abeyance for the present.

The reason of the conduct of the Spanish authorities soon transpired. A treaty of peace had been signed by Napoleon and the captive King Ferdinand at Valençay, by the terms of which the sovereignty of the latter and the integrity of Spain were recognised, and it was stipulated that the French and British troops were to quit the country simultaneously. The Spanish Regency declined, however, to ratify the treaty, but men's minds were disturbed. General Copons, commander of the 1st Spanish Army in Catalonia, gave no notice to Lord Wellington of the arrival of Ferdinand's envoy. Rumours of peace were rife, but the British Commander was not consulted, and the latter writing to his brother at Madrid, in the middle of January, 1814, remarked that he had "repeated intelligence and warning from the French of some act of treachery meditated by the Spaniards." The whole state of affairs was most unsatisfactory, and Wellington dreaded the return of Ferdinand on the ground that at best the war would be rendered "so difficult as to be almost impracticable and without hope of success."

Negotiations for a general peace had also been carried on between the Northern Powers and the Emperor; but the Allies do not seem to have been sincere in their efforts, and the matter fell through.

Meanwhile, Lord Wellington, stinted of money, neglected by the Admiralty, opposed by his Allies, was being driven nearly mad by the wild schemes of the British Ministers, who, instigated by the Czar, were urging him to advance into France with greater rapidity; and of their own egregious folly, pressed him at the same time to detach largely from his army for the sake of a campaign in Holland. The following letter, written in reply to their suggestions, deals clearly with the whole situation:—

" *To Earl Bathurst.*

St. Jean de Luz,
December 21, 1813.

" My dear Lord,—I have received your Lordship's letter of the 10th instant, and I beg you will assure the Russian Ambassador that there is nothing that I can do with the force under my command to forward the general interests that I will not do. I am already farther advanced on the French territory than any of the Allied Powers, and I believe I am better prepared than any of them to take advantage of any opportunities which may offer of annoying the enemy, either in consequence of my own situation, or of the operations of the Armies of the Allies.

"Your Lordship is acquainted, by my last despatches, with the nature and objects of my recent operations, and with the position in which we were at their close. The enemy have since considerably weakened their force in Bayonne, and they occupy the right of the Adour as far as Dax. I cannot tell what force they have in Bayonne, or whether their force is so reduced as that I can attack their entrenched camp.

"In military operations there are some things which cannot be done; one of these is to move troops in this country during or immediately after a violent fall of rain. I believe I shall lose many more men than I shall ever replace by putting any troops in camp in this bad weather, but I should be guilty of a useless waste of men, if I were to attempt an operation during the violent falls of rain which we have here. Our operations, then, must necessarily be slow, but they shall not be discontinued.

"In regard to the scene of the operations of the Army, it is a question for the Government and not for me. By having kept in the field about 30,000 men in the Peninsula, the British Government have now for five years given employment to at least 200,000 French troops of the best Napoleon had, as it is ridiculous to suppose that either the Spaniards or Portuguese could have resisted for a moment if the British force had been withdrawn. The armies now employed against us cannot be less than 100,000 men, indeed more, including garrisons; and I see in the French newspapers that orders have been given for the formation at Bordeaux of an army of reserve of 100,000 men. Is there any man weak enough to suppose that one-third of the numbers first mentioned would be employed against the Spaniards and Portuguese if we were withdrawn? They would, if it were still an object to Bonaparte to conquer the Peninsula. And he would succeed in his object; but it is much more likely that he would make peace with the powers of the Peninsula, and then have it in his power to turn against the Allied Armies the 200,000 men, of which 100,000 men are such troops as those armies have not yet had to deal with.

"Another observation which I have to submit is, that in a war in which every day offers a crisis, the result of which may affect the world for ages, the change of the scene of the operations of the British Army would put that army entirely *hors de combat* for four months at least, even if the new scene were Holland; and they would not then be such a machine as this Army is.

"Your Lordship very reasonably, however, asks what objects we propose to ourselves here which are to induce Napoleon to make peace? I am now in a commanding situation on the most vulnerable frontier of France, probably the only vulnerable frontier. If I could put 20,000 Spaniards into the field, which I could do if I had money and was properly supported by the fleet, I must have the only fortress there is on this frontier, if it can be called a fortress, and that in a very short space of time. If I could put 40,000 Spaniards into the field, I should most probably have my posts on the Garonne. Does any man believe that Napoleon would not feel an army in such a position more than he would feel 30,000 or 40,000 British troops laying siege to one of his fortresses in

Holland? If it be only the resource of men and money, of which he will be deprived, and the reputation he will lose by our being in this position, it will do ten times more to procure peace than ten armies on the side of Flanders. But, if I am right in believing that there is a strong Bourbon party in France, and that that party is the preponderating one in the South of France, what mischief must not our Army do him in the position I have supposed, and what sacrifices would he not make to get rid of us?

"It is the business of the Government, and not my business, to dispose of the resources of the nation; and I have no right to give an opinion on the subject. I wish, however, to impress upon your Lordship's mind that you cannot maintain military operations in the Peninsula and in Holland with British troops; you must give up either the one or the other, as, if I am not mistaken, the British establishment is not equal to the maintenance of two armies in the field. I began last campaign with 70,000 British and Portuguese troops, and taking away the German troops, and adding to me what could be got from the Militia, and by enabling me to bring up the Portuguese recruits, I expected this year to take the field with 80,000 men; but this is now quite out of the question. If you should form the Hanoverian Army . . . I shall not take the field with much more than 50,000 men, unless I shall receive real and efficient assistance to bring up the Portuguese recruits, and it will then be about 55,000, or if our wounded recover well, and we have no more actions, about 60,000 men.

"Then I beg you to observe that, whenever you extend your assistance to any country, . . . the service is necessarily stinted in all its branches on the old stage. I do not wish to make complaints, but if you will look at every branch of the service here now, you will find it stinted, particularly the naval branch, and those supplies which necessarily come from England. . . . Nearly all the great-coats are deficient. The reason of this is, that the inferior departments do not observe that when British exertion is to be made on a new scene, the old means are not sufficient. . . .

"The different reports which I have sent your Lordship will show how we stand for want of naval means, and I beg you to take the state and condition of the ships on the stations . . . and you will see whether or not there is reason to complain. But whatever may be the numbers employed, I complain that there are not enough, because they do not perform the service. This is certainly not the intention of the Admiralty.

"Since we have established our posts on the upper part of the Adour, the French have again begun to use the navigation of the coast from Bordeaux to Bayonne.

"Your Lordship is acquainted with the state of our financial resources. We are overwhelmed with debts, and I can scarcely stir out of my house on account of the public creditors waiting to demand payment of what is due to them. Some of the muleteers are twenty-six months in arrears, and only yesterday I was obliged to give them bills upon the Treasury for a part of their demands, or lose their services, which bills they will, I know, sell at a depreciated rate of exchange to the *sharks* who are waiting at Passages, and in this town, to take advantage of the public distresses. I have reason to suspect that they become thus clamorous at the instigation of British merchants."

To induce the British Government to concentrate its efforts on a single well-planned enterprise was, however, impossible. The politicians at home had no sympathy with the difficulties of the Commander in the field, or with the methods by which his resourceful mind over-

774 WELLINGTON'S OPERATIONS

came those difficulties. We have seen that at an earlier period dread of offending the British merchants in Portugal had made our Government prohibit the trading in corn, by which not only the Army but a great part of the civil population was fed. With a view to drawing money and supplies from the South of France, Lord Wellington had now granted certain licences to a limited number of French ships to trade along the coast. The matter was arranged through a banker at Bayonne, and the best effect was hoped therefrom, but the English Ministers at once prohibited the practice.

About the same time they sent out Colonel Bunbury, the Under-Secretary for War, an able man, to confer with Wellington on various questions; and to him the British Commander was able to point out that the Government was not aware of, and did not realise, the difficulty in which he was placed for want of money; and that their frequent disapprobation of his action arose through failure to appreciate his necessities. Nevertheless, their conduct must have been extremely annoying.

The casualties during the year 1813 had been very heavy. The number of deaths in the British Army alone—apart from those actually on the battlefield—had amounted to 6,791; the greatest sufferer being the 1st Battalion of the 1st Guards, which had hardly been in action. On the other hand, a few battalions had been sent by way of reinforcement, and the English Militia had been invited to volunteer for active service. It was hoped that 30,000 men would respond, but only 8,000 did so. Of these, three provisional battalions were formed, regarding which the Military Secretary to the Commander-in-Chief wrote to Wellington: " I hope when they reach you they will fight well; but at present they are more

IN THE PENINSULA

troublesome than the whole army put together." And Wellington, for his part, was not over anxious to get them, for he remarked that the Militia had all the vices of the regular Army, with some peculiar to themselves in addition.

The following was the "State" of the Anglo-Portuguese Army on the 16th of January, 1814:—

CAVALRY DIVISION.
Lieutenant-General Sir Stapleton Cotton, K.B.

		Effective Rank and File.	Absent Sick.	Total Strength of the Divisions.
Maj.-Gen. O'Loghlin	1st Life Guards	217		
	2nd ,, ,,	260		
	Roy. Horse Guards, Blue	277		
Major-General Hon. W. Ponsonby	5th Dragoon Guards	336		
	3rd Dragoons	358		
	4th ,,	386		
Maj.-Gen. Vandeleur	12th Light Dragoons	387		
	16th ,, ,,	415		
Major-General Hon. H. Fane	13th ,, ,,	348		
	14th ,, ,,	417		
Colonel Vivian	18th Hussars	427		
	1st ,, K.G.L.	426	292	10,179
Major-General Bock	1st Dragoons ,,	339		
	2nd ,, ,,	332		
	3rd Dragoon Guards	350		
	Royal Dragoons	359		
Major-General Lord Edward Somerset	7th Hussars	513		
	10th ,,	459		
	15th ,,	466		
Viscount Barbacena	1st Portuguese Cavalry	255		
	6th ,, ,,	268		
	11th ,, ,,	172		
	12th ,, ,,	199		
		7,966		

WELLINGTON'S OPERATIONS

INFANTRY DIVISIONS.
1st Division.
Major-General Hon. E. Howard.

		Effective Rank and File.	Absent Sick.	Total Strength of the Divisions.
	1st Batt. 1st Guards	785		
	3rd ,, ,,	776		
Major-General Hon. E. Stopford	1st Batt. Coldstream Gds.	767		
	1st Batt. 3rd Guards	864		
	1 Co. 5th Batt. 60th Rifles	50	511	7,401
Major-Gen. Hinuber	1st Line Batt. K.G.L.	574		
	2nd ,, ,, ,,	532		
	5th ,, ,, ,,	482		
	1st Light ,, ,,	568		
	2nd ,, ,, ,,	585		
		5,983		

Unattached Brigade.

Major-General Lord Aylmer	1st Batt. 62nd	427		
	76th	546	228	2,349
	77th	170		
	85th	430		
		1,573		

2nd Division.
Lieutenant-General Hon. Sir William Stewart, K.B.

Maj.-Gen. Barnes	1st Batt. 50th	345		
	1st ,, 71st	498		
	1st ,, 92nd	391		
	1st Company 60th	49		
Major-General Byng	1st Batt. the Buffs	530		
	1st ,, 57th	438		
	1st Provisional Batt.			
	2nd Batt. 31st	271		
	1st ,, 66th	278	2,670	10,629
	1 Company 60th	45		
Major-Gen. Pringle	1st Batt. 28th	485		
	2nd ,, 34th	410		
	1st ,, 39th	565		
	1 Company 60th	47		
Colonel Harding	6th Line Regt. Portuguese	715		
	18th ,, ,, ,,	901		
	6th Caçadores ,,	302		
		6,270		

IN THE PENINSULA

3rd Division.

Lieutenant-General Sir Thomas Picton, K.B.

		Effective Rank and File.	Absent Sick.	Total Strength of the Divisions.
Maj.-Gen. Brisbane	1st Batt. 45th	496		
	74th	438		
	1st Batt. 88th	788		
	4 Co.'s 5th Batt. 60th	197		
Colonel Keane	1st Batt. 5th	640		
	2nd ,, 83rd	371	1,740	7,797
	2nd ,, 87th	305		
	94th	350		
Major-Gen. Power	9th Line Regt. Portuguese	783		
	21st ,, ,, ,,	784		
	11th Caçadores	215		
		5,317		

4th Division.

Lieutenant-General Hon. Sir G. L. Cole, K.B.

		Effective Rank and File.	Absent Sick.	Total Strength of the Divisions.
Major-General W. Anson	3rd Batt. 27th	564		
	1st ,, 40th	468		
	1st ,, 48th	413		
	2nd ,, 53rd } 2nd Provisional Batt.	276		
	2nd Regt. }	204		
	1 Company 60th	45		
Major-General Ross	1st Batt. 7th Fusiliers	604	2,314	8,434
	20th	395		
	1st Batt. 23rd Fusiliers	420		
	1 Co. Brunswick Oels	42		
Col. Vasconcellos	11th Line, Portuguese	794		
	23rd ,, ,,	899		
	7th Caçadores	265		
		5,389		

5th Division.

Major-General Hon. Charles Colville.

		Effective Rank and File.	Absent Sick.	Total Strength of the Divisions.
Maj.-Gen. Hay	3rd Batt. 1st	320		
	1st ,, 9th	482		
	1st ,, 38th	364		
	2nd ,, 47th	256		
	1 Co. Brunswick Oels	25		
Maj.-Gen. Robinson	1st Batt. 4th	344	2,827	7,515
	2nd ,, 59th	268		
	2nd ,, 84th	294		
	1 Co. Brunswick Oels	20		
Colonel de Regoa	3rd Line, Portuguese	608		
	15th ,, ,,	427		
	8th Caçadores	189		
		3,597		

6th Division.

Lieutenant-General Sir Henry Clinton, K.B.

Major-General Pack	1st Batt. 42nd	669		
	1st ,, 79th	594		
	1st ,, 91st	458		
	1 Company 60th	37		
Maj.-Gen. Lambert	1st Batt. 11th	477	1,590	7,687
	1st ,, 32nd	474		
	1st ,, 36th	365		
	1st ,, 61st	438		
Colonel Douglas	8th Line, Portuguese	724		
	12th ,, ,,	820		
	9th Caçadores	231		
		5,287		

IN THE PENINSULA

7th Division.
Major-General Walker.

			Effective Rank and File.	Absent Sick.	Total Strength of the Division.
	1st Batt. 6th		709		
	24th ,, (3rd Provisional Batt.)		271		
	2nd ,, 58th		184		
	9 Cos. Brunswick Oels		250		
Major-Gen. Inglis	51st		268	1,707	7,756
	68th		238		
	1st Batt. 82nd		489		
	Chasseurs Britanniques		288		
Colonel Doyle	7th Line, Portuguese		684		
	19th ,, ,,		854		
	2nd Caçadores		374		
			4,609		

Light Division.
Major-General Baron Charles Alten.

		Effective Rank and File.	Absent Sick.	Total Strength of the Division.
Major-Gen. Kempt	1st Batt. 43rd	724		
	1st ,, 95th Rifles	422		
	3rd ,, 95th ,,	365		
Colonel Colborne	1st Batt. 52nd	714	1,144	5,827
	2nd ,, 95th	350		
	17th Line, Portuguese	611		
	1st Caçadores	421		
	3rd ,,	318		
		3,925		

Portuguese Division.
Major-General Le Cor.

		Effective Rank and File.	Absent Sick.	Total Strength of the Division.
Brig.-Gen. Da Costa	2nd Line, Portuguese	971		
	14th ,, ,,	831		
Brig.-Gen. Buchan	4th ,, ,,	888	851	5,019
	10th ,, ,,	909		
	10th Caçadores	172		
		3,771		

Unattached Portuguese Brigades.

		Effective Rank and File.	Absent Sick.	Total Strength of the Division.
Maj.-Gen. Bradford	13th Portuguese	547 ⎫		
	24th ,,	609 ⎬ 696		2,395
	5th Caçadores	293 ⎭		
Maj.-Gen. Campbell	1st Portuguese	563 ⎫		
	16th ,,	676 ⎬ 363		2,295
	14th Caçadores	222 ⎭		
		2,910		

Total of Effective Rank and File, 56,597; gross total, 85,283.

In addition to the combatant troops were the following:—

| Lieut.-Col. Dundas | Royal Staff Corps | 154 |
| Captain Gibson | Veteran Battalion | 871 |

The Spanish troops under Wellington's immediate command were these:—

Army of Galicia	General Freyre	12,000 men.
Division	,, Morillo	4,000 ,,
,,	,, O'Donnell	6,000 ,,
,,	Prince of Anglona (detached from 3rd Spanish army)	8,000 ,,
	Total	30,000 ,,

The Department of the Basses Pyrenees is watered by a number of rivers, of which the principal are the Nive, the Joyeuse, the Bidouse, the Gave D'Oleron, the Gave de Pau. These all take their rise in the spurs of the Pyrenees, and after running nearly parallel in a northwesterly direction, empty their waters into the Adour. That river is navigable up to Dax, about thirty-five miles above Bayonne. Part of Soult's magazines were established at this point; part at Peyrehorade, twenty-four miles from Bayonne, at the junction of the Gave de Pau with the Gave D'Oleron, and about five miles above

IN THE PENINSULA

their confluence with the Adour. Up to this point the Gave de Pau was also navigable. Both Dax and Peyrehorade had been fortified; and to facilitate communication a bridge was constructed at Port de Lanne on the Adour, just above its junction with the Gave de Pau.

At the beginning of January, 1814, the Divisions of Foy, D'Armagnac, and Boyer were posted on the right bank of the Adour from a point opposite Urt to the Port de Lanne. On their left, Clausel, with Treilhard's Division of Dragoons and two of Infantry, was on the Bidouse. General Paris's Division connected Clausel with St. Jean Pied de Port, which was occupied by a strong garrison, and formed the extreme left of the French line. Headquarters were at Peyrehorade. Reille held the entrenched camp at Bayonne with four Divisions.

Soult relied for his supplies on the coasting trade between Bordeaux and Bayonne (which was not interrupted by the British Navy) and on the navigation of the Adour from its mouth. But the supplies were brought up under the guns of the Allies, and he felt his position uneasy. The French Marshal therefore brought up his left and left centre to the Bayonne–St. Jean Pied de Port road, occupying Hellette, Mondionde in the first line; Bonloc and La Bastide Clairance in the second; and by so doing threatened the British right. The principal points on his line were fortified.

Wellington thereupon made corresponding dispositions. Once or twice a general action seemed imminent, but, partly by reason of the weather, nothing serious took place, though Harispe, with Paris's Division and Dufaure's Brigade, harassed Mina and Morillo on the extreme right of the line of the Allies.

The difficulties with which Soult had to contend were even greater than those of his opponent. He had been ordered to send a Division of Cavalry and two of Infantry to reinforce the Emperor; and with numbers reduced to 40,000 it was impossible to hold on much longer to Bayonne. He believed Wellington to have 120,000 men, and he made up his mind to leave the fortress to its own resources, garrisoned by Abbé's Division, Conscripts, National Guards, &c., to the number of 14,000, and to retire with his field army into the interior. Under these circumstances he wrote to the Emperor proposing to raise a partisan warfare with a view to harassing Wellington's flanks, rear, and communications in case of the Allies following him up; while, with the main body of his Army, he (Soult) marched to Paris to aid in the central defence of the country; for by this time the Austrian, Russian, and Prussian Armies were about to overrun the north-eastern provinces.

The plan was vigorous and able. A partisan warfare seems to have been dreaded by Wellington, and might have been prolonged for as many months as that of the Boers. But Napoleon, knowing the state of chaos into which France would drift by its adoption, would not countenance the suggestion.

By the middle of February, 1814, Wellington was ready to advance. He had received £400,000 in gold, and through the clever expedient of establishing a mint of his own, converted the gold into napoleons, thus enormously increasing the circulating medium. The coins received a private mark to enable them to be called in at any time if desired; but every care was taken to avoid fraud by making them of the correct weight and fineness; and by the circulation a boon was conferred not only on his Army, but on the inhabitants generally. Pitt began the war by forging the French

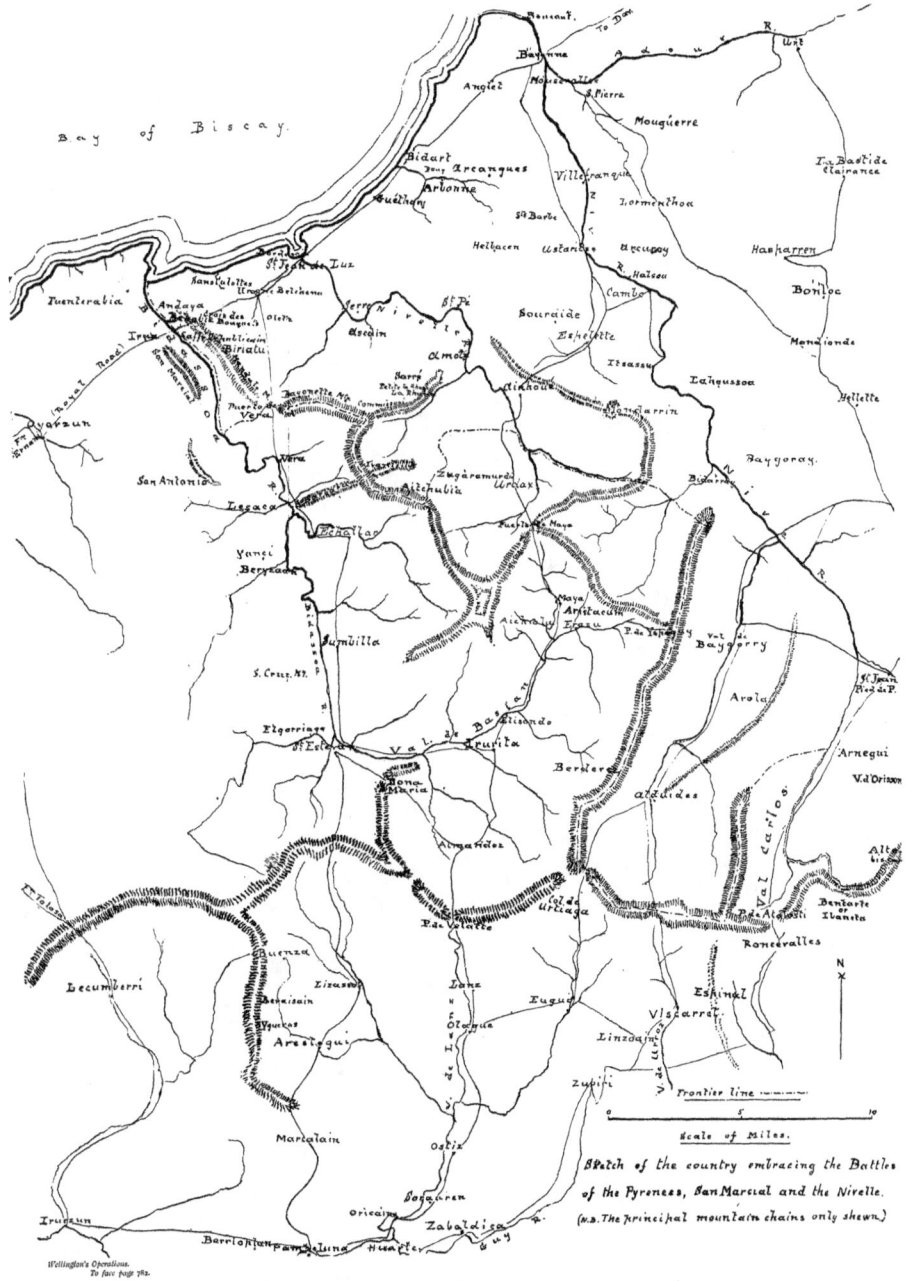

IN THE PENINSULA 783

paper issues. Wellington ended it by adopting a policy marked by scrupulous good faith and honesty.

The Duc D'Angoulême had now joined the Allied Army. Wellington had no partiality for any of the Bourbons, but, as an additional resource, counted on the hope of raising a Royalist party hostile to Napoleon.

"The English chief," says Napier, "now only waited for practicable roads to take the offensive with an army superior in every way to Soult's; for that Marshal's numbers were about to be reduced, his conscripts were deserting, and the inclemency of the weather was filling his hospitals; but the bronzed veterans of his adversary, impassive to fatigue, patient to endure, fierce in execution, were free from serious maladies, and able to plant their colours wherever their General listed. All the country was, however, a vast quagmire; it was with difficulty provisions or even orders could be conveyed to the different quarters, and a Portuguese Brigade on the right of the Nive was several days without food from the swelling of the rivulets which stopped the commissariat mules."

The same writer (bk. xxiv. ch. 2) thus describes the strategical problem :—" Wellington designed to force Soult over the Garonne, and, if possible, upon Bordeaux; because it was the direct line, the citizens inimical to the Emperor, and the town, lying on the left bank of the river, not to be defended; because a junction with Suchet would thus be prevented; and if he could throw the French into the Landes, where his own superior Cavalry could act, they would probably be destroyed. To operate against Soult's left towards Pau was the obvious method of preventing a junction with Soult, and rendering the fortified positions on the Gaves useless. But the investment of Bayonne required a large force; which was yet

WELLINGTON'S OPERATIONS

weak against an outer attack, because separated in three parts by the rivers; hence a wide movement on Pau would have let Soult place the Adour between himself and Wellington while he fell upon Hope. This rendered it necessary to cross all the Gaves on a contracted line of operations, and to collect the principal mass of troops on the right by the help of the great road leading to St. Jean Pied de Port. Rapid marches and reiterated attacks then forced the passage of the rivers above the points which Soult had fortified for defence, and so turned that General's left with the view of finally cutting him off from Suchet and driving him into the wilderness of the Landes."

The first object of the British Commander was to cross the Adour, "a great river with a strong current, and well guarded by troops and gunboats above Bayonne; still greater below the town; there the ebb tide ran seven miles an hour; there also were gunboats, a sloop-of-war, and merchant vessels which could be armed and employed to interrupt the passage." "To throw his bridge above Bayonne involved the carrying of his materials across the Nive and through the deep country on each side, and the driving of Soult entirely from the Adour and all its confluents; but his own convoys between the bridge and the seaport magazines would then be unsafe and uncertain, having to lend their flank to Bayonne and cross several rivers liable to floods" (Napier). To cross the river below Bayonne might well appear impossible, but if achieved the advantage would be great. The mouth of the Adour would give Wellington a harbour, and the Royal Road would be available for his land transport. He therefore determined to make the attempt at a convenient moment.

IN THE PENINSULA 785

During the second week of February a frost dried the roads, and enabled Wellington to begin operations. Soult could now put into the field only 35,000 men, with 40 guns, and was consequently limited to defensive action. Wellington, on the other hand, had 70,000 Anglo-Portuguese troops and 95 guns; 30,000 Spaniards with 5 guns. His gross available force for the approaching campaign was thus 100,000 men and 100 guns. But from these numbers large deductions had to be made. For the investment of Bayonne 28,000 men were required. The Divisions of De la Bispal, Anglona, and half of Freyre's Army were not employed in France. Detachments watched St. Jean Pied de Port and one or two other places in the Pyrenees. Several British regiments had been marched to the coast to get their new clothing, and the force with which Wellington began his advance against Soult can hardly be reckoned at 45,000 men.

His initial operations were directed to turning the rivers beyond the Nive near their sources. On the 12th and 13th of February Sir Rowland Hill, having been relieved on the Adour by the 6th and 7th Divisions, concentrated his Corps and the 3rd Division—20,000 men and 16 guns—at Urcuray and Hasparren. On the 14th he drove Harispe from Hellette to Meharin, turned the Joyeuse River, and cut the direct communication between Soult and St. Jean Pied de Port. Pursuing his advantage, Hill next day occupied Meharin, marched to the Garris mountain, eleven miles distant, where Harispe with 4,000 men had taken up a position, and after a sharp combat drove him over the Bidouse to St. Palais with the loss of 500 men.

On the same day Soult, who expected Wellington to attempt the passage of the Adour above Bayonne, had taken up a position on the Lower Bidouse with four Divisions, his centre being at Bergoney. D'Erlon, with the rest of the Army, was on the right bank of the Adour. The French were in a position to strike a heavy —possibly a fatal—blow at Wellington's left wing, for Beresford had only the 7th Division in hand to oppose to the whole of the enemy's right and centre, while the 6th Division might have been simultaneously assailed in his rear by the Bayonne garrison from Mousseroles. A disaster to Beresford and the interposition of Soult between Hill and Hope would have ruined the plans for the Adour bridge. Wellington, feeling the danger, ordered up the 4th and Light Divisions; but on the 16th Soult, over-estimating Beresford's strength and fearing for his left flank, abandoned the line of the Bidouse and retired across the Gave d'Oloron. D'Erlon crossed the Adour on the 17th by the bridge at Port de Lanne and took post on the left bank. On D'Erlon's left, General Foy held the line of the Gave as far as Peyrehorade, while Taupin and Villatte continued the line thence along the Gave D'Oloron up to Sauveterre, a distance of about fourteen miles. Advanced parties were still retained on the Lower Bidouse, while on the extreme left Harispe held the line of the Soissons. Headquarters were at Orthez, on the Gave de Pau.

On the 16th Hill had crossed the Bidouse at St. Palais. The 4th Division and part of the 7th were at La Bastide de Clairance on the right bank of the Joyeuse. On the 17th Hill, supported on the left by the 3rd Division, carried the bridge over the Soissons at Arriverete. On the same day the fort of Jaca in the Pyrenees capitulated.

On the 18th Harispe and Villatte held the bridge-head at Sauveterre on the Gave d'Oloron, but Hill occupied the road running thence southward to the Fort of Navarrenx, which was still in the enemy's hands.

IN THE PENINSULA

The 4th, supported by the 7th and Light Divisions, came up to the Bidouse at Bidache, communicating with Hill by the Hussar Brigade and the 3rd Division at Somberraute.

Soult was completely puzzled whether he was to be attacked on the left or centre, or whether Wellington's object was to hold him in check while Hope assaulted the entrenched camp at Bayonne. That his adversary's manœuvres were intended to cover the construction of a bridge across the Adour below Bayonne did not occur to him. Nevertheless, the British Commander returned to St. Jean de Luz to carry out that incredible operation; but a snowstorm necessitated its postponement, and he came back to the Bidouse. Beresford, with the 4th and 7th Divisions, menaced the French centre at Hastingues and Oyergave, but the Light and 6th marched up the Bidouse; and on the 23rd Wellington concentrated on Gave d'Oloron, between Sauveterre and Navarrenx, the Cavalry under Cotton, 4 British Divisions (2nd, 3rd, 6th and Light), and those of Le Cor and Morillo.

Wellington's line from Navarrenx to the confluence of the Gaves de Pau and d'Oloron extended over twenty-five miles. By judicious demonstrations with his left and centre he drew the attention of Soult from his main force at Navarrenx, and though that fort was still held by the French, succeeded in carrying his Army with little loss across the Gave d'Oloron by the fords in its vicinity. Covered by Clausel, Soult, whose extended line had been too weak at all points to admit of effective opposition, then retired, and, with a view to resuming the offensive, concentrated his whole Army at Orthez, on the right bank of the Gave de Pau, twelve miles north-east of Sauveterre. Wellington, wheeling up his right, occupied the line Loubieng-Sauveterre, fronting nearly due north. Morillo was left to invest Navarrenx.

788 WELLINGTON'S OPERATIONS

Wellington's operations had had the desired effect of diverting Soult's attention from Bayonne. During this time Sir John Hope had been doing great things. As far back as the 15th he had occupied the heights of Anglet, two miles south of Bayonne, with the 1st Division. On the 21st the 6th Division marched to join Wellington, but was relieved at Mousseroles by the 5th under Colville; while Freyre with two Divisions of the Army of Galicia was called up from the Bidassoa and posted at Arcangues. Hope's Army Corps now consisted of 28,000 men with 20 guns; being made up of Vandeleur's Cavalry Brigade, the 1st and 5th Divisions, in addition to Freyre's Spaniards and the unattached Brigades of Aylmer, Bradford, and Campbell.

During the night of the 22nd-23rd the 1st Division with an 18-pounder and a rocket battery—leaving Bayonne on its right—was brought down through the pinewoods to the Adour at a point opposite the village of Beaucaut. Unfortunately the pontoons stuck fast in the deep sand of the road, and did not reach the river bank till 10 a.m. on the 23rd. In order to divert the enemy's attention the batteries opened fire and false attacks were made, some of which extended even beyond the Nive; while General Thouvenot the Governor, was further deceived by a report that 15,000 men had been embarked with orders to land at Cape Breton, a few miles north of the Adour.

Wellington's arrangements had provided for the co-operation of gunboats at the mouth of the Adour, and for *chasse-marées* loaded with material for rafts; but the vessels were wind-bound, and Hope, feeling the urgency of the case, determined with the courage of splendid genius to effect the passage of a river 300 yards wide without them. The enemy's flotilla on the river opened fire at 9 a.m., but Hope's batteries replied with such

IN THE PENINSULA 789

effect that 3 gunboats were destroyed and a sloop compelled to retire up the river.

Sixty men belonging to Stopford's brigade of Guards were now rowed across the river in a pontoon—reminding one of the officer and 25 men of the Buffs at the passage of the Duero in 1809. The men landed without opposition on the part of the French picquet which retired on their approach. A raft was then made with the pontoons, and a hawser stretched across the river. In the afternoon Stopford gradually brought 8 companies of his Brigade over to the right bank. In the evening he was attacked by General Maucomble with two battalions, but repelled the assailants.

During the night Stopford was reinforced, and the passage was continued while the low tide served, until midday on the 24th, when the British flotilla appeared at the mouth of the river. With great danger and difficulty the vessels crossed the bar. Some were dashed to pieces; but the wind suddenly lulled and the remainder took up their position three miles below Bayonne. By the evening of the 25th, 2 Squadrons, 2 guns, the 1st Division and the Brigades of Bradford and Campbell—8,000 men in all—had crossed the Adour. Next day they invested the fortress on the right bank.

The next object was the construction of the bridge. " Twenty-six *chasse-marées*, moored head and stern at distances of 40 feet, reckoning from centre to centre, were first bound together with ropes; two thick cables were then carried loosely across their decks; and the ends being cast over the walls in each bank were strained and fastened in various modes to the sands. They were sufficiently slack to meet the spring tides which rose 14 feet; and planks were laid upon them without any supporting beams." This bridge was constructed by Major Todd, R.E., upon the plan of Colonel Sturgeon,

790 WELLINGTON'S OPERATIONS

at a point three miles below Bayonne where the bank was revetted with a wall, and the river somewhat contracted to a breadth of 800 feet. It was completed on the 26th. Thus ended an enterprise reflecting equal credit on Wellington and Sturgeon for its conception, and on Hope and Tod for its execution.

On the 27th Sir John contracted his investment line to within 900 yards of the French walls. In the course of this operation a severe fight took place at St. Etienne—an important post on high ground commanding the roads leading to Bordeaux and Peyrehorade—which was gallantly carried by the King's German Legion under General Hinuber and successfully held against a counter-attack led by General Thouvenot, Governor of Bayonne, in person. The church and village of St. Etienne were then entrenched and formed the centre of Hope's position on the right bank of the Adour. On the left bank the line of investment, extending from Urdains to Anglet, was formed by Lord Aylmer, the 5th and a Spanish Division. On the same day Vandeleur's Cavalry Brigade established communication with the 7th Division by the Peyrehorade road.

During this period Wellington had not been idle. On the 25th he drove Clausel's Corps, forming the French rearguard, across the Gave de Pau at Orthez. He then brought up Fane's Cavalry Brigade and the 2nd, 6th, Light, and Portuguese Divisions to the left bank. Lord E. Somerset's Cavalry and the 3rd Division reached the broken bridge of Berenx, five miles below Orthez. Vivian's Brigade with the 4th and 7th Divisions were concentrated in front of Peyrehorade.

On the 26th Beresford with the left wing crossed the Gave unopposed, and advanced along the Orthez road, driving the enemy's rearguard before him, to the village

IN THE PENINSULA 791

of Baights where he halted for the night. The 3rd Division, thus covered by Beresford's advance, crossed the Gave de Pau at Berenx where a pontoon bridge was then constructed. By these movements Beresford, Picton, and Hill were again concentrated; and to ensure direct communication with Hope, orders were given to erect a permanent bridge over the Adour at Port de Lanne, for the temporary one had been washed away. Hope's line of investment was already too long for the strength of his force; but Wellington, fearing that Soult might be reinforced by Suchet, ordered Sir John to send Freyre to join him with two Divisions and a Portuguese battery. The Count de la Bispal and the Prince of Anglona were also warned to be ready to enter France if required. But so greatly did Wellington dread guerilla warfare on the part of the French peasantry that he only sent for the Spaniards when he had received a large sum in gold and was able to pay them regularly. Even then, in order to guard against the disorders to be feared from his allies, he authorised the people of France to take arms under command of their mayors for the preservation of order.

Soult was holding a strong position behind the Gave de Pau. His centre was at Orthez; his left, $1\frac{1}{2}$ mile distant on the Pau road. His right extended to the heights of St. Boës, more than three miles from Orthez in the direction of Dax. But for the neglect of his cavalry to report Beresford's advance until 3 p.m. Soult would have been in a position to fall upon that officer and on Picton with 20,000 men. Even on receipt of the report it was not too late to strike a heavy blow. But the marshal hesitated, and by Beresford's movement his right was uncovered. Still he was determined to fight. He brought up his troops from the Pau road to Orthez where Pierre Soult's Cavalry Brigade and the Division

792 WELLINGTON'S OPERATIONS

of Harispe, which now formed part of Clausel's Corps, represented the new left of the French line. D'Erlon's Corps occupied the centre of the position, with the Division of Foy in the first, and that of D'Armagnac in the second line. On the right Reille, now commanding the Divisions of Taupin, Roguet, and Paris, held the heights of St. Boës. Villatte had been placed under the orders of Clausel and formed a general reserve in rear of the centre. The position was taken up on strong ground covered in front by marshes, and faced nearly due south. The Cavalry took post with Villatte. Of the artillery, 12 guns were attached to Harispe, and 12 to Foy. Sixteen were held in reserve behind the centre, where they commanded the approach by the Dax road. The country in general was open heath. The line of retreat ran directly to the rear through Sault de Navailles to Mont de Marsan where Soult had now established part of his magazines; part being at Aire on the road to Nogara.

The object of Wellington's strategy was to drive Soult into the sandy desert of the Landes near Bordeaux and hem him in between the Garonne and the sea. Beresford's was therefore a false line of advance, and would not have been permitted had he encountered any resistance, or had Wellington not received a report that Soult was retiring from his position.

At daylight on the 27th the 6th and Light Divisions, the latter weakened by the absence of the 43rd and 1st Battalion, 95th (which with three other battalions had been sent to get its new clothing at St. Jean de Luz), crossed the Gave de Pau by the pontoon bridge at Berenx and proceeded to join the 3rd Division on the Peyrehorade road opposite Foy. Beresford was at St. Boës approaching Reille by the Dax road. An interval of a mile and a half separated him from Picton and the 3rd Division; but on an old Roman camp, half way between the two,

IN THE PENINSULA

Wellington in person was watching the enemy's dispositions and had realised that a battle for which he was hardly prepared was now inevitable. Napier states that even in point of numbers he was inferior to Soult, having only 37,000 men with 48 guns against 40,000 and 40 guns; but in his reckoning it is not quite clear whether the French 40,000 are "sabres and bayonets" only, or include officers, artillerymen, &c., in which case for the sake of fair comparison an addition of about 20 per cent. should be made to Wellington's numbers.

Pending the arrival of the 6th and Light Divisions, Picton was in imminent danger of being attacked in overwhelming force by D'Erlon; but Wellington, without showing the slightest sign of anxiety, pushed forward his skirmishers, and by bluff tided over the crisis which lasted for two hours, for the rocky approach through a narrow defile contracted the front of the approaching Divisions, and the troops could only come up by driblets. At length they were ready. Then, leaving the 6th Division with Picton, Wellington posted the Light Division behind the Roman camp, and by so doing helped to fill up the gap between the left and centre.

On the extreme right Sir R. Hill's Corps was drawn up opposite the bridge of Orthez and the ford of Soarnes a mile higher up the river. The bridge was too strongly fortified to be forced, and the river spread out widely with flat banks.

The problem before Wellington was no easy one. The enemy's front was almost entirely covered by marshy ground. His left at Orthez was protected by the old fortifications of the town and by the river. The right flank at St. Boës was almost equally strong, for even if the village were forced the assailants would be compelled to advance through a narrow ravine commanded by the fire of the 16 guns in reserve. The whole line of Soult extended over about three miles.

WELLINGTON'S OPERATIONS

Wellington determined to attack the right and centre. Sir Lowry Cole, with the Fusilier Brigade under Ross and the Portuguese under Colonel Vasconcellos carried the village of St. Boës after a vigorous resistance. The 3rd and 6th Divisions advanced against Foy. But in each case the difficulties in the way of development proved insurmountable. Five times the 4th Division attempted to form line beyond the village, and five times it was driven back. At length the Portuguese Brigade gave way in disorder, and that of Ross was with difficulty extricated from the streets. In the centre Picton and Clinton were not only brought to a standstill, but suffered heavily in a counter attack by Foy.

Three hours had been spent in fruitless efforts, but Wellington had still large reserves in hand. Directing Picton and Clinton to make a renewed attack on Foy, he brought up the 7th and the remaining Brigade—W. Anson's—of the 4th Division to assail the flank of Reille once more. At the same time he pushed the 52nd under Colborne from Barnard's Brigade of the Light Division, straight across the marsh to support both attacks. Hill was ordered to force the passage of the river. These dispositions proved completely successful. Colborne, having with great difficulty pushed his way through the marsh, appeared where least expected by the enemy, penetrated between Reille and D'Erlon and threw both Corps into disorder. The 7th Division under General Walker gained possession of St. Boës and deployed on the French side unmolested. At the same time Picton seized a point of vantage whence his guns enfiladed Foy's line. Soult found himself compelled to fall back and rally his troops on a new position. Beresford and Picton continuing to advance, joined hands; and Hill who had by this time forded the river at Souarnes above Orthez, seized a height on the right bank and threatened to sever

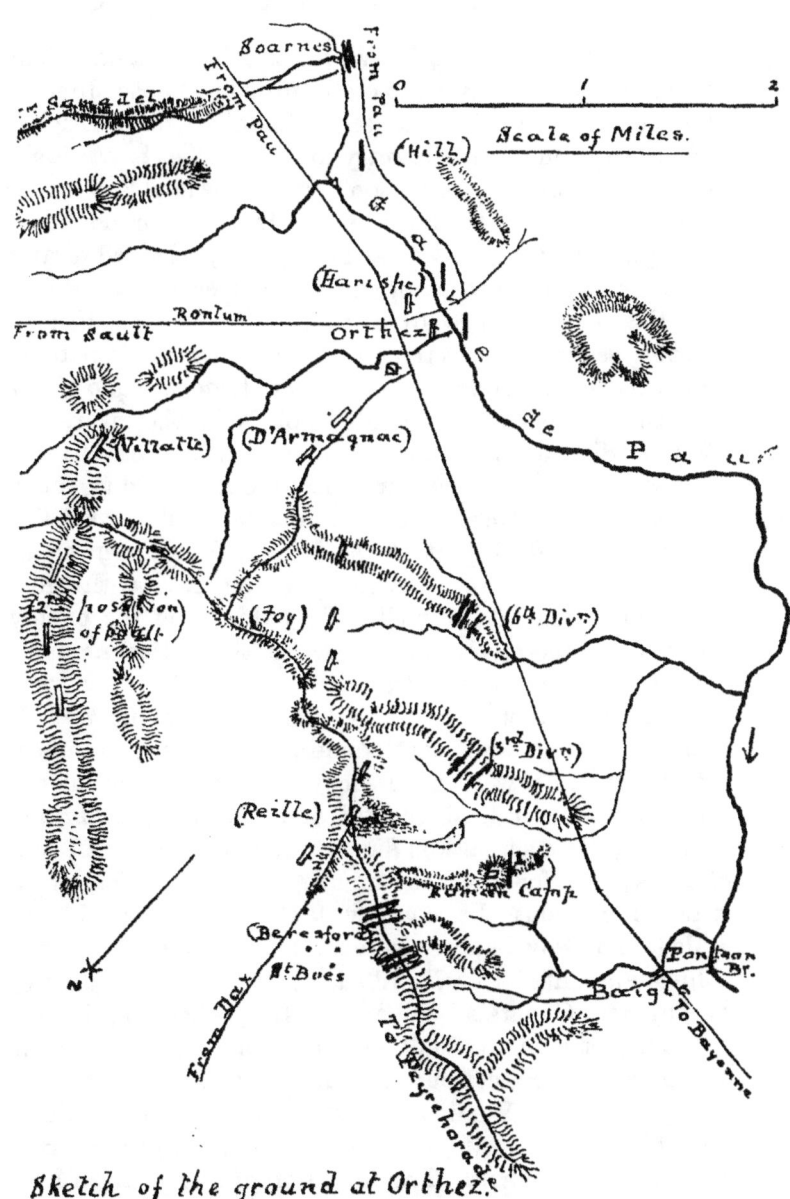

the French communication with Sault de Novailles. The flank of Harispe was completely turned. Clausel directed him to retire upon Villatte, and attempted with a Brigade of Cavalry and one of Infantry to keep Hill at bay. Soult, however, coming up in person, felt that he could no longer make head against the Allies. He gave orders for a general retreat which was at first conducted in admirable order; but on approaching the deep river called the Luy de Bearn, five miles from the battlefield, the French troops, seeing their retreat threatened by Hill's parallel line of advance, broke and in scattered mobs made either for the bridge or the fordable points of the river. At 5 p.m. Sir Rowland was in possession of the Orthez-Marsan road. The country, being enclosed and intersected by deep ditches, was most unfavourable for cavalry action, but at dusk part of the Hussar Brigade in small parties succeeded in attacking the fugitives with great effect near Sault de Novailles. By this time the enemy seemed completely dispersed; but at the critical moment Wellington for the third time during the war was struck by a bullet and rendered for the moment *hors de combat*. "Whereby," says Napier, "the vigour and unity of the pursuit were necessarily abated." The enemy in consequence rallied quickly, and destroyed the bridge at Sault. His actual loss did not exceed 4,000 men and 6 guns; but for the next month 3,000 conscripts were straggling about the country. General Bechaud was killed and Foy badly wounded. The casualties of the Allies amounted to 277 killed, 1,923 wounded—among whom were Generals Walker and Ross—and 70 missing.

During the night Soult retreated to St. Sever, fifteen miles beyond Sault, on the Adour, at the edge of the sandy Landes. Wellington, who had so nearly gained the object of his strategy, followed him on the 28th. But the French Marshal had no intention of being driven into the desert. Evacuating St. Sever, he marched up the right bank of the Adour, posted Reille at Barcelonne, and D'Erlon at Cazeres, while he directed Clausel to cross the river and take post on the left bank at Aire. By this movement he had, it is true, abandoned his magazines at Mont de Marsan, but was free to march either northward by Roquefort and draw nearer the Emperor, who was now fighting against enormous odds on the Seine and Aube, or southward upon Pau or Tarbes and communicate with Suchet. By the slowness of the pursuit Wellington had therefore lost his strategical object. He crossed the Adour, however, soon after midday on the 1st of March, pushed a column along the right bank to Cazeres, ordered Beresford to seize the stores at Mont Marsan, and Hill to advance to intercept the enemy in his retreat upon Aire. No doubt the order reached Hill after he had quitted Samadet, for instead of marching thence directly upon Aire, he first moved to the Adour, opposite Grenade, and by this circuitous route missed the whole object.

A heavy storm, which washed away the pontoons, delayed these movements, but D'Erlon was pushed back from Cazeres to Barcelonne, and the road to Bordeaux by Roquefort occupied by the Allies. At 3 p.m. on the 2nd Hill reached Aire, where he found Clausel in occupation of a line of heights behind the Grave river, covering the town. After a stiff contest Clausel was driven from his position, the magazines at Aire were seized, and Soult retreated up the Adour.

Napier remarks that between the 14th February and the 2nd of March "Wellington travelled with his right wing eighty miles, passed five large and several small rivers, forced the enemy to abandon two fortified bridge-heads and many minor works, gained one great battle and two combats, captured six guns and 1,000 prisoners, seized the magazines at Dax, Mont Marsan and Aire, forced Soult to abandon Bayonne, and also cut him off from Bordeaux. And in this time he threw his stupendous bridge below Bayonne, and closely invested that fortress."

During these operations Wellington had been obliged to pursue two, to some extent, divergent objects. The principal one was to separate Soult from Suchet and drive the former into the Landes, where he would be in a country not only devoid of resources but also partly hostile to the Emperor. To this end it was necessary to turn his left flank; but until communication with Hope could be established by the right bank of the Adour, the turning movement had to be followed with caution, and the left of the Allies kept well forward to prevent Soult interposing between Wellington and Hope. The communication was successfully effected; but when the ulterior object of pushing the French into the desert seemed also nearly assured, Soult by rapidity of march escaped the toils. It was unfortunate that Hill was not directed straight upon Aire from Samadet. He would then have intercepted not only Clausel, but the whole French Army.

CHAPTER XLVII

Beresford enters Bordeaux—Operations of Lord Dalhousie in the neighbourhood—Soult resumes the offensive against Wellington—Retires towards Toulouse—Wellington follows—Skirmish at Vic en Bigorre—Death of Colonel Sturgeon, R.E.—Skirmish at Tarbes—Advance on Toulouse—Wellington fails to cross the Garonne above the town—Crosses it below—Battle of Toulouse—Soult evacuates the town—Abdication of Napoleon—Cessation of hostilities.

THE successive defeats of the French were reflected in the conduct of Soult's army. Its magazines having been lost, supplies became irregular, and the troops got out of hand. Wellington's policy in maintaining discipline and in enforcing cash payment of requisitions went far to reconcile the civil inhabitants to the invasion of their country, and stop all danger of partisan warfare in his rear.

On the 4th of March Soult took up a position from Marsiac on the Adour to Maubourget, covering Tarbes. Here he received a letter from the Emperor directing him to leave only a small garrison in Bayonne, to resume the offensive and to fall upon one or other of the Allied wings, as occasion might offer. The letter was written under a misapprehension of Soult's position. It also came too late. Otherwise Abbé's Division, which had been thrown into Bayonne, might have been saved for the field army. In reply Soult wrote an explanatory letter, pointing out the extent to which he was able to carry out Napoleon's orders, and observing that the position which he had taken up enabled him to attack the flank of the Allies should they march upon Toulouse, or their rear if they moved against Bordeaux.

Meanwhile Lord Wellington was feeling the want of the force necessary to carry on operations under present conditions. He desired to reach the Lower Garonne and seize Bordeaux, but the detachment of 12,000 men with that object would leave him with barely 30,000 to oppose Soult, while he believed the latter to have been reinforced by 10,000 men from Suchet's army. He had been led to expect the addition of 20,000 men from England and Lisbon, but they had not arrived. In addition to the two divisions under Freyre, Wellington therefore called up a brigade of Morillo from Navarrenx; and, concluding that one result of the battle of Orthez would be the evacuation by Suchet of Catalonia, ordered General William Clinton to send him, by way of the Ebro, two battalions of the 27th, the 44th, 58th and 81st, the 4th Battalion K.G.L. and three batteries—about 5,000 officers and men—and to embark the rest of his army for Sicily or Gibraltar.

The march of the Spaniards was accompanied by all kinds of irregularity, and the conduct of some of the British troops, hitherto good, deteriorated and gave great anxiety to Lord Wellington, who took the strong measure of advising that two Colonels of Byng's Brigade should in consequence be deprived of their commissions.

The project of getting possession of Bordeaux and the mouth of the Garonne had much to recommend it. It would materially widen the base of operations, it would encourage the royalist party to assert itself, and would thereby tend to the protection of his left flank. It was known that a force under General L'Huillier was being collected on the further side of the Lower Garonne. Beresford, with Vivian's Brigade and two squadrons of

IN THE PENINSULA 801

Vandeleur, the 4th and 7th Divisions, was accordingly despatched, by way of Roquefort and Captieux, to seize Bordeaux. His Cavalry entered it unopposed on the 12th. The Bourbon dynasty was then proclaimed by the Duc D'Angoulême, and the local authorities, contrary to the wishes of Lord Wellington, who was quite ready to make use of any party opposed to Napoleon, but had no intention of encouraging measures which might perforce be afterwards repudiated; for the Allied Powers were still treating for peace with the Emperor, and it soon indeed became evident that the mass of the people was loyal to him.

Beresford, with the 4th Division and Vivian's Brigade, was now recalled by Wellington, while Lord Dalhousie, with the 7th Division, was left in the neighbourhood of Bordeaux. But for the early termination of the war Dalhousie might have found himself in a position of some difficulty, for Napoleon at once organised a force at Libourne under General Decaen called the Army of the Gironde, the nucleus of which was formed by gensd'armes, National Guards and a Division of Suchet's army 6,000 strong, under General Beurman, which had been at first despatched to Lyons, but was believed by Wellington to have joined Soult.

L'Huillier, retiring behind the Dordogne, took up a position at St. André de Cubzac. On the 27th Admiral Penrose entered the mouth of the Garonne with a line-of-battle ship and two frigates. This eased Dalhousie. He pushed two or three squadrons over the Dordogne as far as Libourne, thus interposing between L'Huillier and Decaen, the latter of whom reached Mucidan with 250 gensd'armes on the 1st of April. Beurman had not yet arrived at Perigueux. Dalhousie then crossed the Dordogne on the 4th near St. André at the head of two brigades and four guns. His apparent intention was to summon the fort of Blaye; but he suddenly attacked

L'Huillier at Étauliers, routed him and took 320 prisoners. The French vessels in the river were then destroyed and the fort of Blaye invested.

Just at this time three provisional battalions of English Militia landed at Bordeaux. They gave proofs, not unnaturally, of a total absence of discipline; but as the war now terminated, their fighting qualities remained unknown. It was unfortunate that they were commanded by Lord Buckingham and other very stout persons, who excited the derision of the ribald populace, which hailed them as "Les Boeuf-gras Anglais!"

For a few days after the fight at Aire neither Wellington nor Soult made any movement of importance. Each overrated the strength of the other, Wellington believing that his opponent had been reinforced by Beurman, Soult being unaware of Beresford's absence. In point of fact the opposing armies were about equal in numbers, each having, perhaps, 32,000 officers and men of all arms. The Allies had 44 guns against 38 of the French.

On the 13th and 14th of March Wellington was joined by Ponsonby's Brigade of heavy Cavalry and 8,000 Spaniards under Freyre; but he still felt anxiety, for his promised reinforcements from England and Portugal had not arrived, and a proposal had been made by Marshal Suchet to evacuate the Catalonian fortresses, provided that their garrisons were allowed to return to France. Wellington, having no desire to see Soult reinforced by 20,000 veteran troops, refused his consent; but the Spanish generals were anxious to accept Suchet's proposal, and there was a fear lest difficulties should arise on the return of King Ferdinand, which was now momentarily expected, in regard to engagements into which he might privately have entered with the Emperor.

To increase his available force the British Commander

called up Giron and the Prince of Anglona from the valley of the Bastan. Headquarters were established at Aire, and a position facing south-east was taken up astride the Adour and Leés.

On the 13th Soult, discovering Beresford's absence, assumed the offensive in accordance with the Emperor's injunctions by attacking Hill's outposts in the hope of seizing a ridge leading to Garlin and Aire, which would place him at right angles to Wellington's line, and enable him to menace his line of communications. Sir Rowland was thereupon reinforced by the 3rd and 6th Divisions. During the next two days Soult continued to threaten the British right, but without much spirit; and on hearing of the fall of Bordeaux retired by the direct Tarbes road as far as Lembeye.

By this time the approach of Beresford and the arrival of the Spaniards and the Heavy Cavalry had increased Wellington's strength to about 55,000 officers and men, with nearly 60 guns, but he would seem to have been slow in resuming the offensive. To some extent he may have been influenced by the bad weather. On the 18th he advanced. Hill, on the right, moved to Conchez; Wellington, in the centre, with the 3rd and 7th Divisions to Mandiran. The Spaniards followed in second line. The Hussar Brigade and Light Division pushed along the right bank of the Adour to Plaisance, followed at an interval of a day's march by the 4th Division and Vivian's Brigade. The direction and arrangement of the columns lent itself to the strategical object of cutting Soult from Toulouse. The Marshal fell back in the night behind the Laiza river. Next day the advance was continued, and Soult suddenly found his right outflanked, and his army in imminent danger of being intercepted in its ultimate line of retreat to Toulouse and into the Pyrenees. D'Erlon with the right wing was at once ordered to occupy Vic en Bigorre, and hold the Allies in check, while Soult himself carried the Corps of Reille and Clausel by a forced march on a circuitous route to Tarbes.

D'Erlon found himself anticipated at Vic en Bigorre by Bock's Cavalry Brigade. He had barely time to expel it when up came Picton with the "Fighting 3rd." A hot fight ensued. D'Erlon's leading Division under Paris was driven in disorder upon D'Armagnac; but the two then held their ground until the arrival of the Hussar Brigade and Light Division at Rabastens, when D'Erlon, seeing his right turned, abandoned his position. But he had done his work, and Soult was enabled to retreat almost unmolested through Tarbes along the St. Gaudens-road and to take up a position for the 20th on the heights of Oleac just in front of Tournay with the Corps of Reille and D'Erlon, while Clausel held on to the town of Tarbes with the Division of Villate, and with that of Harispe occupied a ridge at Orleix on the Rabastens-road with a view to making head for a time against Hill and Wellington respectively.

During the skirmish at Vic en Bigorre fell Lieut.- Colonel Henry Sturgeon, R.E., Assistant Quartermaster- General on the Headquarters Staff, an officer of great talent and resource, whose name has been repeatedly mentioned in these pages in connection with enterprises demanding the highest skill, and whose opinion is said to have been "often asked and sometimes followed" by Wellington himself. His death took place under painful circumstances. In addition to his other appointments Sturgeon had been appointed to the command of the Corps of Guides. Among his duties was that of organising relays of couriers along the line of communications to escort officers charged with despatches. After the battle of Orthez Wellington, desirous of sending off his

IN THE PENINSULA

messenger, called for Sturgeon, but found to his surprise and annoyance that the latter, absorbed in the grand manœuvres of the army, had entirely forgotten all about the Guides. It was a grave error, and Wellington, whose temper was perhaps affected by the pain of his wound, forgetting all he owed to the Colonel, reprimanded him in the presence of a large number of officers with such violence that Sturgeon, stung to the quick, took the earliest opportunity to seek death among the enemy's skirmishers. To make matters worse, Wellington, on hearing of this gallant officer's fall, made no allusion to him in his despatch, and receives a well-deserved rebuke in the observation of Sir W. Napier that "the whole army felt painfully mortified that Sturgeon's merits were passed unnoticed." It has been said of Wellington that he kept two sets of Staff Officers—one for work, the other for promotion. The latter were for the most part relatives of titled nonentities. The system has been not altogether unknown in more recent times.

At midday on the 20th, Clinton with the 6th Division turned Harispe's right, while the Rifle battalions of the Light Division attacked and broke his centre. Hill forced the passage of the Adour. Villatte and Harispe retired in confusion along the Tournay road, but deep ditches prevented the British Cavalry acting with effect; Clausel showed his usual skill in a difficult situation, and eventually brought his Corps safely under the protection of Soult's main body on the heights of Oleac, which checked the pursuit. It was now dusk, and Wellington bivouacked on the bank of the Arros.

But during the day Soult had heard of Vivian and Cole in Miélan, whither they seem to have been directed by an after-order. The 6th Division was at Coussan, five miles due north of Tournay. A large body of the Allies being thus on the chord while the French Army was traversing the arc, was in a position to intercept Soult's retreat on Toulouse at Muret. The French Commander therefore, without more ado, evacuated his position during the night and reached St. Gaudens next day after a march of thirty-five miles, covered by Clausel, who formed the rearguard and halted at Montrejeau, where he was joined by the Cavalry Division under P. Soult, which had been detached in observation along the Trie road, and had been cut off from the main body by the direction of Clinton's advance.

Wellington, however, did not follow up the enemy very rapidly. He was by this time over a hundred miles from his base at Passages, and his communications were liable to attack on both sides. He had great difficulty in keeping his troops in order. The Portuguese behaved admirably, but the British Cavalry, particularly Ponsonby's and the Hussar Brigade, gave cause for complaint, and the Spaniards committed every excess that could not be stopped. The danger of exciting the peasantry to partisan warfare would have been much increased had it not been that the French in their retreat had incensed their countrymen by their depredations and thus counter-balanced the irregularities of the Allies.

Under all the circumstances, good policy seemed to dictate short marches with a view to keeping the men in hand and saving them from fatigue and sickness. Strategy was therefore made a secondary consideration, and Wellington failed to intercept the French at Muret. The course which he took was no doubt right; but Napier points out that without deviating from his principle, more use should have been made of the Cavalry, and that the enemy should not have been allowed to get away scatheless. The reason of the apparent want of energy was probably that lack of confidence in his Cavalry leaders, by which he had been influenced on former occasions.

IN THE PENINSULA 807

On the 21st the Allies advanced on a front of about fifteen miles. Beresford on the left, with the Cavalry Brigades of Ponsonby and Somerset and the 6th Division, was about Castelnau, the 4th Division and Vivian's Brigade being in second line at Trie. The Cavalry Brigades patrolled the roads leading to Masseube and Boulogne. Bock's Brigade, the Light and 3rd Divisions, forming the centre, were between Gaussan and Lannemazan. Hill, on the right, was near the latter place.

On the 22nd the left and centre halted, while Hill pushed along the St. Gaudens road to Montrejeau. The two Cavalry Brigades under Fane, attached to Hill's Corps, reconnoitred St. Gaudens, where two squadrons of the 13th in a brilliant charge defeated four of the enemy, driving them through the town and taking 102 prisoners.

On the 23rd Beresford reached Puymaurin, followed at an interval of a day's march by Cole. The centre was about Boulogne, the right wing at St. Gaudens.

The advance continued unopposed. On the 24th the right wing was at St. Martory, the left at Lombez, the centre five miles east of L'Isle en Dodon.

Next day Beresford, who had been joined by the 4th Division, reached St. Foy, supported by the Light and 3rd Divisions at Samatan. Hill was at Cazeres. On the 26th Beresford entered St. Lys and found himself in presence of the French Army drawn up behind the Touch, a tributary of the Garonne, covering the city of Toulouse.

Soult had effected his retreat with skill, and was again in a position to choose his own line of operations. He could retire down the Garonne and join Decaen; he could move either by Alby to join Augereau at Lyons, or by Carcassonne to join Suchet. He could at his pleasure fight or avoid a battle. He had all the advantage of holding an important strategical point. Toulouse had a population of 50,000. It "commanded the principal passage of the Garonne, was the centre of a number of roads on both sides of the river, and the chief military arsenal of the South of France. Here he could easily feed his troops, arm and discipline the conscripts, control and urge the military authorities."

A force under General Loverdo was posted at Montauban, who was ordered to construct a bridge-head on the left bank of the Tarn, and by so doing secure the passage of the river and form a rallying point for the detachments observing the Lower Garonne. "To maintain Toulouse was a great political object. It was the last point which connected him at once with Suchet and Decaen." "Toulouse was not less valuable as a position for battle. The Garonne on the west presented to the Allies a deep loop, at the bottom of which was the bridge, completely covered by the suburb of St. Cyprien, itself protected by an ancient brick wall three feet thick, and flanked by two massive towers: these defences Soult had improved and added a line of exterior entrenchments. Beyond the bridge was the city, surrounded by an old wall flanked with towers, and so thick as to admit 16- and 24-pound guns. The great and celebrated canal of Languedoc, which joined the river Garonne a few miles below the town, wound for the most part within point blank shot of the walls, covering them on the north and east as the Garonne and St. Cyprien on the west; and the suburbs of St. Stephen and Guillermerie, between which the canal ran, furnished outworks on the east; for they were entrenched and connected with the fortified hills of Sacarin and Cambon, which crossed the suburbs and flanked the approaches to the canal above and below." (Napier, bk. xxiv., ch. 5.)

Half a mile beyond these hills a series of entrenchments

IN THE PENINSULA

extended along the rugged ridge of Mont Rave, overlooking the marshy plain of the Hers. "On the south side of the town, the St. Michael suburb formed one advanced work, beyond which were the Pech David heights trending to the Garonne." (Col. W. H. James.)

To await the fall of Bayonne or the arrival of the rest of the Spaniards, would merely give Soult time to strengthen his position. It was indispensable to the Allies to cross the Garonne. Strategy dictated a passage below the town, for it was more important to deny Soult access to the interior of France than to stop his junction with the small force now commanded by Suchet.* But the south side of the city was the weakest, and on the 27th Lord Wellington tried to throw a pontoon bridge six miles up-stream, yet failed, for the Engineer Officer, miscalculating the width of the river, had brought up an inadequate number of pontoons. An eye-witness says that he had never seen Wellington so enraged.

Compelled to change his plan, the British Commander drove the enemy from the Touch on the 28th, massed his left and centre about Portet, six miles above Toulouse, and drew back Hill's Corps to Roques. During the night of the 30th Sir Rowland, with Fane's Cavalry, the 2nd Division and those of Le Cor and Morillo, eighteen guns and a rocket battery, crossed first the Garonne by a new bridge at Pensanguel, and then the Ariège, with the intention of marching down the right bank to attack the suburbs of St. Michel and St. Etienne, while Wellington assailed St. Cyprien. But the marshy ground bordering the Ariège stopped the movement, and Hill recrossed the two rivers.

This delay gave Soult time to complete his defences.

* Wellington believed Suchet to have 12,000 or 14,000 men. He had in reality only about 3,000 remaining.

He resolved to give up his communication with Montauban and hold on to Toulouse to the last, hoping for the arrival of Suchet, whom he had repeatedly begged to join him. His army was composed as follows:—

Lieut.-Gen. Count D'Erlon	{ 1st Division	... General	Darricau (late Paris)
	{ 2nd ,,	,,	D'Armagnac
,, Count Reille	{ 4th ,,	,,	Taupin
	{ 5th ,,	,,	Maransin
,, Baron Clausel	{ 6th ,,	,,	Villatte
	{ 8th ,,	,,	Harispe
	Reserve of Conscripts	,,	Travot
	Light Cavalry Division	,,	Pierre Soult

Wellington now made up his mind to cross the Garonne below Toulouse. The river was swollen, and the difficulties had increased; but, as already noticed, from the strategical point of view a passage below the city was preferable to one above it. A bridge was thrown across at Grenade, fifteen miles down-stream. Its construction occupied several days. Wellington was constantly present in person to see the progress made. The further bank of the river was lined by the enemy's videttes. Once a shot was fired at his lordship. A non-commissioned officer immediately ran up to apologise for the violation of etiquette established between the two armies. "Pardon, monsieur," said he, "c'est un nouveau." On another occasion Wellington was in danger of being shot by one of his own sentries. Fortunately recognising his visitor, the man expressed his delight in homely phrase—"I would rather see your long nose than ten thousand men"!

On the 4th of April, in presence of thousands of spectators, while the regimental bands played "The British Grenadiers," the Cavalry Brigades of Somerset, Vivian, and Ponsonby, the 3rd, 4th, and 6th Divisions—the whole under Beresford—passed over to the further bank of

IN THE PENINSULA 811

the Garonne. Before the Light Division and Spaniards could follow, the river, which had fallen slightly, rose again. The pontoons had to be taken up and the detachment was exposed to the attack of the whole French Army. But the danger was apparent rather than real. Beresford—or rather Wellington, for the latter constantly crossed to and fro in a boat, and would certainly have taken command in the event of an action—had upwards of 20,000 men, with 18 guns, and was flanked by 30 more on the left bank. He had a line of retreat across the Hers; while, on the other hand, Soult would have been obliged to march 15 miles to the attack, and in his absence St. Cyprien was open to assault by Hill with 15,000 men. It is said that the Marshal was pressed by his officers to take the risk, but replied, "The British Divisions would not be conquered as long as there was a man of them left to stand, and I cannot afford to lose men now."

On the 8th the bridge was laid again, and Wellington, having reinforced Beresford with Freyre's troops and the Portuguese artillery, advanced by both banks of the Hers upon Toulouse. Vivian seized the bridge at Croix d'Aurade and established communication between the two columns. Wellington halted within five miles of the town. He shortened his communication with Hill by throwing a new bridge over the Garonne at Seille, half way between Toulouse and Grenade, intending to call up the Light Division and attack Soult on the 9th. But the Engineers again disappointed him. The bridge was not finished in time, and the battle had to be postponed till the 10th—much to Wellington's annoyance, for he had already lost valuable time, and any day might bring Suchet to the aid of his colleague.

On the other hand, observes Napier, "Soult's combinations were now crowned with success. He had, by means of his fortresses, his battles, the sudden change of his line of operations, his rapid retreat from Tarbes, and his clear judgment in fixing upon Toulouse as his next point of resistance, reduced the strength of his adversary to an equality with his own. He had gained seventeen days for preparation, had brought the Allies to deliver battle on ground naturally adapted for defence, well fortified, and where one third of their force was separated by a great river from the rest—they could derive no advantage from their numerous cavalry, and were overmatched in artillery, notwithstanding their previous superiority in that arm."

His dispositions for battle were as follow: Reille with the Divisions of Taupin and Maransin occupied the suburb of St. Cyprien on the left bank of the Garonne. D'Erlon held the line of the canal on the north side of the town from its junction with the river at the bridge of Jumeaux to that of Matabian on the Alby road, with Darricau's Division, retaining D'Armagnac in reserve. Clausel held the fortified heights east of Toulouse, Harispe being posted along the whole length of Mont Rave except the spur jutting out towards the Croix d'Aurade, called La Pugade, which was occupied by a Brigade of Villatte, the rest of whose Division was held in reserve. General Travot with about 7,000 conscripts manned the walls of the enceinte.

Including these conscripts, Soult had an available force of 49,000 officers and men (of whom upwards of 40,000 were actually engaged in the ensuing battle), supported by 56 field guns and about 30 guns of position.

Lord Wellington's primary object was to enclose the enemy within the walls of the city. He wished to make his principal attack upon the south front, as being least strongly fortified; but the deepness of the ground and other circumstances prevented his approach and compelled him to assail Mont Rave on the east side. His army was thus composed (*vide* Napier, vol. vi. app. ii., No. 7) :—

Cavalry.	Officers, Sergeants, &c.	Rank & File.	Total.	Guns.
Bock's Brigade (Lieut.-Col. Bulow commanding)	112	694	806	
Ponsonby's Brigade (Lord C. Manners commanding)	188	1,221	1,409	
Fane's Brigade, British	} 240	1,506	1,746	
,, ,, Portuguese				
Vivian's Brigade (Col. Arenschildt commanding)	128	960	1,088	
Lord E. Somerset's Hussar Brigade	214	1,691	1,905	
Total of Cavalry	882	6,972	6,954	
Infantry.				
2nd Division, British	715	4,123 }	6,940	
,, ,, Portuguese	235	1,867 }		
3rd Division, British	529	2,741 }	4,679	
,, ,, Portuguese	226	1,183 }		
4th Division, British	531	3,028 }	5,383	
,, ,, Portuguese	239	1,585 }		
6th Division, British	558	3,233 }	5,681	
,, ,, Portuguese	246	1,644 }		
Light ,, British	378	2,469 }	4,318	
Le Cors ,, Portuguese	231	1,240 }		
,, ,, Portuguese	455	3,507	3,962	
Total of Infantry	4,343	26,620	30,963	
Artillery (approximately)			1,500	64
Spaniards under Freyre and Morillo			14,000	
Grand Total			53,417	64

N.B.—The numbers of the Cavalry are taken from the "State" of the 15th of May; of the Infantry, from that of April 10th.

On the left bank of the Garonne Sir Rowland Hill was directed to threaten the suburb of St. Cyprien. The 3rd and Light Divisions supported by Bock's Cavalry Brigade were to demonstrate against the canal on the north side of the town from the Garonne to the Croix d'Aurade road. Freyre, who had demanded the honour of making the first attack, was ordered to drive the enemy's brigade off La Pugade and cover the march of the 4th and 6th Divisions under Beresford, who was directed to move along the low ground by the Hers past Mont Rave, and then wheeling to the right attack the fort of St. Sypière on the southern spurs of the Mont Rave ridge. The Hussar Brigade moved up the left bank of the Hers; that of Vivian—now commanded by Col. Arenschildt—by the right bank to keep off the enemy's Cavalry.

The fact that Napoleon had abdicated on the 6th and that the war was at an end ought to have been known to Wellington. But no authentic news had arrived, although both he and Soult seem to have been aware that Paris had been captured by the Allies.

At 6 a.m. on the 10th—Easter Day—the various columns pressed forward to the attack. The preliminary objects were easily attained. The enemy's advanced posts were driven across the canal by the 3rd and Light Divisions: Hill had no great difficulty in forcing the outer line of entrenchments at St. Cyprien: Freyre occupied La Pugade almost unopposed. During this time Beresford was slowly making his way along the Hers. He reached Montblanc, but shortly afterwards found himself in marshy ground and decided to leave his artillery behind. Arenschildt drove the French Cavalry over the river at Bordes, but failed to stop the destruction of the bridge. Somerset, with the Hussars, seized that of Montaudran, two miles up-stream.

Beresford's progress was slow, and Freyre " either from error or impatience " prematurely assaulted the northern end of the Mont Rave ridge. The attack was made with much spirit; but at length, met by a deadly fire from front and flank, the Spaniards, after suffering terrible loss,

IN THE PENINSULA 815

broke; and though they rallied, and again gallantly assailed the entrenchments, a charge of the enemy's supports hurled them back once more in the utmost confusion. The 52nd had barely time to make way for the flying mass; and as Wellington saw the stream of fugitives heading for the Alby road he remarked with acid pleasantry that in his experience he had seen many curious things, but never 10,000 men starting on a race, and that he doubted whether they would be brought to a standstill by the very Pyrenees!

The enemy followed in hot pursuit, but was checked by a Brigade of the Light Division and the Portuguese guns on La Pugade. Wellington then restored the fight by bringing up the reserve Artillery and the Brigade of Heavy Cavalry commanded, in Ponsonby's absence, by Lord Charles Manners.

But matters were going badly. Picton had carried his demonstration to a length unwarranted either by his instructions or by the general situation, and was repulsed in an attack upon the strongly fortified bridge of Jumeaux. Hill was not strong enough to attack the inner line of St. Cyprien. Musketry fire almost ceased, though the cannonade continued without intermission. Picton's repulse had deprived Lord Wellington of his reserve. Apart from the Light Division, which could not be spared from the point vacated by the Spaniards, the 4th and 6th Divisions under Beresford alone remained intact, and their strength, about 11,000 of all ranks, seemed hardly adequate to turn the scale. These two Divisions were executing the very manœuvre which had recoiled with such fatal effect upon Marmont at Salamanca. But Soult was not a Wellington, and in any case had not a sufficiency of force to crush the turning movement as it had been crushed by the British Commander. Still, the French Marshal had no intention of allowing it to be carried out with impunity. Observing that Hill could make no further progress, and that Beresford's column, slowly toiling through the deep ground, sometimes under musketry fire, never let alone by the guns posted on Mont Rave, was continually lengthening out in spite of repeated halts for the purpose of closing up the ranks, Soult called up Taupin's Division and a Brigade of Maransin from Reille's Corps; and was in a position to assume the offensive with these troops as well as with the Divisions of Villatte and D'Armagnac hitherto held in reserve, and the Cavalry—an aggregate force of 15,000 men. Victory seemed assured; but instead of using his strength *en masse*, Soult merely brought Taupin to St. Sypière; and flanking him with the Cavalry, directed that General alone to fall upon Beresford. But Taupin's artillery had not yet come up. Some little delay occurred; and thus it happened that when he "poured down the hill" to attack, Beresford had gained time to complete his march and wheel into line—the 6th Division on the right, the 4th on the left flanked by Somerset's Hussars.

Taupin was received with a heavy musketry fire. Then the rocket battery opened, and the missiles (being happily induced to go in the right direction) spread astonishment and terror in the enemy's ranks. Lambert's Brigade of the 5th Division and part of Anson's (belonging to the 4th) "rushed forward with a terrible shout, and the French fled back to the upper ground." Taupin, sharing the fate of nearly all the Divisional Generals in what had formerly been "the Army of Portugal," was killed; and though a Cavalry regiment, attempting to intercept Beresford's line of retreat, charged, it was repulsed by the Brigade of the 6th Division under Pack. Sir Lowry Cole captured the St. Sypière redoubt, and the two Divisions established themselves on Mont Rave.

IN THE PENINSULA 817

Soult brought up the remaining Brigade of D'Armagnac, rallied the fugitives and sent part of Travot's conscripts to defend the Demoiselles bridge over the canal (southeast of the town) now menaced by Cole and Arenschildt. The 6th Division, wheeling to the right, attacked Clausel. It was about 2.30 p.m. A desperate struggle ensued. The Calvinet and Columbette redoubts were taken and retaken. General Harispe, who commanded in person, at this point was badly wounded, and the French at length fell back. But this time Clinton's Division was exhausted and Wellington had no further reserves. At 4 p.m. the northern end of Mont Rave was still in the hands of the French; and as the Divisions of Villatte and D'Armagnac were still intact it would seem that Soult still held the advantage. Had Wellington been the defender it may be taken for granted that he would have made a bold bid for victory. But after a time the 6th Division, supported by the 4th, began to advance again. Picton still kept Darricau employed. The Spaniards most gallantly prepared to attack once more. Soult then abandoned the contest at 5 p.m. and withdrew the whole of his army behind the canal. He had lost a gun and 3,239 officers and men killed and wounded. The casualties of the Allies reached 4,659, distributed thus :—

	British.	Portuguese.	Spanish.
Killed	312	78	205
Wounded	1,795	529	1,722
Missing	17	1	

Considering that Picton lost 400 and the Spanish 1,500 men in their first attack, the casualties of the Allies must be deemed comparatively light. Those of the French seem unexpectedly large.

Although Wellington was successful his combinations were marred by the failure of the Spaniards and Picton, and his conduct of the action has been severely criticised not only by Napier but by other competent authorities such as Sir H. Smith and Lord Seaton. Smith remarks that it was the only one of Lord Wellington's battles in which he had not sufficient weight of reserve, and Seaton considers that he deserved to have been beaten. Although for different reasons, neither Hill's Corps nor the Light Division could take any active part in the engagement, and the latter would have been hard put to it to cover Beresford's retreat had he been defeated. Whether in such a case Wellington would have succeeded in uniting his two wings on one or the other side of the Garonne must be a matter for pure conjecture.

The fact is that the British Commander had not a large enough force for the operation, and his courage in undertaking it is more to be admired than his mode of execution. But Wellington was always an excellent judge of the moral strength of his opponent, and in the full tide of victory felt himself able to attempt what might otherwise have been impossible. To use his own words, he had an army which "could go anywhere and do anything," and his confidence was not misplaced.

By the time Soult had effected his retreat daylight had failed. The occupation of Mont Rave had given Wellington an invaluable foot-hold, but the northern and western fronts of the city were still too strong to be attacked. To complete the success and gain a footing on the south side it was essential to force the Port des Demoiselles. But while a chance remained Soult declined to own himself beaten, and resolved to fight again next day for the possession of Toulouse. The 11th, however, passed without renewal of the battle. Wellington's ammunition was expended and he could not get a fresh supply till the afternoon. The attack had, therefore, to be postponed till the following morning. But the day

IN THE PENINSULA

was not wasted. The Hussar Brigade was despatched in the direction of Caraman and Alby to give notice of the approach of any reinforcement to the enemy from that direction. Arenschildt moved up the canal. He was intended to endeavour next day to occupy the great road to Castelnadaury forming Soult's sole remaining line of retreat, and was to be supported by Hill and Beresford. But the preliminary movement was enough for the French Commander. Soult fully appreciated the advantages of his entrenched position at Toulouse, but, with better judgment than that of Bazaine at Metz, had no intention of allowing himself to be closely invested within its walls. Leaving behind him 8 guns and 1,600 badly wounded men, including Generals Harispe, Baurot, and St. Hilaire, he retired during the night of the 11th upon Villefranche, 22 miles distant, and on the 13th took up a position in front of Castelnadaury, once more urging Suchet to join him, but still receiving no reply.

On the 12th Lord Wellington entered Toulouse, but in the afternoon messengers arrived with news of the Emperor's abdication. They were at once sent on to the French armies. Marshal Suchet, whose conduct had been supine throughout the campaign, on hearing of the change of government at once acquiesced in it. Soult, from the tenor of his previous advices, thought a trick was being played on him, and very properly declined to abandon the cause of his master while any shadow of doubt remained. He requested an armistice; which Wellington with equal propriety refused. The British troops were then pushed forward. One or two skirmishes took place, but the authentic nature of the tidings was soon established beyond dispute, and on the 18th a Convention was signed by the terms of which lines of demarcation were fixed between the opposing armies, and hostilities ceased.

The French agreed to evacuate the Spanish fortresses of which they still held possession. On the western side Santona, which was blockaded by the Spaniards and would probably have fallen in a few days, alone remained in their hands; but on the eastern, Figueras, Barcelona, Tortosa, Morella, Peniscola, Saguntum, and Denia were still surmounted by the tricolor. In France neither St. Jean Pied de Port, Navarrenx, Blaye, Lourdes, nor Bayonne had been captured by the Allies.

What would have ensued had hostilities been continued can be only a matter for conjecture. Soult and Suchet would ultimately no doubt have joined hands, but their relations could hardly have been harmonious, and Napoleon would probably have recalled one or the other. Napier is prejudiced in Soult's favour, and that Marshal certainly seems to deserve every praise for his loyalty to his sovereign and country and for the undaunted courage with which he fought the losing campaign for so long; but it is curious that Napoleon felt no great confidence in him at the end and contemplated his supersession by Suchet.

Wellington, for his part, would no doubt have made a great effort to hem the enemy in between the Pyrenees and the Golfe du Lion. Had he succeeded, the French, with the Allies in their front and the Spaniards in their rear, would have been in an awkward position and would probably have dispersed or surrendered *en masse*. After disposing of the French "Army of Spain" Wellington's intention was to advance to the Loire, forming a new base at Nantes, and one may feel confident that he would have made further brilliant illustration of the art of war.

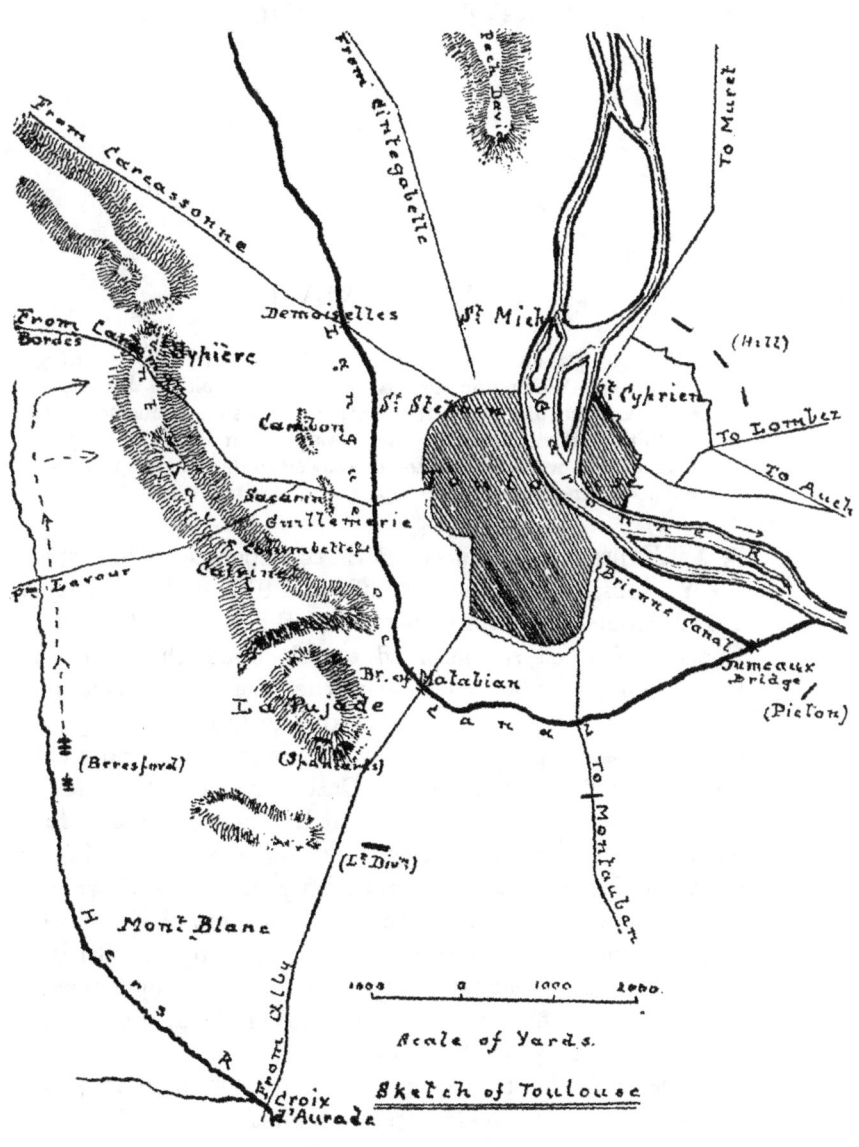

CHAPTER XLVIII

Operations in Catalonia—Treaty of Valençay—Release of King Ferdinand—Wellington directs Clinton to break up his Army and reinforce him with the British regiments—Conclusion of hostilities—Sortie from Bayonne—Capture of Sir John Hope—End of the war—Wellington's farewell order to his troops—Sails for England—Conclusion.

WE brought the account of the operations in Catalonia down to the end of 1813. In January, 1814, General William Clinton and the Spanish General, Copons, planned a combined attack upon the enemy's force—3,000 or 4,000 strong—on the Llobregat. But the operation failed in consequence of the failure of Copons to co-operate; partly, as it would seem, from political motives, for the Duque de San Carlos had recently passed through the French and Spanish lines *en route* for Madrid, bearing the Treaty of Valençay negotiated between Napoleon and Ferdinand, by the terms of which the latter was to be restored to the throne of Spain on condition of the evacuation of the country by the British troops. This Treaty was approved of by Copons and other general officers, but, as already noticed, was eventually rejected by the Regency.

Another draft—to the extent of 10,000 men and 80 guns—was now made upon Suchet's army by the Emperor; and the Marshal, having increased the garrison of Barcelona to 8,000 men, sent word to the governor of

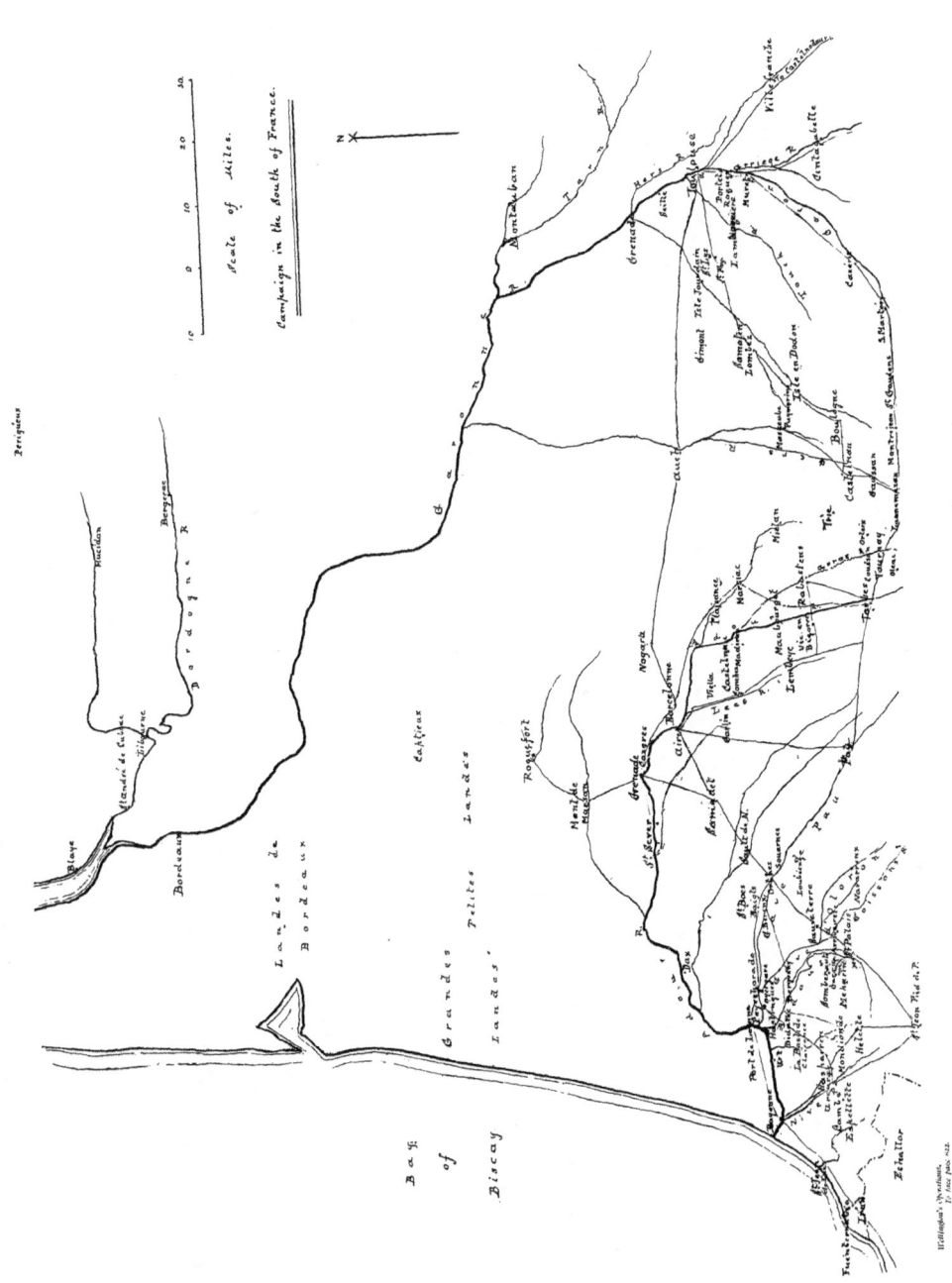

IN THE PENINSULA 823

Tortosa to hold out as long as his provisions lasted and then, after gathering the garrisons of Mequinenza and Lerida, to retire by way of Venasque into France.

On the 4th of February Clinton passed the Llobregat without opposition. On the 7th Barcelona was blockaded by the Allies. Mequinenza and Lerida fell into the hands of the Spaniards about this time through the medium of a forged despatch.

Early in March yet another draft of 10,000 men was made by Napoleon, but, as already noticed, was eventually diverted to Bordeaux. It was at this time that Suchet proposed to give up all the fortresses still held by the French, excepting Figueras and Rosas, on condition that the garrisons were allowed to join him. Copons gave a provisional assent, but the question had to be referred to Lord Wellington, who had no hesitation in declining the proposal. Suchet then evacuated Gerona and Rosas and concentrated at Figueras in the Pyrenees, where he remained inactive, making no attempt either to relieve the blockade of Barcelona and Tortosa or to send aid, in accordance with repeated entreaties, to Soult.

On the 30th of March King Ferdinand, having been released unconditionally by Napoleon, passed through General Clinton's camp at Esplugas. He then resumed the throne and with it every species of that tyranny and superstition from which Napoleon had desired to liberate the people of Spain.

Leaving a Division of about 6,000 men in Figueras, Suchet now retired into France with the remnant of his Army, by this time not much more than 3,000 strong.

Early in the month of March Wellington, under the impression that Suchet had already retired from Catalonia, had sent orders to Clinton to break up his army by

824 WELLINGTON'S OPERATIONS

sending the British regiments—viz., 2 Battalions of the 27th, 44th, 58th, 81st, 4th Batt. K.G.L., and 3 Batteries —*viâ* Tudela, to join their comrades in France, and the foreign legions back to Sicily. Clinton himself was offered a Division in Wellington's Army. When the orders were received the state of affairs made it impossible to comply with them at the moment. But when Suchet had at length recrossed the frontier and Copons had assented to Clinton's repeated requests by relieving the Anglo-Sicilians in the blockade of Barcelona the British General lost no time in executing Wellington's instructions, and on the 14th of April his army was broken up.

An order from the Emperor reached General Robert, commandant at Tortosa, to break out and gain Barcelona, after which the combined garrisons were to force their way back into France. Robert made no attempt to comply, but General Habert, Governor of Barcelona, made a sortie, and though driven back, inflicted on the Spaniards a loss of 800 men.

News of peace arrived four days afterwards, and the fortresses still in the hands of the French (Figueras, Tortosa, Morella, Peniscola, Saguntum, Denia, and Barcelona) were in due course evacuated. Habert wisely declined to give up Barcelona until assured that the other garrisons had reached France in safety, and finally struck his flag about the end of May.

Thus ended the operations on the eastern side of Spain—operations which had been terribly mismanaged except by Clinton, and which give a pretty good idea of the fate of the Peninsula generally had it been entrusted to other hands than those of Wellington or Moore.

Clinton proved that his diffidence was misplaced, and Wellington, in his dispatch to Lord Bathurst on the

IN THE PENINSULA

19th of April narrating the last events of the war, took occasion to pay a graceful compliment to the General and his troops.

The last word only remains to be told, and it is one of misfortune. Sir John Hope had, as we have seen, established the investment of Bayonne with Vandeleur's Cavalry Brigade, the 1st and 5th Divisions, Lord Aylmer's Brigade of young soldiers, the Portuguese Brigades of Wilson and Bradford, and two Divisions of the 4th Spanish Army. In due course Hope perfected his communication with Wellington on the east and Dalhousie on the north, but in the absence of a siege train was unable to begin active operations against the citadel, situated on the right bank of the Adour. Preparations were, however, nearly complete, when news (which, though not authentic, proved well founded) arrived of Napoleon's abdication and the cessation of hostilities. These rumours were informally mentioned to the French outposts, but General Thouvenot, like a good soldier, declined to be influenced by reports which were not substantiated.

At 1 a.m. on the 14th of April a deserter brought word to General Hay, whose Brigade furnished the outposts at St. Etienne, that a sortie was about to be made in force. Hay probably disbelieved the story; he took no additional precautions, but General Hinuber, commanding the K.G.L., which formed a support, being not too proud to conform to the rules of his profession, at once put his Brigade under arms. The officer commanding the Brigade of Guards—posted in reserve—did the same. At 3 a.m. the French, 3,000 or 4,000 strong, burst out of the citadel. Hay's outposts were surprised and broken; the whole village of St. Etienne, with the exception of one house occupied by a Company of the 38th, was lost, the line of the Allies pierced and thrown into dire confusion. Desperately, however, the British veterans fought, and though overpowered, exacted life for life. Then Hinuber came up with his Brigade, rallied Hay's men, and, with the aid of a battalion sent by Bradford, recaptured St. Etienne.

On the British right the Guards were also broken, "and the battle was most confused and terrible; for on both sides the troops, broken into small bodies by the enclosures and unable to recover their order, came dashing together in the darkness, fighting often with the bayonet; and sometimes friends encountered, sometimes foes; all was tumult and horror." The guns of the citadel and of the gunboats poured in their fire, sometimes indiscriminately, sometimes upon Hope's supports now arriving on the scene.

Having put his reserves in motion, Sir John attempted to reach St. Etienne; but the road was already in possession of the enemy. The British Commander found himself in the midst of the French. A shot struck him in the arm. His charger was killed, and being unable to extract himself as it fell, he was made prisoner.

The moon rose and day began to dawn. General Howard, in command of the 1st Division, brought up the reserves of the Guards and drove the enemy back into his works with the loss of over 900 men. The British casualties amounted to 150 killed, 457 wounded, and 236 prisoners. General Hay paid for his lack of vigilance with his life. He is rescued from oblivion by a remarkable monument in St. Paul's Cathedral, which represents the General falling into the arms of a man who (being in a state of nature) presumably belonged to one of the surprised picquets, and had violated the orders prohibiting

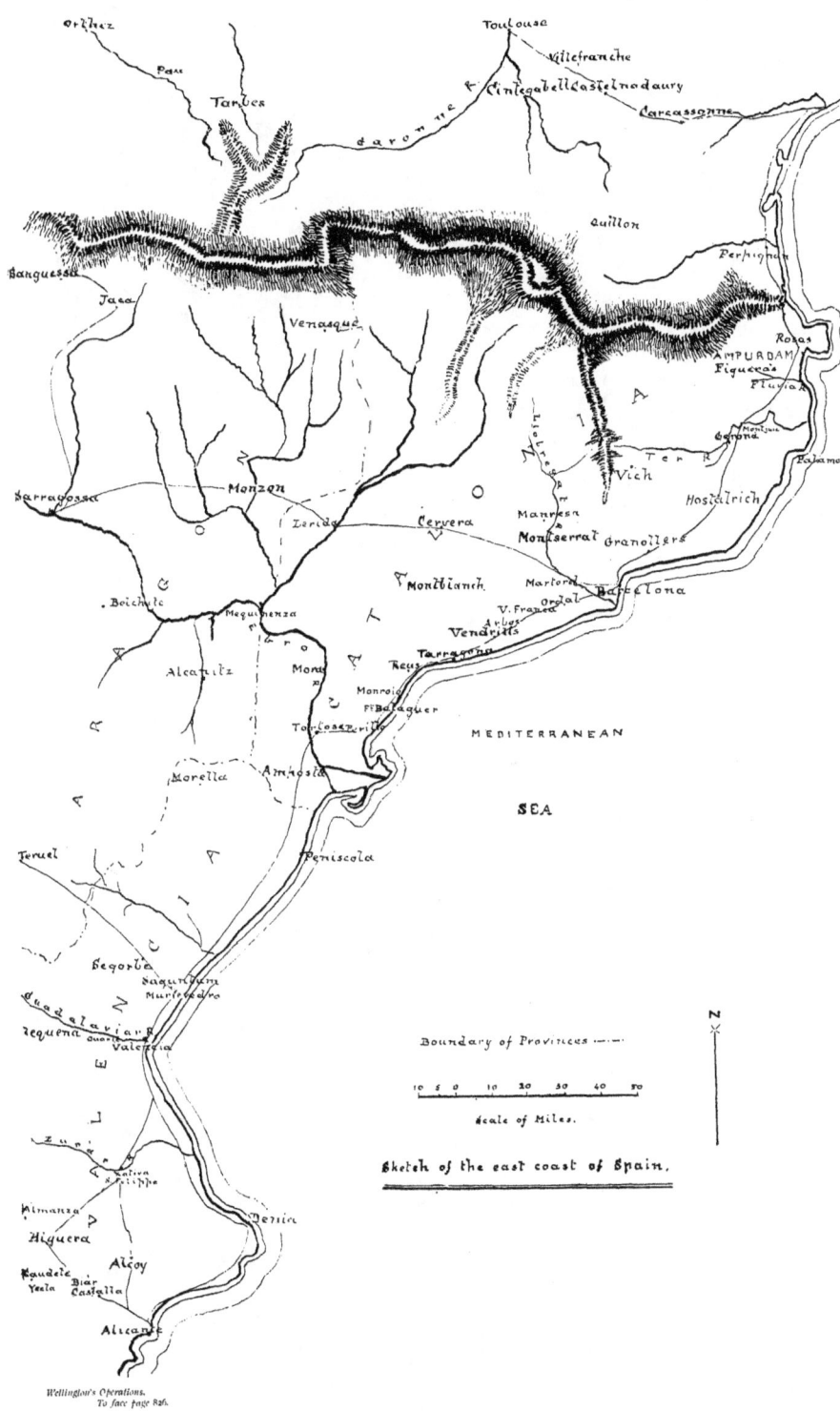

men on outpost duty from laying aside their clothing or equipments. Another soldier, fully accoutred, stands close by, taking no interest in the proceedings and apparently asleep. Distressing, however, as is the monumental fate of Hay, still worse is that of William Ponsonby in the same transept. Ponsonby (killed at Waterloo in command of the Union Brigade) is portrayed in sculpture without a stitch of clothing, squatting on his haunches beside his charger—which his servant had evidently forgotten to saddle or bridle—and stretching out his hand for a wreath proffered by an Angel who does not seem to have enjoyed the immunity generally accorded to the celestials, for she has lost three fingers which no doubt were shot away in traversing the field of battle. As a record of English taste and English art, these monuments may be regarded as gems; but whatever were his shortcomings as a cavalry leader, poor Ponsonby at all events lost his life in the service of his country, and it is hard that he should be thus condemned to do public penance, possibly for centuries! So terrible a punishment might be thought more appropriate for, say, a Secretary of State who absented himself from his post at the critical moment when his country was on the point of embarking on a life or death struggle.

It is rather curious that out of the five officers who acted as second in command to Wellington, two should have been taken prisoners. It will be remembered that Sir Edward Paget was captured during the retreat from Burgos in 1812. On at least three occasions Wellington himself was within an ace of being taken.

Major-General Colville succeeded Sir John Hope in command of the Army Corps at Bayonne. For a few days longer shots were exchanged, but eventually General

Thouvenot satisfied himself that peace was really made, and ceased fire.

On the termination of the war Lord Wellington received a dukedom, and the officers who had commanded Army Corps or their equivalent, viz., Sir J. Hope, Sir S. Cotton, Sir R. Hill, Sir T. Graham, and Sir W. Beresford, were raised to the peerage. A large number of others were admitted to the various degrees of the order of the Bath; but more than a quarter of a century elapsed before the junior officers, N.C.O.'s, and men received even a medal for the glorious Peninsular campaigns as the meed of their country's gratitude which they had so magnificently earned. "Yet," in Napier's words, "those veterans had won 19 pitched battles and innumerable combats; had made or sustained 10 sieges and taken four great fortresses; had twice expelled the French from Portugal, once from Spain; had penetrated France, and killed, wounded, or captured 200,000 enemies—leaving of their own number 40,000 dead, whose bones whiten the plains and mountains of the Peninsula."

Of the army now about to be dispersed, three battalions only, viz., the 1st of the 40th and 45th, and the 5th of the 60th, had disembarked at Montego Bay in 1808, and had served without intermission in the Peninsula to the end of the war.

Of the various Divisions, the 3rd, 4th, and Light were certainly the most distinguished, though all were good at the end. The 1st was usually held in reserve, and was comparatively seldom in action, but the honourable traditions of the Foot Guards in the zealous performance of their duty, however irksome or inglorious, were as well maintained as at the present day.

The Artillery always did well, but the comparative

IN THE PENINSULA

power of the arm—particularly in the British Army where the proportion of guns to bayonets was so small —was much less than in recent times.

The Cavalry failed to add much to the laurels which it had gained in the Corunna campaign. Whether Moore understood the branch better than Wellington; whether his regiments were better than those of his successor; or whether Paget was a better Cavalry General than Cotton must be matter for conjecture;* but the fact remains that in spite of a few isolated cases of brilliant action such as that of the 13th at Campo Mayor and St. Gaudens, or Cotton's charge at Salamanca, the performance of the British Cavalry as a whole was disappointing. The K.G.L. regiments were good, and took their profession seriously.

A rather remarkable feature of the war was the comparative youth of the officers on either side. Wellington was under 45 at the battle of Toulouse. Soult was the same age. Clausel was 42; Reille 39; Fane and Pakenham about 35. Yet all had been general officers for years past. Graham and Rey were over 60, but their cases were exceptional. Cotton commanded the Cavalry at the age of 37. Marmont was a Marshal at 35. Many regimental Colonels were about 30. William Napier commanded the 43rd at Salamanca—as a Major— at the age of 26.

No words could describe the army as a whole better than Wellington's expression in later years, that it was one which " could go anywhere and do anything." It was not less terrible in attack than immovable in defence, and its fire power and discipline are admitted by its enemies to have been of the highest order.

* The writer once asked a distinguished cavalry officer his opinion of the comparative merits of Paget and Cotton. Unfortunately he had never heard of either.

During the recent Boer war a storm of censure was poured upon our troops, particularly upon the officers. Some stigmatised them as bookworms, others ridiculed them as the most ignorant of their species. But though the grounds of censure were diametrically opposed to one another, all agreed in condemnation. Yet from the letters published and the talk indulged in, the writer is convinced that a large proportion of those who criticised so glibly and sought to take away the reputation of the officers fighting their country's battles under great difficulties, had no knowledge of military matters beyond what they had acquired at school or college in studying the combats of Hector and Achilles. Some strictures were, however, undoubtedly well founded, and that a higher standard is attainable no one will dispute. But the improvement made by soldiers both before and during the war has hardly been appreciated. During the last ten or fifteen years probably no body of men has made greater progress in the study of the theory and practice of its profession.

Before our next European war break out—and there are even now signs that a continental power, like France a century ago, is preparing a contest with England for commercial and colonial supremacy—it is to be hoped that we may have a commander of Wellington's calibre and an Army like his, but strengthened in quality and numbers by a public opinion making it a point of honour that every Englishman contribute something of personal service towards his country's defence. In such a case England will have nothing to fear.

On the 14th of June the Duke of Wellington (who had just returned to his army after transacting political business both at Paris and Madrid, and had now com-

IN THE PENINSULA

pleted his arrangements for sending the Portuguese troops home, and the British Infantry either to America, the Netherlands or England), issued his farewell order.

GENERAL ORDER.
BORDEAUX, 14*th June*, 1814.

"1. The Commander of the Forces, being on the point of returning to England, again takes the opportunity of congratulating the Army upon the recent events which have restored peace to their country and to the world.

"2. The share which the British Army has had in producing these events, and the high character with which the Army will quit this country, must be equally satisfactory to every individual belonging to it, as they are to the Commander of the Forces; and he trusts that the troops will continue the same good conduct to the last.

"3. The Commander of the Forces once more requests the Army to accept his thanks.

"4. Although circumstances may alter the relations in which he has stood towards them, so much to his satisfaction, he assures them that he shall never cease to feel the warmest interest in their welfare and honour; and that he will be at all times happy to be of any service to those to whose conduct, discipline, and gallantry their country is so much indebted."

The Duke embarked for England the same day. Lord Hill had already preceded him; and Lord Dalhousie was left in command to superintend, with the assistance of the Headquarter Staff, the arrangements for the embarkation of the Infantry at Bordeaux. The Cavalry marched through France to Boulogne, whence it was conveyed by ship to England.

The Peninsular War was at an end. Among the many names of men who had played a distinguished part in it may be selected for special admiration on the side of France, those of Masséna, Soult, Clausel, Gazan, and Reille; on that of England, those of Hill, Hope, George Murray, Colborne, Sturgeon, and—last but not least—that of the invaluable diplomatist, Sir Charles Stuart. But the central figures must ever be those of Moore and Wellington. Of the former it is unnecessary now to speak; of the latter, impossible. For no one—least of any the present writer—can attempt to gauge the depths of Wellington's character, or do justice to his astonishing combination of qualities—business capacity, method, industry, foresight, resolution, statesmanship—all welded together by the incomparable cement of patience.

And so the writer takes leave of those whose careers he has followed, most feebly indeed and most inadequately, but with such surpassing interest that the heroes of the great drama almost appear to be old and intimate friends.

"The knights are dust, their good swords rust;
Their souls are with the saints we trust."

In this world it may not be possible to get answers to those inquiries which alone can enable us to take a correct and impartial view of the past; and, more particularly, to decide whether our policy of hunting Napoleon to death was that most conducive to the interests of our country; or whether statesmanship might not have found a means by which we could have gone hand-in-hand on the path of civilisation and progress with the most sagacious and far-seeing genius which the earth has seen, and by so doing have solved in their infancy some of those problems which after the lapse of a century weigh so heavily upon us.

Index

A

Abercrombie, Sir R., off Cadiz, 7
Albuera, battle of, 410
Aldea Ponte, skirmish at, 454
Almada, defences of, 447
Almaraz, surprise of, 517, &c.
Almeida, fall of, 287
Alten, V., posted on the Yeltes, 485
  ,, abandons his position, 511
Amarante, abandoned by Loison, 167
Andalusia, invasion of, 231
Anglo-Sicilian army, state of, 578
Angoulême, Duc d', joins Allies, 783
Areizaga, General, advances against Madrid, 228; defeated at Ocana, 230
Armies, Spanish, 182
Army, British, states of, 154, 158, 196, 262, 281, 429, 486, 548, 775, 813
  ,,   ,, armament of, 184
  ,, French, states of, 284, 457, 530, 650, 747
  ,, British, General Foy's notes on, 189
Army, French, General Foy's notes on, 187
  ,, Spanish, ,, ,, 194
Army of Reserve enters Spain, 20
Aroyo des Molinos, surprise of, 464, &c.
Artillery, British field, 184
Asturian deputation in England, 42
Augereau, Marshal, captures Gerona, 226

B

Bacellar, General, commands militia in the Tras os Montes, 257
Badajoz, captured by Soult, 355; first British siege of, 407; second ditto, 426; value of, 472; third siege of, 493; taken by storm, 500
Barossa, battle of, 380
Bâsle, treaty of, 36
Baylen, capitulation of, 69
Bayonne, preparations at, 82; sortie from, 827
Beresford, Lieut.-Gen. (afterwards Sir W. Marshal in Portuguese service) commands Portuguese

army, 146); question regarding his rank, 180; captures Campo Mayo, 385; at Albuera, 409; at Salamanca, 561; crosses the Gave de Pau, 790; at Orthez, 792; sent to take possession of Bordeaux; his successful movement at Toulouse, 815

Bessières, Marshal, his victory at Rio Seco; commands the Northern Governments, 387; refuses to aid Masséna, 398

Bidassoa, passage of, 742

Blake, Spanish General, at Albuera, 411; captured at Valencia, 460

Bonaparte, First Consul, makes proposals of peace to England, 9 (*Vide* Napoleon)

Brennier, General, escapes from Almeida, 401

British Infantry, its accurate marksmanship, 405

Burgos, Castle of, besieged, 591; retreat from, 598, &c.; castle blown up, 675

C

Cadiz, British force refused admission to, 145

Castille, Council of, proclaims Joseph Bonaparte king, 26

Casualties, British, 1809–11, 471

Cazal **Nova**, rearguard action at, 352

Charles IV., King of Spain, abdicates, 21

Cintra, "Convention of," 70, &c.

Ciudad Rodrigo, taken by Masséna, 275; value of, 472; taken by Wellington, 479

Clausel, General, takes command of the Army of Portugal, 559; retires over the Duero, 575; operates on Wellington's line of communications, 588; appointed to the Army of the North, 653; marches to join the king at Vitoria, 696; retires into the Pyrenees, *id.*; at Sorauren, 714; at the Nivelle, 756; at the Nive, 759; at Orthez, 792; at Toulouse, 812

Clinton, General W., commands Anglo-Sicilian force, 630, 727; directed to reinforce Wellington, 800; crosses the Llobregat, 823; breaks up his army, 824

Colborne, Colonel, feat of, 743

Cortez, National, assembled at Cadiz, 421

Corunna, battle of, 104

Cotton, Sir S., his charge at Salamanca, 560

Cradock, Sir J., appointed to command in Portugal, 143

Craufurd, General Robert, his operations on the Coa and Agueda, 270, &c.; driven over the Coa, 277; at Busaco, 304; killed, 479

Cuesta, Spanish General, commands Spanish Army of the Centre, 178; co-operates with Wellington, 202, &c.

D

Dalrymple, Sir H., 70

Discipline enforced, 174

INDEX

Dorsenne, General, commands Army of the North, 439

Douro, passage of the by Wellesley, 164

Dupont, General, marches into Andalusia, 34; capitulates at Baylen, 36

E

El Bodon, skirmish at, 480

Espinosa, battle of, 83

F

Ferdinand VII., not recognised by Napoleon, 24; re-enters Spain, 825

Figueras, captured by the French, 4

Fontainebleau, Treaty of, 16

Forces, French, 30

Foz de Aruce, skirmish at, 357

Fuentes d'Onoro, battle of, 393, &c.

G

Galicia, its importance, 445

Geborah, battle of the, 336

Gerona, gallant defence of, 226

Godoy, Emanuel, Prince of the Peace, proclamation of, directed against France, 13

Graham, Lieut.-Col., afterwards Sir T., at Barossa, 380; commands left wing of the army, 666; at Vitoria, 687; attacks Foy on the Royal Road, 695; quits the army, 743

H

Hardinge, Colonel, at Albuera, 413

Hill, Lieut.-Gen., afterwards Sir R., commands a corps on the Tagus, joins Wellington, 291; relieves Beresford, 418; surprises Girard at Aroyo des Molinos, 464; attacks Almaraz; ordered to Madrid, 587; directed to join Wellington on the Adaja, 602; forms junction at Alba de Tormes, 619; at Vitoria, 686; his position in the Pyrenees, 702; at the battle of the Nivelle, 751; attacked at St. Pierre, 761; crosses the Bidouse, 786; at Orthez, 793; directed upon Aire, 797; at Toulouse, 814

Hope, Lieut.-Gen., afterwards Sir J., his skilful march, 102; commands the army on Moore's death, 126; joined the army under Wellington, 744; his passage of the Adour, 788, &c. taken prisoner at Bayonne, 826

J

Joseph Bonaparte, proclaimed King of Spain, 26; flees from Madrid, 36; resigns the throne but resumes it, 422; advances to help Marmont, 576; abandons the capital, 577; advances against Wellington, 608; prepares to resist the advance of the Allies in 1813, 672; takes post at Pancorbo, 677; defeated at Vitoria, 681, &c.; retires from the scene, 699

Jourdan, Marshal, Chief of the King's Staff, 75; advises direct attack on the Allies, 613

836 INDEX

Junot, General, occupies Portugal, 17; marches against the British, 64; defeated at Vimeiro, 65; commands the 8th Corps under Masséna, 266

M

Macdonald, Marshal, commands the 7th Corps, 420; retakes Figueras, 421

Madrid, riot at, 24; entered by the Allies, 578; evacuated by Hill, 608

Maitland, Lieut.-Gen., in command of Anglo-Sicilian force, sails from Tarragona, 579; lands at Alicante, id.; declines to march against Suchet, 587

Marmont, Marshal, succeeds Masséna in command of the Army of Portugal, 403; joins Soult near Badajoz, 428; retires into the valley of the Tagus, 439; revictuals Ciudad Rodrigo, 448; his operations on the Portuguese frontier, 449, &c.; retires to Salamanca, 455; advances to Celorico, 511; retires into Spain, 512; starts to relieve the Salamanca forts, 539; retires across the Duero, 541; advances again, 546; defeated at Salamanca, 558; Napoleon's comments on, 564

Masséna, Marshal, appointed to command the Army of Portugal; concentrates on the Mondego, 288; defeated at Busaco, 304; follows Wellington to the Lines of Torres Vedras, 310; takes post at Santarem, 326; retreats from Portugal, 340, &c.; advances to relieve Almeida, 388; attacks Wellington at Fuentes d'Onoro, 393; superseded by Marmont, 403

Mendizabel, General, defeated at the Gebora, 336

Military road, the, 265

Militia, English battalions land at Bordeaux, 802

Moncey, General, afterwards Marshal, forces the passage of the Deva, 5; attacks Valencia, 33

Moore, Sir John, appointed to command a force in Spain, 94; reaches Salamanca, 99; marches against Soult, 105; retreats, 111; reaches Corunna, 121; his death and character, 128

Murray, Sir John, takes command at Alicante, 642; at Castalla, 643; besieges Tarragona, 644; raises the siege, 647

N

Napoleon, the Emperor, fails to get possession of the Danish and Portuguese fleets, 15; his views on Spain and Portugal, 16, &c.; enters Madrid, 90; marches against Moore, 111; halts at Astorga, 114; his orders to Marmont, 512, &c.; hears of the battle of Vitoria; despatches Soult to Spain as his lieutenant, id.; instructions to Soult, 799; abdicates, 814

Ney, Marshal, quarrels with Soult, 176; drives Craufurd over the Coa; his attack at Busaco, 302;

INDEX 837

at Redinha, 349; superseded for insubordination, 814
Nive, battle of the, 749, &c.

O

Ocana, battle of, 230
Oporto, capture of, by Soult, 138
Ordenanza, correspondence on between Wellington and Masséna, 293
Orthez, battle of, 793, &c.

P

Paget, Lieut.-Gen. (afterwards Sir E.), commands the rearguard, 115, &c.; wounded at the Douro, 166; rejoins the army, 587; taken prisoner, 616
Paget, Lord, commands the Cavalry Division, 109
Pakenham, Major-Gen., his attack at Salamanca, 558
Pampeluna, surrenders, 748
Partidas, inefficiency of, 235; menace the French communications, 521; on the east coast, 522; operate against Suchet's communications, 629, 641
Peninsula, strategic position of, 1
Picton, Major-Gen., afterwards Lieut.-Gen. Sir T., in Masséna's retreat, 353, &c.; takes post at Sorauren, 711; at Vic en Bigorre, 804; his failure at Toulouse, 815
Pombal, rearguard action at, 349
Portugal, appeals to England, 9
Portuguese army, starving, 585
Pyrenees, battles of, 710, &c.

R

Redinha, rearguard action at, 349
Reille, General Count, commands the Army of Portugal, 629; his position, 639; at Vitoria, 687; at Orthez, 792; at Toulouse, 812
Reinforcements for Wellington, 433, 443, 634
    ,,   ,, French, 332
Reynier, General, his attack at Busaco, 301; defeated at Sabugal, 362
Rio Seco, battle of, 38
Roads between France and Spain, 28
Romana, Marquis of, in command of a Spanish Corps, 113, &c.
Roriça, rearguard action at, 61

S

Sabugal, fight at, 362
St. Cyr, General Gouvion, besieges Gerona, 224
St. Ildefonso, Treaty of, 5
Salamanca, battle of, 554, &c.
San Marcial, battle of, 738
San Sebastian, besieged, 730; taken, 736
Sarragossa, attacked by Verdier, 37; taken by Lannes, 135
Seville capitulates, 232
Silveira, Portuguese General, driven across the Tamega and Douro, 139
Skerrett, Colonel, pusillanimous conduct of, off Tarragona, 428
Slade, General, defeated at Maquilla, 523
Somers Cocks, Captain, his reconnaissance, 290
Souham, General, commands the

838 INDEX

Army of Portugal, 595; follows up Wellington, 598; superseded by D'Erlon, 613

Soult, Marshal, follows Moore, 115; invades Portugal, 137; driven from Oporto, 166; retreats from Portugal, 167, &c.; attacks the Allies in rear, 215; at battle of Ocana, 230; captures Olivenza, 335; captures Badajoz, 355; at Albuera, 410; joins Marmont near Badajoz, 428; his conduct and ability, 436; marches to relieve Badajoz, 507; ordered to abandon Andalusia, 580; recalled from Spain, 641; appointed Lieutenant of the Emperor, 699; takes post in the Pyrenees, 701; attacks the positions of the Allies, 710, defeated at Sorauren, 715, &c.; retreats, 718; driven from his lines on the Nivelle, 751; takes up a position on the Nive, 755; attacks Wellington, 759; retires over the Gave d'Oleron, 786; attacked at Orthez, 793; takes post on the Adour, 799; resumes the offensive, 803; is outflanked, *id.*; retires on Toulouse, 806; his skilful combinations, 811; attack at Toulouse, 814; abandons his position, 818; evacuates Toulouse, 820

Spain, population and geography of, 4

Spanish Armies, 80, 182, 635

„   treasure ships seized by England, 12

Spencer, Major-Gen. joins Wellesley in Mondego Bay, 53

Strategic lines of operation in Spain and Portugal, 48, &c.

Stuart, Lieut.-Gen. Sir C., captures Minorca, 6; takes a force to Portugal, 8

Stuart, Mr., afterwards Sir C., son of above named, appointed British Minister at Lisbon, 238; takes his seat on the Board of Regency, 318

Sturgeon, Colonel, commands the Corps of Guides, 657; his death, 804

Suchet, General, afterwards Marshal, captures Tortosa and Tarragona, 420; captures Valencia, 460; recognises the new government, 820; retires into France, 823

Supply depôts, 258

T

Talavera, battle of, 206
Tarifa, defence of, 469
Torres Vedras, Lines of, 310, &c.; planned, 240
Toulouse, its importance, 808; description of, *id.*; battle of, 814
Trant, Colonel, harasses Masséna's columns, 291; captures the enemy's sick and wounded at Coimbra, 308; defends the frontier against Marmont, 511

U

United States declare war against England, 526

V

Valençay, Treaty of, 822

INDEX 839

Valencia, operations in, 459
Vic en Bigorre, skirmish at, 804
Victor, Marshal, defeats Cuesta at Medellin, 141; at Talavera, 208, &c.; invests Cadiz, 233; defeated at Barossa, 380, &c.
Vimeiro, battle of, 65
Vitoria, battle of, 686, &c.; consequences of, 692

W

Waters, Colonel, A. A. G., 364
Wellesley, Lord, envoy to the Spanish Government, 238
Wellesley, Sir A., appointed to command a force in Portugal, 46; lands in Mondego Bay, 54; superseded by Sir H. Dalrymple, 55; defeats Junot at Vimeiro, 65; his memorandum on the defence of Portugal, 148; takes command of the Army in Portugal, 152; his orders for the march, 160, &c.; advances against Oporto, 163; forces the passage of the Douro, 165; drives Soult from Portugal, 170; advances along the Tagus, 202, &c.; defeats Joseph at Talavera, 206; his army starving, 219; takes up position near Badajoz, 220; comparison of his campaign with that of Moore, 222; created LORD WELLINGTON, 223; the King's opinion of, 240; leaves a wing of his army on the Tagus under Hill, and takes the other into Beira, 251; his preparations for defending the frontier, 254, &c.: his annoyance at Crauford's action, 279; retires before Masséna, 290; his victory at Busaco, 300; resumes his retreat, 306; enters the Lines of Torres Vedras, 310; follows up the French in their retrograde movement, 337, &c.; joins Beresford at Badajoz, 386; returns to Beira, *id.*; his want of money, 389; joins Beresford at Albuera, 418; takes post on the Caya, 434; returns to Beira, 443; operations against Marmont, 451; captures Ciudad Rodrigo, 480; and Badajoz, 500; his plans for taking the offensive, 515; preserves the neutrality of Portugal in the contest between England and the United States, 526; his distress for money, 528; crosses the Agueda, 534; enters Salamanca, 536; captures the forts, 538; battle of Salamanca, 554, &c.; enters Madrid, 578; marches against Clausel, 589; failure at Burgos, 592, &c.; appointed Commander-in-Chief of the Spanish Armies, 594; raises the siege and retreats, 598; concentrates on the Arapiles, 615; resumes his retreat into Portugal, 616; goes into winter quarters, 619; his circular, 621; goes to Cadiz, 635; prepares to resume the offensive, 653; crosses the Duero, 668; crosses the Ebro, 676; establishes a new base at Santander, *id.*; defeats Joseph at Vitoria, 686, &c.; made Field-Marshal, 692; misconduct of his troops, 697; reaches Sorauren, 714; pushes the enemy back to

the frontier, 722; crosses the Bidassoa, 742; attacks Soult on the Nivelle, 749; advances on Bayonne, 755; at the battles of the Nive, 758, &c.; foresees danger from the Spanish Government, 767; replies to the views of the British Ministry, 769; his strategical objects, 788; advances against Soult, 785; attacks him at Orthez, 792, &c.; directs W. Clinton to reinforce him, 800; crosses the Garonne, 800; attacks Soult at Toulouse, 814, &c.; follows him up in the direction of Castelnadaury, 820; concludes a convention, *id.;* his farewell order, 831

Wilson, Sir R., acts on Wellesley's left flank, 203

Y

York, Duke of, his orders to Wellington, 697